AUG 1 1 2017

P9-DTA-102

NAPA COUNTY LIBRARY
580 COOMBS STREET
NAPA, CA 94559

Roots, Radicals and Rockers

by the same author

THE PROGRESSIVE PATRIOT
A LOVER SINGS: SELECTED LYRICS

BILLY BRAGG

ROOTS, RADICALS AND ROCKERS

How Skiffle Changed the World

FABER & FABER

This edition first published in the UK in 2017
by Faber & Faber Ltd, Bloomsbury House,
74–77 Great Russell Street, London WC1B 3DA
First published in the USA in 2017

Typeset by Ian Bahrami
Printed in the UK by CPI Group (UK) Ltd, Croydon CR0 4YY

All rights reserved
© Billy Bragg, 2017

The right of Billy Bragg to be identified as author of this work
has been asserted in accordance with Section 77 of the Copyright,
Designs and Patents Act 1988

*This book is sold subject to the condition that it shall not, by way
of trade or otherwise, be lent, resold, hired out or otherwise circulated
without the publisher's prior consent in any form of binding or cover
other than that in which it is published and without a similar condition
including this condition being imposed on the subsequent purchaser*

A CIP record for this book
is available from the British Library

ISBN 978–0–571–32774–4

FSC
www.fsc.org
MIX
Paper from
responsible sources
FSC® C020471

For every kid who picked up a guitar
after hearing Lonnie Donegan

CONTENTS

ILLUSTRATIONS

ILLUSTRATIONS

ILLUSTRATIONS

INTRODUCTION

'Dead ground' is a term that I first came across during my brief spell as a trainee tank driver in the early 1980s. It refers to an area that is hidden from the observer due to undulations or obstacles in the terrain. You can see what is in the distance, but between there and here, things that stand in plain sight are obscured by the prominence of nearer objects, drowned in the contours of the landscape.

Skiffle exists in the dead ground of British pop culture, between the end of the war and the rise of the Beatles. It's a landscape dominated by Elvis and his British acolytes – Cliff Richard, Billy Fury, Marty Wilde – but beyond Tommy Steele, the terrain falls quickly away. In the distance, surrounded by a blue haze of sentimentality, looms the Second World War. In the dead ground between are those everyday features of post-war life that have proved immune to nostalgia: conscription; cod liver oil; smog; carbolic soap; polio; Izal medicated toilet paper; the gallows.

That skiffle should be among them is no surprise. The vast majority of its practitioners were boys in their early to mid teens, whose amateur performances in youth clubs, school gyms and church halls left no permanent marks on our culture. Just as the soft parts of ancient organisms don't fossilise, so there is little tangible evidence of the contribution made by tens of thousands of skiffle-mad kids, save for a few black-and-white photos of earnest youths posing with washboards, tea-chest basses and cheap acoustic guitars.

Of the handful of skiffle artists who did make the charts, only

Lonnie Donegan is remembered, and rightly so because he kicked the whole thing off and was by far the most successful proponent. Yet his later decline into singing novelty songs has tarnished the whole genre. Just as Elvis became a parody of himself when he went to Hollywood and made *Clambake*, so Lonnie betrayed his skiffle roots when he took 'My Old Man's a Dustman' to the top of the charts.

As pop became profound in the 60s, artists who had learned their chops playing skiffle tended to leave it out of their biographies. If you wanted to be taken seriously, better to claim you were initially inspired by Chuck Berry and Buddy Holly rather than Chas McDevitt and Nancy Whiskey. Thus skiffle became a bit of an embarrassment for Britain's 60s rock royalty, like an awkward photo from a school yearbook, a reminder of the shabby realities of post-war, pre-rock Britain.

Even when credit was given, skiffle often found itself edited out in the search for a snappier soundbite. Take George Harrison's famous quote about how his band was influenced by the blues: 'No Lead Belly, no Beatles.' What Harrison actually said was: 'If there was no Lead Belly, there would have been no Lonnie Donegan; no Lonnie Donegan, no Beatles. Therefore no Lead Belly, no Beatles.' Due to the key role it played in the founding of the Fab Four, skiffle cannot be completely ignored by pop historians, but too often Donegan's success with 'Rock Island Line' in 1956 is portrayed as a singularity, unfettered by history or context.

Yet every now and then, it is possible to catch glimpses of how deeply skiffle affected the generation who first encountered this exciting music in the cultural desert of the BBC-mediated 1950s. When, in the last days of the twentieth century, I was invited by John Peel to have dinner with him and Lonnie Donegan, I was surprised to find that Peel said barely a word during the meal. It transpired that he was such a fan of Donegan that he needed me to be there so that he could listen to the great man talk, being too awestruck to engage his hero in conversation himself.

In many ways, skiffle is just the sort of music that Peel championed during his years as a major taste-maker. It was the first to reach the UK charts that hadn't been spoonfed to record-buyers by Tin Pan Alley; it sounded rough and ready compared to the lushly produced hit records of the day; most of the songs were little more than a high-tempo three-chord thrash; and it fiercely resisted any notions of commerciality – the audience who booed Bob Dylan for playing an electric guitar at the Manchester Free Trade Hall in 1966 had likely been turned on to folk music by skiffle.

Most importantly, skiffle was the first music *for* teenagers *by* teenagers in our cultural history. Not willing to sit passively and wait to be told what to listen to, this first generation of British teens took the initiative and created a do-it-yourself music that crossed over racial and social barriers. Taking their songs from black blues, gospel and calypso and white folk and country music, and their instruments from the jug bands and spasm groups that played in the streets of the American south, the skiffle groups mixed them together to create a sound that had never been heard in these islands before. In doing so, they faced resistance from generational forces that sought to control and dictate youth culture.

We're so familiar with the story of the Beatles and the Stones that we take it for granted that British kids always played guitars and wrote their own songs, that the spirit of self-realisation was somehow coded into their DNA. Yet that is not the case. It was skiffle that put guitars into the hands of the war babies, and this book aims to place that empowering moment in its proper context in our post-war culture, illuminating the period when British pop music, for so long a jazz-based confection aimed at an adult market, was transformed into the guitar-led music for teens that would go on to conquer the world in the 1960s.

ROOTS, RADICALS AND ROCKERS

1

THE ROCK ISLAND LINE

Anyone who knows anything about skiffle will tell you that its genesis occurred on 13 July 1954, when Lonnie Donegan recorded 'Rock Island Line', Lead Belly's song about the wily train driver who fools the operator of a big tollgate just outside of New Orleans. Except the Rock Island Line doesn't go to New Orleans and there never were any tollgates on American railroads. And Lead Belly didn't write that song. So what is really going on here?

To get to the bottom of the story, we have to go back almost exactly one hundred years before that historic recording, to 10 July 1854, when the Chicago & Rock Island Railroad was officially opened. For two years, work gangs had been laying steel rails forged in England along a 181-mile route due west across Illinois from the city of Chicago to Rock Island on the banks of the Mississippi. The plan was to cross the mighty river and bring the iron road to the American west.

For the men who owned the railroads, the Mississippi presented a formidable physical barrier, still half a mile wide at Rock Island, a thousand miles upstream from the Gulf of Mexico. Beyond it, the western plains were beginning to be settled and, in 1846, the land across the river from Illinois became the state of Iowa. Riverboats had a monopoly on transport across and along the Mississippi, but the intentions of the owners of the Chicago & Rock Island Railroad became clear in 1851 when they asked the Iowa legislature to grant them land to build a depot in Davenport, directly across the river from Rock Island.

Based on a topographical survey conducted in 1837 by Lt Robert E. Lee, engineers had chosen a prime spot to build the first bridge across Big Muddy and construction began in July 1853. The largest island in the whole of the Mississippi, Rock Island offered a sturdy jumping-off point for the 1,528-foot wooden bridge, which was supported by six granite piers. The first train crossed over to the Iowa shore on 21 April 1856, linking up with the Mississippi & Missouri Railroad, which was making heavy going of building a track across Iowa towards Council Bluffs on the eastern bank of the Missouri River. Several other railroads had reached the Mississippi, but none had managed to cross it. The Chicago & Rock Island Railroad had brought the possibility of transcontinental trade a step closer.

Before the coming of the railroad, rivers provided the main form of transport in the American interior, with a network of canals connecting tributaries and lakes, ferrying goods and people inland from the coast. But this distribution network was subject to seasonal changes: rivers in the north would freeze in the winter; some in the south would run dry in the summer. Many were prone to flooding. The railroad offered an all-weather form of transport and, since 1830, tracks had been laid linking eastern cities to the Atlantic coast.

Their livelihoods threatened by the railroad, the riverboat owners opposed the bridge from the outset, arguing that it would cause an impediment to navigation. Informing their complaints was a struggle over trade routes across the US. The southern states had built their distribution networks on a north–south axis using riverine routes. In the north, the east-to-west expansion of the railroad threatened southern interests. Most vocal among those opposing the bridge was US Secretary for War Jefferson Davis, who would go on to lead the Confederacy during the Civil War. As the issue of slavery became increasingly divisive, southern legislators, fearful of being dominated by the more populous north, sought to ensure that any new states joining the union would be pro-slavery. Davis used his office to promote a southern transcontinental route for the railroads in the hope that the west would be settled by slave-owning southerners. When the notion of a river crossing in the upper Mississippi presented a threat to his plans, he took legal action to stop the Chicago & Rock Island Railroad from building their bridge.

He was ultimately unsuccessful, but other interests were more determined. Just two weeks after the bridge was opened, on the night of 6 May 1857, the steamboat *Effie Afton* had passed beneath the open draw of the bridge when she suddenly veered to the right. Her starboard engine stopped, power appeared to increase in the port engine and she hit the pier next to the open draw. A stove in one of the cabins was overturned and soon the entire boat was aflame, with fire spreading to the wooden superstructure of the bridge, destroying one of the spans. Immediately suspicion fell on the riverboat owners. What was the *Effie Afton* doing so far north from her usual route between Louisville and New Orleans? Why was she out on the river long after other boats had tied up? How did she burn so quickly? And was she drifting helplessly or deliberately driven into the pier?

When it took just four months to repair the bridge, the riverboat owners resorted to the courts, demanding damages for the loss of the *Effie Afton* and seeking to prove that the bridge was a hazard. The Chicago & Rock Island company hired an experienced Illinois railroad lawyer to be their lead counsel. Abraham Lincoln had handled a number of cases concerning rights of navigation around railroad bridges on other rivers, some of which had gone all the way to the Supreme Court.

The judge dismissed the case after a trial that lasted fourteen days and resulted in a hung jury. Seen as a moral victory for the railroad, the Rock Island Bridge case drew national attention, helping to establish Lincoln's reputation ahead of his bid for the presidency in 1860.

The riverboat owners kept up their legal opposition for another decade, finally conceding defeat in December 1867. By that time there were several other bridges across the Mississippi and a transcontinental railway was being constructed between Sacramento, California, and Council Bluffs. The Mississippi and Missouri Railroad, in its attempt to cross Iowa ahead of competing railroads, had hit financial difficulties and was absorbed by the Chicago & Rock Island Railroad, whose track-laying gangs finally reached Council Bluffs on 10 May 1869.

This event was overshadowed by news that, just the day before, the final spike had been driven on the transcontinental railway at Promontory Point in Utah, uniting the Union Pacific and Central Pacific Railroads. Where once wagon trains had taken six weeks to cross from coast to coast, the steam trains had now cut the journey to just six days.

In the railroad boom years that followed, the company, changing its name to the Chicago, Rock Island & Pacific Railroad, began building lines that radiated out from the Rock Island crossing: north to Minneapolis, west to Denver and south across the Missouri River into

Ride it like you're flying: a Rock Island locomotive, *c.*1880

Kansas. In 1882, a song appeared extolling the virtues of the network, written by one J. A. Roff:*

> *Now listen to the jingle,*
> *The rumble and the roar*
> *As she dashes through the woodland*
> *And speeds along the shore;*
> *See the mighty rushing engine,*
> *Hear her merry bell ring out*
> *As they speed along in safety*
> *On the Great Rock Island Route.*

Shortly after the song was published, the track gangs reached Herington, Kansas, where the line split, one branch heading southwest towards New Mexico while the other dived due south towards Oklahoma. This southern spur followed the Chisholm Trail, used by cattle herders to bring their stock to railheads in Kansas and Missouri. Crossing Oklahoma, the tracks reached the Texas border in late 1892. By the end of the century, the Rock Island Railroad operated 3,568 miles of track, all of it west of Chicago, and had an annual turnover of $20 million.

In the early years of the new century, the company pushed south across Texas, heading for the Gulf port of Galveston. In 1904, it purchased the Choctaw, Oklahoma and Gulf Railroad, allowing it to link Memphis, Little Rock and Oklahoma City with Tucumcari, New Mexico, from where passengers could transfer to Southern Pacific trains serving California. In the same year, the Rock Island Employees

---

* In 1904, William Kindt would publish a version of the song, with the same tune and slightly changed lyrics, under the title of 'Wabash Cannonball'. Over time, and with many more lyrical changes, it would become one of the most famous songs in American folk music.

Club was founded at the company's headquarters in Chicago and, within a decade, had expanded to involve all levels of workers across the network, from brakemen and porters to engineers working in train yards. With separate organisations for black and white employees, the clubs staged social events such as picnics and sporting competitions between various depots.

In 1920, the company was actively encouraging employees to 'boost' the Rock Island brand. Music was at the forefront of this effort, with choirs and singing groups sent to perform at public gatherings, their members encouraged to write material that promoted the railroad. One of these booster groups, the Rock Island Colored Quartet, was formed by workers from the company's central freight yard and repair shops at Biddle,* just outside Little Rock, Arkansas. In January 1930, the *Rock Island Magazine* reported that a member of the Quartet, engine wiper Clarence Wilson, had composed a booster song entitled 'Buy Your Ticket Over Rock Island Lines', which was being performed in the Little Rock area. The verses spoke of the different characters that worked out of the Biddle depot, while the chorus extolled the virtues of the railroad:

> *Rock Island Line is a mighty good road*
> *Passengers get on board if you want to ride*
> *Ride it like you're flying*
> *Be sure you buy your ticket*
> *Over the Rock Island Line*

––––––

* Biddle Shops served the Rock Island's Arkansas–Louisiana Division as a central repair works and roundhouse for the trains that ran west to Memphis, Tennessee, and south to where passengers could catch the Southern Pacific's 'Sunset Limited' train that ran from New Orleans to Los Angeles at Eunice, Louisiana.

In the north-west of the state, straddling the Texas–Louisiana border, lies Caddo Lake. At the end of the nineteenth century, the area was home to rural communities of African Americans who made up 65 per cent of the local population. It was in this secluded area, near the town of Mooringsport, that Huddie Ledbetter was born in January 1888. From an early age he showed an aptitude for singing and playing guitar, making a name for himself as a 'musicianer' by performing at social gatherings. He also gained a reputation as someone who would never back down from a fight. In the early years of the twentieth century, Caddo Lake still had the aura of a frontier town, where men were expected to resolve their differences without recourse to the law. By the age of sixteen, Huddie carried a pistol as well as a guitar to local dances.

In 1910, he travelled to Dallas, where he teamed up with a teenage blues singer named Blind Lemon Jefferson. In the following decade, Jefferson would rise to fame as the first country blues artist, but during their time together, he and Huddie were just a couple of musicianers earning whatever they could by playing wherever they happened to be. A tall, well-built man with a strong singing voice, Huddie needed a powerful instrument to put his songs across, and during his time in Dallas he acquired the twelve-string guitar that was to become his trademark.

In 1915, Huddie was settled with his wife of seven years, Lethe Henderson, in Marshall, Texas, just across the state line from Mooringsport. Their lives were shattered when Huddie was involved in an altercation that resulted in him being convicted of carrying a pistol and sentenced to thirty days on the chain gang. Unable to countenance the treatment meted out to him, he escaped after just three days, heading eighty-five miles north to live with members of his extended family in De Kalb, Texas. There he worked as a cotton picker under the assumed name of William Boyd. While walking to

9

a dance with a group of friends in December 1917, Huddie, never the most faithful of husbands, became involved in an argument with one of his companions, Will Stafford, over the affections of a young woman. The dispute quickly escalated, violence ensued and Huddie pulled out his pistol and shot Stafford down. Convicted of murder, Huddie was sentenced to serve seven to thirty years and soon found himself Sugarland bound.

The Central State Prison Farm, just west of Houston, took its familiar name from nearby Sugar Land, a company town built by the Imperial Sugar Company in the first decade of the twentieth century to process sugar cane from the surrounding fields. A humid, subtropical climate made labouring in the fields a challenge, but Huddie rose to become a team leader of a work gang. Realising that he would be at Sugarland for a long time, he used his talent as a performer to win a small degree of liberty within the prison regime. On Sundays, he was allowed to travel unaccompanied to other camps within the prison to entertain inmates with his songs and stories.

It was during this time that he picked up the nickname by which he would come to be known around the world: Lead Belly. Many of the songs that he later popularised came from his time in Sugarland. Most famous of them all was 'Midnight Special', which took its name from a Southern Pacific train that left Houston every night around 11 p.m., heading west for San Antonio. Its lights would sometimes flicker on the walls of inmates' cells as the train passed the prison, giving rise to the belief that if the light from the Midnight Special fell on you, you would be next for parole.

In January 1924, Texas Governor Pat Neff visited the prison and Lead Belly was called upon to provide some evening entertainment. Desperate for his freedom, Lead Belly composed a song asking to be pardoned for his crime, singing, 'If I had you Governor Neff like you got me, I'd wake up in the morning and set you free.' Although he impressed the governor with his ability to write songs, Lead Belly had to wait a whole year before he got his pardon, signed by Neff on his last day in office. During his time as governor, Neff signed very few pardons, and the fact that he made an exception for Lead Belly is probably a sign of his generosity towards the convict musician – although any suggestion of excessive clemency is tempered by the fact that Lead Belly would have been eligible for parole just four months later, having served the minimum seven years demanded by his sentence.

Lead Belly headed back to Mooringsport, where the discovery of oil had created an economic boom. He worked as a roustabout, performing at night in local barrelhouses. He again found himself in trouble with the law in January 1930, when he was arrested following an altercation with a group of white men. According to the press report of his trial, the trouble began when Lead Belly came upon the local Salvation Army band playing on a street corner one Saturday night. When he began to dance in time to their music, some white bystanders took exception, presumably thinking he was being disrespectful. When they told him to move along, he did so, but carried on dancing, provoking a group of men to go after him. When knives were pulled, Lead Belly drew his in self-defence and, in the scuffle that followed, he received a gash to the top of his head, while one of his attackers, Dick Ellet, had his arm slashed.

When word spread that a 'drunk crazed negro' had attempted to murder a white man, an angry mob descended on the parish jail where Lead Belly was being held. Only the swift action of the law enforcement officers guarding the jailhouse saved him from being lynched. Knife fights had always been a part of Lead Belly's life. His body bore the scars of many barrelhouse brawls. He'd often go and report what had happened to the local sheriff's office, only to be told to stay out of town for a while. But this was different. Unlike his other victims, Dick Ellet was white and, as a result, Lead Belly

11

would have to face the full force of the law. Convicted of attempted murder in a trial lasting just a day, he was sentenced to serve six to ten years' hard labour.

At the age of forty-three, Lead Belly found himself in one of the most notorious prisons in the whole of the US – Angola State Penitentiary. Here, the regime made Sugarland seem easy by comparison. Slavery may have been abolished at the end of the Civil War, but sixty-five years later, its practices were still being employed at Angola. Shackled together with chains, working in the fields from dawn to dusk in sweltering heat and humidity, at night inmates slept on the floor of dormitories that held seven hundred men, where the lights were never switched off. Surrounded on three sides by the Mississippi River and the tangled forest of the Tunica Hills in the east, there was very little opportunity for escape.

As in Sugarland, Lead Belly soon gained a reputation as a talented performer whose skill on the twelve-string guitar drew the attention of prisoners and guards alike. When song collectors from the Library of Congress arrived at the prison in July 1933, looking to record vernacular material, Lead Belly was an obvious candidate for their project.

John Lomax was a sixty-six-year-old college professor and folklorist researching African American work songs for the Archives of Folk Music at the Library of Congress. Equipped with the latest portable recording technology and assisted by his eighteen-year-old son Alan, Lomax toured labour camps across the south in search of material. His focus soon turned to prisons, where incarceration isolated singers from the popular music of the day. At Angola Lead Belly impressed the Lomaxes with the breadth of his repertoire and his storytelling skills. Among the seven songs he recorded that day was the one that would become his signature tune: 'Goodnight Irene'.

Believing that it had been his songwriting that got him out of

Sugarland, Lead Belly resolved to try the same method to secure his release from Angola. When the Lomaxes returned to the prison in June 1934, Lead Belly recorded a song asking Louisiana Governor O. K. Allen for a pardon, which he asked John Lomax to take to Baton Rouge and present to Governor Allen himself. Lomax duly delivered the recording and within a month – on 1 August 1934 – Lead Belly was set free.*

He immediately wrote to John Lomax, offering to work as his 'man' – driving his car and carrying the heavy recording equipment. Lomax was in need of assistance. About to set off on another field recording expedition, his son Alan had been taken ill and was unable to accompany him. He hired Lead Belly and soon the pair were headed for Arkansas. Immediately Lomax realised what an asset he had. Rather than have to explain the nature of his project in patrician tones to often bemused and sometimes hostile prison staff, who in turn would order inmates to comply, he was able to send Lead Belly into the dormitories to tell the prisoners what was happening and to play them examples of the kind of songs Lomax was looking for.

In the first week of October 1934, at Cummins State Farm near Pine Bluff, a twenty-one-year-old convicted burglar named Kelly Pace came before Lomax's recording machine, leading a group of seven fellow convicts. In close harmony, they sang 'Rock Island Line' in a call-and-response style. This wasn't the first time Lomax had heard the song. It was among those he had collected at Tucker State Prison, some fifty miles north, just the week before. In the five years since it was written by Clarence Wilson in the Biddle Shops, 'Buy Your Ticket on the Rock Island Line' had been transformed from a

* There is no evidence that Allen ever heard the record. Lead Belly was not pardoned; rather, he gained his release under a programme that sought to cut the sentences of well-behaved prisoners to save state expenditure during the Great Depression.

Rock Island Line
LEADBELLY
Huddie Ledbetter Memorial Album, Vol. 2
Notes by FREDERIC RAMSEY, JR.
FA 2014 1-10" L.P. 33⅓ RPM record
Folkways Records & Service Corp., N.Y.

Cotton Song, Ha Ha This Way,
Sukey Jump, Black Girl, Pigmeat,
Rock Island Line, Blind Lemon,
Borrow Love and Go, On A Monday,
Shorty George, Duncan & Brady,
Old Riley, Leavin' Blues

booster tune into a song offering redemption from sin. In Lead Belly's hands, that process would continue.

In many ways, Lead Belly was more of a song collector than John Lomax. While the learned professor needed to record performances in order to study them, Lead Belly could play a song after hearing it just a few times, appropriating material as he needed it. 'Rock Island Line' soon joined others in his song bag, although with just two verses it felt a little short. A talented improviser, Lead Belly had no compunction in extemporising a few extra verses, borrowing from children's nursery rhymes and the blues tradition.

When their work in the prisons ended, Lomax invited Lead Belly to come north with him to appear at an academic event in Philadelphia organised by the Modern Language Association. He would be required not only to perform the songs but to give some context to their origins.

Over the next few months, Lead Belly would accompany John and Alan Lomax to such august venues as Harvard University, where folklorists were bowled over by the depth of his repertoire and the power of his performances. For many of them, Lead Belly was the first vernacular singer they had seen, and his back story of plantation and prison offered them an insight into the daily lives of the rural African American community.

Lead Belly realised that the academics wanted to hear the stories behind his songs. Some, like those he had learned in childhood, were simple to explain. A song like 'Rock Island Line', however, had no background. Neither he nor Lomax had bothered to ask Kelly Pace where he had first heard the song, nor enquired whether it was used for work or pleasure. Recalling that the recording sessions at Cummings had been held next to the log pile, Lead Belly introduced 'Rock Island Line' as a chopping song. In June 1937, when he first recorded 'Rock Island Line', Lead Belly, singing a cappella, explained how a gang of men preparing a log would use the song to time the swing of their pole-axes.

When Alan Lomax arranged for the Golden Gate Quartet, a popular vocal group, to back Lead Belly on a recording of 'Rock Island Line' in June 1940, he dispensed with any spoken introduction, performing the song in its original call-and-response style. Lead Belly's January 1942 recording for Moe Asch featured a whole new introduction concerning a train driver and a depot agent. It contains the list of livestock familiar from later versions, but fails to explain their significance. Things became clearer in October 1944, when Lead Belly, out in Hollywood hoping to make a career in movies, recorded the song for Columbia Records, backed by Paul Mason Howard on zither. He begins the introduction by telling us that the Rock Island train is out of 'Mule-een' – possibly a reference to Moline, the largest city in Rock Island County, Illinois. The depot agent throws a switch over

15

the track to send the train 'into the hole'.* Instructed to pull into a siding, Lead Belly tells us, the train driver explains to the depot agent that he's carrying cows, horses, hogs, sheep and goats. Due to animal welfare considerations, trains hauling livestock were given priority over ordinary freight and so the agent lets the train pass. As he picks up speed, the driver calls back, 'I thank you, I thank you.'

Five months later in San Francisco, Lead Belly records the song again, starting his introduction with the wood-chopping story before segueing into the tale about the train. This time, however, the driver fools the depot agent, calling back that he's carrying 'all pig iron' – possibly a livestock pun. The definitive version of 'Rock Island Line' is recorded in the summer of 1947 in New York City. Again, Lead Belly mentions that the train is coming back from 'Mule-een'. Again, the depot agent tells the driver to take the train 'into the hole'. Told

* During the Golden Age of the railroad, before the post-war development of the interstate highway system made car travel more attractive, freight trains had to give way to the more lucrative passenger services, pulling into a siding – going 'in the hole' in railroad slang – to wait while the express thundered past.

that the train is hauling 'all livestock', the depot agent waves it past, only to be told, 'I fooled you! I fooled you! I got all pig iron.'

It's highly likely that it was on this performance that Lonnie Donegan based his version of 'Rock Island Line'. Folkways released the 1947 recording in 1953, four years after Lead Belly's death aged sixty-one. It was the title track of the second in a series of Huddie Ledbetter memorial albums. According to Chas McDevitt, this 10" thirteen-track record was a key source of inspiration for skiffle groups. Listening today, it's easy to imagine that Donegan could have mistaken 'Mule-een' for 'New Orleans', given that Lead Belly himself hailed from Louisiana. Not so easy to imagine is where Donegan found the idea of the 'big tollgate'. Lead Belly never mentions it, nor does he ever suggest in any of his recordings that a payment may have been due. In fact, there never were any tollgates on American railroads. Trains were charged to use tracks owned by other companies, but this was part of a contractual 'trackage rights' agreement, not a train-by-train cash fee.

However, by extemporising a story that made sense to his audience, Donegan was doing no more damage to the song than Lead Belly did when he introduced it to the staid New England academics at Harvard. Kelly Pace had also taken someone else's song and shaped it into something that made sense in his environment. Who is to say that Clarence Wilson, the engine wiper at Biddle Shops, didn't base his lyric on a popular tune of the day? Before commerce made ownership the key transactional interest of creativity, songs passed through culture by word of mouth and bore the fingerprints of everyone who ever sang them.

Little of this story was available to the young Englishmen who avidly collected American jazz and blues records in the 1930s. For them, a single recording was definitive, offering an insight into a culture that seemed to offer more excitement than the bland music they heard on BBC radio. Like members of an underground cult, they collated details of recording sessions, trying to discern the landscape of a musical form that they found so invigorating, yet so distant. Frustrated in their attempts to understand what it was that so moved them, some began to pick up instruments in the hope of emulating the primal sounds of New Orleans jazz.

2

RATION BOOK JAZZ

Bill Colyer was the Godfather of Skiffle. He was present at its birth and presided at the christening, naming this purely British phenomenon after a distant American relative of whom he was very fond. This role fell to him due to his deep knowledge of American roots music, stretching back to when he began collecting jazz records as a teenager.

His interest began in the 1930s, when he lived with his family in Soho, then the most multicultural district of London, where jazz had taken hold following the British debut of the Original Dixieland Jazz Band in 1919. In *Madness at Midnight*, his salacious memoir of London low life, Jack Glicco describes the multitude of clubs that sprang up in Soho between the wars: jazz was played until 4 a.m. in tiny rooms, most no more than twenty-five feet square and crammed with smoke, noise and people. A few tables were scattered around the walls and, on a small rostrum in an alcove at the far end of the room, a band played 'like men possessed'.

Too young to enter such places, Bill often loitered with his friends by the grating of a club called Jigs in an alleyway between Dean Street and Wardour Street, listening to the hot music rising up from basement sessions. Once a month, he'd cycle down to Levy's music store in Whitechapel to spend whatever money he'd saved from his job as a trainee electrician on a 78 rpm jazz record.

In 1938, when the Colyer family moved out of Soho to a housing estate in Cranford, west of London, Bill, then aged sixteen, had a collection of thirty or so records, which he kept in an old orange box lined with oilcloth. Every evening after work, he had a set time in which he was allowed to listen to jazz on his HMV wind-up gramophone, changing the Songster needle after every play, carefully wiping each record clean before it went back in the box. His younger siblings, Bob, Ken and Valerie, were all under strict instructions to never, ever touch any of Bill's records.

The Colyer children had endured a chaotic upbringing. Their father had drifted in and out of their lives, while their mother had suffered from bouts of ill health. At one point in the early 1930s, the boys were left to fend for themselves while their mother was in hospital with kidney failure, the three brothers, two of them under the age of ten, living rough in a disused railway carriage in the rural backwater of the Laindon plotlands in Essex.

Moving to leafy Cranford offered the Colyers comparative stability even as events elsewhere were drifting towards conflict. Around the time the family arrived in the area, the plane carrying British Prime Minister Neville Chamberlain home from Munich after negotiations with Adolf Hitler landed at nearby Heston Aerodrome. Chamberlain emerged waving an accord signed by the German Chancellor, proclaiming it would guarantee 'peace in our time'. The crowds at Heston cheered, unaware that Hitler had other intentions.

When war broke out in September 1939, Bill Colyer soon got his call-up papers, his brother Bob following shortly after. With their father again absent, youngest brother Ken was left to be the man of the house, looking after his infirm mother and younger sister.

Ken Colyer was born in 1928 in Great Yarmouth, Norfolk, at the home of his maternal uncle, William Ehrhardt. His mother, unable to cope on her own, had put his two elder brothers into children's homes at the time of his birth. Eleven years old when war broke out, Ken was quick to adapt to the new realities. With his mother preferring to remain in the house during air raids – some householders feared blackout burglars more than bombs – Ken took ownership of the air-raid shelter at the bottom of the garden, using it as a gang hut for his pals in the village.

It was here that Ken discovered his musical ability. A neighbour gave him an old harmonica, which he quickly mastered. Then, with money earned from a paper round, he bought himself a second-hand guitar from Shepherd's Bush market. Being left-handed, he had to restring the instrument so he could play the chords, but he was soon whiling away the time in the bomb shelter learning to strum tunes.

By the time Ken left school aged fifteen in 1943, Hendon Aerodrome was home to squadrons of Spitfires and Hurricanes. But instead of the RAF, he attempted to join the Merchant Navy, despite being under-age. His deception was discovered and he saw out the war as a milk-man, doing a horse-and-cart round for the Co-op.

In 1944, Bill Colyer took part in the Normandy landings, fighting inland as far as Brussels. Due some leave, he wrote to his mother to tell her he was coming home.

'Now don't be angry,' she wrote back, 'but Ken's been playing your records.'

Bill was seething. He'd survived D-Day, the house in Cranford had made it through the Blitz, but this was one bombshell that he was not prepared for. That little toerag had been playing his precious records!

'He's been treating them with great respect,' she continued, 'wiping them clean and using new needles.' Any sense of calm reflection that these details may have brought was shattered by his mother's further shocking revelation: 'But also, your brother Bob took your racing bike out from the shed and has had a little accident and buck-led the front wheel.'

Clearly, on getting home to Cranford, the first thing Bill Colyer needed to do after kissing his mother was give his two little brothers a clip round the ear. However, by the time he arrived back, the wheel had been repaired, and once Bill saw that his record collection had been shown the same level of respect that he himself had lavished on it, he calmed down.

Talking to Ken, he was intrigued to discover which records he had been playing. From the age of twelve, the youngster had been imbibing the country blues of Sleepy John Estes, the guitar-driven gospel of Sister Rosetta Tharpe and the boogie-woogie piano blues of Champion Jack Dupree. Not only was he listening to Bill's records, he was learning to play along with them too. By the time Bill came home on leave, Ken had acquired a second-hand trumpet and was trying to make it sing. To encourage the lad, Bill bought him Nat Gonella's tutorial *Modern Style Trumpet Playing*, but Ken never learned to read music, preferring instead to play by ear.

The two brothers didn't have much time to discuss their common interest in jazz and blues. As soon as Bill and Bob returned from the war, Ken was finally accepted into the Merchant Navy, joining his first boat as a cabin boy on VE Day. He had just turned seventeen.

The *British Hussar* was a rickety old oil tanker built in 1923, and for the first year he was aboard Ken saw the canals of Venice, the Old City of Trieste, the troubled port of Haifa – restless under the British Mandate – Port Said, gateway to the Suez Canal, and the Arabian Gulf ports of Abadan and Aden. Merchant seamen don't get to pick and choose which ships they work on. They sign up to the 'pool', are given the next available job and have to take it, no matter where the voyage may be headed. Frustratingly for a young man who longed for the jazz clubs of Chicago and New Orleans, the old bucket only seemed capable of sailing eastward.

On returning home to Blighty, Ken enrolled himself in the Merchant Navy's cookery school in the hope of escaping the lowly position of cabin boy. He managed to get a job as a galley lackey on the *Waimana*, a cargo ship that had been roaming the seas since before the First

22

World War. Again his hopes of seeing America were thwarted when the ship headed south around the Cape of Good Hope to Australia.

Ken had taken his guitar and trumpet to sea, and when he wasn't strumming the blues on one, he was trying to find his tone on the other, studiously learning his craft seven days a week.

Finally, he was able to find a boat to take him west. The *Port Sydney* was a refrigerated meat carrier, thirty years on the high seas and somewhat worse for wear. Ken didn't mind at all, because this baby was going to take him across the Atlantic. The *Port Sydney*'s first destination was Montreal, where Ken witnessed a teenage Oscar Peterson pounding out boogie-woogie at the Café St Michel.

Now elevated to the role of second cook, Ken's dreams came true when he learned that the *Port Sydney* would next be heading for New York. In the years after the Second World War, New York became not only the biggest city on earth but also the most vibrant. While the European capitals struggled to piece their cultural life back together after the chaos and destruction of the war years, the Five Boroughs were busy creating the sounds of a new world.

Swing music and jump jive kept the Manhattan ballrooms jammed with dancers, and modern jazz was emerging from after-hours clubs in Harlem. Frank Sinatra crossed the river from Hoboken to win the hearts of young girls everywhere, and Woody Guthrie blew in from California to ride the subways, his guitar emblazoned with the slogan 'This Machine Kills Fascists'. Guthrie was a merchant seaman himself during the Second World War, working in the galley just like Ken. Had Colyer arrived a few years earlier, he might have heard the Dust Bowl Balladeer performing in one of the seamen's bars near the 14th Street Pier where the *Port Sydney* was docked.

When the twenty-year-old Ken Colyer arrived in the spring of 1948, Woody Guthrie was still living with his wife and kids in the flat on Mermaid Avenue in Brooklyn. He could have looked him up in the

New York area phone book. Instead, he went to the first phone box he saw, opened the directory and looked for Mr Edward Condon – the simplest way to find the address of his club.

Condon was synonymous with the switch from Chicago to New York that jazz made in the late 1930s. Born in 1905, he played guitar and specialised in a sophisticated version of the Dixieland style that harked back to the early days of jazz in New Orleans. Ken knew of him thanks to a series of concerts that Condon recorded at the New York Town Hall, broadcast in England by the BBC. In 1945, he opened his own jazz club on West 3rd Street in Greenwich Village. Heading to the venue Ken discovered he was in luck – Eddie Condon was hosting one of his jam sessions that very night. Managing to get a seat close to the band, Ken had a night he would never forget.

'Within a couple of numbers, the band were playing with a power, swing and tonal quality that I would not have believed possible. It struck me for the first time that the gramophone record is badly misleading when it comes to jazz. No recording could ever capture the greatness of this music.

'As each number got rocking, I seemed to be suspended, just sitting on air. And when the music finished, I just flopped back on my chair as though physically exhausted. The sensation I got from hearing Wild Bill Davison for the first time was a sort of numb joy that such a man lived and played.'

Three years at sea had inured Ken to the effects of strong drink, but after nursing a few expensive beers for the whole night at Condon's, he left dizzy from the emotional high.

Ken became a fixture at the club, only wandering further into Manhattan when he learned that Eddie Condon always played a show at Town Hall on the first day of the month. To his delight he arrived to find a placard outside announcing that Condon's special guest was Lead Belly, the acclaimed blues and ballad singer from Louisiana.

His euphoria was short-lived, however: the concert was already over. Jazz musicians tended to work nights in bars and clubs. If they gave concerts, they'd happen during the day. For the rest of his life, Ken would regret the fact that he'd missed seeing Lead Belly, one of the greatest blues singers of all time, by just a few hours. He was, though, able to pick up one of the albums that Lead Belly recorded for Moe Asch, as well as a first edition of the jazz hipster's bible, *Really the Blues* by Mezz Mezzrow.

Milton 'Mezz' Mesirow was the middle-class son of Russian Jewish immigrants, born in Chicago in 1899. A fairly proficient jazz clarinettist, he founded one of the first interracial jazz bands and financed recording sessions for New Orleans jazz men Tommy Ladnier and Sidney Bechet. His greatest claim to fame, however, is as the author of *Really the Blues*, his autobiographical exploration of urban African American culture, heavily focused on the jazz scene. Like Woody Guthrie's *Bound for Glory* and Jack Kerouac's *On the Road*, it fired the imagination of a generation of readers who, in the stuffy atmosphere of the late 1940s and early 50s, yearned to find an exciting life beyond the four walls of their boring adolescent bedrooms.

In his book, the hippest of the hip are always seeking Mezz out, conversing with him in jive. A quick look in the glossary will reveal that they're mostly enquiring if Mezz has any marijuana to sell them: he's a dealer in 'hay'. Published just a few years before Ken Colyer visited New York, the jive section may have given Ken some new slang words to use aboard ship, but the deep appreciation of New Orleans jazz that runs through the book would have given him greater insight into the music he loved.

When Bill Colyer read his brother's letters from New York, with their excited accounts of spending nights enthralled by the most scintillating jazz he had ever heard, he too resolved to sign up for the Merchant Navy as soon as possible. After what he later referred to as 'a lot of argy-bargy', Bill was able to join Ken on the *Port Sydney* as a stoker, shovelling coal in the bowels of the ship, four hours on, eight hours off, every day.

On the 'corned beef run' to South America, Ken and Bill teamed up with another shipmate, second cook Les Mullocks, for jam sessions below deck – Ken on trumpet, Les on banjo and Bill keeping the rhythm on a suitcase using wire brushes. Month after month they jammed, night after night, until Ken could play any song he heard by ear after just a couple of listens. Impressed by his brother's talents, Bill began to wonder – with all the connections he had in the nascent London jazz scene, maybe the two of them could get a few gigs.

Back in England, the first tentative stirrings of what would become the trad jazz boom were being made by pianist George Webb. He and his band began playing in a Dixieland style during 1943, eschewing the swing sound that was popular at the time, taking inspiration instead from the New Orleans revival. After seeing Webb's Dixielanders perform at King George's Hall, just off Great Russell Street in central London, while on shore leave in late October 1948, Ken decided to quit the Merch and look for work in a band playing New Orleans jazz.

Despite the fact that a National Federation of Jazz Organisations of Great Britain had been formed just a few months previously, there were very few active bands looking for new members. Most outfits were little more than a bunch of jazz-loving pals who got together to jam wherever they could.

For Ken, unable to read music and with no experience of blowing with other brass musicians, ensemble playing presented a considerable challenge. Offered the chance to try out for a band called the Jelly Roll Kings, Ken failed the audition. After years of playing to be heard above the thrum of a ship's engine, he was simply too loud, and when he improvised he changed key without realising. But it wasn't just his playing that put the Jelly Roll Kings off – there was also the matter of Ken's temperament. For Dave Stevens, pianist with the band, the problem was really lack of communication. 'Ken said very little to us, and we responded the same way.'

By the end of 1948, Ken was living back in Cranford, working as a carriage cleaner on the London Underground. At the time, Cranford, although just fifteen miles from central London, was little more than a village on the main trunk road to the west. Other than the traffic rattling along the A4, there wasn't much happening. Three pubs provided the nightlife, and there was the Continental Café for the teenagers to hang out in, but if you wanted to see a movie or visit a dancehall, it was a Green Bus ride away.

Like all such communities, everyone of a certain age was just a few degrees of separation away from each other, and for someone with the advanced social skills of Bill Colyer, those networks were likely to be large. Bill liked to chat, especially about jazz, and as a consequence he knew most of the players in the area. His vast knowledge of styles and genres, coupled with his now formidable record collection, meant that he could often introduce other jazz buffs to rare 78 cuts that they would never hear on the radio. When he found out that one of his local contacts had a younger brother who played a bit of jazz, he suggested Ken go round and get acquainted.

One Saturday afternoon, Ben Marshall answered a knock at the door to find a young man with a trumpet case and slicked-back hair. 'My brother knows your brother and he tells me that you play guitar.' Ben invited the stranger in and soon the two of them were jamming a twelve-bar on trumpet and piano.

'We chatted and got along quite well,' Marshall said of his first encounter with Ken Colyer. 'Very enthusiastic he was. A little bit introverted, as he always is – he couldn't really open up to you. Lived in this world that he'd created for himself. He was telling me he wanted to get a band together to play New Orleans music, which meant nothing to me at that point, really.'

That soon changed. Ben had been playing with a group of friends, who had up to then been trying to master a mixture of swing and modern jazz. Ken introduced them to the music of the Crescent City. Playing along with 78s on Bill Colyer's portable Dansette record player, the band was soon brought round to the Colyers' way of thinking.

Looking to escape the confines of their parents' back rooms, they began to search for a rehearsal space where they could really let rip. In early March 1949, they secured the use of the British Legion hut next to the White Hart pub in Cranford, for a regular Tuesday-night get-together.

Initially there were just four of them: Ben Marshall on banjo, Ron Bowden playing drums and Sonny Morris and Ken on trumpet. For such a small jazz band, it was unusual to have two horns, but Ben and Ron were insistent that Sonny should stay, and Ken, for once, acquiesced. What else could he do? He just wanted to play New Orleans jazz and these guys seemed willing.

In May, Ken heard that John R. T. Davies, a multi-instrumentalist member of Mick Mulligan's Magnolia Jazz Band, lived a few miles up the road in Longford. Ken paid him a visit, and within a week Davies had left Mulligan and was rehearsing with the lads in the White Hart hut, with his younger brother Julian in tow.

John R. T. was just what the band needed. A privately educated, classically trained musician, he pointed out, ever so politely, their beginner's mistakes. 'There's no key change in that tune,' he told Ken at their first rehearsal. 'What key change?' Ken replied. Lacking any formal knowledge of music, the lads had been inadvertently breaking the rules, playing free-form jazz long before it became fashionable.

The arrival of the Davies brothers had the effect of gelling this bunch of players into a viable unit. All they needed now was a name. On the summer nights when they couldn't get access to the hut, they would take their instruments into the fields, walking down to the banks of the Crane River that had given Cranford its name. This minor tributary of the Thames, more of a stream than a river, now marks the eastern boundary of Heathrow Airport, but in 1949 it ran through a wooded vale on open heath land.

Although Ken was clearly the leader of the band, in the spirit of democracy they decided against naming it for him and instead settled on the Crane River Jazz Band, adopting the old spiritual 'Down by the Riverside' as their theme tune. The locals, hearing them playing to the cows on the heath, thought they were mad, but on the Tuesday nights when they rehearsed in the hut behind the White Hart, drinkers would wander in with their pints and listen to the band. One night, a clarinet player by the name of Monty Sunshine came along to check them out and was invited to sit in. By the end of the evening, he was a member of the band.

Eventually, so many people were wandering in – mostly teenagers unable to enter the pub – that someone suggested they charge a door fee, and so the Crane River Jazz Club was founded. To begin with, punters just watched the band rehearse, but slowly one or two began to dance to their tunes. If, while trying to master a number, they had to stop and start again, the dancers didn't seem to mind. They just waited while the band discussed what was wrong, then carried on dancing once the music resumed.

Now they had an audience, the Cranes' playing took on a new dynamic, as they were able to see the effect their music had on the crowd. But pushing their performance to the next level put a huge strain on tired lips so, to give the band a break, Bill Colyer was drafted in to provide a record recital based on his extensive collection of jazz 78s.

Record recitals were a familiar aspect of the late-40s revivalist jazz scene in Britain. Fans eager to hear music that they had hitherto only read about would attend lectures by respected jazz critics such as Sinclair Traill, James Asman and Albert McCarthy, who played records from their personal collections to a seated audience. Between platters, they would discuss the different styles and genres and examine the lives of the great jazz musicians. These were well attended, stand-alone events: one man with a gramophone and a love of jazz.

While the Cranes headed into the White Hart to refresh themselves ahead of their second set, Bill Colyer would offer the audience the benefit of his knowledge, playing his cherished records on a portable Colaro electric turntable.

'We're talking about kids – fifteen, sixteen, seventeen,' Bill said of the crowd who gathered round to hear his recitals. 'I would be playing 78s in the interval, entertaining if you like, but teaching too. I played the music I liked; it made me happy and it made other people happy and it always used to go down well. I'd do my thirty minutes, or whatever, then the band would come on again.'

When drummer Ron Bowden left the Cranes to play a more modern jazz, Bill Colyer was drafted in as a stopgap, playing washboard in the rhythm section. Reminded of the days when they used to jam together in the Merchant Navy, Bill suggested to his brother that, instead of playing the records during the interval, the two of them could perform some American roots music on guitar and washboard, and if Julian Davies wanted to join in on stand-up bass, they'd have a great little breakdown group.

It made a lot of sense to Ken. Not only would he get to rest his lips, he would also be introducing material to an audience that would have only previously heard the songs on record, if at all. And with Bill giving some background to each number, the process of enlightening the young jazz club members would continue.

The breakdown sessions mostly featured Lead Belly songs like 'Midnight Special', 'Take This Hammer' and 'John Henry'. Big Bill Broonzy was another favourite, as were Brownie McGhee and Lonnie Johnson. The breakdown group was the first of its kind in the UK and, from October 1949, it became a regular feature of the Crane River Jazz Band. Though no one was calling it skiffle back then, Bill and Ken Colyer, through their urge to spread the gospel of the roots of jazz, had planted the seeds of a movement that would one day inspire a generation of British kids to pick up a guitar and play rock 'n' roll.

———

As the new decade opened, the Crane River Jazz Band took to the road, playing various halls and clubs across west London as well as the occasional art school dance. Eventually they took up residency in the cellar of 11 Great Newport Street in Covent Garden. Appearing every Monday night for a year, they finally came to the attention of the jazz establishment.

James Asman, founder of the Jazz Appreciation Society, loved their spirit but wrote that they were 'rough and incredibly crude'. James Berman of *Melody Maker* dismissed their 'primordial sense of jazz'. But the Cranes didn't care, they were insurrectionists, a revolutionary cadre come to save jazz from commercialism by taking it back to basics, recreating the sound of the rowdy clubs of Storyville in turn-of-the-century New Orleans.

An invitation to perform at the prestigious Royal Festival Hall in 1951 in the presence of two royal princesses did nothing to dent Ken Colyer's outsider persona. 'The Cranes were grudgingly allowed to play,' he later wrote, 'although there was strong opposition from some quarters. We were a bunch of roughnecks playing a purpose-fully primitive music. We might dirty up the place and offend the

The Crane River Jazz Band, *c.* 1950

ears of Princess Margaret and Princess Elizabeth.' In the event, a photographer was able to capture an image of a tieless Colyer and a fur-wrapped Princess Elizabeth smiling at one another during introductions at the after-show reception. A little over six months later, she would be queen and he would be back in the Merchant Navy.

That gig was part of the Festival of Britain, a year-long celebration of British culture and ingenuity that sought to draw a line under the war years, encouraging its audiences to look to the future. But for Ken Colyer and the Crane River Jazz Band, there was to be no future. The Festival Hall gig was the last time the friends from Cranford performed together. Earlier in the year, Ken, Ben Marshall and pianist Pat Hawes from the Cranes had done some recordings with members of Humphrey Lyttelton's jazz band. The records were very well received, and when two of Lyttelton's musicians, brothers Keith and Ian Christie, approached the Crane boys with a view to forming a permanent group, Colyer jumped at the chance, taking Hawes and Marshall with him.

The Christie Brothers Stompers were formed in July 1951, and the money they were offered to play a residency at the 100 Club on London's Oxford Street meant that the former Cranes could afford to give up their day jobs. And Bill Colyer came along too, playing the occasional washboard on recordings. They based their style on that of Kid Ory's Original Creole Jazz Band, who featured one of Ken's heroes, Mutt Carey, on trumpet.

The Crane River Jazz Band had tried to stay true to their ideals, relying on collective improvisation around a theme to produce peaks

The Crane River Jazz Band open for Big Bill Broonzy, February 1952

of excitement without solos. 'A good New Orleans band has no stars,' Ken told the Cranes. 'It's the ensemble sound that is important.' And while he was initially at home in the Christie Brothers Stompers, he was ever watchful for deviations from the traditional New Orleans style. When Keith Christie began introducing other elements into their sound, Ken knew it was time to move on.

But where? Nobody in Britain was performing the kind of music that Colyer wanted to play. The most successful bandleader from the revivalist scene was Humphrey Lyttelton. An old Etonian and former officer in the Grenadier Guards, Humph was all the things that Colyer was not: suave, sociable and blessed with the boundless self-confidence that comes from a public-school education. George Melly, in his autobiography *Owning Up*, described Lyttelton's relationship with Colyer in a telling passage: 'Even Humph, although he always denied it, was affected by Ken's ideas. For a month or two he stopped to look over his shoulder. The ghost of Mutt Carey whispered in his ear. Then he turned away, and swam slowly and deliberately into the mainstream.'

In Colyer's eyes, Lyttelton was an apostate, someone who believed that leaving New Orleans for the bright lights of Chicago was the best thing Louis Armstrong had ever done.* Unfortunately for Ken, almost everybody in the UK revivalist movement agreed with Humph.

———

Ken Colyer's biggest hero was Bunk Johnson, a jazz trumpeter born in 1879 and active in turn-of-the-century New Orleans. In 1910, Johnson left the Crescent City to tour with minstrel shows and circuses, never

* Armstrong was the first great jazz soloist, stepping out of the ensemble and into the spotlight, undermining what Colyer believed to be the original ethos of jazz – that all are equal on the bandstand.

to return. In the decades that followed, he became a legendary figure among the fans of New Orleans jazz.

In the late 1930s, two American jazz buffs, Frederic Ramsey and Charles Edward Smith, set out to write the first comprehensive history of the genre. Their book, *Jazzmen: The Story of Hot Jazz Told in the Lives of the Men Who Created It*, published in 1939, sealed the reputation of New Orleans as the home of jazz. As they conducted interviews with the old-timers who had been playing in the early days, one name kept coming up – Bunk Johnson. But nobody knew what happened to him.

Then, one night in 1937, Louis Armstrong was playing a show with Luis Russell's Orchestra in New Iberia, a rural town about ninety miles west of New Orleans. A thin old man with no teeth came close to the bandstand to listen and during the interval called out to Armstrong. It was Bunk Johnson. Having lost his front teeth in a barroom brawl, he'd been unable to play and was making a living driving sugar cane trucks for local farmers.

With his re-emergence, the authors of *Jazzmen* had access to a gold mine of memories from the dawn of jazz. Johnson brought first-hand experience to their narrative. His assertion that Buddy Bolden was the first person in New Orleans to play what we now know as jazz, and that he, Bunk Johnson, was right there playing second trumpet when it happened, ensured his legendary status.*

The jazz buffs who had rediscovered Johnson raised the money to buy him a new set of false teeth and a serviceable trumpet and, to their delight, they found his playing still had enough tone and drive

---

* Over time, Johnson's claims have been contested. What scant evidence has since come to light suggests that Bunk was actually born in 1889, ten years later than he claimed. If true, this seriously undermines his claim to have been playing jazz in Buddy Bolden's band in 1895. On hearing of his elaborations, clarinettist Wade Whaley, who worked with Johnson in the early years of the twentieth century, was heard to comment, 'In New Orleans, we didn't call him "Bunk" for nothing.'

to lead a band. He played in an archaic, almost primitive style that allowed the young enthusiasts to believe that this was how jazz must have sounded before Armstrong went north. Excitedly, they began making plans to record their rediscovered legend.

The musicians assembled to work with Johnson were chosen from among those who had never left New Orleans, middle-aged men who held down menial day jobs while playing for a dollar a night in hole-in-the-wall joints in the city's rougher districts: George Lewis on clarinet, Jim Robinson on trombone, Lawrence Marrero on banjo, Warren 'Baby' Dodds on drums, Alcide 'Slow Drag' Pavageau on bass and Alton Purnell on piano.

The initial recordings that Bunk made were greatly appreciated by the small clique of New Orleans jazz fans, but it was only after he appeared in New York City that the revival really got under way. In September 1944, Bunk Johnson and His New Orleans Band created

Bunk Johnson and Lead Belly with (*in background*) George Lewis (*left*) and Alcide Pavageau, Stuyvesant Casino, New York, *c.*June 1946

a sensation, playing four nights a week at the disused Stuyvesant Casino on the lower east side.

Shortly before their New York engagement, most of these players had backed Bunk at the San Jacinto Hall in New Orleans on sessions later released on the American Music label. It was these recordings that caught the ear of the young Ken Colyer. Ken listened closely to Bunk's playing, trying to translate the tone and feel of what he heard into sounds on his own trumpet. It was a frustrating process. There were no handy guides on how to play New Orleans-style. The best education was to watch someone actually playing.*

Sadly, Ken never had the chance to see Bunk Johnson perform. The veteran trumpet player died in July 1949, and, despite telling one gullible journalist that he'd once toured England with a circus led by a famous Russian strongman and made the sour-faced Queen Victoria smile with his parlour tricks, Bunk never graced our shores.

Even if he had been inclined to take a trip to Britain, he wouldn't have been able to perform. Since its creation in 1921, the Musicians' Union had worked hard to protect its members from foreign competition. In the early 1920s this competition had mostly come from European orchestras, but as the decade wore on and jazz became increasingly popular, audiences in the UK began to clamour for American bands. In March 1923, the MU met with Sir Montague Barlow, Minister for Labour in Stanley Baldwin's Conservative government, to argue that foreign musicians should only be admitted under strict conditions.

A new policy was developed, aimed specifically at American musicians, stipulating that work permits should be issued for eight weeks only; any American band performing at a particular venue had to

---

* Years later, Ken recalled the night he saw Oscar Peterson playing piano at the Café St Michel in Montreal. 'You see those fellows standing behind him?' someone at the bar had asked him. 'They're all pianists trying to watch his hands.'

return home before they could be replaced by another band from the US; where an American band was employed in a ballroom or night-club, a British band had also to be employed; where any American musicians were to be employed in an otherwise British band, there should be an equal number of British players.

While the key aim was to protect the livelihood of MU members – which is the whole point of forming a union – there is evidence that the policy was used to keep out a certain type of music. A later Tory Minister for Labour, Sir Arthur Steel-Maitland, explained the permit system to Parliament in February 1929 thus: 'If the employer desires to bring in a complete band to play for dancing, he is required to engage, or to continue to engage, a British band equal in size to the alien band . . . Complete bands to play symphony or national music are admitted on assurance that no British band or British player is being displaced and that the alien band will not play for dancing.'

The emphasis on dancing suggests that the MU was seeking to resist the tide of modernity that swept through the Roaring Twenties. Such a policy, however, whether by design or by accident, carried a racial dimension. Symphony orchestras and national bands were exclusively made up of white musicians, playing music from the classical canon. Popular dance bands from the US, however, would be playing music either written or inspired by African American musicians and might even include some among their number. The discriminatory nature of this policy is brought sharply into focus by the fact that, during the 1920s, the MU had no British dance bands among its membership.

The situation was not helped by the attitude of the American Federation of Musicians, the US equivalent of the MU, who sought to block any application for a foreign band to tour the US. It was a tactic that proved remarkably successful. In the 1920s, over fifty American bands toured the UK, yet not a single British band worked in America during the same period.

While the US Department of Labor appeared willing to issue work permits, the threat of strike action by the AFM made the granting of visas almost impossible. One British bandleader who performed in the US in 1934, Ray Noble, was not permitted to take his own musicians with him and had to use American players. A further stipulation was that he take American citizenship.

Things came to a head in June 1933, when Duke Ellington brought his band to the UK. The British press made much of the fact that Jack Hylton, the UK's top bandleader, had recently been denied a work permit to tour the US. Despite the public outcry about the lack of reciprocity, the AFM refused to budge, and when another British tour was proposed for Ellington in 1934, the MU put pressure on the Ministry of Labour to get tough.

While ministers had so far resisted an embargo on American bands, news from across the Atlantic forced their hand. In late 1934, the US Labor Department announced that it would no longer consider any work permit applications from British bands. In January 1935, the British government responded by announcing that it would oppose any applications from American musicians.

So began the AFM/MU ban, lasting two decades during which British audiences were forced to go to Paris if they wanted to hear American artists. Some performers were brought in under an exemption for variety acts, which at the time included solo performers – a fact that enabled Fats Waller to visit Britain in 1938, a rare treat witnessed in Soho by a teenage Bill Colyer. In 1949, Sidney Bechet appeared unannounced on stage in London with British artists the Wilcox Brothers. The crowd of over 1,700 were ecstatic (and clearly all in on the plot), but the promoter was found guilty of contravening the 1920 Aliens Order and heavily fined.

For Ken Colyer, this was doubly frustrating. It was hard enough to bear the knowledge that he would never see the musicians he loved playing a gig in England. Harder to deal with was the thought that they were still out there, playing two or three times a week, in the US.

Bunk was dead, but his band, now led by clarinettist George Lewis, were back in New Orleans, gigging in those same old joints they'd always performed in. These weren't young men: Alcide 'Slow Drag' Pavageau was born in 1888. Soon they'd be gone and the way they played would be lost for ever. In order to fulfil his artistic potential, Ken realised he needed to see these guys playing their chops, up close; to talk to them; maybe even sit in with them.

But how to get to New Orleans? A visa for travel to the US cost a small fortune, and even if by some piece of luck he was granted permission, where was he going to find the money to pay his fare?

Whereas young Americans take to the road when they want to discover their destiny, young Britons have traditionally taken to the sea. In November 1951, having quit the Christie Brothers Stompers, Ken Colyer packed his trumpet into his kit bag, went down to the Victoria Docks and signed back on for another spell in the Merchant Navy. He later explained his reasoning to *Melody Maker*: 'In England, owing to the unfortunate restrictions, the jazz musician has no teachers to go to for the necessary tricks-of-the-trade. Records and articles gave me something, but I believed that only by mixing and playing with American musicians would I be able to round out my jazz education. With so much to learn, I felt I had to go to the only authorities I recognise.'

3

BLUES IN BRASS

The popular music industry was born in the United States during the late nineteenth century, when syncopation – the displacement of beats or accents so that strong beats become weak, or weak strong – released first rhythm and then melody from the formalities placed upon it by European culture to create ragtime.

The use of syncopated rhythms wasn't new. Classical composers had for centuries been writing pieces that surprised the listener by placing the accent on weaker beats. For the likes of Bach and Mozart, syncopation was a way of introducing some variety into their pieces.

Ragtime was different in that it was an entire style of music based on syncopation and, unlike the classically trained musicians who played those cleverly off-beat pieces, the African American artists who developed it weren't performing someone else's music written out for them and rehearsed in advance. Ragtime was all about improvisation, a rejection of formality in favour of feel, a change underscored by segregation. In the late nineteenth century, formal music tuition was simply not affordable for most African Americans. And even if they had the means, 'Jim Crow' laws designed to keep them in their place continually set obstacles in their way. With little access to formal training, the vast majority of African Americans were forced to play by ear, improvising melodies when asked to play popular tunes at dancehalls and parties within their own community.

In the years following the American Civil War, slave songs had been carefully arranged in the European classical style. Smartly

41

dressed choirs of students from 'negro' colleges were highly popular with white audiences. At the same time, minstrel shows toured the rural areas, offering a parody of black racial stereotypes as a form of entertainment. While whites lapped up these bowdlerised versions of black culture, the African American community were not only busy creating a style of music that was destined to become hugely popular, they were doing so on their own terms.

The word 'ragtime' doesn't appear in mainstream American culture until 1897, but as early as 1891 African American newspapers were using the word 'rag' to describe a grassroots social function at which string bands performed.* They were by all accounts roughhouse affairs. The *Kansas City Star* newspaper noted on 29 December 1893 that 'when an Aitchison fiddler plays at a rag, he always sits by the door so he can get out when the fighting starts'.

Two years later, the *Leavenworth Herald* carried a report of a rag held on Christmas Eve, noting that 'the orchestra was composed of three pieces, a fiddle, bass fiddle and a triangle . . . that ever favourite dance, the "possum a la" was introduced, and it seemed to carry the house by storm.'

The 'Possum a La', a black vernacular dance song better known as the 'Pas Ma La', is regarded by many as the earliest indicator of what would later be termed 'ragtime'. Its appearance at this festive rag may be explained by the fact that African American entertainer Irving Jones published the first version of the song in 1894. The *New York Clipper* reported on 25 November 1893 that Jones was enjoying success with his new song, 'The Parsamala Dance', in Louisville, Kentucky, where he was performing with the Creole Burlesque

---

* In their comprehensive study of the emergence of African American popular music, *Out of Sight*, Lynn Abbott and Doug Seroff note that before the word 'rag' came into fashion, the most common term used to describe these informal events was a 'breakdown'.

Company. The Creole connection and the fact that the phrase 'Pas Ma La' sounds very much like a phonetic corruption of a colloquial French term suggest the possibility that the dance may have originated in New Orleans.

Forgive the qualifications that surround that last statement. Since the publication of *Jazzmen* identified New Orleans as the place where jazz was born, almost everyone who has written on the subject has felt the need to either uphold or debunk that narrative. For jazz, just like punk rock, didn't originate in any one place in particular. There was no moment when jazz 'began'. The musicians who we now consider to have been playing jazz in the early days actually called their music 'ragtime'. 'Jazz' as a musical term was rarely heard before 1920.

It was only when Tom Brown's Ragtime Band went north in 1915 that they found they were playing a new kind of music. Five white New Orleans musicians, performing what we would now describe as 'Dixieland', they were booked into Lamb's Café in Chicago for a six-week run. As non-union out-of-towners, they faced organised opposition from the local musicians' union. When protesters gathered outside the cafe, one of them held a placard that read: 'Don't Patronise This Jass [*sic*] Music'.

Whether it began as a derogatory term or was a slang word for the band's vigour and pep, the term 'jazz' doesn't come from New Orleans. What is undeniable is the fact that all of the early jazz stylists did.

New Orleans in the nineteenth century had a social history unlike any other city in North America, not least because of its strong cultural connections with the Caribbean. Founded by the French in 1718, the city was ceded to Spanish control under the Treaty of Fontainebleau in 1762. Following defeat by the British in the French and Indian Wars, Louis XV of France realised that, having already lost his territories in Canada to Britain under force of arms, he was likely to lose the rest of his North American empire – known as the Louisiana Territory – during the peace negotiations that followed. Preferring to do business with his Catholic Spanish allies rather than hand a vital trading link with the Caribbean to the hostile British, Louis secretly passed Louisiana to Charles III of Spain.

When peace between Britain and France was signed in Paris in 1763, provision was made to allow French colonists who didn't want to live under British rule the freedom to move to other French colonies in the Americas. Many headed to Louisiana from the north-eastern maritime province of Acadia, becoming 'cajuns' in the local vernacular. Although Spain remained in control of the city until the end of the eighteenth century, this influx of French-speaking refugees ensured that New Orleans retained its French identity.

In 1800, in return for agreeing to establish the Spanish Bourbons in Tuscany, Napoleon Bonaparte secretly took control of the Louisiana Territory in the hope of re-establishing French power in North America. Before his plans could be put into action, however, a slave revolt in the French possession of Haiti was successful in overthrowing colonial rule. Having lost his most important base in the Caribbean, and with war against Britain once again looming, Napoleon decided to cash in his chips, selling the Louisiana Territory to the United States government in 1804 for $14 million.

New Orleans immediately became the biggest city in the US after those in the original thirteen colonies, and this new metropolis of the south was unlike any that America had seen before. Most of the inhabitants spoke French as a first language, the dominant religion was Catholicism and the city retained an aristocratic class of the sort that had been turfed out of the thirteen colonies by the Revolutionary War.

The white ruling class in New Orleans referred to themselves as *creoles*, a French adoption of the Spanish term *criollo* – a person of Spanish descent born in the West Indies or Spanish America. The meaning of the term *creole* was broadened in 1804 with the arrival and swift integration into Louisiana society of the wealthy French-speaking slave owners who fled Haiti in the wake of the victorious slave revolt. They were followed by mixed-race Haitians, who feared for their safety now that darker-skinned former slaves had taken control of the island.

In the French colonies, people of mixed race were categorised as *gens de couleur libres* – free people of colour – and they occupied a place in society above freed slaves. With the declaration of the Haitian slave republic, thousands of free people of colour fled to Louisiana, and in New Orleans they found that an urban coloured community was already thriving in the city.

Despite the fact that it had always been a major slave-trading port, decades of rule by France and then Spain had produced a greater degree of integration in New Orleans than in other cities in the US. When the Spanish ruling class sought to marginalise French settlers in the late eighteenth century, it reached out for support to the black population of the city, allowing many slaves to buy their freedom.

By 1840, New Orleans was booming, the third largest city in America, behind only New York and Baltimore. The commercial centre of the south, its prosperity was based on the slave trade. The American Civil War brought an end to that inhumane business in April 1862, when Union forces captured the city in the sea-bound assault that left its antebellum architecture intact.

The Union was initially committed to integrating slaves freed by the victory of 1865, but within a decade of emancipation, reformers had grown exhausted trying to ensure that everyone enjoyed the freedoms guaranteed in the Constitution. Federal troops remained in New Orleans until 1877, but once they left, as in so many places in the south the white population of the city began constructing barriers to reassert the pre-war racial hierarchy.

In most places in the southern states, the question of who was white and who was not was relatively straightforward. In New Orleans, however, the French-speaking free people of colour had become an educated artisan class, used to enjoying a social status above that of African Americans.

As English became more commonly heard in the city, free people of colour found themselves being referred to as 'creoles of colour', differentiating them from their fellow French speakers in the white upper class. In the difficult years following the withdrawal of Union troops, with segregation creeping into New Orleans society, 'Creole' became a catch-all term to describe the Francophone community in Louisiana, but one that was particularly applied to those of mixed race. Slowly, the restrictions that had previously applied only to African Americans began to eat away at the freedom of Creoles until, in 1894, those formerly regarded as free people of colour found themselves reclassified as 'negro' by Louisiana state law.

The Creoles were shabbily disenfranchised by segregation, but the presence in New Orleans of an educated, mixed-race community existing in its own social space between whites and blacks was unique in the United States and played an important role in bringing jazz to a wider audience.

Prominent among Creole musicians working in New Orleans around the end of the nineteenth century was John Robichaux. In a posed photograph from 1913, he and his six-piece band are shown playing their instruments while reading music from stands. Renowned scholar of early New Orleans jazz Samuel Charters observed that this was the only picture from the period that shows a local band reading music. The implication is clear: the John Robichaux Orchestra are professionally trained musicians who won't lower the tone of your event by vulgar improvisation.

Robichaux built his reputation on musical literacy, ordering all of the latest published dance arrangements from New York, and this soon found him playing at white society functions. However, his up-to-date repertoire failed to find favour with African American audiences. As trumpeter Lee Collins recalled, Robichaux was 'a very high-class musician. He was the most respected musician among both white and colored [Creole], and his orchestra played for the white society dances. But most negroes didn't care for his music; it was more classical.'

For the African American community of New Orleans, the place to go to hear the latest sounds was Storyville. In the final years of the nineteenth century, in an attempt to better regulate prostitution and gambling within their bustling port city, the elders of New Orleans delegated City Councilman Sidney Story to draw up a series of guidelines legalising both practices in an area of the city referred to as the Restricted District. Officially established on 6 July 1897, and bounded by Robertson, St Louis, Basin and Iberville Streets, the area soon became known as Storyville. Adjacent to one of the main railway stations, by 1900 this red-light zone was generating more revenue than any other district of the city. Most of the bars and brothels had a resident piano player and maybe a small string band. It was these string ensembles, variously consisting of mandolin, fiddle, guitar and double bass, that had been instrumental in the spread of ragtime from the country rag breakdowns into the urban dancehalls. And in turn-of-the-century Storyville, ragtime was king.

From its inception, ragtime had been associated with loose morals. The *Freeman*, the nationally distributed African American newspaper, carried an editorial in 1901 that denigrated ragtime as a celebration of 'open and notorious depravity'. One of the foremost ragtime bandleaders was Buddy Bolden. It was said of him that 'he played nothing but the blues and all that stink music, and he played it very loud' – a habit he'd acquired from performing in rowdy red-light district dancehalls.

Bolden was an African American cornet player, born in New Orleans in 1877. Thanks to Bunk Johnson singling him out for special praise some sixty years later, he is cited by many as being the first musician to 'swing the beat' of ragtime in a manner that later became recognised as jazz. Although Bolden died long after the gramophone had been invented,* he made no recordings. But one tantalising photograph of the band he led, Professor Bolden's Orchestra, survives from around 1900. The ensemble consists of two clarinettists, a trombone player, a guitarist, a double bass player and Bolden himself on cornet. This is clearly a jazz band. The stringed instruments have been relegated to the rhythm section, while the brass and woodwind have been brought to the fore. Was this Bolden's innovation or was he simply following fashion? We'll never know. But what is clear from the testimony of those that heard him is that Bolden excelled in playing the blues.

When they spoke of 'the blues', African American musicians in turn-of-the-century New Orleans weren't referring to the three-chord, twelve-bar form that has since become synonymous with the term. That genre didn't emerge until later in the twentieth century. For Bolden and his contemporaries, 'blues' was the way they described a loosely played melody that wasn't formally orchestrated. As Kid Ory observed, Bolden relied on improvisation: 'He wasn't really a [trained] musician, he didn't study. He was gifted, playing with effect, but no tone. He played loud.'

Trombonist Edward 'Kid' Ory was born on the Woodland Plantation at La Place, a day's walk from New Orleans, on Christmas Day 1886. Like many of the tenant farmers on the plantation, Ory was mixed-race, his first language French, and all his life he identified as Creole. He got his nickname from the fact that he was playing music from an early age, he and his friends constructing rudimentary

---

* Bolden was declared insane and committed to an asylum in 1907, remaining there until his death in 1931.

48

musical instruments from discarded cigar boxes and fruit crates they found on the plantation.

It wasn't uncommon in the south to see kids busking for pennies on the streets, playing home-made instruments. Known as 'spasm bands', the more proficient were hired by bars and vaudeville shows as novelty acts. Ory's spasm band organised gigs in an empty house, charging admission and selling fried fish that they had caught themselves. Soon they had earned enough money to buy real instruments. When bands from New Orleans made whistle stops in La Place, Ory and his friends went along, watching the players closely, trying to pick up new tricks.

Ory made his first trip to New Orleans in 1905, to buy a trombone from Werlein's music store. His sister Lena was living on South Robertson Street and it was there that he went with his new instrument. While he was practising, a knock came at the door. It was Buddy Bolden. The bandleader was passing by and heard Ory's playing, promptly offering him a job in his band. But Lena was having none of it. Telling Bolden that Ory was only eighteen years old and had to go back home, she ushered the man they called King Bolden out of her house.

The encounter with Buddy Bolden only whetted Ory's appetite for music. Lena lived near Lincoln Park, a combination skating rink, vaudeville theatre and amusement park that opened in 1902. Operated by people of colour, it featured concerts by both Creole and African American musicians. Soon Ory and his bandmates from the plantation were heading to the park on a Sunday afternoon to hear John Robichaux's Orchestra playing in the dance pavilion. As the day turned to evening, Buddy Bolden's band would set up in the skating rink and, once they started playing their down and dirty music, the crowds that had been dancing to Robichaux's more formal arrangements would push their way to the ice rink to hear the King. It was

Bolden's loud playing that caught their ear – a trick that the great man himself referred to as 'calling my children home'.

Ory and his friends became regular visitors to New Orleans, watching and learning in venues from Storyville to Perdido. They were such a familiar sight at Lincoln Park that, in 1908, the band were hired by the manager to play on the park's advertising wagons that toured the city streets drumming up custom. Arriving for their first gig, they found that the manager had placed a painted sign on the wagon announcing 'Kid Ory's Brown Skinned Babies'. A photo taken around this time reveals that the band, four of whom were African Americans, consisted of trombone, clarinet, trumpet, guitar, double bass and drums.

Ory moved to New Orleans with the band in 1910 and they were soon appearing at Lala's in Storyville, playing gut-bucket blues, all improvised as none of them could read music. Although Ory greatly admired Buddy Bolden, he also brought elements of John Robichaux's more formal style to the band. He referred to this mixture of influences as 'soft' ragtime, and such was its success that within three years, just like Robichaux, Kid Ory's Brown Skinned Babies were playing for white audiences.

In the years that followed, a series of New Orleans greats passed through the bands that Ory led: Mutt Carey, the first trumpet player to mute the sound of his horn and make it moan; Joe Oliver, a musician so sensational that he would one day be acclaimed King; and Louis Armstrong, the first superstar soloist. The reason why Ory had to keep replacing his trumpet players was simple: the rest of the US had developed an appetite for the hot music coming out of New Orleans. Chicago had been drawing musicians north since Tom Brown's Ragtime Band had taken residency at Lamb's Café in 1915, but jazz became a nationwide phenomenon – and entered the lexicon – in 1917 with the release of the first jazz record.

One of the most problematic issues in the early history of New Orleans jazz is the question of the role white players had in its development. However, given the Jim Crow laws that prevented African Americans from fully participating in society, it was surely inevitable that the first jazz record would be made by a band of white musicians.

At the turn of the century, when Buddy Bolden was in his prime and Kid Ory was playing a guitar made out of a cigar box, most of the white musicians playing hot music in New Orleans were working for Jack Laine. Born in 1873, Laine was a bass drum player in marching bands, parades being very popular across the city. Working by day as a blacksmith, Laine formed his own Reliance Brass Band in the late 1890s and, when he had more offers for bookings than he could fulfil, began to assemble bands for each occasion from a pool of white musicians that he knew, many drawn from the communities of European immigrants that were springing up in New Orleans.

It was one such booking in 1915 that led to a watershed moment in the history of jazz. A Chicago cafe owner, in New Orleans to see a prize fight, by chance encountered Laine's band playing in the streets to advertise the event. Highly impressed with the way the trumpet player performed, he asked Laine if the band would be interested in coming north to Chicago. As ever, Jack Laine already had more work than he could handle in New Orleans, but he told the cafe owner that he could ask the horn player if he was interested. He was.

Nic La Rocca was the son of Italian immigrants and, like many white musicians in the city, had been playing for Jack Laine since he was a boy. The band that he would lead would go on to define the sound of jazz for a generation.

Their initial engagements in Chicago were successful, but arguments over money led to divisions. Other white musicians from New Orleans working in the city came and went from the line-up until it settled on La Rocca on trumpet, Tony Sbarbaro on drums, Eddie Edwards on trombone, Larry Shields on clarinet and Henry Ragas on piano. La Rocca and Sbarbaro were Sicilian by descent, Edwards the son of an English immigrant. Shields was an Irish American, and Ragas's family hailed originally from Spain. Looking for a name that described their sound, and feeling that the terms 'New Orleans' and 'Louisiana' were too regional, they decided to call themselves the Original Dixieland Jazz Band.

While the music they played was gaining popularity, there was still a sense that jazz bands were a novelty. When the Original Dixieland Jazz Band played their first gig in New York in January 1917, the music was so unfamiliar to the wider public that advertising copy-writers were unsure of how to spell this new buzzword. The ad for their debut appearance at the Paradise Ballroom read: 'The First Sensational Amusement Novelty of 1917 "The JASZ Band"'. The first number that the band tore into – the old New Orleans staple 'Tiger Rag' – so shocked the audience that they were unsure if they were to dance to this music or laugh at it. It was only when the man-ager appeared at the end of the tune and announced that this was music for dancing that couples began to take to the floor.

The idea that jazz wasn't really music, that the whole thing was a bit tongue-in-cheek, comes over in subsequent adverts for the band, one of which describes them as 'Untuneful Harmonists Playing "Peppery" Melodies'. The novelty aspect was underlined by their first single, recorded just a month after they arrived in New York. 'Livery Stable Blues' featured members of the band making comedy animal noises – a rooster's crow, a horse's whinny and the moo of a cow. The impression given was that, rather than representing the birth of a new music, the band were playing a souped-up version of novelty ragtime, a staple of vaudeville shows of the time.

The musicians who heard that first jazz record were of a different opinion. In New Orleans, they immediately recognised the Original Dixieland Jazz Band as representing a more formalised version of the music they had been playing for two decades. However, such was the popularity of recorded jazz that soon bandleaders like Kid Ory and King Oliver, forced to meet the public's expectations of what jazz was supposed to sound like, were having to modify their sound to match that of La Rocca's band.

Numerous arguments and disputes rage around the true origins of jazz, and there are those who claim others were the first to put what we now call jazz on record. What is indisputable is that the 1917 Victor Records releases by the Original Dixieland Jazz Band are the earliest examples that we can hear today of a New Orleans jazz band playing the hot music of the Crescent City.

The record's success sent a stark message to those still plying their trade in and around Storyville: if they wanted to make recordings and become famous, they had to leave New Orleans. This was doubly true for Creole and black musicians. New York had a large coloured population and Chicago was growing all the time as African American workers left the south to do war work in the city's factories. King Oliver headed north in 1919, calling Louis Armstrong to join him three years later. Kid Ory left his band and headed west to California.

While the pull of popularity was strong, changes in New Orleans also forced jazz musicians to look elsewhere. On 6 April 1917, the United States entered the First World War, mobilising hundreds of thousands of young men. To protect their morals, a law was passed prohibiting prostitution within five miles of any military or naval base. On 2 October 1917, New Orleans City Council adopted an ordinance abolishing the Restricted District. At the sweep of a pen, Storyville was no more.

While the prostitutes simply moved into other parts of the city, the musicians who gathered to improvise gut-bucket jazz suddenly found many of their best venues had disappeared. Prohibition, introduced in 1920, further undermined their opportunities for work, to the extent that, in the 1930s, it was easier to find a band playing New Orleans-style jazz in Chicago or New York than it was in the Big Easy.

By the mid-1930s, jazz had evolved into swing – large ensembles including saxophones, grand pianos, strings and vocalists performing sophisticated arrangements of the dance tunes of the day. Hugely popular in the years leading up to the Second World War, swing's dominance split jazz purists. Some felt that the genre was in a rut, that innovation had been sidelined in the pursuit of popularity; others felt that jazz had lost the raw edge of the early days. While both camps were dismayed at the commercialisation of the genre, their reactions couldn't have been more different.

Those wanting greater innovation started pushing at the boundaries of musical form. In the early 1940s, young swing musicians working in New York began heading to jam sessions in Harlem after hours, where their improvisations gave rise to a new form of modern jazz called bebop. Meanwhile, those who believed that commercialism had robbed jazz of its essential spirit had set out to revive the music of the early days, seeking out musicians who still played in the traditional style. That search had led them to New Orleans and Bunk Johnson.

When Johnson's clarinettist George Lewis was tracked down, he was working as a stevedore. The revivalists were relieved to find that, unlike almost every other clarinet player in New Orleans, he hadn't traded in his instrument for a saxophone with the advent of swing. Lewis was in his forties, still playing the old-style jazz for middle-aged dancers in the tiny bars of the city's rougher districts.

As word spread that there were young white jazz buffs looking for traditional players to record, more of the old-timers came forward.

Johnson and Lewis recorded together as the revival built momentum, but it was their trip to New York in 1945 that brought the New Orleans sound back to prominence.

Just as the Original Dixieland Jazz Band had done decades before, Bunk Johnson and his New Orleans Band stunned Manhattan audiences with the dynamic power of their playing. Having been accustomed to the smooth sound of swing, the crowds at the Stuyvesant Casino were once again captivated by peppery melodies played by untuneful harmonists.

Throughout the late 1930s and early 40s, musicians from turn-of-the-century New Orleans were re-emerging into the spotlight: Jelly Roll Morton turned up at the Library of Congress in Washington, DC, telling Alan Lomax that he, Morton, had invented jazz; Sidney Bechet was able to quit his job in a tailor shop and find fame in France; Louis Armstrong became the first jazz musician to appear on the cover of *Time*; Kid Ory, who had quit music in 1933 and had been raising chickens in Los Angeles, went back into the studio to record for Nesuhi Ertegun, son of the Turkish ambassador, who founded the Crescent record label especially to release Ory's music.

Sadly this resurgence of interest came too late for one of the New Orleans greats: King Oliver was working as a janitor in Savannah, Georgia, when he died in 1938, too poor to afford medical treatment.

Soon the revival spread to Europe. In 1942, George Webb, a twenty-five-year-old pianist from London, was working as a machine-gun fitter at the Vickers-Armstrong armaments factory in Crayford, Kent. From among his fellow workers he pulled together a small band that played lunchtime concerts in the factory. After work, they got together in the cellar of a local pub to play revivalist jazz. They were the quintessential definition of an amateur jazz band: just a bunch of fans who had access to some musical instruments. They were often out of tune and their sense of rhythm was hampered by the fact that the bass parts were played on a sousaphone, but they were defiantly making music that they loved.

Dave Gelly, writing in his exploration of post-war jazz in Britain, *An Unholy Row*, sums up the attitude of the revivalists thus: 'Rather like a primitive religion, it was a mechanism for explaining a phenomenon that was real to them but which they could not account for. They had found this music that moved and excited them, which they had come to value highly, amid the puerile trivialities of early twentieth century music. This was a way of extracting it, bringing it to light and according it the status of an art.'

George Webb's Dixielanders set out to replicate the recordings that King Oliver's Creole Band, Jelly Roll Morton's Red Hot Peppers and Louis Armstrong's Hot Five and Hot Seven had made some twenty years before. Like Bunk Johnson did in New York, the Dixielanders played with a rough edge that enthralled young British audiences. Uncompromising in his pursuit of that 1920s sound, Webb was known to upbraid band members who strayed in the direction of swing.

Ken Colyer was just as dogged in his commitment to New Orleans jazz, but the two bandleaders ended up on opposing sides of a rancorous dispute that still echoes in the British jazz scene today. Fans of the revival were like treasure hunters, seeking out the original 78s, cataloguing their serial numbers, memorising the line-ups of bands, obsessing over particular sessions. Though they collected music from all over the US, at the heart of the revival were a handful of greats who had left New Orleans to seek fame and fortune in Chicago, New York and California: King Oliver, Louis Armstrong, Jelly Roll Morton and Kid Ory.

Ken Colyer didn't subscribe to this belief. He felt that something had been lost in the migration north, believing style and commitment had been traded in for popularity and commercial success. The recording sessions, where technological limitations forced the musicians to play far apart, had compromised the unity of the music, depriving it of its internal rhythms.

As far as Colyer was concerned, real New Orleans jazz never left the Crescent City. In late 1951, he set out to discover if it was still there.

PILGRIMAGE TO NEW ORLEANS

Having rejoined the Merchant Navy as a galley cook, Ken Colyer hoped to find a ship that would take him to the Gulf of Mexico, although this was by no means guaranteed. But then Colyer, without work and living in digs that gave him the creeps, couldn't really afford to be choosy, and anyway, after quitting the Stompers, he just wanted to ship out.

He was fortunate in finding a berth on the *Port Lyttelton*, a brand-new ship, built in the late 1940s as Britain sought to regain the tonnage lost due to enemy action in the Second World War. It was much more comfortable than the hulks that he sailed on in his early spell in the Merch, but after the six-week voyage he found himself back looking for work in the pool.

The vagaries of a seaman's life are illustrated by the fact that not only did Colyer initially refuse the next offer of work, on the *Llandovery Castle* headed for Cape Town and home via the Suez Canal, but the ship's chef didn't want to employ him either. Both were overruled by the Clerk of the Pool, who got on the phone and told the reluctant chef, 'You'll get what men I send you and you'll accept them.'

The third vessel Colyer signed up for, the *Tamaroa*, took him even further from New Orleans, shipping British émigrés to New Zealand. Back in Blighty looking for work again, he heard about a vacancy for second cook on the *Empire Patrai*, operating out of the Gulf port of Mobile, Alabama. That was good enough for Ken.

They flew him out to Mobile, where the ship was being loaded with mining equipment bound for the Venezuelan city of Puerto Ordaz, a hundred miles up the Orinoco River in South America. Once back in Mobile, the *Patrai* had a week-long stopover while the boat was reloaded. Colyer took the opportunity for a day trip to New Orleans.

Although he knew no one in the Crescent City, he had come prepared. Before he left England, he had visited the Westminster Public Library, where they kept telephone directories for the major cities of the US. There was a considerable number of people in New Orleans named George Lewis, making it impossible for him to find the clarinettist who'd once played with Bunk Johnson.

He was, however, able to find a phone number for Doc Souchon. Born in 1897, Souchon had played guitar in the Six and Seven-Eighths String Band around New Orleans in the years immediately prior to the First World War. From old French stock, Souchon's family boasted a legend that told how an ancestor had saved the life of Napoleon during the Egyptian campaign.

Souchon would have been known to Colyer as someone who had played an important part in the New Orleans revival, helping to establish the National Jazz Foundation. He wrote on the subject for several publications and had a radio programme on the WWL station. And 'Doc' wasn't a nickname – he was a qualified MD, which was how Colyer had been able to find his number in the telephone directory, listed under 'Doctors'.

Initially confused as to why this English sailor was calling him at his surgery, once the penny dropped Souchon told him that George Lewis and his band were due to play that same day at the International House. As soon as he'd finished his shift, Colyer cleaned up and headed to the Greyhound Bus Station in downtown Mobile to buy himself a return ticket to New Orleans.

After a three-hour drive, from Alabama across Mississippi into Louisiana, Colyer went directly to the International House. He arrived too late to hear Doc Souchon perform with Johnny Wiggs and was disappointed to hear that George Lewis wasn't appearing after all. Nevertheless, there were a number of New Orleans jazz greats in the room and he got to meet them all. The event was a reception for some visiting NATO dignitaries and the New Orleans Jazz Club had pulled in as many of its members as it could muster. Tom Brown, who had led the first jazz band north in 1915, was there, as was 'Papa' Jack Laine. Colyer also heard Creole chanteuse Lizzie Miles sing in both English and her native tongue.

Afterwards, Doc Souchon took Ken on a tour of the Vieux Carré, regaling him with tales of the times he saw King Oliver and Jelly Roll Morton. Colyer ended the evening at the Paddock on Bourbon Street, listening to seventy-three-year-old Alphonse Picou, who had played clarinet with Bunk Johnson in the early days.

Colyer arrived back aboard the *Empire Patrai* at eight thirty the next morning to find the crew preparing their own breakfasts, as the cook was having a day off. Despite being in trouble with his shipmates, he was in heaven. He had visited the city of his dreams, if only for a few short hours. Over the following weeks, all he could think of was how to get back to New Orleans.

The next trip down to Venezuela was arduous. Just as they reached Puerto Ordaz, the *Empire Patrai* developed serious engine trouble. It had broken a piston rod and was forced to limp back across the Caribbean at snail's pace. Provisions began to run short and tempers started to fray. By the time they returned to Mobile, Colyer had made up his mind to jump ship. On 25 November 1952, having been granted a month-long visitor's visa by US immigration, he went down to the Greyhound Bus Station and bought another ticket to New Orleans – this time one-way.

No sooner had Colyer arrived in the city than he learned that the George Lewis Band were playing in town that very evening. He hurried

The Guv'nor. Ken Colyer in New Orleans, 1952

to the Mardi Gras Club to find Lewis on stage with most of the band that had backed Bunk Johnson at their legendary stand in New York. Colyer found a seat within touching distance of banjo player Lawrence Marrero. Alcide 'Slow Drag' Pavageau stood behind Marrero playing an upright bass. Pianist Alton Purnell sat to their right, facing the band, with drummer Joe Watkins at the front, to Marrero's right. Alongside the drummer sat trumpet player Percy Humphries, trombonist Jim Robinson and, on clarinet, George Lewis himself.

One year and five days after Ken Colyer had gone to sea in search of the real New Orleans jazz, he had finally found his holy grail. 'I ordered a drink,' he wrote to his brother Bill of the moment he encountered his heroes, 'and almost went into a trance.'

61

When Bill Colyer read his brother's account of meeting the George Lewis Band, he knew what he must do. Prior to leaving England, Ken Colyer had built a reputation as a leading light of the burgeoning trad jazz movement. Yet he had walked away from the scene, heading out onto the high seas in a quest for a more perfect sound. Conscious that the fans Ken had left behind had heard nothing for over a year, Bill Colyer offered his brother's letters for publication to the editor of the premier weekly music paper in Britain.

———

Melody Maker was founded in 1926 and, until its demise in 2000, it was always a musician's paper. Virtually unchallenged as a weekly until the emergence in 1952 of the pop-orientated *New Musical Express*, *Melody Maker* was, for the first twenty-five years of its life, a paper read by most jazz players and fans.

In the early 1950s, big bands led by the likes of Ted Heath and Jack Parnell were hugely popular in Britain. Their domesticated version of swing dominated the airwaves, and *Melody Maker* reflected this trend. Dickie Valentine, a velvet-voiced singer from Marylebone, topped the *MM* poll as best vocalist of 1952.

While the general public seemed content to consume the white-bread pop music served up by the mainstream, beneath the surface a war was going on, one that kept exploding on the pages of *Melody Maker*. Headlines such as 'This Dixie v Modern War Must End' appeared above articles that sought to smooth the waters between fans of trad and bebop. The modernists dismissed the traditionalists as 'mouldy figs'; trad fans responded by insinuating that the music the modernists played was not really jazz.

No matter how much some musicians might have stressed the fact that all jazz is good jazz, the argument over the best way to counter the commercialisation of swing only became more heated. It didn't help that, within the traditionalist camp, there was another divisive split. To their lasting frustration, history has labelled all those British musicians who played in the New Orleans style as being tradition-alists. The so-called 'trad boom' of the 1950s encompasses everyone from Kenny Ball to Ken Colyer, and to the uninitiated they can often sound as if they're all playing the same kind of music. But to those who really care about these things – and nobody cares more about variations of style than jazz aficionados – Ball is a formalist, a fol-lower of the more sophisticated practitioners of the New Orleans style whose music accommodated a broader public taste, such as Louis Armstrong. Colyer, by contrast, is a naturalist, rejecting the way in which jazz developed after it left New Orleans, preferring to take his cue from the more primitive style of Bunk Johnson. Never mind that Bunk, a great admirer of Armstrong, was comfortable playing both formalist and naturalist arrangements. The naturalists drew their metaphorical line in the sand on the banks of Lake Pontchartrain, just north of New Orleans. Anyone who crossed that was *outré*.

When Ken Colyer left the Christie Brothers Stompers, British fans of the back-to-basics style were left without a champion. Since his disappearance, all his followers knew was that he was living the life of an ascetic, destined to roam the seven seas until he found enlighten-ment. This monk-like silence was broken on 13 December 1952, when *Melody Maker* gave a whole page to Ken's report of his first encoun-ter with the George Lewis Band. 'A Letter from New Orleans', read the bold headline on page five. 'British cornettist Ken Colyer sends this first-hand account of life today in the Crescent City.'

For most British jazz fans, New Orleans was a distant, mythical place, one which they could never aspire to visit themselves. To hear that Colyer had made it to Bourbon Street was akin to hearing that he had reached the summit of Everest. The subheadings of the article underlined the semi-religious nature of the experience. 'I was near Marrero', read one, suggesting that Colyer had touched the hem of his garment. 'What Picou said', read another, implying that Ken had conversed with the ancient sages.

If Colyer's adventures were causing a stir back home, in the bars on Bourbon Street he was becoming a minor celebrity. The old guys were tickled pink that this English kid knew their stuff. After years of being more or less ignored by local youngsters, the fact that someone from so far away should be interested in what they were doing, well, it made them all smile.

And Ken really *was* interested. Not only did he seem to know the names of all the musicians they'd played with back in the day, he knew the tunes they played too, and recognised the arrangements. He actually appreciated what they were doing. It was only a matter of time before he was invited to sit in and play a couple of numbers. For Ken, this was a dream come true, but in the segregated south of the mid-50s, the idea of black and white musicians playing together was fraught with problems.

The laws of the state of Louisiana enforced a 'colour bar' to keep black and white citizens apart: separate school systems, separate swimming pools, separate counters in diners, separate seats on public transport – segregation reached into every social space. New Orleans liked to think of itself as different. Race laws might be violently enforced in other parts of the south, but this was the Big Easy; people were more relaxed about the issue here. In truth, however, while the racism encountered by the black community might have appeared on the surface to be of a less formal, more personal ilk, it was no less pernicious than that meted out elsewhere.

The authorities were relaxed about white patrons visiting black bars on Bourbon Street, but any Caucasian American would think twice before sharing a stage with black musicians. Fred Hatfield, a white American jazz buff who befriended Colyer in New Orleans, recalled that the musicians kept themselves apart too. '[Ken and I visited] places like the Barn on Franklin Avenue; that was usually a white band – white musicians. Luthgens was black, of course, and it varied, depending on where you went, but we never saw blacks and whites playing together. That was sort of verboten. I always looked forward to the day when we could have a mixture, you know, of just good musicians playing together.'

Ken's willingness to defy the colour bar didn't go unnoticed in certain quarters. 'I was given a quiet word of warning one day, that it was going around that I was a nigger-lover and should play with white musicians more. I quietly explained that this was what I had come to New Orleans for and nothing was going to deter me.'

This act of defiance would cost Ken his liberty.

Five months before Ken arrived in New Orleans, the United States Congress had enacted the Immigration and Nationality Act of 1952, known as the McCarran–Walter Act after its two Democrat sponsors, Pat McCarran, a senator from Nevada, and Francis Walter, a Pennsylvanian. Aimed at removing the racial restrictions imposed on immigration to America since the 1790 Naturalisation Act, McCarran–Walter sought to shift the focus of border controls to prioritise those who were willing to assimilate into US society, while denying entry to those considered unlawful, immoral, diseased or politically radical.

McCarran–Walter was a product of the Red Scare, coming at a time when the United States felt threatened by anyone who expressed 'un-American' sentiments. Francis Walter was a prominent member of the House Un-American Activities Committee, tasked with investigating US citizens whose views were considered to be left-wing. Pat McCarran was an outspoken admirer of the Spanish fascist dictator Francisco Franco and led investigations into left-wing influence in the administrations of Franklin D. Roosevelt and Harry Truman.

McCarran–Walter made it possible for the US government to deport immigrants who were felt to be engaged in subversive activities. No one would ever accuse Ken Colyer of being a communist sympathiser, but by playing with black musicians he was seen as taking a stand against segregation, which in the post-war south was about as subversive as you could get. Without him realising, his card had been marked.

Merchant seamen usually had little trouble in getting their visas extended, especially in a port city like New Orleans, and so Ken wasn't worried when his expired on Christmas Day 1952 – he'd simply go downtown and ask for an extension. Sure, he was a couple of days late, but the immigration office was closed for the holidays, so he felt he had a cast-iron excuse when he turned up on the first day it reopened. Unfortunately for him, the McCarran–Walter Act had come into force on 24 December.

Whereas detainees had previously been kept under house arrest in a hotel until they could be processed, the local authorities decided the new Act allowed them to make use of the parish prison. Ken was transferred into the custody of the sheriff and a bond of $500 was set for his bail. Rather rashly, he told his captors that it was his intention to stay in New Orleans and study jazz. To the authorities, that was just confirmation of his subversive intentions. As a result, he was three times refused bail, despite a friend coming up with the required cash. This was such an exceptional circumstance that a local newspaper, the *New Orleans Item*, ran an article questioning why this jazz-loving British seaman was being held for thirty-eight days and denied bail.

The fact that Ken was languishing in the pen was unknown to the readers of *Melody Maker*, who were being treated to his letters from New Orleans throughout January 1953. His column of 3 January gave a first-hand account of a classic Crescent City funeral parade he attended, led by John Casimir's Young Tuxedo Band.

Three weeks later, the paper carried the article that helped to seal the legend of Ken Colyer. Having told his readers he had seen the band that backed Bunk Johnson on the American Music recordings, he now revealed that he had been invited by leader George Lewis to get up and play a few tunes with them. For British fans of New Orleans jazz, this was an epochal event. Not only had their hero been to the mountaintop and conversed with the gods, he had actually sat in with them.

And not just the once. The column nonchalantly began, 'The first time I sat in with the George Lewis Band . . .' This was clearly a regular occurrence – Ken had been accepted by the old players on Bourbon Street as an equal. Two weeks later, by way of proof that such an unimaginable event had actually occurred, *Melody Maker* printed a photo of Ken sat between Lewis and trumpeter Percy Humphries. From now on, Colyer was considered by jazz fans in the UK to be the Guv'nor of the New Orleans style.

Then, on 21 February, news of Ken's incarceration reached the UK. *Melody Maker* splashed the story across its front page: 'British Jazzman Held in New Orleans Jail for 38 Days'. If playing with George Lewis had given Colyer the authority to make genuine New Orleans jazz, his time in prison gave him a special insight into the blues. Who else in the British music scene could introduce a Lead Belly prison song by referring to his own time in a southern jailhouse?

Ken Colyer had left England a disillusioned man, unable to make his mark on the fledgling British trad jazz scene. Following his adventures in New Orleans, he would return to the UK a hero. A roustabout seaman who took his trumpet to the Crescent City and blew with the Old Masters till they put him in jail, he had transformed himself into a character from the pages of Mezz Mezzrow's *Really the Blues*.

All he needed to do on his return was form a band of hot musicians whom he could mould into the best New Orleans-style outfit in the

UK. But this was not as simple as it seemed. He'd burned quite a few bridges when he lit out in November 1951. Fifteen months had passed since then – new players might have emerged, other trad styles could have taken precedence. He had much to mull over as he sat in the parish prison.

While he was waiting to be deported, a letter arrived from England with an offer of a place in a young band of professional musicians who were dedicated to playing in the New Orleans style. Dated 17 February 1953, it came from Monty Sunshine, who had played clarinet with Colyer in the Crane River Jazz Band. Sunshine spoke excitedly of the potential of the new line-up:

'The people in the group are Ron [Bowden] and I plus the following. Chris Barber who is a much improved player and can hold his own with anyone playing our music in England and his style is now very much turned towards what we always wanted to hear from a trombone. On banjo and guitar is Tony Donegan, who is a much soberer and better banjoist than he used to be and who also sings well now. Our bassist is Jim Bray who even Bill considers to be the finest in the tradition in the country. Ever since we heard of your plans from Bill we have been more or less banking on your returning here very soon and taking the group over under your leadership – we planned to call it Ken Colyer's All Stars.'

It was an offer that was too good to resist – especially as it had come endorsed by his brother Bill. Ken had a ready-made vehicle with which to spread the gospel of true New Orleans jazz. But before he was deported, there was to be one more twist to his tale.

When finally released on bail, Ken once again sought out his heroes in the George Lewis Band, who were preparing to leave for a tour of California. Lewis was sorry to hear that Ken was being sent home because he had hoped Colyer would come on tour with the band in place of his regular trumpet player, Percy Humphries, who couldn't make the trip. For Ken it would have been the ultimate dream come true – to become an official member of the George Lewis Band, not just some kid from England who sat in with them now and again. But Fate and the US Department of Immigration had other plans, and on 3 March 1953 he arrived in Ellis Island, New York, to await a ship to take him home.

In an irony that would not have been lost on someone who had spent so much time at sea below decks, Ken's transport home was the luxury liner SS *United States*, holder of the Blue Riband for fastest Atlantic crossing. It was a classy way to cross the ocean, but knowing that his visa misdemeanour meant that he might never again be given permission to visit the US, it's fair to assume that Colyer would have willingly swapped his spacious cabin for a cramped seat on the Lewis Band tour bus.

BACK TO BASICS

The band that awaited Colyer when he arrived in England on 13 March 1953 worked along co-operative lines, but it was very much the creation of trombonist Chris Barber. Barber was born in Welwyn Garden City in 1930 to left-wing parents; his father was an economist who became secretary of the Socialist League in the 1930s, while his mother taught at the King Alfred Grammar School in Golders Green, which he attended.

During the Second World War, the school moved out of London to escape the Blitz, setting up temporary home near Royston in Hertfordshire. With their parents involved in war work, Barber and two other boys were billeted at the house of one of the teachers until the end of hostilities.

Three miles north of Royston, near the village of Bassingbourn, there was a huge air base, home to the USAAF Eighth Air Force, from which B-17 Flying Fortress bombers flew in vast formations to attack Germany on nightly raids. Chris and his two friends would often cycle to the airfield perimeter before breakfast and lie in a ditch to watch as the returning bombers flew just a few hundred feet above their heads before touching down on the runway across the road. He later recalled that, as they came in, he and his friends sometimes saw, in the shattered gun cupola below the cockpit, that the nose gunner had been killed during the raid.

Another attraction of the Bassingbourn base was the propensity of the US airmen to throw away things that were everyday items in

America, yet impossible to find in English shops. One such trip to the base's rubbish dump provided Chris with a copy of Mezz Mezzrow's *Really the Blues*.

At the time, swing was the most popular dance music and interest in traditional jazz was a serious pursuit that involved much listening to archaic recordings and chin-stroking discussions. Most of its aficionados were students and, as a result, record shops in Cambridge often stocked a few trad titles. Barber attended violin lessons in the university city once a week and he soon worked out that, if he cycled the fifteen miles from Royston, he'd be able to spend the bus fare on a 78 rpm jazz record.

By the time the war ended and he was sent back to London, he had amassed a collection of sixty or seventy records. Not bad for a fifteen-year-old kid. As all of that material had been recorded by American artists in the 1920s, it never occurred to the young Barber that there might be anyone playing this kind of music now, in England. So he was surprised to see, in Dobell's Record Store in central London, a leaflet advertising a band playing 'A Varied Selection of Stomps, Rags, Blues, Cakewalks and Marches'. Chris had never heard a live jazz band, so he immediately bought a ticket to see George Webb's Dixielanders.

The Dixielanders offered Chris Barber the first opportunity to hear the music he loved being performed live. The difference between the scratchy old 78 rpm records he played on his wind-up gramophone and what he later described as the all-enveloping sound of a real live band was nothing less than sensational. The Dixielanders had taken a huge leap forward when Humphrey Lyttelton joined on trumpet in 1947. Humph would be responsible for taking jazz into the mainstream in the decades that followed, but for now he was bringing some much-needed professionalism to the emerging British trad scene.

Still a teenager, Barber became an avid fan of Lyttelton's playing and, as there was no one giving jazz lessons at the time, he would sit on the edge of the stage while the band performed, watching closely, trying to work out the trumpet player's technique. To get a better view, Barber would sit at a slight angle to Lyttelton, in front of Harry Brown on trombone. One night, Brown leaned over to him and asked, 'Do you want to buy a trombone, son?' Nonplussed, Barber asked how much. 'Five pound ten,' was the reply. By chance, he had that exact amount in his pocket and, as he admitted in his autobiography, he couldn't think of a good reason for not buying it. It was, by his own admission, a terrible trombone, but from this impulsive purchase a career in music was born.

Like many musicians, Barber learned his instrument by playing along with records. His violin lessons as a kid had made him aware of musical scales, and he soon found some like-minded teenagers to play along with. Leaving school at eighteen with an aptitude for maths, he found work in an insurance company. However, the Clerical Medical Life Assurance Society was a little too staid for a jazz-loving youth and, aged twenty, Barber was fired after failing company exams twice in succession.

His father, recognising that Chris had a talent for music, offered to pay for him to go to music college. The Guildhall School of Music and Drama was very keen on Barber joining their ranks, as they had no brass players in the entire school. When he was asked to choose a second instrument he at first decided on violin. The school was most disappointed as they already had dozens of highly trained violinists, so instead he put his name down for the most common stringed instrument in the jazz world – the double bass.

Barber spent three years as a student at the Guildhall School, all the time playing in small jazz bands with friends he'd found on the scene. Among them was Alexis Korner, described by the impresario Harold Pendleton as 'strange, wild, smoking black cigarettes, [who] grew his hair shaggy for those days. Demonstrably a foreigner and weird. He looked like a Balkan terrorist.'

Born in Paris in 1928, Alexis Korner was the son of a Jewish Austrian father and a mother from the Greek community of Constantinople (now Istanbul). Though born in France, he was an Austrian national who had become a naturalised British citizen. During the war, the family dropped the umlaut from their name, which changed its pronunciation from 'Kerner' to 'Korner'. Alexis had attended the King Alfred Grammar School at the same time as Barber, but their paths had never crossed.

In 1950, Chris Barber and his New Orleans Jazz Band featured trombone, clarinet, two trumpet players, banjo, piano, double bass and drums. Because he wanted to play blues numbers as well, Barber invited Korner to join on electric guitar. Like other trad jazz bands of the time, their set included a breakdown session, which featured blues songs by the likes of Tampa Red and Big Bill Broonzy. This was a four-piece set-up – Korner on guitar, Barber on double bass, along with the band's pianist and drummer. Asked in later years what the young Alexis Korner sounded like, Barber sheepishly admitted that he couldn't hear him – but then, given that Korner was playing an electric guitar without an amplifier, nor could anyone else.

Korner was one of a number of peripheral figures who came and went from Chris Barber's band in its earliest years. The jazz scene at the time was wholly amateur and the realities of day jobs, education and conscription into the armed services would often cause band members to drop out. Korner only got the gig with Chris Barber because the band's regular guitar player, Tony Donegan, had been sent overseas on national service.

Tony Donegan was born in Glasgow on 29 April 1931, the son of an Irish mother and Scottish father. Donegan senior was a professional musician who played violin with the Scottish National Orchestra, but the economic chaos that followed the Wall Street Crash of 1929 meant that work was hard to come by. In the hope of finding better times in London, the family moved to Wilton Road in East Ham when Tony was two years old, where his father took a number of jobs, eventually joining the Merchant Navy.

The outbreak of the Second World War saw the mass evacuation of schoolchildren from the East End of London. Surrounded by docks, car factories and the largest gasworks in Europe, East Ham would be hit hard by the Blitz. With his father away at sea, Tony and his mother headed back to Glasgow, but when that too became a target for the Luftwaffe, Tony was sent to live with his uncle in Altrincham, in the Cheshire countryside near Manchester.

His mother returned to the East End, renting a flat in Rosebery Avenue, Manor Park, which would become home to Tony in the years following the war. The conflict had played havoc with his education, resulting in him only attending school for a year during his stay in Altrincham. Despite this, he was intelligent enough to secure a job as an office boy at a firm of stockbrokers in the City of London.

One of his young workmates played guitar in a dance band and, bringing his instrument into work, would show Tony how to place his fingers on the fretboard to make a chord. When the time came for him to buy a new guitar, Tony bought his old one for thirty shillings.

The best way to teach yourself how to play a guitar is to find someone whose songs you love and to learn their repertoire. In my case that artist was Rod Stewart. For Tony Donegan it was Frank Crumit, a singer of novelty songs who hailed from Jackson, Ohio. Crumit was born in 1889 and performed on the US vaudeville circuit. He made several popular recordings during the 1920s of humorous songs such 'Abdul Abulbul Amir', 'What Kind of Noise Annoys an Oyster?' and 'The Prune Song'. Taking a break from the comedy tunes, Crumit scored a hit in 1927 with the blues standard 'Frankie and Johnny', the story of Frankie Baker, a young prostitute who killed her man in the red-light district of St Louis because 'he done her wrong'. Although the young Donegan loved Crumit's novelty songs, when he had the opportunity to make his first recording, in a booth on Southend Pier, it was 'Frankie and Johnny' that he chose to perform, in the hope of impressing a girl who had accompanied him to the Essex seaside town.

By the time he was seventeen, Donegan was attending jazz gigs at the 100 Club in Oxford Street, home to Humphrey Lyttelton and his band, making sure to stand as close as possible to guitarist Nevil Skrimshire, the better to study the chords he was playing. One night, heading home on the Tube, he got chatting with a lad whom he recognised as a 100 Club devotee like himself. Alex Revell was a member of an amateur jazz band that got together to play for fun once a week at a school hall in Gants Hill, on the eastern fringes of London. Hearing that Tony played guitar, Alex invited him over for a jam session.

As often happens, playing with other musicians had a hugely beneficial effect on Tony's technique. Revell gave him a sheet of chords to practise and soon he became a regular member of the band. Chris Barber also entered Revell's orbit, venturing over from north-west London a couple of times to join the session.

In the interests of authenticity, Donegan was encouraged to buy a banjo, the mainstay, along with the double bass and drums, of the New Orleans jazz band rhythm section. He duly obliged, underlining his commitment to the music of the Crescent City. Before the band could perform any gigs, however, its members began to be picked off by conscription.

In 1948, the British government, facing a shortage of volunteers for the armed forces, introduced legislation which required every male between the ages of seventeen and twenty-six to register for compulsory national service of eighteen months' duration. There were exemptions for certain trades such as farming and coal mining, and those who went into higher education, as Chris Barber did at the Guildhall Music School, were allowed to defer their call-up until they had completed their studies.

Like the rationing that was a feature of British life well into the 1950s, conscription into the armed forces was one of the things that lingered on long after hostilities had ended, preventing people's lives from returning to the normality they had enjoyed before the war. National Service taught teenagers to take orders, forcing them into a rigid world of hierarchy, authority and discipline. The whole process seemed to be designed to make you behave just like your parents. By the time conscription ended in 1960, over 2 million teenagers had served in the armed forces. Some saw out their time bored stiff in barracks in the UK and Europe, while others were sent overseas to fight in the jungles of Malaya or on the frozen hillsides of Korea.

When Tony Donegan was called up in 1949, he took his banjo with him. After basic training, he was sent to serve in the Royal Army Medical Corps, based at Woolwich Barracks in south London, within easy reach of the 100 Club. Back in the Soho jazz scene, he began asking around if anyone needed a banjo player and ended up joining in breakdown sessions with Chris Barber and his New Orleans Jazz Band.

His sojourn with Barber was abruptly terminated after six months when Donegan was sent to Austria, despite his best effort to avoid the posting by purposefully failing an army exam. When his ruse was discovered he was charged with insubordination and immediately shipped out, giving Alexis Korner the opportunity to join the Barber band. Like Berlin, Vienna had been divided into four sectors by the victorious allies – British, French, Russian and American – but unlike the German capital it had not been the scene of a full-scale battle. As a result, much of the city was intact, making it a rather cushy posting.

Even under post-war occupation, Vienna was still the city of Schubert, Strauss and Klimt, yet such iconic figures made little impression on Donegan. For him, the great cultural attraction of Vienna was the proximity of the Americans. The occupying powers went to great lengths to ensure that their servicemen enjoyed the standard of living they were used to at home. For British squaddies, this meant a regular supply of things like tea and digestive biscuits. For the American GIs, it meant ice cream, hot dogs, bubblegum and popular music.

The American Forces Network radio station broadcast the US pop hits of 1950 across the divided city, and Donegan, having got himself a job as a storekeeper, listened avidly. Gospel songs and mainstream jazz numbers rubbed shoulders with tracks by Nat King Cole and the Weavers. None of this was to be heard on the boring old BBC. With many American servicemen coming from rural communities, country music was very popular on AFN – Donegan heard Hank Williams, the Carter Family and Tennessee Ernie Ford for the first time, as well as blues singers such as Josh White, Big Bill Broonzy and, a particular favourite, Lonnie Johnson.

Although he never performed any gigs in Austria, his talent was much in demand in the barrack room, where he led singing sessions that helped while away the boredom that was a major part of a national serviceman's lot. In many ways, Tony Donegan's time in Vienna provided him with a musical education. When he returned to civvy street in 1951, he'd adopted the nasal, high singing style he'd heard on AFN's country programmes and given himself a new moniker. The nervous conscript came back a confident performer, knowledgeable about American roots music and determined to make a living playing jazz. Looking for gigs on the London scene, he began introducing himself to people as Lonnie Donegan.

His first break came at the Fishmonger's Arms in Wood Green,

77

which hosted a jazz night. Lonnie, carrying his guitar, talked the promoter into letting him get up and sing a few songs in the interval. Opening with 'Frankie and Johnny', he showed how much he'd grown since first recording the song on Southend Pier years before. Frank Crumit was no longer his point of reference – he was now trying to channel Lead Belly.

While his playing lacked polish, Donegan's enthusiastic performances of American folk songs began to attract an audience. 'At Wood Green, I would sing the songs with a mixture of ineptitude and amateurism,' he reflected years later, 'but with plenty of enthusiasm and I think that is what brought the punters back from the bar. I mean, when the band came off, there would always be a mad rush to the bar, it was empty room time, but over the weeks, more and more would trickle back to see me.'

Soon he found himself a gig with Bill Brunskill's Jazz Band, one of the numerous New Orleans-style outfits playing around London for fun. But Lonnie was after more than fun. Driven by the urge to earn a living in music, he took over the job of getting the band work. The promoter at the Wood Green Jazz Club was happy to give his successful soloist a few gigs and, as other paid work appeared, the band was renamed the Tony Donegan Jazz Band (he had asked his new bandmates to call him Lonnie, but he wasn't yet brazen enough to advertise his metamorphosis in lights).

Not only was Donegan now running the band, he was also giving himself a solo spot at every gig, playing his American roots music during the interval. And he was clearly getting better at it, for out of the blue he got a call from promoter Maurice Kinn, offering a gig at the Royal Albert Hall on 2 June 1952. The fee was £4 10s. Complaining that this wasn't much for a six-piece band, he was told, 'No, I just want you. You do that thing with the guitar, don't you? We need someone to come out between the bands while they're changing over.'

His first gig as Lonnie Donegan was to be at the most prestigious venue in the country, playing a ten-minute set along with seventeen other bands in what was billed as 'the greatest jazz event ever staged in Great Britain'. The only solo performer on the bill, he walked out in front of seven thousand people and performed with the same naïve enthusiasm that had worked so well for him at the Fishmonger's Arms.

'OK, I was terrible,' he later admitted. 'Just an arrogant little strummer who didn't know any better. I shudder to think what my voice sounded like in a place that big, but the response was as if I'd just raised the *Titanic* single-handedly. It was enormous, gigantic! The audience adored me!'

Lonnie must have been pleased when Ernest Borneman, reviewing the gig for *Melody Maker*, described his performance as 'a cowboy-styled blues vocal'. Brilliant! 'It had echoes of Jimmie Rodgers and the hillbilly parade, falsetto notes and all.' Praise indeed! And then the sucker punch: 'Really dreadful.' All the things that Lonnie had been reaching for, the reviewer had hated. There was no mention of the fact that his performance had gone down a storm.

Such a damning review at an early stage can seriously dent a performer's confidence, but Lonnie had that massive audience response to comfort him. The *Melody Maker* could go to hell. His burning self-belief was vindicated when, a few weeks later, he found himself invited to play the second-biggest venue in London, the newly opened Royal Festival Hall.

The National Federation of Jazz Organisations – the nearest thing the UK jazz scene had to an organising body – had been negotiating with the Ministry of Labour to promote a concert featuring both British and American artists. The ministry had agreed to provide work permits for the foreign performers, but the Musicians' Union was opposed to the event. The ban on British artists touring in the

US, instigated in the 1930s by the American Federation of Musicians, was still in force, leaving the MU little choice but to reciprocate.

British jazz fans found the stand-off immensely frustrating. If they wanted to see the latest American stars, they had to travel abroad. Paris was a regular stop-off for US musicians on tour, but strict rules on currency exchange made it almost impossible for the average fan to organise and fund a cross-Channel trip.

Musicians themselves were just as put out. As Ken Colyer had shown, in order to learn how to perform this stuff correctly, you needed to see and hear the experts playing it live. The stuffed shirts who ran the union couldn't understand that, on this issue, they were actively holding their members back.

Angry at this ongoing state of affairs, the NFJO decided to push the boundaries. Having secured the necessary work permits for their American performers, they went ahead, booking the best British jazz bands as supporting acts. No sooner had the tickets gone on sale than the MU issued a statement threatening to blacklist any members who appeared on stage with the Americans. For the young men who were desperately trying to make enough money playing jazz to survive, this was something they had to take seriously. As members in good standing of the MU, they could demand better fees and conditions and get representation if disputes arose. Being a jazzer in the mid-50s was still a precarious occupation – to be blacklisted would be the kiss of death to most careers.

As their British acts began to withdraw under MU pressure, the NFJO began to scout around for artists who weren't union members. Although he'd been playing gigs for five years, Lonnie Donegan was still classed as an amateur musician and as such wasn't a member of the MU. When the call came through asking him if he'd like to appear on stage at the Royal Festival Hall, and with his hero Lonnie Johnson no less, Donegan leapt at the chance.

As it had been at the Royal Albert Hall, his performance was well received, but his encounter with the star of the show left him underwhelmed. Lonnie Johnson had first visited Britain back in 1917, to play for the troops heading for the trenches. The records that Donegan loved had been recorded in the 1920s and 30s, when his sound was edgy and raw. Now sixty-two years old, he appeared in a well-cut white suit and a bow tie, playing in the smooth style that he'd developed in east coast supper clubs over the past decade.

While he may have been disappointed with Johnson's set, his appearance on the same bill gave Donegan the first building block in his legend. In the years that followed, he would tell anyone who asked that he got his new name when the MC at the Festival Hall gig got him mixed up with Johnson, introducing him to the audience as 'Lonnie Donegan'.

In truth, he'd appeared under that name on the bill for the Royal Albert Hall a month earlier. However, when you've got snotty reporters asking – by implication – how a jumped-up little herbert from East Ham, whose real name was Anthony, came to have a name that sounded like something out of the American south, you can understand why said little herbert might want to use a bit of synchronicity to build a protective myth around himself.

Having played two of the biggest gigs in London in the space of a few weeks, Lonnie must have thought he was on the up. But then he received a buff envelope from the War Ministry. The government required all those who had completed their national service to remain on call as reservists. Lonnie had to report to his depot for three weeks' training. When he returned, he found that he'd been fired from his band, which was now called the Geoff Kemp Band. Lonnie wasn't too disappointed because he'd recently renewed his acquaintance with Chris Barber, playing banjo and singing blues songs like Blind Blake's 'C.C. Pill Blues'.

Barber was becoming increasingly frustrated with his band's lack of progress. Rehearsing just once a week was holding them back. In September 1952, he became convinced that the only way for the band to improve would be for them to turn professional.

They say that the most dangerous part of any flight is not the time spent at altitude, but the moment when the wheels leave the ground. It's the same for a band. When you've been playing together for fun with the same bunch of people over a long period, the suggestion that you should all give up your day jobs and make a living playing music can be highly destabilising. Some members might be in an apprenticeship or a steady job with good prospects for the future. Their parents or spouse might be relying on them to bring in regular money. Performing on stage is a wonderful thrill, but the notion of leaving a stable environment for a throw of the dice in the capricious music industry doesn't appeal to everyone who enjoys doing gigs.

Barber's band thought he was mad. 'None of us believed that it was possible to make a living playing jazz,' recalled clarinettist Alex Revell. 'We knew that even our hero King Oliver had ended up working as a janitor in a Georgia pool room.' One by one, the people that Barber had played jazz with since his teens fell away. But not Lonnie. After years of low-paid work in retail, scrabbling around trying to form bands, get gigs and organise the logistics himself, in Chris Barber Donegan had finally found someone as driven to succeed as he was.

Having decided they wanted to turn professional, they started sounding out other musicians who might share their dream. Chris recruited Ken Colyer's old clarinettist, Monty Sunshine. Lonnie called the bass player from the Tony Donegan Jazz Band, Jim Bray, who couldn't wait to leave his job as a researcher at Shell. The rhythm section was completed by Ron Bowden, another former member of the now defunct Crane River Jazz Band.

82

When they were unable to find a regular trumpet player, Barber pulled out a couple of old 78s made by the Eclipse Alley Five, an old-time New Orleans quintet led by George Lewis. If he could make jazz without trumpets, Barber declared, then so could they. 'Straight away we sounded marvellous, light years ahead of what any of the other bands were doing. And it made us work harder: in that line-up, you couldn't hide bad phrasing behind somebody else, it was just too transparent.'

At the time, Lonnie was dating the girl who would later become his first wife, Maureen Tyler. Her father was the landlord of the Prince Albert pub in Mile End, a working-class district of east London. Mr Tyler loved a bit of jazz, so was happy to have the band rehearsing in his first-floor function room – he even sent up crates of beer to keep the lads happy. They seemed like a band that had it all: great musicians, limitless rehearsal time, free beer. Yet the lack of a horn restricted the scope of their material. Eventually, Barber recalled the name of the impressive trumpet player he used to see when his old band played at the White Hart in Southall: Pat Halcox jumped at the chance to go professional.

The band was constituted as a co-operative – all decisions taken together and all profits equally shared – and made its debut with two consecutive Friday-night gigs at the Club Creole, Harold Pendleton's new venue at 44 Gerrard Street in Soho. The first was on Christmas Eve 1952, and the audience response was very positive. When the reaction to the second gig, on New Year's Eve, was even better, the band were convinced that they had made the right decision. 1953 was going to be their year.

The previous September, Chris Barber had accepted an invitation to make a trip to Denmark, where he toured as a guest with a Danish jazz band. When the promoter, Karl Emil Knudsen, heard about the new band that Barber was forming, he invited them to Denmark at

Easter 1953 for an extensive tour. It would be pretty low-key, travelling by rail and sleeping on floors in the homes of local jazz fans, but it was just what the band needed – three weeks on the road, playing every night, honing their skills and defining their repertoire before launching themselves on the UK jazz scene.

This was the moment that Barber had been waiting for – in Denmark he would finally become a professional musician. The band were busy handing in their notice, resigning from college or notifying their next of kin when Pat Halcox dropped a bombshell: his mum and dad wouldn't let him go. They had scrimped and saved to get him through college and he felt that he would be grievously letting them down if he chucked in his job at Glaxo.

This was a potential disaster – Barber had already booked the travel tickets and the gigs were on sale. A band meeting was hastily convened, just as news broke in *Melody Maker* that Ken Colyer had been jailed for violation of his visa conditions in New Orleans. The band realised that there could only be one outcome for Colyer – he would be deported from the US and back home soon.

The weekly reports in *Melody Maker* had greatly enhanced Colyer's reputation. He would return to England as the high priest of the New Orleans sound, come to show his people the true path, like some trad jazz Moses come down from the mountain. Whatever he chose to do next, it would be big news – any band led by Colyer would be the hottest on the scene. All of this must undoubtedly have been on their minds when they deputised Ken's old bandmate Monty Sunshine to write, offering him not only a place in the band, but his name on the marquee: Ken Colyer's All Stars.

WHAT KIND OF MUSIC ARE THEY PLAYING?

The news that Ken Colyer had returned from New Orleans was splashed by *Melody Maker* on 14 March 1953, the day after he had disembarked from the SS *United States* at Southampton. Waiting for him on the quayside were his brother Bill and new bandmates Chris Barber and Monty Sunshine, who filled him in on the band's plans as they travelled back to London. Bill Colyer, who had kept his name in the papers and parlayed a radio programme based on Ken's trip onto the BBC, made sure that *Melody Maker* stayed abreast of the latest developments.

The following week, the paper announced the formation of Ken Colyer's Jazzmen (they must have baulked at calling themselves 'All Stars') under the headline 'New Colyer Band for LJC and Danish Clubs': 'Cornettist Ken Colyer, who returned to Britain last week from New Orleans, has formed his new band and begun rehearsals,' it stated. 'The Jazzmen will leave on 30 March for the Danish jazz clubs and hope to play concerts in Germany and Holland on their way back. When they return at the end of April, the Jazzmen take up residency at the London Jazz Club.' Colyer told *Melody Maker*, 'We are going to try to popularise New Orleans music without distorting it, aborting it, or slapping any gimmicks on it.'

Before they left for Denmark, the band made their radio debut, interviewed by Denis Preston on the BBC's *World of Jazz* programme on 28 March 1953 – billed in the *Radio Times* as Monty Sunshine's Jazz Band. For, although he spoke on air about his time in New

Ken Colyer's Jazzmen, 1953: (*left to right*) Monty Sunshine, Lonnie Donegan, Ken Colyer, Ron Bowden, Chris Barber and Jim Bray

Orleans, Ken declined to perform. The following week's *Melody Maker* explained why: 'Colyer obeyed decisions made by manager/brother Bill and did not play. His first public appearance will be when the new outfit take over the resident job at the London Jazz Club following their trip to the continent.'

Now that Ken had returned from his great adventure, his elder brother was determined to stoke the Colyer legend. And *Melody Maker* seemed only too happy to oblige. For now, 'with the glamour of his New Orleans adventure behind him', it purred in conclusion, 'Ken Colyer will remain the mystery man of the British traditionalist jazz world'.

The Danish tour was not without its mishaps – Donegan missed the ferry, and when the band arrived for their first gig a huge banner announced the appearance of 'The Chris Barber Crane River Jazz

86

Band' – but the gigs were a huge success. And from the beginning, they included a breakdown set.

'Playing every night in Denmark, the band got better and better,' recalled Barber. 'It started to sound like a proper group. We also introduced [breakdown] sessions into our concerts. I'd been doing blues sessions with my previous band, when Alexis Korner sang a short blues set between numbers, backed by our pianist and me on bass, then with Lonnie. We wanted to do some of the best of the classic blues. We felt it was part of what you had to do, that without the blues you couldn't possibly understand New Orleans jazz. The two things went hand in hand. The only real difference between blues and New Orleans jazz is the instruments it's played on. It's mostly the same music, but played on guitars, not trombones.'

For Lonnie Donegan, the Danish tour was his chance to shine. 'Whenever there was a gap [in the performance] I would sing my little songs and people either liked it or went for a beer – and I got better at it. Chris would join in on the bass when he felt like it, Ken would join in on the guitar when he felt like it and his brother Bill would join in on the washboard or sometimes my bass player would play – it was very much an ad-lib situation. But it's all on record – on the "Danish" record.'

The record that Donegan is referring to was the work of Karl Emil Knudsen, who organised a recording session for the band in the ballroom of the Gentofte Hotel in the suburbs of Copenhagen. Armed only with a domestic Grundig tape recorder, Knudsen was able to release several successful records of the band, allowing him to start his own jazz label, Storyville.*

Although Knudsen recorded the band's whole set, the subsequent Storyville releases only featured the trad jazz numbers – it would be

---

* Decades later both Colyer and Donegan were still to be heard bitterly complaining that they were never paid for the recordings.

years before the songs recorded during the breakdown sessions came to light. In 2008, Acrobat Music produced a comprehensive collection of Lonnie Donegan's early work over three CDs entitled *Midnight Special: The Skiffle Years 1953–1957*. The album kicks off with the songs he recorded with the Colyer breakdown band at the Gentofte Hotel fifty-five years before. The first track, 'Hard Time Blues', features Lonnie singing high and lonesome, in a voice reminiscent of the great Appalachian banjo-playing balladeer Roscoe Holcomb. A double bass is just about audible in the background. The song had originally appeared on the Paramount label in 1931, sung by Charlie Spand, a boogie-woogie piano player who specialised in the barrel-house style.

The second track, 'Nobody's Child', is an orphan's lament that had been a hit for Hank Snow and His Rainbow Ranch Boys in 1949. Donegan always had a weakness for a maudlin country song but here he plays the banjo too heavily to give the lyrics the pathos they require. He's much better on 'You Don't Know My Mind', an up-tempo blues originally recorded by Virginia Liston for Okeh Records in New York in 1923. His heavy strum drives the song forward, waking up the bass, which seemed to be dozing off during the two earlier tracks.

In the last of the songs from the Gentofte sessions, Ken Colyer takes the lead vocal on Lead Belly's 'Midnight Special'. His rather pedestrian delivery simply can't compete with Donegan's hillbilly howl, the song only really coming to life when Lonnie starts to sing harmony.

The band came back from Denmark earlier than intended, such was the clamour in London to hear Ken Colyer play the way he'd learned in New Orleans. The London Jazz Club had just relocated to the crypt of the Church of the Annunciation in Bryanston Street, near London's Marble Arch. They made their debut on May Day 1953, and the response was immediate.

The *New Musical Express* noted that 'from the first stomp the six-piece Colyer outfit went with a swing which the packed enthusiasts greeted with the fervour it deserved'. James Asman, jazz critic of *Record Mirror*, was even more fulsome in his praise: 'This was the nearest thing we have heard to genuine New Orleans music. The spontaneous applause and the entranced faces of the crowds told us that Ken's adventures across the Atlantic had not been in vain. In fact it was the best thing we have yet heard by British musicians. It sounded very much like jazz.'

The breakdown group played a big part in the success. Lonnie Donegan takes centre stage in a photograph from the period, playing guitar and singing into the mic. To his right, Alexis Korner plays mandolin and Ken Colyer strums the guitar slung across his knee. To his left, Bill Colyer sits playing a washboard, while Chris Barber plucks

The founding fathers of British rock: (*left to right*) Ken Colyer, Alexis Korner, Lonnie Donegan, Bill Colyer (*seated*) and Chris Barber play together in Ken Colyer's Skiffle Group, 1953

a stand-up bass. This picture embodies a revolutionary moment in British popular music, when the guitar, for so long stuck at the back of the bandstand, an often inaudible part of the rhythm section, comes to the front and takes control.

A young Pete Townshend was there to witness this paradigm shift. The future powerhouse guitar player of the Who was just a school-boy when he saw Ken Colyer's Jazzmen at Acton Town Hall in west London. At the time, his father was a professional musician, perform-ing with the Squadronaires big band. Used to the smooth, sophis-ticated swing played by his father, Townshend was shocked by the primitive nature of the Jazzmen and their crowd.

'I was used to the tidy music of my dad's era,' he told me in 2008, during an interview conducted for a radio documentary about Ken Colyer. 'It was messy. He [Colyer] was messy. The band were messy. The audience were messy.' In scenes of seeming chaos that would not have been out of place at a punk gig twenty-five years later, Townshend described how the men in the audience were drunk, they wore cheap rough duffel coats, some had wet themselves, and instead of wearing wrist watches some had alarm clocks hanging around their necks.

Disorienting though these scenes must have been for the young Townshend, what made a lasting impression on him was the sight of the guitarist taking control of the gig by bringing his instrument to the front of the stage. In that moment, he grasped the enormity of what was happening. 'This instrument was going to change the world. For me, this was absolutely massive because my father was a saxophone player. I could see the end of my father's world – I was going to get this guitar and it was going to be bye-bye, old-timer, and that's exactly what happened.'

Around this period the Ken Colyer Jazzmen recorded a radio ses-sion for the BBC, and the breakdown band tracks, which appear on *Midnight Special,* are audible evidence of how far the band had progressed since their Danish recordings. Colyer's vocal on 'Midnight Special' is much more lively and Donegan's backing vocals provide a high-energy counter to Colyer's lead. On the band's performance of the American folk song 'John Henry', Donegan offers the first example of the vocal style that would become his trademark. Compared to the suave big-band singers of the day, Donegan sounds like a wild man. And his performances were driving the audiences wild too.

In June 1953, shortly after the Jazzmen had taken up their residency in the crypt on Bryanston Street, *Jazz Journal* reported on the sensation that the breakdown band were creating:

'The skiffle group which takes over during the intervals at the London Jazz Club is obviously going to be the success of the year. It's getting so that more people flock into the club for the interval than for the rest of the session. The group varies but it's always based on the guitars, banjos and vocals of Ken Colyer, Alexis Korner and Lonnie Donegan.' The article goes on to name some of the numbers performed, among them Trixie Smith's 'Freight Train Blues' and Woody Guthrie's 'New York Town'. 'If you don't believe this kind of music could be a draw in London – and I don't blame you for doubting – then drop in and feel the electric atmosphere that builds up during Lonnie Donegan's version of "John Henry".'

What is remarkable about this short report is not just the prescience of the author in recognising the potential of this music some thirty months before it took the country by storm; Brian Nicholls was also the first journalist to use the word 'skiffle' in reference to music played by British musicians. The word was so unfamiliar to the sub-editors at *Jazz Journal* that rather than use it, they chose to headline the article 'The New Sound'.

In memoirs and interviews over the years, those who were there at the time tend to credit Bill Colyer as the man who introduced the term 'skiffle'. Although Ken was familiar with the concept – in his last

91

Melody Maker dispatch from New Orleans he'd used it to describe music he'd heard improvised on home-made instruments – it was Bill who first applied it to the guitar-led music that the breakdown band were playing in the UK.

During an overseas broadcast for the BBC World Service in 1953, the session producer recognised that the breakdown band had a different line-up from the jazz band and clearly weren't playing jazz. 'So who should the song be credited to,' asked the producer, 'and what kind of music are they playing?'

As manager, Bill informed the producer that this was the Ken Colyer Skiffle Group. Put on the spot, he could have given a number of answers: blues, folk, country, gospel – their material came from many different traditions. Years later, Bill wondered why he hadn't called them the Spasm Band. Instead, he chose an archaic musical term that had fallen into disuse and, in doing so, christened a new movement.

———

The word 'skiffle' first appeared in the America of the Roaring Twenties as a term for the rent parties thrown by urban blacks hoping to raise enough money to pay the landlord when things were tight. In *The Story of the Blues*, Paul Oliver describes how, during the years of Prohibition, a tenant looking to rustle up a month's rent would brew up some moonshine liquor, engage the services of a barrelhouse piano player and charge people twenty-five cents for admission. Oliver lists the slang terms for such events: 'the "parlor social", the "gouge" and the "percolator", the "skiffle" and the "too terrible party" were all names for the function most commonly termed a "boogie" or "house rent party"'.

The term first became associated with music on a 1929 release by Paramount Records. 'Hometown Skiffle', described on the label as a novelty record, was a promotional recording that brought together the label's biggest stars on a two-part 78 rpm single. An MC acts as host of the 'skiffle', introducing each artist, who then plays a brief snatch of material. The Hokum Boys sing a couple of verses about having a party and selling bootleg liquor, Will Ezell hammers out some boogie-woogie piano and Blind Blake plays a little ragtime guitar. Someone impersonates the then familiar guitar style of Paramount's biggest-selling star, Blind Lemon Jefferson, whose name appears on the label but who had passed away just before this session was recorded. Charlie Spand, whose repertoire provided Lonnie Donegan with a song for his recording debut in Denmark, plays a few verses of barrelhouse piano blues. The recording ends when the police arrive. On hearing their knock at the door, the MC declares, 'It must be Johnny Nabbs. He broke up the hometown skiffle. See you in jail.'

In this original context, rather than being attached to a particular style of music 'skiffle' is descriptive of an event – a slang word to describe a social occasion that involved informal music and dancing. 'Hometown Skiffle' was part of Paramount's legendary 12000 series of 'race' records that came to define the best jazz and blues music of the 1920s. The label floundered in 1935, just as the more sophisticated sound of swing was winning the hearts of American record buyers. With Paramount's demise, the term disappeared from musical vocabulary for a decade.

———

By 1945, the trad jazz revival was well under way in the United States. Researchers were rediscovering artists who had been present in the early days of jazz, some of whom had never been recorded. It was in this environment that a successful African American journalist and publisher decided to get together with friends to record some of those old good-time tunes that he used to play in the 1920s.

Dan Burley was born in Kentucky in 1907 and as a teenager played piano at rent parties in and around Chicago, working for the city's *Daily Defender* newspaper, where he became sports editor at the age of twenty-one. He was manager and co-owner of the *New York Age* and editor of *Ebony* magazine from the late 1930s. A Renaissance figure of African American culture, he acted, wrote poetry, was the author of *Dan Burley's Original Handbook of Harlem Jive* and performed with such jazz greats as Duke Ellington, Cab Calloway and Ella Fitzgerald.

In June 1946, Burley got together with brothers Sticks and Brownie McGhee on acoustic guitars and Pops Foster on stand-up bass to record *Southside Shake*, an album of barrelhouse piano tunes for New York's Circle label. Looking for a name that would evoke those good old rent-party days of his youth, Burley chose to call his ensemble the Skiffle Boys. Again, the context here is that of an event. Burley isn't claiming to be performing a style of music called skiffle; he's declaring that he and his band are playing music *for* a skiffle. A British band that came together for the same purpose in the mid-1940s might have called themselves Dan Burley and His Knees-Up Boys.

Bill Colyer, who had been collecting jazz records since he was a teen, worked in the record department of the International Bookshop, the forerunner of Collets, in London's Charing Cross Road. Here, his deep knowledge of jazz styles was put to good use, serving the small but growing number of fans eager to learn more about the history of the genre. Working in a record shop that prided itself on having the latest imports from the US, he would have been familiar with the name Dan Burley and His Skiffle Boys. However, to those outside the clique of trad jazz fans who used the shop as a kind of social club, the word 'skiffle' would have been meaningless.

Such was its obscurity that when Bill Colyer plucked the term out of the air to describe the music played by the breakdown band for the producer of that BBC radio session, no one batted an eyelid. In an instant, Colyer had changed the meaning of the word, from arcane black American slang for a rent party to a contemporary British term describing guitar-led, roots-based music. It was a sleight of hand that made a lot of sense to the trad jazz coterie, for it provided a ready-made mythology that linked them to the roots of the music they so passionately loved.

Was Bill Colyer aware of what he'd done? Among all of the young faces on the scene, he had the most authority when it came to nuances of style and genre. Had he been searching for a better term to describe what the breakdown band were doing – something that evoked the spirit of the Lead Belly songs that they were performing? Or was it simply that he knew he and his brother would be laughed out of town, losing all the credibility they'd carefully built, if he were so outlandish as to claim that these nice English lads were playing the blues?

The BBC producer was probably quite happy with the term 'skiffle'. It had an onomatopoeic quality suggestive of the frantic strumming of several tightly strung guitars against the metallic scrape of an old washboard. And, more importantly, it gave him something to write in his studio notes.

———

The notion of sticking an old label on something new is not unheard of in the music industry. The *New Musical Express Book of Rock*, originally published in Britain in 1973, has an entry for 'punk rock', some two years before the Sex Pistols made their debut. For the journalists who compiled this first rock encyclopedia in the early 70s, 'punk rock' was a term they gave to the white guitar bands that formed all over America in the wake of the Beatles-led British Invasion. These were predominantly garage bands, suburban kids with long hair and cheap guitars who won the local talent show and got to make a record that was a regional hit before disappearing back into obscurity. With its simplistic riff, staccato Vox organ and snotty-nosed vocals, 'Louie Louie' by the Kingsmen came to typify this almost wilfully dumb approach to music-making.

It was this attitude that the Ramones were seeking to reconnect with when they began playing loud, fast and unintelligible pop music as a response to the deification of musicianship that was a central feature of mainstream 70s guitar rock. Journalists looking for a term for their back-to-basics style didn't take long to come up with a name. Leather jackets? Check. Cheap guitars? Check. Early-60s haircuts? Check. And that wilfully dumb attitude? What else could they call it but punk rock?

When Eddie and the Hot Rods started playing 60s garage band tunes real fast at the Marquee Club in London in 1976, it seemed like this new punk rock had crossed the ocean. The arrival in England around the same time of the Heartbreakers – consisting of former members of the New York Dolls, themselves a throwback to the 60s – only gave substance to the term. However, it took the Sex Pistols to transform the meaning of punk rock from what seemed initially to be a revivalist tendency into a new dynamic movement that sought to sweep away everything that had gone before. What had begun as a homage to an earlier style had suddenly taken on a very contemporary resonance.

———

When questioned about the term 'skiffle', Bill Colyer always cited Dan Burley and His Skiffle Boys as its source. But he didn't only lift

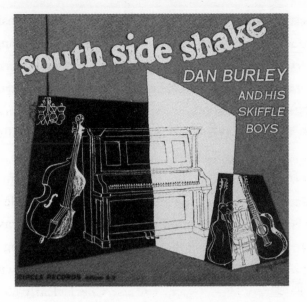

the word, he also appropriated the back story, probably straight from the liner notes that Rudi Blesh wrote for Burley's *South Side Shake* album, which appeared on Circle Records in 1947 and was, according to Blesh's biographer, a big seller in England.

'From 1910 to about 1933,' wrote Blesh, 'Chicago, at the confluence of rivers and railroads to the south, became the center of a great northward industrial migration of the Negroes and thereby a meeting place for barrel-house and boogie-woogie players. The great South Side institution of "rent party" (locally known as "skiffle," "shake," or "percolator") run by the landlady, paid the rent by the proceeds from the sale of homecooked food and nefarious, bootleg liquor, and was the scene of gambling, dancing, brawls and "good time." These social affairs of a submerged, underprivileged, and partly expatriate dark population were the haven of those piano blues players who, making the rounds of the innumerable "skiffles," subsisted on the free food and drink and the large tips from those who emerged as winners in the crap game.'

Pretty soon, everyone was repeating this story as the origin myth of British skiffle music: that it originated in the Chicago rent parties of the 1920s. Sure, that's where the *word* came from, but the style of music being played by Colyer's breakdown band – though it had many antecedents on both sides of the Atlantic – was a new and wholly British phenomenon.

STUMBLING TOWARDS A NEW DAWN

In the Coronation summer of 1953, the fresh sound of the Ken Colyer Jazzmen added to the feeling that the nation was beginning to emerge from the shadow of war. On 1 August, it was announced that they would be making an album for Decca Records. This was a breakthrough, as *Melody Maker* noted: 'An LP of New Orleans jazz by a British band would be something of a departure for the local record companies.'

Recorded in London on 2 September 1953, *New Orleans to London* was released six months later on 10" vinyl. There was no sign of the skiffle that had been electrifying audiences at Bryanston Street – all eight tracks were traditional New Orleans style. And in vindication of Ken Colyer's pilgrimage to the Crescent City, the record won rave reviews.

James Asman, writing in his weekly jazz column in *Record Mirror*, saw the band as nothing less than the saviour of British jazz. 'At a time when the early promise of such groups as George Webb's Dixielanders, the Yorkshire Jazz Band, the Saints, the Crane River Jazz Band and Humphrey Lyttelton's outfit with Keith Christie has not been fulfilled, along comes this swinging and startlingly authentic music.'

Thou preparest a table for me in the presence of mine enemies; thou anointest my head with oil, Colyer must have thought. *My cup runneth over.*

Asman was in no doubt about the significance of *New Orleans to London*: 'Let us not carp, gentlemen. This is the most exciting record ever issued by a British jazz band without exception.'

The lead track from the album, a reworking of the 1930s tune 'Isle of Capri', was released as a single and was picked up by the crustiest of BBC DJs, Jack Payne. The old trouper, who had been a bandleader between the wars, played the song every week on his show until it shaded into the Top Ten. The future seemed bright for the Ken Colyer Jazzmen.

Below decks, however, all was not well. Ken thought everyone was against him. His wife Delphine said as much in Mike Pointon and Ray Smith's oral history of his career, *Goin' Home*: 'I don't think he thought many people were on his side.' Early years spent in children's homes and the Merchant Navy had left Colyer with a contempt for authority, religion and anyone who had been privately educated. Before he went to New Orleans, he had already shown the extent of his uncompromising nature, walking away from bands that didn't live up to his expectations.

If anything, his time in the Crescent City only fuelled his determination to do things his way. All of Pointon and Smith's interviewees agreed that Ken was utterly dedicated to his music, even as they described him as taciturn, cussed, moody and diffident. On his return from the US, with so much expected of him, these unfortunate traits came to the fore.

Ken's real problem was that he struggled to make himself understood. The fact that he couldn't read music had never been a problem before. Everyone he'd played with in England had been making it up as they went along too. And anyway, none of his heroes could sight-read. But when you've set yourself up as the only guy in England who truly knows how to play original New Orleans jazz, that's simply not good enough. People are going to ask you technical questions, about what you are playing, about how they are playing, about the overall arrangement of tunes.

Chris Barber respected him and wanted to get the music exactly how Colyer thought it should be, so he took notes and asked questions, and when something was settled, he'd go around the other band members and alter their arrangements accordingly. He was trying to be helpful, but all Colyer saw was this highly trained musician – ex-private school, never worked a bleedin' day in his life – constantly putting him on the spot and forcing him to play these rigid arrangements.

The other problem Colyer had, one that seems to have been there from the very beginning, was Lonnie Donegan. Barber easily identified the cause of the friction: 'Lonnie is a dedicated cheeky chappie; his idol was Max Miller.' Colyer despised Donegan because he was a wind-up merchant, always ready with some smart-arse remark. It was a hatred compounded by his inability to come up with a swift riposte that would cut Donegan down to size.

Intimidated by Barber, wound up by Donegan and frustrated by his own inability to articulate his vision, Ken came to rely on his brother to speak for him. While Bill Colyer was very knowledgeable about jazz records, he wasn't really a musician. When it fell to him to critique the band's playing, tempers frayed.

The frustration wasn't all one way. As the band became popular, Ken's insistence on playing traditional New Orleans jazz left them unable to respond to an audience which wasn't only interested in that style. When they performed in dancehalls outside of London, dancers wanted to hear material that they were familiar with. For the more commercially minded Barber and Donegan, it made sense to accommodate public taste. People needed to be entertained. But Colyer was having none of it.

In May 1954, with the band riding high on the success of their debut album, things came to a head. Bill Colyer took Chris Barber for a quiet drink and told him that his brother had decided to fire the rhythm section. Bass player Jim Bray didn't swing; drummer Ron Bowden was too modern in his playing; Donegan had to go because Ken hated his guts. 'Well, that's not difficult,' Barber later reflected.

101

'Anyone who's ever dealt with Lonnie hates his guts, but that's no reason to fire him.'

Barber didn't take kindly to Ken unilaterally deciding to fire half the band. Yes, his name was on the posters, but that didn't mean he was in charge. The band was a co-operative. Barber consulted the other members and they voted for a different solution. They fired Ken Colyer and his brother Bill.

On 23 May 1954, *Melody Maker* reported the split under the headline 'Colyer Breaks Up: Barber to Lead': 'The cooperative band hitherto known as Ken Colyer's Jazzmen has severed connections with Ken and Bill Colyer by unanimous decision of its members.' Ken was quoted as saying: 'While the band has made great progress in the year that it's been going, I have been well aware of its shortcomings from the New Orleans jazz point of view. We have tried a variety of styles, playing ragtime, Ellington numbers and so on, and I think this has been a mistake.'

In his autobiography, *When Dreams Are in the Dust*, Ken Colyer was disdainful of the time he spent with the band, referring to it as a wasted year. In their own memoirs, his erstwhile bandmates didn't share that opinion. Lonnie Donegan, who could be forthright in his opinions, called Ken 'the best ever in Europe, even to this day. If you're talking about pure New Orleans jazz, I don't think he's ever been equalled.' Chris Barber was no less effusive. 'For that kind of music, Ken would still be the best today, were he alive. He had a perfect understanding of how to make a New Orleans band swing – while doing almost nothing. He was a marvellous musician who became a pain in the arse.'

The band's bass player, Jim Bray, caught something of the enigma of Ken Colyer when he observed that '[Ken] always had to have a lot of people he hated. It was necessary for him to hate people. And none of those people he hated did anything but admire and like him.'

In the wake of Colyer's departure, Pat Halcox, whose parents had refused to let him quit his job at Glaxo to join the band in early 1953, was invited to play trumpet. This time, he didn't bother to ask his mum and dad, and the newly christened Chris Barber Jazz Band made its debut on 31 May 1954 at the 100 Club.

———

Bill Colyer's first move on hearing that he and his brother had been sacked was to go to Decca Records and offer to make a follow-up to the reasonably successful *New Orleans to London*. Such was the power of Ken Colyer's name, Decca were only too happy to agree, even if the Jazzmen were now a completely different outfit.

On 25 June 1954, less than a month after the sacking, Colyer assembled the new line-up of his band at the Decca Studios in the London suburb of West Hampstead. Trombonist Ed O'Donnell and clarinet player Bernard 'Acker' Bilk joined him in the front line, while Diz Disley (banjo), Dick Smith (bass) and Stan Gregg (drums) made up the rhythm section. The studio was housed in a large late-Victorian building situated at 165 Broadhurst Gardens which had originally been built in 1884 as the Falcon Works, a space for local craftsmen to ply their trade. When the owners went bankrupt, the building was converted into West Hampstead Town Hall, which despite its civic title never housed local government. It was a venue that could be hired for social functions. In 1928, the building was bought by the Crystalate Recording Company and converted into a studio complex, and when the company was sold to Decca for $200,000 in 1937 it became their main recording studio.

The new Jazzmen had the same instrumental line-up as the original band, but were they as good? When the subsequent album, *Back to the Delta*, was released in late 1954, the sleeve notes reveal that this unspoken question cast a shadow over proceedings:

'From the start of this session, the music would not flow; the tension was too stringent. For the other five members of the band it was a case of "first night nerves"; for Ken it was more difficult. This record had to disprove the criticism which had been generally leveled at him for disbanding his first group. Many people accused him of wilfully breaking up the finest jazz band that Britain had produced and, furthermore, they said that he would never find five other men in this country who could play this music with any degree of success. Part of this criticism was justified for Ken did, after much thought, leave the first band [whoever wrote these sleeve notes is being economical with the truth: Colyer was fired]; he did so, however, for a very good reason. He wanted to get back to the original jazz, with a more buoyant beat, less arranged passages and a freer atmosphere: a regression in time but not in quality.'

The stakes were high. If Ken really was the true prophet of the original New Orleans style, then he should be able to work his wizardry with any bunch of competent players. If not, if he faltered, the

104

crown would pass to Chris Barber, and the dedication and sacrifice that Ken had put into his pilgrimage to the Mississippi Delta would have been squandered.

The sleeve notes state that the session was saved by the simple expedient of getting the band to sit down while they played. That, however, is being a little bit disingenuous. In truth, Colyer was so disappointed with the results that the session was scrapped, the band returning to the studio in September to attempt the songs again. It was at that subsequent session that someone suggested it might help if the band sat down to play.

The only material on the album that was actually recorded on 25 June were the three songs credited to Ken Colyer's Skiffle Group. This is borne out by the presence of double bass player Mickey Ashman, brought into the original session at short notice to deputise for Dick Smith, who was stricken with a burst appendix. Frustrated by the failure of his new band to swing in the studio, Colyer was worried that the whole thing had been a waste of time. Desperate to salvage something from the session, he decided to play a few of those skiffle songs that were going down so well with his teenage audience.

Calling in his old friend Alexis Korner to play guitar and mandolin, and with his brother on washboard, Ashman on double bass and Ken himself on guitar and vocals, they became the first skiffle band to be recorded for disc. 'Midnight Special' kicked the set off, followed by a version of 'Casey Jones' with spoken verses and a gentle take on 'KC Moan', which had originally been recorded by the Memphis Jug Band in 1929.*

———

* Bandleader Will Shade formed the Memphis Jug Band in 1926 from an ever-changing crew of African American musicians in and around Memphis. They made many recordings for the Victor label.

Ken Colyer's Skiffle Group, 1953: (*left to right*) Lonnie Donegan, guitar; Bill
Colyer, washboard; Ken Colyer, guitar; and Chris Barber, bass

The album that the original Colyer/Barber Jazzmen had made, *New
Orleans to London*, had appeared on Decca Records thanks to the
efforts of Hugh Mendl. Born in 1919, Mendl had been a friend of
Chris Barber's since they met collecting jazz records in 1949. An
Oxford graduate whose grandfather had been a chairman of Decca,
he began in the post room, worked as a radio plugger and by 1950 was
producing records for the likes of the Trinidadian pianist Winifred
Atwell – in 1954, she became the first black person to top the UK
charts with 'Let's Have Another Party', a medley of knees-up tunes.

When Mendl heard that Colyer had been fired, he was quick to offer
the Chris Barber Jazz Band an opportunity to make *New Orleans
Joys*. They had been playing six nights a week since Pat Halcox had
replaced Ken Colyer on trumpet and had developed a style of their
own. On Tuesday 13 July 1954, the band assembled at Broadhurst
Gardens, in the same Studio 2 where Colyer's skiffle band had been
recorded just a couple of weeks before.

106

The session was engineered by Arthur Lilley, who, like many of his profession at the time, wore a white coat and cotton gloves while going about his duties. The band would be recorded live onto a two-channel EMI quarter-inch tape recorder. As he positioned the mics around the band – Chris Barber on trombone, Monty Sunshine on clarinet, Pat Halcox on cornet, Lonnie Donegan on banjo, Jim Bray on double bass and Ron Bowden on drums – Lilley had no idea that, before the session was over, he would have made the most significant recording of his long career.

Much has been written about what transpired in Studio 2 on 13 July 1954. Lonnie Donegan made a living telling tall tales and his version of events has come to be both the best known and, at the same time, the most disputed account. In it, he's the little guy, trying to get his music heard in the face of resistance from the big bad record company man. In reality, the birth of skiffle in the UK – and Donegan's role in it – was more a series of cock-ups and coincidences than anything else. Given the facts, you can understand why Donegan wanted to make it more of a drama.

On the fiftieth anniversary of the session, I interviewed Hugh Mendl for an article that appeared in the *Guardian*. He was living in Devon at the time, having retired from the record business to run an antiques shop. He told me that he wasn't supposed to record trad jazz as it was deemed subversive by his superiors and didn't sell. 'There were rules about the sort of people who were allowed to make records and trad jazz was really contrary to that.'

Mendl chafed against the staid conventions that shaped public taste. 'Every song came out of Tin Pan Alley and had a chorus and a verse. You didn't open with the verse, you had to open with an intro and the chorus.' Hoping to break out of this straitjacket, he had been asking Decca to let him record some of the young turks he'd seen at the 100 Club whipping up a storm playing traditional New Orleans jazz to teenage audiences. They finally relented, on the understanding that the record would cost no more than £35 to make.

Just as Ken Colyer had felt the pressure weeks before, now Chris Barber's reputation was on the line, arguably more so because he'd retained most of the band that had made *New Orleans to London* such a success. Were they a great band, or was it the presence of Ken Colyer, the Guru of Trad, that had made them shine? It was a classic case of second album syndrome: you've made a great record and gained everyone's attention – now they all want to know if you can top it.

The key to success would be the material. Barber didn't want to just play New Orleans standards, he wanted to take the idea forward. He also had to choose songs that weren't regularly played by other trad bands. By early evening, they had recorded an eclectic collection of tracks: a King Oliver number called 'Chimes Blues', Jelly Roll Morton's 'New Orleans Blues', 'The Martinique', a tune by Wilbur de Paris, Duke Ellington's 'Stevedore Stomp' and a trad arrangement of 'Bobby Shaftoe', a folk song from the north-east of England.

'At this point, it became clear that the band didn't have enough material,' recalled Mendl. A 10" 33 rpm album required a minimum of four songs per side. When no new tunes were forthcoming, Mendl sent the band to the Railway Arms pub next door to come up with a solution. The tactic paid off – they returned and jammed a lively number they called 'Merrydown Rag' in honour of the cider that was popular with the students who frequented jazz clubs. One tune, however, wouldn't be enough to save the record. There was a terrible hiatus. 'No one knew what to suggest. There was a feeling that everybody should just pack up and go home, but there was too much money involved.'

Arthur Lilley was looking at his watch and one or two band members were eyeing the door when Donegan suggested they record some of their skiffle songs. Barber, faced with blowing his first chance to make a proper album, liked the suggestion. Sending the rest of the band home, he phoned blues singer Beryl Bryden, who lived round the corner in Maida Vale. Could she come down to the studio and bring her washboard?

While waiting for her to turn up, Donegan grabbed his guitar and Barber picked up Jim Bray's double bass to rehearse a couple of songs. When Mendl questioned his abilities on the bass, Barber assured him that he'd had a few lessons from a classical player and would be fine with the instrument. In truth, he'd been playing bass in the breakdown band for over three years.

When Bryden arrived, the trio recorded a version of 'Rock Island Line', with Donegan recounting the tale of the train driver who tricks the toll booth operator. Mendl remembered that there was some lengthy discussion about whether the long spoken introduction should be included. Eventually agreeing that it should stay, they nailed the song in two takes, going on to record 'John Henry' and 'Wabash Cannonball'. Donegan rounded things off with a version of 'Nobody's Child' accompanied by Barber on the bass – a much superior version to that recorded on the early Danish tour. The session saved, Hugh Mendl brought proceedings to an end just before 10 p.m.

As he locked the soundproof door of Studio 2, Arthur Lilley may have chuckled to himself about having to mic up a washboard. After all, he was responsible for the lush sound of the current number one single, 'Cara Mia' by David Whitfield. Recorded with the hugely popular Mantovani and His Orchestra in the spacious Studio 1 that sat at the centre of the recording complex, 'Cara Mia' stayed at number one for ten weeks.*

---

* That summer, Whitfield, a tenor from Hull, held off competition from Doris Day, Perry Como, Johnnie Ray, Al Martino, Billy Cotton and the Obernkirchen Children's Choir, earning himself the first gold disc for record sales ever awarded to a British male vocalist.

The trio that recorded 'Rock Island Line': (*left to right*) Chris Barber on bass, Beryl Bryden on washboard and Lonnie Donegan on guitar (1954)

In July 1954, pop music meant a well-turned-out male or female singer performing a big ballad backed by the massed strings of a light orchestra, and Arthur Lilley was a master at creating that sound. He could have no way of knowing it as he left Broadhurst Gardens that night, but he'd just played a small part in the creation of a movement that would sweep Whitfield and Mantovani out of the pop charts for ever.

———

Elsewhere, others too were stumbling towards a new dawn. Just a week or so earlier, on 5 July, in Memphis, Tennessee, record producer Sam Phillips had conducted an audition for a nineteen-year-old guitar-playing truck driver with a singing voice that was hard to pin down. Phillips called in a couple of young local musicians to back the kid up on electric guitar and double bass, and together they were trying to cut a version of Ernest Tubb's 1949 hit 'I Love You Because'. Half a dozen times they recorded the song, but the kid just couldn't seem to convey the words.

Exasperated, Phillips told the band to take a break. While the rhythm section sucked on a couple of Cokes, the kid picked up his acoustic guitar and began goofing around on a blues song recorded some eight years earlier by Arthur 'Big Boy' Crudup. Laughing at the incongruity of the moment, the bass player picked up his instrument and began playing in a similarly exaggerated style. The guitarist put down his Coke and joined in.

Hearing this spontaneous revelry, Phillips, who was busy in the control room, stuck his head round the door and said, 'What are you doing?'

The band replied, 'We don't know!'

'Well, back up,' said Phillips. 'Try to find a place to start and do it again.' In a couple of takes, Elvis Presley, Scotty Moore and Bill Black recorded 'That's All Right', and rock 'n' roll was born.

Lonnie Donegan and Elvis Presley had little in common, except a young man's love of roots music. Both had called on that love to salvage recording sessions that were going nowhere. Fronting guitar-led trios without the need of a drummer, both sang with a frenzied passion of the kind that never encroached on the genteel world of the BBC Light Programme. 'Rock Island Line' and 'That's All Right' were the first tremors of an earthquake that would shake the world. But on that hot summer night, David Whitfield and Mantovani could sleep soundly in their beds, for it would be another eighteen months before Donegan and Presley crashed into the UK charts.

8

THE NEW EDWARDIANS

On 15 March 1954, the *Daily Sketch* reported that a bunch of teenagers had tried to sneak into a cinema in south London without paying. This sort of behaviour was not unusual. Sunday afternoons in the 50s were dreadfully dull. The places where young people often gathered – cafes, shops and arcades – were closed. Cinemas offered the one source of entertainment still available, and if you could get your mate to open one of the exit doors to let you and your pals in for nothing, then what a lark!

What was so different about this particular group of bored kids that it merited their elevation into the pages of a national newspaper? Their choice of attire. 'A cinema used barbed wire yesterday to keep out a gang of youths in Edwardian clothes,' declared the introduction to the article. Mr Morley Clarke, manager of the Eros Cinema, told the *Sketch* reporter, 'Most of the cinemas around here are barring these Edwardian-suited hooligans.'

The garment that made these neo-Edwardians stand out from other run-of-the-mill teenagers was the drape, a formal jacket that extended down the body as far as the fingertips of a fully extended arm. At a time when men's jackets barely covered their trouser pockets, these extra few inches of fabric were seen as a brazen affront to civilised society.

The Edwardian look had been introduced by Savile Row tailors shortly after clothes rationing ended in March 1949. Pitched at young aristocratic men about town, the look was soon adopted by stylish officers from the Brigade of Guards. It featured a long jacket, narrow trousers and ordinary shoes, topped off with a fancy silk waistcoat. Shirts were white with cutaway collars and ties were fashioned with a Windsor knot.

These dashing young turks were known across fashionable London as the Guardees and the message they sought to convey by dressing in the Edwardian style was both sartorial and political. Sartorially, it harked back to what many remembered as a golden age. Modernism seemed to have arrived with a whizz-bang at the outbreak of the First World War, and what followed was a marked decline in the British way of doing things. For those who longed for the old order to be restored, references to the Edwardian period evoked both a sense of lost innocence and a whiff of the glory days of imperialism.

Politically, the long jacket and fancy waistcoat were a slap in the face of the austerity that the 1945 Labour government had imposed in order to get the country back on its feet following the damage done during the war. If you could cover your body with more cloth than anybody else, your attire could send a clear message to the rest of society. With their long drapes and fancy waistcoats, the Guardees were sticking two flamboyant fingers up at the authorities.

At the opposite end of the class system was a figure who also expressed disdain for government-imposed austerity by dressing to impress. The spiv emerged from the dog tracks and gambling dens of pre-war London to make a living on the black market. Once rationing was imposed at the outbreak of the Second World War, these 'wide boys' gained a reputation for being able to provide things that were scarce.

Appreciating the difficulty of supplying an island during wartime, most British people had grudgingly accepted the necessity of rationing. However, when the war ended in 1945 and controls were not eased, many understandably began to chafe against restrictions. It was in this environment that attitudes to black marketeers became somewhat ambiguous.

In the drab, war-weary Britain of the late 1940s, the spiv took on the air of a glamorous outlaw, attracting clients and lovers alike with his flashy attire. But as a petty criminal, he also had to intimidate his customers to ensure they didn't grass him up to the authorities. This archetypal tough-guy spiv provides the central character in the classic British film noir *Brighton Rock*. Pinkie Brown is a razor-wielding teenage thug, dressed to kill in a long, double-breasted pinstripe suit with padded shoulders, garish tie and trilby hat. Played by Richard Attenborough, Pinkie exuded a moody menace that made *Brighton Rock* Britain's most popular film of 1947.

Just a few years later, teenagers in the tough, working-class areas of south London were crossing the flamboyance of the Guardee with the menace of the spiv to come up with a style all their own. Some have assumed that this new mode of dress was imported from the US, but study of contemporary sources reveals their inspiration to be wholly indigenous.

Like the drape suits they wore, the crepe-soled shoes favoured by these new Edwardians were first produced in England by the Northamptonshire firm of George Cox in 1949 under the brand name 'Hamiltons'. Crepe is a crinkly lace-like rubber that offers greater grip on polished dancefloors than that provided by standard leather soles. This was ideal for the energetic jiving that was increasingly popular among teenagers in the early 50s. Although additions such as the black 'gambler's' tie were later imported from America, the original Edwardians took their cues from the streets of London.

As with all styles that come from the streets, the exact moment of its conception is hard to pinpoint, but newspaper cuttings suggest that the look was visible enough to gain national attention by late 1952. On 11 January 1953, in an article comparing contemporary fashions

WHY ALL THIS TALK OF CHANGE?

By PETER WRIGHT

IN grandfather's day, a young man was not in the running unless he could lay claim to being bold. Bold in his clothes and bold in the way he went about the business of living.

So far as clothes are concerned half a century doesn't seem to have changed the basic styles.

Item by item, there isn't much to distinguish between the sartorial ideas of 1903 and today. Consider the present fashions.

TOP COATS: Lightly made, of gaberdine material. Knee-length with four pockets (probably flap). Velvet collar butting on to short lapels. Full-length sleeves with ends folded over and buttoned. Colour probably black or maroon

♦ ♦ ♦

WAISTCOATS: Corduroy is a popular material. Four pockets and the normal arrangement of buttons. If corduroy, it will be self-coloured—black

SHIRTS: Gaberdine shirts with attached collars opening wide allow for a tie with a large Windsor knot.

♦ ♦ ♦

TIES: Hand-knitted type, silk, with a bold vertical design

♦ ♦ ♦

SHOES: Here, perhaps, the resemblance to anything Edwardian is not so noticeable! But the thick crepe-soled shoes with a plain or semi-brogue front suit the general style.

Progress. Or is it? Left, the early 1900's and, right, the not so different 1950's.

The *Sunday Pictorial* compares the old Edwardians with the new, 11 January 1953

with those from fifty years before, the *Sunday Pictorial* newspaper printed an illustration of a neo-Edwardian youth with an accompanying description of his outlandish costume: hair piled in a quiff, long sideburns, a drape jacket with a velvet collar, a silk waistcoat, drainpipe trousers and crepe-soled shoes. Clearly, all of the classic elements of Teddy Boy style had already entered the public consciousness over a year before the press first adopted the term and a full two years before the arrival of rock 'n' roll in Britain.

The Teddy Boy began his journey from fashion curiosity to folk devil in September 1953, when the national press made a connection between the clothes worn by a group of youths from Clapham in south London and the violence they visited on four young men who were more conventionally dressed. In a case that became known as the Clapham Common Murder, seventeen-year-old John Beckley, one of the four, was stabbed to death in a brutal gang attack. The initial suspect in the murder inquiry was fifteen years old.

Casual violence between groups of young men has always been the dark side of male adolescence and post-war Britain had its fair share of hooligans. Hitherto the press had labelled them spivs, 'cosh boys' or 'creepers'. The Clapham Common Murder offered the tabloid papers another dimension with which to sensationalise their reports and they grabbed it with both hands.

'Flick knives, dance music and Edwardian suits', screamed the front page of the *Daily Mirror* when the case came to court. Over the next few months, reports of Edwardian-suited youths involved in acts of vandalism and violence began to appear regularly in the press. But the new moniker was a real mouthful and not nearly as headline-friendly as 'cosh boy'.

If the lurid story of the Clapham Common Murder had identified this new menace to society, it was the report of the kids bunking into the cinema in Catford that named them for the public. Pushed for space, the *Daily Sketch* headline writer condensed the phrase 'Edwardian-suited youths' down to the bite-size 'Teddy-suited gang'. Soon the term 'Teddy Boy' began appearing in tabloid reports. The first teenage subculture in post-war Britain had arrived.

The Teds would go on to become synonymous in most people's minds with the rock 'n' roll era, yet here they were, fully formed, before Bill Haley and his Comets had been heard in the UK. Ken Mackintosh was leader of a big band from Halifax, whose single 'The Creep' hit the UK charts in January 1954. There is nothing creepy about the sound of this saxophone-led instrumental, reminiscent of the theme tune to an American detective series, but it struck a chord with the Teddy Boys, who danced a slow smooch to it with their girl-friends. It may have been the popularity of 'The Creep' that gave the Teds' crepe-soled shoes their nickname of 'creepers'.

Big bands like that led by Ken Mackintosh provided the popular music of the day. When a song was a hit, every dancehall band would buy the sheet music and include it in their set. The average big band could play a number of different musical styles, but their aim was to get people dancing. In the Britain of the early 50s, that dancing was strictly ballroom.

A photograph taken from a balcony of the Tower Ballroom, Blackpool, in 1954 shows perhaps a thousand couples on the dance-floor. On the bandstand, clearly visible, is a sign that reads 'No Bop. No Jive.' The choreography of ballroom dancing is circular; while the couples dance with one another, they also move around the floor in one great rotational sweep, like stars in a spiral galaxy. Jiving, how-ever, requires the dancers to remain more or less in one place, and so it was seen as a disruptive force, not to be tolerated. Its athletic moves were viewed as physically dangerous and, for many Britons, it was associated with black American culture, making it even more troublesome.

Fortunately, British kids didn't want to copy the formal dances of their parents' generation. They wanted something more exciting.

It wasn't only bop and jive that were banned from Britain's ball-rooms. Within weeks of the Teddy Boy being identified as a trouble-maker, signs began going up in dancehalls and ballrooms across the country: 'Youths wearing Edwardian dress will not be admitted'; 'No Edwardian clothes, crepe or rubber-soled footwear please'.

Excluded from the adult world, teenagers sought out those places where they could hear up-tempo music, places where nobody would scold them if they wanted to jive. In the pre-rock 'n' roll 50s, the hot-test music in Britain was being played in the trad jazz clubs. These often took place in the function room of a public house, where wedding receptions and birthday parties were held. Because these rooms could be rented out for family occasions, licensing laws made provision for

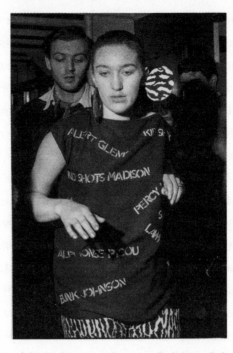

A trad jazz fan in home-made attire: Delphine Colyer, 1954

unaccompanied sixteen-year-olds to attend such events. As jazz clubs were viewed as private functions, teenagers could legally attend, unlike in the US, where stricter liquor laws restricted access for those under the age of twenty-one.

In March 1954, two young, aspiring film-makers approached the British Film Institute with an idea for a documentary about the teenage trad jazz scene. Karel Reisz was a programmer at the National Film Theatre and Tony Richardson worked as a television director at the BBC. Though neither had made a film before, they were bored by the conservatism of mainstream British cinema and the patronising way that it portrayed working-class life, believing they could do better.

Momma Don't Allow, the short documentary they made, was shot on 16 mm film in the winter of 1954–5 in the upstairs room of the Fishmonger's Arms in Wood Green, where Lonnie Donegan had performed his first solo gigs three years before. Reisz and Richardson set out to challenge negative views of working-class youth, a point they made explicit in interviews: 'We did not need to take up the conventional class attitudes of British film-making, we felt free not to disapprove of the teddy boys, not to patronise shop-girls, not to make sensational or hysterical a subject which is neither (but is almost always shown so).'

The twenty-two-minute film has no dialogue, relying for a soundtrack on live performances by the Chris Barber Jazz Band that had recorded *New Orleans Joys* earlier that year – Barber on trombone, Monty Sunshine on clarinet, Pat Halcox on cornet, Lonnie Donegan on banjo, Jim Bray on double bass and Ron Bowden on drums – with vocals from Ottilie Patterson, who had joined the group in December 1954.

The film opens with the band sound-checking at the pub. As Donegan picks out a tune on the banjo, the scene is intercut with images of teenagers at work. A young woman cleans an empty British Rail dining car; a young man cuts a leg of beef at a butcher's shop; another young woman assists a dentist at his surgery, while her boyfriend waits outside for her to finish work. We cut back to them as each returns home to get ready for a night out at the Wood Green Jazz Club.

The scene shifts to the club and as the tempo of the music quickens, teenagers take to the dancefloor to jive. Girls dance with one another, while lads sporting greased-back hair and velvet-collared drape jackets watch eagerly from the sidelines.

Outside, some upper-class teenagers arrive in a 1930s Rolls-Royce Phantom. The young women are wearing furs and carrying small dogs. One of the young men removes the RR marque from the bonnet of his car before entering the club, for fear of it being stolen in this rough neighbourhood. Once inside, the toffs stand awkwardly about before attempting some half-hearted jiving, but it's obvious they're not taking it as seriously as the cool working-class kids spinning on the dancefloor.

Unable to make either an impression or a connection of any kind, the young toffs leave just as the Barber band kick into a rousing version of 'Mama Don't Allow'. As if sensing some kind of victory over their upper-class contemporaries, the kids at the jazz club go into a frenzy of celebratory jiving.

Reisz and Richardson initially struggled to get their film screened, until they joined forces with two other young independent film-makers, Lindsay Anderson and Lorenza Mazzetti, whose work had also been focusing on the lives of ordinary working people. In February 1956, they staged a joint screening at the National Film Theatre under the title 'Free Cinema' – a reference to the fact that each of the films had been made free from the pressures of the box office. Inspired by the new wave film movements that had revitalised post-war European cinema, they came up with their own manifesto:

> As film makers, we believe that:
> No film can be too personal.
> The image speaks. Sound amplifies and comments.
> Size is irrelevant. Perfection is not an aim.
> An attitude means a style. A style means an attitude.

Those last two sentences could have featured in the Teddy Boy manifesto, had such a thing ever been written.

————

In May 1954, a four-page feature claiming to tell 'The Truth About Teddy Boys and Teddy Girls' appeared in the popular weekly magazine *Picture Post*. Amid pictures of the new Queen Elizabeth and her children, adverts for Brylcreem – 'it grooms by surface tension' – and a competition for people whose name was Smith, staff writer Hilde Marchant reported from the front line of this new troubling youth cult, the Mecca Dance Hall in Tottenham, north London.

Picture Post appears to take a certain pride in the fact that these juvenile delinquents are a product of native genius – 'the dance is contemporary jive, but the suit is an adaptation of the Edwardian "masher's" outfit. It is also English in conception and, unlike recent men's fashions, owes nothing to Hollywood.' And while Marchant reports with some credulity that the Teds prefer mineral water to beer, there is very little sensationalising in the feature. What does stand out is the fact that these teenagers claim to be earning between £5 and £12 a week. These figures will have raised eyebrows at a time when average adult earnings were around £550 per annum.

By the mid-1950s, a post-war consumer boom was under way. This called for cheap, mass-produced goods that required lighter forms of industry and a less skilled workforce. Most kids left school at fifteen with few qualifications and had little difficulty finding employment, and, as they were almost all living at home with their parents, they often had money to spend once they'd given their mother the weekly housekeeping.

In the late 50s, the London Press Exchange, Britain's largest advertising agency, commissioned a study of the spending power of young people. *The Teenage Consumer* offers a snapshot of life at a time when young people were beginning to emerge as a distinct social group. Although not an academic study, it represents the first attempt by mainstream culture to take seriously the newly identified phenomenon of the British teenager.

The report begins by stating that, in 1958, there were 5 million unmarried teenagers in the UK, who together earned £1.48 billion per annum. Compared to 1938, the real value of teenagers' earnings had increased by 50 per cent – double the rate of growth for adult wages. Using these figures, the study estimated that, after their expenses were taken into account, teenagers had roughly £17 million every week to spend at their own discretion. Unsurprisingly, it was found that much of this went on clothes, drinks, sweets and records.

For teenagers in the mid-50s, the sudden abundance of consumer goods and their ability to afford them was a stark contrast to the austere childhoods that most had endured. Rationing began in January 1940, but the first years of peace brought restrictions that, in some cases, were even more severe than those imposed during wartime. Clothing, fuel and furniture were still restricted and, in July 1946, for the first time, bread was added to the list of foodstuffs that required coupons.

For children growing up in Britain during these years, treats were hard to come by. Sweets and chocolate were rationed from 1940 and

Lonnie Donegan gets the kids jiving, 1954

the manufacture of ice cream was banned in 1943. When restrictions on sweets were lifted in April 1949, demand was such that they had to be swiftly reimposed. Sugar remained rationed until as late as September 1953, and it was only when butter, margarine and cooking fat became freely available in May 1954 that fancy cakes made a welcome reappearance in bakery windows across the country. Rationing finally came to an end on 5 July 1954, a week before Lonnie Donegan recorded 'Rock Island Line'.

Although rationing had ended, the war still cast a shadow over the lives of teenagers in the late 50s. National service continued until 1960, and waiting for the call-up could be a frustrating business. Leaving school at fifteen and earning decent money, but faced with the prospect of conscription, many a lad went looking for his kicks now, before being dragged off to face two years of military discipline. One teenager told *Picture Post* in April 1957 that he felt he might as well have a good time 'before I get called up, blown up or married'.

National service was an overwhelmingly working-class experience. Middle-class boys avoided the call-up by remaining in education much longer than their working-class contemporaries. This fact, along with the tendency of middle-class career structures to deliver higher wages later in life, meant that middle-class kids were by and large excluded from teenage consumer culture in the mid-1950s.

Bill Osgerby, in his 1998 study *Youth in Britain Since 1945*, cited a passage from the memoirs of an ex-public schoolboy from Dorset, who said of his school days in the 50s: 'teenagers, viewed from the shelter of this middle-class enclave, were a working-class phenomenon . . . Boys like me tried to dress (tweed jackets and flannel trousers) and talk like men . . . There was no space between being a boy and becoming a man for any distinctive style or assertion of identity.'

The Teddy Boys were post-war Britain's first visible expression of a sensibility that was neither child nor adult; while waiting to be forced into the uniform of their country, they adopted a different uniform, one that declared they were not like their parents. By the simple act of wearing stylish clothes, the Teds were able to challenge the authority of the generation that had won the war.

THE HIGHBROW OF SWING

Denis Preston is probably the most influential figure in British pop music that you've never heard of. He's the reason why much of the best British jazz in the 1950s was recorded; he is credited with being the key figure in the development of black music in the UK; he was a pioneer of what we now call 'world music'; he produced the first skiffle records; he encouraged his engineers to experiment with sound. Although his name features in so many remarkable stories from the first decades of British pop, his significance can only really be discerned by reading the credits on obscure records from sixty years ago and joining the dots. Record producer, label boss and pioneer studio owner, he also worked as a music journalist and radio broadcaster. In 1962, the *Sunday Times* noted that he mixed 'considerable technical expertise with business flair and a flamboyant personality'.

Preston's real talent was a wilful determination to push popular taste towards experimentation and diversity. On the stuffy airwaves of the BBC in the 1940s, he played the hipster, championing the best modern music made by African Americans. When he was producing calypso records, he consciously booked musicians from differing West Indian communities, throwing artists from Trinidad, Jamaica and Guyana together, encouraging them to inspire one another. When trad became the hip sound in the early 50s, he sought to push British jazzers out of their comfort zone by putting them in the studio with West Indian musicians. He set up his own jazz label and proceeded to release records by modernists, traditionalists and mainstream players, forming a loose ensemble that played in different styles. With his eclectic tastes, broadcasting acumen and enthusiasm for the new, Denis Preston is the John Peel figure of pre-Beatles British pop, an independent spirit constantly at odds with the musical mainstream.

Born in London in 1916, a cousin of Marxist historian Eric Hobsbawm, Preston was a jazz critic who had been broadcasting on the BBC since 1940. His efforts to elevate artists like Duke Ellington to the heights of intellectual sophistication earned him the nickname 'the Highbrow of Swing'. Initially styling himself St Denis Preston, he affected a bohemian style that was at odds with the clipped tones expected of BBC presenters, leading the *Daily Mail* to condemn his *Radio Rhythm Club* broadcasts as 'un-British'. Just a few weeks after the defeat of Nazism, on 22 July 1945, he staged a concert that featured Freddie Grant and his West Indian Calypsonians, the first hint of the key role the broadcaster would play in the development of calypso in post-war Britain.

On 21 June 1948, the *Empire Windrush* docked at Tilbury in Essex, an event now recognised as the starting point of the mass migration of West Indians from the Caribbean to the UK. On board were two of Trinidad's finest exponents of the calypso style, Lord Beginner and Lord Kitchener. The latter was famously filmed on the deck of the *Windrush*, singing his newly composed song 'London Is the Place for Me'. When this newsreel was shown in cinemas around Britain, calypso was presented to the native population as the identifying culture of the new West Indian arrivals. Preston, a committed anti-racist who penned editorials for *Jazz Music* magazine condemning the treatment of African Americans in the US and campaigned for *The Story of Little Black Sambo* to be removed from schools, saw an opportunity to break down barriers using music. He convinced EMI to let him record Beginner and Kitchener at the company's London studios in Abbey Road on 30 January 1950, a session that resulted in four 78 rpm singles for the Parlophone label. Preston took the credit of 'recording supervisor', a role we would now describe as freelance producer.

In the summer of 1950, the West Indian cricket team defeated England for the first time and then went on to win the Test series 3–1. The final match at the Oval, close to where many Caribbean immigrants had set up home in south London, became a celebration of West Indian culture. Calypso, which had developed in Trinidad as a means by which the people could verbally challenge the ruling class, rose to the occasion. Lord Beginner quickly composed 'Victory Test Match Calypso' (aka 'Cricket, Lovely Cricket'), recording it with the Calypso Rhythm Kings, supervised by Preston, for Melodisc, the largest independent record label operating in the UK.

Russ Henderson, a jazz pianist and steel pan player who came to London from Trinidad in 1951, saw how these records helped integrate the West Indian community. 'What we were doing at Melodisc helped English people to get to know us more, because they didn't have a clue about calypso. It introduced Caribbean culture to the English.' Henderson went on to talk of the Melodisc label as a big melting pot,

Denis Preston

alluding to the records that Denis Preston recorded with Ambrose Campbell and his West African Rhythm Brothers, who mixed the highlife and palm wine styles of Africa with calypso and jazz.

Preston furthered his goal of breaking down racial barriers in 1952, when he supervised a session that twinned Humphrey Lyttelton's musicians with a West Indian rhythm section led by Guyanese-born Freddy Grant. The record appeared on Parlophone, credited to the Grant-Lyttelton Paseo Band, and Preston put together a touring band to promote it featuring Trinidadian vocalist Young Tiger, Jamaican Tony Johnson and veteran Guyanese singer Bill Rogers, whose popular hit 'Weed Woman' he later recut for Parlophone.

When the two owners of Melodisc Records, Emil Shalit and Jack Chilkes, parted company in late 1952, Preston followed Chilkes to the Lyragon label, where he supervised a recording of the risqué calypso 'Don't Touch Me Tomato' by the American singer and dancer Marie Bryant. Lyragon, set up specifically to release material aimed at the West Indian market, was an offshoot of Polygon Records, a British independent founded in 1949 by Alan A. Freeman and Leslie Clark. The main aim of the label was to facilitate the recording career of Clark's daughter Petula, who had been a child star during the 1940s.

Throughout this period, Denis Preston had continued to broadcast on BBC radio, presenting programmes about the many facets of jazz. After *Radio Rhythm Club* ended in 1947, Preston hosted *Radio Blackbirds*, 'a half hour of record entertainment by coloured artists', as the *Radio Times* explained. In October 1952, he was engaged as editor and occasional presenter of *World of Jazz*, a regular Saturday-evening programme on the Light Service. It was in this capacity that he broadcast a programme based on Ken Colyer's letters from New Orleans in early 1953.

While working as a freelance producer on his calypso recordings, Preston had realised that, if he funded the sessions himself and then

Denis Preston with Mike McKenzie and Marie Bryant, *c.*1952

licensed the resulting material to whichever label was willing to release the songs, he could avoid the stodgy playing of the middle-aged, middlebrow musicians that the major labels employed on almost every session, whatever the style. On 14 December 1954, Preston set up Record Supervision Ltd and, in doing so, became the first independent record producer in Europe.

A big part of this decision was his frustration with the attitudes of the major labels. Preston was very impressed with the Chris Barber Jazz Band and couldn't understand why Decca hadn't signed them to a long-term contract after the recording of *New Orleans Joys*. He had good contacts at Decca, having worked for the label as their New York representative in the late 1940s. However, when the label showed no interest in his ideas for Barber, Preston approached Columbia Records, who released a series of 78s by the band for export only.

One of these was 'On a Christmas Day', a song that Lead Belly had recorded for Moe Asch in 1941. The Barber band version begins with

Lonnie Donegan singing and strumming a mid-tempo banjo, but soon the band take over, turning the song into a trad jazz romp. The 10" 78 released in December 1954 was backed with the popular gospel song 'Take My Hand, Precious Lord', which again began with Donegan singing at slow march pace, eventually overtaken by Barber and the boys blowing up a storm. In hindsight, it's possible to hear Donegan's skiffle sound trying to escape the trad scene, only to be overwhelmed by the enthusiastic playing of his bandmates. The record failed to capitalise on the festive spirit, but it remains significant as the first recording credited to Lonnie Donegan.

This wasn't the first time the public at large had the opportunity to hear Donegan's distinctive voice. In cinemas across the country, he could be heard singing the title song from *The Passing Stranger*, a British-made film noir which went on general release in November 1954. Starring glamour girl Diane Cilento, the plot of this forgotten B movie concerns a GI deserter, played with smouldering menace by Lee Patterson, who, having stolen guns from his barracks, goes on the run with Cilento, a waitress from a transport cafe.

The soundtrack was composed and largely performed by Ken Sykora, a popular jazz guitarist who would later find fame as the host of *Guitar Club*, teaching 'Spanish to skiffle' on the BBC Light Programme from 1957 onwards. The movie's title song is an adaptation of an old ballad, long popular in the Appalachian Mountains of the United States. Recorded by Clarence Ashley in 1929 as 'Dark Holler' and by the Carter Family in 1934 as 'East Virginia Blues No. 1', a version by Buell Kazee was included by Harry Smith in his 1952 collection, the *Anthology of American Folk Music*.

Whether Donegan had heard this record is moot, but his impression of the high lonesome singing style that typifies the versions recorded by white ballad singers from the Appalachian region is decent enough. Not that anyone was particularly impressed by his performance

– 'The Passing Stranger' wasn't issued on record until 1956, when it was oddly coupled with the theme tune to another British film noir, performed by Canadian harmonica virtuoso Tommy Reilly, entitled 'The Intimate Stranger'. If Oriole Records were hoping to cash in on Donegan's sudden fame, they were wasting their time – mournful and jazz-tinged, 'The Passing Stranger' had nothing in common with the frantic energy of his skiffle hits.

In January 1955, six months after it had been recorded, Decca finally decided to release *New Orleans Joys*, the debut album by the Chris Barber Jazz Band. The sleeve featured a scary clown acting as a puppeteer to a bunch of silhouetted jazz musicians. Two of the tracks, 'Rock Island Line' and 'John Henry', were credited to the Lonnie Donegan Skiffle Group, which was a little unfair, because this was really the skiffle group in Chris Barber's Jazz Band. Still, Lonnie was the featured vocalist and so, as often happened in those days, he got the credit. The sleeve notes played up the skiffle band, claiming that their version of 'Rock Island Line' was 'one of the finest skiffle numbers ever recorded in this country'. Given that the only other skiffle

numbers to have been recorded in Britain at this point were the three tracks that featured on Ken Colyer's *Back to the Delta* album, this wasn't really saying much.

While the reviews were broadly positive, there were one or two raised eyebrows about the appropriation of the term 'skiffle' to describe guitar-led music of the kind played by artists such as Lead Belly. Humphrey Lyttelton, reviewing both the Colyer and Barber LPs in the same *NME* column, argued that technically it should only be used to describe the instrumental piano music made by the likes of Dan Burley. 'Isn't it time to call a halt to this sloppy use of the term "skiffle" before it changes its meaning altogether? Country folk songs and urban rent-party music are not the same thing.' Humph complained in vain; that horse had already bolted.

The arrival of Ottilie Patterson had also brought a new dimension to the Barber band. Ottilie was a young trainee teacher from County Down in Northern Ireland who had come to London hoping to sing some jazz. Though she looked demure, Patterson had a voice reminiscent of Bessie Smith, rich and soulful, ideally suited to singing the blues and gospel songs that Barber was introducing into the band's repertoire. With the twenty-four-year-old from Newtownards singing a bluesy counterpart to Donegan's reedy treble, Chris Barber now had two powerful voices fronting his band.

This adventurous approach, mixing blues, gospel and skiffle in with traditional jazz, drew enthusiastic audiences across the country. The band were playing over three hundred gigs a year, from smoky clubs to large seated concert halls. Their popularity was such that *New Orleans Joys* would go on to sell over sixty thousand copies in its first year of release. Yet Decca weren't interested in the band, putting their weight behind Ken Colyer and his purist New Orleans approach.

Decca's Director of Artist Development, Hugh Mendl, thought it was a huge mistake to let Chris Barber walk out the door. When he approached his boss, Edward Lewis, on the matter, the response was dismissive. 'Give the boy a radiogram,' he was told. Rather than offer Barber a properly funded recording contract, Lewis expected him to be awed by a freebie from Decca's extensive range of domestic gramophones. 'I think he already has one,' replied an exasperated Mendl, knowing that Barber had one of the most extensive record collections in the country and that Edward Lewis couldn't care less.

Denis Preston's enthusiasm was about to come to Chris Barber's aid. Having set up his independent record production company, Preston had struck a deal with Polygon Records, convincing them to give him his own sub-label, Jazz Today. Employing talented graphic designer Ian Bradbery, who was responsible for the best-looking jazz magazine of the period, *Jazz Music*, Preston set about creating a house style that still looks cool today. Photographer Walter Hanlon took moody portraits of jazz musicians in action, all light and shade and with great depth of field. These were put to good use by Bradbery, who let the photos bleed to the edge of the sleeves, their freshness and verve making the designs that Decca produced for the Barber and Colyer albums look quaint by comparison.

After years of working without credit as a freelance producer, Preston made damn sure that his name was on the sleeve, a privilege he extended to everyone involved in making the record: on his recordings, listeners would know the names of the backroom boys who engineered the tracks, as well as who created the artwork.

Ensuring everyone got a credit was crucial to Jazz Today, as the majority of their releases were recorded by an ever-changing line-up of talented soloists whom Preston brought together under the title the Jazz Today Unit. Featuring some of the best mainstream performers and modernists in British jazz, the ensemble had room for old-school players like Jimmy Skidmore, as well as Jamaican-born Joe Harriott, whose alto sax was bebop cool.

After Ottilie Patterson's show-stopping major-venue debut fronting the Chris Barber Jazz Band at the Royal Festival Hall in January
1955, Preston was anxious to let the record-buying public hear her
amazing voice. Thus the Barber band's first release on Jazz Today
was a showcase for their new singer. Recorded in March 1955, *That
Patterson Girl* was a 7" 45 rpm EP that included versions of Bessie
Smith's 'Poor Man's Blues' and the Richard M. Jones standard
'Trouble in Mind'.

The Barber band had been the first to record for the new label,
at a session on 13 January 1955, but bass player Jim Bray's ancient
station wagon had broken down in west London on the day, leaving
everyone twiddling their thumbs in the studio. Undeterred, Barber
picked up the double bass, as he had done on the Decca session six
months before, and led the band through a couple of improvised numbers. The results were issued by Jazz Today in August 1955, on an EP
entitled *Chris Barber +1–1* (the +1 being cornettist Ben Cohen, who
joined the band for a couple of tracks, the -1 being the missing Jim
Bray).

Released in the summer of 1955, *Chris Barber Plays the Music of
Clarence and Spencer Williams* was an album of New Orleans standards composed by the aforementioned (but unrelated) Clarence and
Spencer Williams. Derek Stewart-Baxter, writing in the trad-friendly
Jazz Journal, thought it the best record that the Chris Barber Jazz
Band had yet made. *Jazz Monthly*, declaring itself to be 'the magazine
of intelligent jazz appreciation', was rather more sniffy: 'The typog-
raphy and design of the sleeve is really first class and it's a pity the
music is not of the same standard.'

Whereas on the first Barber album Lonnie Donegan had taken
the vocal chores, now Ottilie Patterson was the featured vocalist and
there was no room for any skiffle. This wasn't because the band had
given up the style – far from it. They had expanded the skiffle group

to include guitarist and backing singer Dickie 'Cisco' Bishop, a goateed and bespectacled devotee of Woody Guthrie and Hank Williams.

Bishop was a good friend of Barber's trumpet player, Pat Halcox. The two had first performed together as members of the Brent Valley Stompers. An eighteen-year-old Bishop had been invited to take photographs of the band; Halcox went round to his house to collect them and, noticing a guitar in the corner, invited Bishop to join the band – on banjo. When the nervous Bishop complained that he didn't know any chords on the banjo, Halcox told him not to worry, the band didn't have a gig for two weeks.

From then on, Dickie Bishop and Pat Halcox were inseparable. If one was offered a gig, he'd only accept if the other could join the band too. Once Halcox hooked up with the Chris Barber Jazz Band, it was only a matter of time before Bishop joined him. There was no place for an acoustic guitar in the jazz band, so Bishop joined Donegan in the skiffle group, waiting patiently by the side of the stage until the brass players took their break. It was Monty Sunshine who gave him his nickname, observing that, when the two sang together in the skiffle group, Bishop was Cisco Houston to Donegan's Woody Guthrie.

Denis Preston was the first to realise that skiffle might have a life of its own beyond the confines of the trad jazz movement. On 19 May 1955, he assembled the four members of the Chris Barber band who played in the skiffle group – Donegan and Bishop on guitar and vocals, Bray on double bass and Barber himself on harmonica – in the IBC Recording Studios at 35 Portland Place in London. With additional vocals from his friend Bob Watson and mandolin from Pete Korrison, Preston created the first-ever stand-alone skiffle record.

Credited to the Lonnie Donegan Skiffle Group, the *Backstairs Session* EP was released on the Jazz Today label in October 1955. The 7" 45 rpm disc came in a black-and-white sleeve featuring a moody portrait by Walter Hanlon. Lit low and from behind, strumming his

guitar almost in silhouette against a wall from which the paint is peeling and torn, Lonnie Donegan would never look so cool again.

And here, at the very beginning, was a selection of material that would set the template for the skiffle boom: a Lead Belly favourite, a folk blues borrowed from Big Bill Broonzy, a song originally collected from a prison work gang by John Lomax, and a tune popularised by Woody Guthrie. What more did the average skiffler need?

The opening track, 'Midnight Special', which had been picked up by Lead Belly when he was serving time for murder in Sugarland, was by now a standard among the handful of bands playing skiffle sessions in the jazz clubs and had already been recorded by Ken Colyer. The sleeve notes state that the second track on the EP had been learned by the band from Big Bill Broonzy when they were backing him on a recent UK tour. 'When the Sun Goes Down', written by pianist Leroy Carr, features harmonica by Chris Barber.

'New Buryin' Ground', the third track, probably began its life as a spiritual, so widely was it distributed across the American south. The lyrics that Donegan sings were taken from a version sung by William Williams and his fellow inmates, recorded by John Lomax in 1936 at the Virginia State Penitentiary. This recording first appeared on the Library of Congress album *Folk Music of the United States Album III: Afro-American Spirituals, Work Songs and Ballads*, edited by Alan Lomax and released in 1942, which is where Donegan is likely to have first heard it.

The final track is the folk song 'Worried Man Blues', which first came to prominence in the repertoire of the Carter Family. However, the version being referenced here is the one recorded by Woody Guthrie and Cisco Houston in New York for Moe Asch's Folkways label just before the two friends shipped out to join the D-Day invasion fleet in 1944. Dickie Bishop takes the lead vocal on this track, with Donegan providing vocal encouragement.

Sam Phillips, boss of Sun Records in Memphis, Tennessee, once mused that if he could find a white boy who sang like a black man, he'd make a million dollars. When he recorded Elvis Presley singing 'That's All Right', he knew he'd caught lightning in a bottle. Denis Preston's reaction to hearing Lonnie Donegan sing 'Midnight Special' is not recorded, but, knowing that there was only a niche market for this kind of trad-based skiffle, he'd probably have been happy just to make his money back.

10

WILL TV KILL THE BRITISH SUNDAY?

Before the term became synonymous with being interested in mathematics, a geek was someone who entertained fairground crowds by committing transgressive acts. Often found as the opener for a live freak show, the geek, a seemingly ordinary, unprepossessing individual, would, for example, chase chickens around a pen before capturing one and biting its head off. The act was often faked, but the notion of the freak who was made rather than born struck a chord with the crowd. There was something enticing about this pathetic figure whose actions were both repulsive and attractive at the same time.

Johnnie Ray was the first geek idol. Whereas 50s crooners tended to be smooth and sophisticated like Frank Sinatra, macho like Frankie Laine or wholesome like Perry Como, Ray had none of these charms. Born in Oregon in 1927, he was a shy, skinny kid prone to tearful breakdowns. A childhood accident cost him half his hearing, forcing him to wear a hearing aid, its thin wire clearly visible as he performed. He wrote his two biggest songs himself – 'Cry' (which he pronounced 'Ker-eye') and 'The Little White Cloud that Cried' – and, most nights, when performing these numbers, he would burst into tears.

In the strait-laced 1950s, such behaviour by a grown man would normally have been frowned upon, but Johnnie Ray's female audience took his emotional collapse as the cue for their own loss of control, screaming, weeping and wailing, reaching out to touch his extended arms. As the hysteria reached its peak, he sang on, his face fixed in a pained expression that suggested he was appalled by his own transgressive behaviour. Johnnie Ray was damaged and his fans loved him for it.

In film, too, the macho swagger of the Hollywood hero had been challenged by sensitive young men like Montgomery Clift. Introspective, asexual and with an acting style that gave the impression his mind was elsewhere, Clift brought a different tone to leading-man roles. James Dean was another star who traded on his vulnerability, reflecting on the insecurities of a generation of teenagers whose parents expected them to be happy in the comfortable conformity that followed the turmoil and tumult of their own adolescence in the 1930s and 40s.

Johnnie Ray embodied this ambivalent attitude to material success. While glossy magazines offered the fans photo spreads of their idols enjoying their stardom, Ray stood in the spotlight and told his audience he was unhappy. Artists had hinted at the sorrow behind the smile before, but no one had ever made it their entire shtick. While there were plenty of idols to worship, they were all marketed as commanding, larger-than-life characters, intimidating to an insecure teenage girl. Johnnie Ray was an altogether different prospect, a complete reversal of what had gone before. Here was a star whose histrionic performances made him appear weak, giving his overwhelmingly female followers the impression that, if only they had the chance, they could help him to be happy. His melodramatic performances unleashed a tsunami of mothering instinct.

When he first came to Britain in 1953, he appeared to be a gawky figure with a mediocre voice, but his act was like nothing that British audiences had seen before. Clenching his fists as he sang, hunching down into himself, clutching his body, falling to his knees, at one point reportedly beating his head against the piano, it was a performance worthy of a fairground geek, all inhibition lost in a desperate attempt to be the centre of attention.

In the right little, tight little world of post-war Britain, where emotions seemed to be on ration along with sweets, nylons and anything else that might be exciting, teenage girls finally had an excuse to release their inhibitions. Wherever he appeared, they tried to grab him, to kiss him, to tear away his clothes. This was a new phenomenon in British culture. When he returned in 1955, his run at the London Palladium beat the box office record set by Danny Kaye. Wherever he went, thousands of fans thronged the streets. In Edinburgh, so enthusiastic were his supporters that he was knocked unconscious when they mobbed him outside his hotel.

While the tabloid press loved the weeping wonder, giving him titles such as 'The Prince of Wails', 'The Howling Success' and 'The Nabob of Sob', British crooners were forced to sit on the sidelines while he was in town, unable or unwilling to compete with his raw, emotional performances. Dickie Valentine, whose single 'Finger of Suspicion' topped the charts just as the Chris Barber Jazz Band's *New Orleans Joys* was released in January 1955, introduced some elements of Ray's stage show into his own performances, but with his matinee idol looks, no one was ever going to believe that Valentine was a vulnerable soul.

The most popular vocalist of his time, Dickie Valentine kept a constant eye on the US charts. Once a song was a hit in America, British artists would rush to release their own versions before the original could be made available in the UK. As a result, it wasn't uncommon for several renderings of the same song to be vying for position in the charts. At one point in 1955, Dickie Valentine, Ronnie Hilton and Nat King Cole occupied consecutive chart positions with different versions of the syrupy ballad 'A Blossom Fell'.

Public taste was largely dictated by a small clique of music publishers based in London's Denmark Street and by the dead hand of the BBC, whose broadcasting monopoly ensured that popular music was kept bland and unthreatening. *Housewives' Choice*, which aired weekday mornings on the station's Light Programme throughout the 50s, reassured the nation that pop was something that housewives listened to during the day while their husbands were out at work.

Just as white kids in the US tuned into black radio stations to hear music their parents despised, so the British youth had to dial beyond the wavelengths of the BBC to find exciting new sounds. Radio Luxembourg had begun broadcasting in English from central Europe in 1933, and in the early 50s transferred its programmes to a new, more powerful transmitter at 208 metres on the medium wave. Because of the distances involved, the station could only be picked up in the UK after dusk, when the signal was able to reach the iono-sphere and bounce down onto British soil. This nocturnal presence, coupled with the fact that Luxembourg carried advertising, forbidden on the BBC, gave teenagers the feeling that they were listening to something clandestine.

Another source of new sounds was the American Forces Network, a series of AM stations broadcasting from US bases across Europe. The aim of the AFN was to give GIs a taste of home and, as most US servicemen were in their late teens or early twenties, and many were black, the station played a healthy mix of the latest jazz, blues, R & B, country and rock 'n' roll. Where they could pick up the signal, teen-agers in Britain were also tuning in.

In late 1954, a record appeared in the UK charts that had never been played on the BBC nor reviewed by the British music press – the demand must have come from the listeners of Radio Luxembourg and AFN. 'Shake, Rattle and Roll' by Bill Haley and His Comets was a sax-led up-tempo twelve-bar that was made for jiving. Like so much of 50s pop, it was a bowdlerised version of a song popular-ised by a black artist, in this case a forty-three-year-old blues shouter from Kansas City named Big Joe Turner. The original was sassy and salacious, with Turner telling his amour that she did something to him that made him roll his eyes and grit his teeth. Haley toned down the lyrics, but somehow kept the energy. The BBC never condescended to play it, but 'Shake, Rattle and Roll' got to number four in the charts.

Bill Haley was born in Detroit in 1925. His father was a Kentucky banjo player, his mother a pianist from Ulverston in the English Lake District. In the late 1940s, he led a western swing band called the Saddlemen, but noticing how the kids at dances kept asking him to play songs by black artists, he recorded a cover of 'Rocket 88', which Jackie Brenston had taken to the top of the R & B chart. By mixing western swing – itself a hybrid of country and jazz – with rhythm and blues, Haley had hit on a revolutionary formula. In 1952, the Saddlemen cut a version of Jimmy Preston's 'Rock the Joint' that became a blueprint for their signature sound.

Changing the name of his backing band to the Comets, he co-wrote their next single, 'Crazy Man, Crazy', which became the first rock 'n' roll record to enter the US pop charts in June 1953. His follow-up single, 'Rock Around the Clock', written for him by the songwriting team of Max Freedman and James Myers, was something of a damp squib, lasting only a week in the national charts. However, the Comets' next release was 'Shake, Rattle and Roll'. A massive hit, it sold over a million copies in the US, yet Haley seemed unsure about what he had started. Having lit the fuse of rock 'n' roll, the next record he released was a mambo.

The mambo craze, originating in the Cuban community in New York City, swept the US in the mid-50s, with big-band leaders adding this Latin rhythm to their repertoire as a novelty. Tin Pan Alley, its eye as always on the big bucks, swiftly added the word 'Mambo' to the title of any corny old song in the hope of seeing it rise up the charts. In his magisterial history of 1950s pop culture in Britain, *The Restless Generation*, Pete Frame lists no fewer than forty-five singles released in Britain during 1955 with 'Mambo' in the title, including 'Ooh and Ah Mambo', 'Middle Age Mambo' and 'I Don't Want to Dance a Mambo Combo'. Bill Haley's job was to play music for people to dance to, so who can blame him for seeking to cash in on the latest dance craze by releasing 'Mambo Rock'?

The switch didn't do him any good – the BBC still refused to play Haley's records and 'Mambo Rock' managed nothing more than a couple of weeks in the UK charts in April 1955. However, the fact that the Comets were able to chart at all suggested that teenage consumers, through their purchasing power, were capable of creating new trends. Just as this phenomenon was building up a head of steam, a rival emerged to challenge the BBC's broadcasting monopoly.

Since its inception in 1922, the BBC had been the prime provider of popular culture in the UK. Adhering to the values of its first director general, John Reith, it sought to educate, inform and entertain. Reith's Scottish Presbyterian upbringing had also given the BBC a strong sense of morality, which led it to eschew anything that might be considered common or vulgar by polite society.

In 1955, the BBC's single TV channel appeared to be aimed at people watching from their drawing rooms. Following a short afternoon interlude for housewives and children, programmes began at 7.30 p.m. with the news and ended four hours later with another news bulletin, broadcast only in sound. In the week that 'Mambo Rock' entered the charts in April 1955, BBC TV featured an opera, three dramas, ice hockey, a visit to the circus, boxing, a piano recital, association football, a wildlife documentary and several light entertainment pieces, in which the participants wore formal dress. Each of these programmes was broadcast live and none was bought in from the United States.

This hearty mixture of the highbrow and the healthy was the BBC's way of mediating public taste and chimed in with the wartime ethos of being happy with what you were given. However, just a few weeks after food rationing finally ended in July 1954, the British government announced the introduction of commercial television. After years of receiving their ration of culture from the Reithian BBC, viewers would be able to sample the delights of a television channel that put popularity before public service.

The 1954 Television Act created a new regulator, the Independent Television Authority, tasked with setting up commercial television in the UK. Hoping to avoid a repeat of the BBC's broadcasting monopoly, the ITA decided to award regional franchises to different TV companies around the country. As a result, the roll-out of commercial television took place over a period of six years, starting from September 1955. The first three companies to be awarded franchises came from diverse backgrounds. Associated-Rediffusion, who won the right to broadcast in the London area on weekdays, was a partnership between Associated Newspapers, the owners of the *Daily Mail*, and Rediffusion, a company which manufactured TV sets. The northern franchise went to Granada, owners of a chain of cinemas, while the Associated Broadcasting Company, a company formed by a consortium of showbiz agents, won the broadcast rights for the Midlands. Each was a classic case of entrepreneurs hoping to avoid the disruption of their own core businesses by investing heavily in the disruptive force.

And there were many who felt that commercial TV would be a very disruptive force. Opponents looked across the Atlantic at the way TV had developed in the US, where the live broadcast of the coronation of Elizabeth II in 1953 had been interrupted by an advert featuring a celebrity chimpanzee. The BBC, funded by a universal broadcasting licence, had never needed to worry about ratings. Guardians of the nation's morals voiced concern that TV stations forced to rely on audience figures to make money would soon be heading downmarket.

The aim of the ITA in setting up the regional model was to encourage the commercial stations to offer more local produce. After years of dining on the cucumber sandwiches offered by the clipped tones of the BBC, regulators wanted the newcomers to serve up black pudding. Instead, from day one, viewers of the independent channels were offered a diet of hamburgers.

When Associated-Rediffusion began broadcasting in the London area on 22 September 1955, their schedules featured a number of new programmes and formats imported from the US. *The Roy Rogers Show*, a cowboy serial which had been running on NBC in the States since 1951, appeared in the children's hour along with *The Adventures of Robin Hood*. The latter, though ostensibly English in its theme and presentation, had an American producer, Hannah Weinstein. She made a point of hiring blacklisted American scriptwriters who were unable to find work in the US due to their left-wing views.

For the first time in the UK, game shows that offered cash prizes were broadcast. The BBC had shown quiz programmes, but in keeping with public service principles, all the winner received at the end of the show was a sense of intellectual superiority. In the first week of independent television, viewers in the London area were treated to a number of new quiz shows in which real money changed hands: *Take Your Pick*, *Double Your Money* and, as part of *Sunday Night at the London Palladium*, *Beat the Clock*. There were jocular hosts, real live members of the public, broad general knowledge questions and moments of genuine excitement – 'Do you really want to open the box?' At the climax of the programme, the studio audience, emerging from a world of make do and mend, would audibly gasp as the curtains parted to reveal 'tonight's star prize'.

By far the most successful programme on the new channel was *I Love Lucy*. The first American sitcom to be shown on British TV, it was shot on 35 mm film and introduced a new standard of production

145

to British television. The star of the show, Lucille Ball, was a highly talented comedienne whose slapstick was light years ahead of the stodgy buffoonery of our own Mr Pastry.

The American influence extended into music programming. Liberace had a weekly show in which he grinned widely while performing classical numbers, jazz and even the occasional boogie-woogie tune. His brand of schmaltz tended to divide audiences along gender lines. The *TV Times* told readers in October 1955 that 'in the United States, Liberace's fans are mostly women. On the other hand American men are a good deal less enthusiastic. Indeed, many of them are said to grit their teeth in baffled fury whenever he appears on the screen.' Liberace's response to such a violent reaction could be found in the theme song from his show: 'I Don't Care'.

With regard to domestic artists, independent television initially echoed the BBC's formal approach to music. *Music Shop*, broadcast on Saturdays at 3 p.m., featured the staid duo of Teddy Johnson and Pearl Carr, while the first edition of the big weekend variety show, *Sunday Night at the London Palladium*, was headlined by wartime favourite Gracie Fields.

The only concession to teenage viewers was a weekly serial in the 7.30 p.m. slot, *Penny for a Song*, described as 'a light musical adventure'. According to the *TV Times*, 'This is the happy-go-lucky romance of pretty, vivacious Penny Lester, who decides to turn an old mews garage into a coffee bar, called "The Rattletrap". In this bright setting we follow, through story, song and dance, Penny's attempts to come to terms with life and the coffee machine.' The star of the show was Shirley Abicair, a twenty-four-year-old Australian singer who had risen to fame in the UK accompanying herself on the zither. In her new role, she was forced to dispense with her instrument, which perhaps wasn't seen as a fitting accoutrement for a cappuccino-drinking teen.

Voices were soon raised in complaint about the threat that

commercial television posed to traditional values. In early December 1955, *Picture Post* asked, 'Will TV Kill the British Sunday?' The hugely popular *Sunday Night at the London Palladium* was held up as an attack on the sanctity of the Sabbath. 'Already we've been given on our screens much more (and much less inhibited) entertainment than you could have regaled yourself with on any British Sunday since the Restoration,' thundered Denzil Batchelor. 'The greater part of these high jinks can be credited to independent TV, who devised the most daring Sunday programme yet: the *Palladium Show* in which people are invited on stage to win £100 for stamping on a balloon encased in a woman's girdle.' This was at a time when Sunday trading was banned, including professional events such as football, racing and theatre. Both the BBC and ITV were required to delay the commencement of their Sunday-evening programmes by order of the government so as not to interfere with the habits of churchgoers. The Lord's Day Observance Society had recently rebuked the Duke of Edinburgh for playing polo on a Sunday. The Queen and the Queen Mother were also criticised for watching him. 'Do we want a Sunday in which we all go to church in the morning and amuse ourselves during the afternoon?' asked Batchelor incredulously. If we did, he declared, Britain would no longer be considered a Christian country.

The same issue of *Picture Post* contained an article entitled 'Has Commercial TV Failed?' Just three months into the new service, the owners of the London franchise were being forced to make changes. Roland Gillett, programme controller for Associated-Rediffusion, explained the lessons he had learned. 'Let's face it now, once and for all: the public like girls, wrestling, bright musicals, quiz shows and good real life drama. We gave them the Halle Orchestra, "The Peaceful Atom", Foreign Press Club, Floodlit Football and the sort of thing I call Visits to the Local Fire Station. Well, we've learned. From now on, what the public wants, it's going to get.'

The news was cut to five minutes, discussion programmes were shunted to Sunday afternoon and more TV serials were bought in from the United States. If you wanted to watch worthy programmes in your drawing room, the commercial stations seemed to be saying, you have the BBC. We're going elsewhere. It was a popular move. By the end of 1955, over half a million households in the London area had converted their TVs to receive independent television. As the new channels were rolled out across the country, it was cinema that would suffer most.

By 1955, the number of tickets sold at the cinema was 1,181 million, down from the post-war high of 1,635 million. Yet film was still the main source of entertainment. That year, the British public were treated to a diet of movies that focused on wartime drama: *The Cockleshell Heroes*, *The Colditz Story*, *Above Us the Waves* and the most popular film of the year, *The Dam Busters*. The heroes were stoical officers with clipped, upper-class accents. While helping to boost the morale of an audience that was chafing against shortages of goods and housing, these films subtly reinforced the idea that the officer class knows what's best for you – even if they no longer wear a uniform.

Teenagers of the period didn't need reminding that their parents had won the war – they'd grown up hearing little else. Push against parental control and you'd be likely to hear how lucky you were even to be living with your parents, given that they themselves had been drafted or evacuated. Refusing to eat your greens would result in a lecture about the privations of wartime rationing. Little surprise then that 50s teenagers should be drawn to movies that challenged authority figures.

Marlon Brando was the star of the 1953 film *The Wild One*, playing the leader of a motorcycle gang that terrorises a small Californian town. In *Rebel Without a Cause*, James Dean plays a mixed-up kid from a dysfunctional family who shuns his parents' world to hang out with the teenage nighthawks in suburban Los Angeles. These films were among the first to highlight the generation gap that had grown between those who had been adults during the Second World War and their children. The American people looked across that gap and saw a new menace threatening the tranquillity that they had fought so hard to achieve: the juvenile delinquent, looking to rebel against whatever you've got. Now Hollywood was bringing that rebellion to the silver screen.

Youths in the UK were somewhat late to the party. *The Wild One* was considered too violent to be shown in the UK until 1968, and when *Rebel Without a Cause* opened in March 1956 its young star had been dead for six months, killed in a car wreck aged twenty-four. The first juvenile delinquent movie to gain wide release in the UK was *Blackboard Jungle*, set in a school in one of the rougher neighbourhoods of New York. Glenn Ford plays Richard Dadier, a Navy veteran retrained as a teacher, tasked with educating a class of anti-social hoodlums. They constantly mock him, pronouncing his name 'Dad-ee-o', and the threat of violence is never far from the surface. Dadier intervenes to stop a student raping a female teacher and is subsequently beaten in a back alley by gang members who are also his pupils. When a bespectacled maths teacher brings his irreplaceable collection of 78 rpm jazz records into class, the students smash them in a forceful rejection of the past. Eventually, Dadier is able to win the respect of one of his tormentors, played by Sidney Poitier, who comes to his aid when the leader of the gang pulls a knife in class.

The producers attempted to avoid any accusations of exploitation by attaching a scrolled preface to the movie which solemnly declared their concerns about the problem of juvenile delinquency. However, any pretence of sociological value this might have given the movie was completely undermined by the fact that the director immediately

149

cut to an opening scene soundtracked by 'Rock Around the Clock'. Bill Haley's single, which had barely made any impression when released in the UK some eight months earlier, sounded a whole lot better when played through massive speakers in a cinema – so much so that some teenagers got up and danced in the aisles.

Blackboard Jungle propelled 'Rock Around the Clock' to the top of the American charts, the first rock 'n' roll record to reach such dizzy heights. When the movie was released in the UK on 17 October 1955, Brunswick Records were looking to repeat the trick. 'Rock Around the Clock' entered the *New Musical Express* charts at thirteen, hitting the number one spot five weeks later. Haley's timing was impeccable. During the first ten months of 1955, over 46 million records had been sold in the UK, 8 million more than in a similar period in 1954. In November, *Record Mirror* reported that 'demand for discs has paralysed supply'. The record-buying public appeared to be undergoing a sea change. On 22 July, 'Rose Marie' by Slim Whitman reached the top of the charts and stayed there for an unprecedented eleven weeks. Whitman, billed as a cowboy singer, sparked a craze in western songs. He was finally ejected from the top spot by a domestic cover of the theme tune to the James Stewart movie *The Man from Laramie* sung by crooner Jimmy Young, who hailed from the wild west of Gloucestershire.

In the months that followed, a number of western-themed songs hit the charts. Mitch Miller reached number two with 'The Yellow Rose of Texas'. Frankie Laine did the same with a song about a man and his mule, 'Cool Water'. Tennessee Ernie Ford took 'Sixteen Tons' all the way to the top and Bill Hayes got to number two with 'The Ballad of Davy Crockett'.

As record sales went through the roof, a significant element of the public, possibly driven by the sudden appearance of various cowboy serials on commercial TV, were moving away from crooners like

Johnnie Ray towards guitar-strumming singers like Slim Whitman. To make it as a crooner you needed a great voice and the ability to look good in a dinner jacket, and, at the time, there were plenty of those kind of guys in the UK. A cowboy singer, however, had to sound like he'd got prairie dust on his boots, like he could round up cattle or ride the rails. And he had to strum a guitar while he sang. So far, Britain hadn't produced any homegrown artists like that. Sure, Jimmy Young had taken a cowboy song to number one, but on his record sleeves he was formally dressed, flashing a smile above his dickie bow. That was the music industry standard in the UK. The press dismissed Slim Whitman as nothing more than a hillbilly.

Despite being held in such disdain, this hillbilly was selling more records than anybody else had ever done, and there were more of his country cousins climbing the chart. British record companies were caught on the hop – there simply weren't any hillbillies in Britain.

Or were there?

Decca Records had a guitar-toting singer on their books who'd done time in a New Orleans jailhouse, a hardscrabble roustabout who'd sailed the seven seas in search of the Devil's music. He was the very epitome of authenticity – and he was English. This may explain why, in the same week that 'Rock Around the Clock' entered their singles chart, the *New Musical Express* carried a Decca Records ad announcing their new releases for the week of 17 October 1955. Squeezed in between Billy Cotton's recording of the theme to the most popular film of the year, 'The Dam Busters March', and a new Bing Crosby 45 was the debut release of Ken Colyer's Skiffle Group.

Coming just a week after Lonnie Donegan's *Backstairs Session* EP hit the shops, it was beginning to look like the emergence of a skiffle scene. The music papers, however, were unimpressed. Only James Asman of *Record Mirror* seemed to notice, featuring both releases on his traditional jazz page. Asman was the owner of a

record store in Covent Garden, the Jazz Centre, and had been an early supporter of Colyer, championing him since the days of the Crane River Jazz Band. He fully recognised that Ken was a prickly personality, but saw that as part of his genius. He once observed that 'there's a demon in this man Colyer, a grinning fearsome monster who pushes and shoves – and gets ahead. Behind the melancholy, sensitive eyes and rugged face is a fierce, almost insane ambition. His history is littered with musicians who found out about the demon and just couldn't live with it.'

Asman was willing to forgive Colyer's behaviour because of his important role in the development of British jazz. Unfortunately, this enthusiasm didn't extend to skiffle. On 12 November 1955, Asman reviewed both the Donegan and Colyer skiffle group releases, observing that, while he was happy to tap his foot and nod his head to trad jazzers playing Lead Belly or Broonzy songs in the convivial atmosphere of a live gig, he didn't need a recording of their antics when he could easily find far superior records made by the original artists.

What's more, he was clearly irritated by the audience that this type of music was drawing to the trad jazz scene. Under a column headed 'Teenagers (!)', Asman wrote that 'the current popularity of "skiffle" music amongst the teenagers who throng the outskirts of British jazz appreciation is having a dubious effect, of which these two records just issued are obvious examples. I would like to put on record my trepidation at the wholesale effect they are having on jazz musicians and groups now playing in Britain.' He went on to decry 'the utterly stupid antics of fans and fannies who cavort and prance like inmates of a mental home during music far beyond their comprehension'.

Like the teacher in *Blackboard Jungle* who thought his rare jazz records would cast a calming spell over the teenagers in his class, Asman was dismayed to find that the skiffle sessions had become more popular than the trad jazz which gave them birth. A week later, his page was headlined 'This Is a Problem of Youth Which Must Be Solved in Order to Keep the True Name and Spirit of Jazz Clean'. The High Priest of Trad was clearly spooked by the popularity of a couple of guys strumming guitars.

The A side of the Ken Colyer Skiffle Group's 78 rpm single, 'Take This Hammer', had originally been recorded in 1941 by Lead Belly, and was backed with a reading of the spiritual standard 'Down by the Riverside'. While Colyer was a great trumpet player, he was a pedestrian singer, even when assisted here by Alexis Korner. There was no way Colyer's low-fi sound could compete with the production values of the hit singles coming out of Nashville. Slim Whitman could rest easy. The two cuts retained too much of their trad jazz flavour to cross over into the mainstream and the single disappeared without trace.

Decca were not put off by this failure. They had another guitar-playing hillbilly singer from Britain on their books and so, a month later, on Friday 11 November 1955, they released 'Rock Island Line' by the Lonnie Donegan Skiffle Group. At first hearing, this was an

153

odd choice for a single – a minute or so of monologue, followed by a frenzy of nonsense lyrics – but however strange this proposition may have seemed, it wasn't completely without precedent. Just a month before, bandleader Billy Vaughn had reached number five in the American charts with 'The Shifting, Whispering Sands', the story of a gold prospector lost in a desert way out west. American voiceover artist Ken Nordine performed the narrative as a dramatic monologue, backed by the strings of Vaughn's orchestra, and took the record into the UK Top Ten. As for the frantic rhythms of the second part of 'Rock Island Line', weren't they reminiscent of the up-tempo western bop records that were becoming popular with teenagers in the US?

'Rock Island Line' starts with Donegan recounting a slow, rambling conversation between two railroad employees, one deceiving the other into letting him pass a toll booth on the way to New Orleans. The narration continues until halfway through the record, when, suddenly, the song begins to pick up momentum like a runaway train. The washboard player scrapes up a storm while the double bass dances around the rhythm. Their vigour seems to possess Donegan, who fires off a few frenzied verses punctuated with yelped vowels and growled consonants. Sixty years later, 'Rock Island Line' still sounds like a song that is about to go off the rails.

Compared to Ken Colyer's restrained take on Lead Belly, Donegan's performance is incendiary. Colyer, however, could not have cared less – he put his heart and soul into New Orleans jazz; Lonnie Donegan put his into skiffle.

Decca's timing could not have been better. The same week that they ran their advert announcing the release of 'Rock Island Line' in *Record Mirror*, 'Rock Around the Clock' hit number one in that paper's singles chart. Had someone at Decca spotted that the word 'rock' suddenly had currency with teenagers? Did they sniff the possibility that rock might be the dance craze to follow mambo's success, its mere inclusion in a song's title making it more likely to be a hit? Sixty years later, it's difficult to discern, but one contemporary journalist, Charles Govey, reported in the *NME* that 'it has even been suggested that "Rock Island Line" is selling on the strength of its title alone'.

Whether it was the coincidence of the two 'Rock' titles, the public's new-found taste for western-flavoured songs or the growing popularity of skiffle among teenagers at jazz clubs that so annoyed James Asman, something clicked for Lonnie Donegan. 'Rock Around the Clock' topped the *Record Mirror* charts for the whole of December 1955, but in the very last week of the year, the follow-up single by Bill Haley and His Comets, 'Rock-a-Beatin' Boogie', leapt into the *RM* chart at number three, above festive-themed platters by Dickie Valentine, Max Bygraves, Pat Boone and the party pianist Winifred Atwell. Also making its chart debut, at number eight, was 'Rock Island Line' by the Lonnie Donegan Skiffle Group.

If Donegan was surprised to find he'd charted with a Lead Belly song he'd recorded eighteen months previously, he wasn't the only one scratching his head. 'Here's a surprise entry!' chirped *Record Mirror*. 'This must surely be the first record of its kind ever to enter the best sellers. It's "Skiffle" music, which, we understand, originated in the old days of New Orleans,' it helpfully informed readers.

James Asman wasn't best pleased to find that a music which had hitherto been the preserve of his trad jazz column had escaped onto the Top Ten page. In his last dispatch of 1955, he admitted to being genuinely amused to see Lonnie Donegan in the charts. 'The general "pop" public,' he grumbled, 'who abhor jazz in any form unless it be thoroughly watered down to suit their feeble tastes, take [Donegan] and his singing to their heart precisely as they did to a third-rate, pseudo hillbilly singer in America called Slim Whitman. Makes a queer world to live and listen in, doesn't it?'

And a Happy New Year to you too, Jimmy.

11

SUNSHINE ON SOHO

Sunshine on Soho, a short documentary on release in cinemas as a B movie in the summer of 1956, described the Soho district of London's West End as 'the most fabulous square mile in the world'. While that claim may have been open to contention, 1950s Soho was undoubtedly the most exotic neighbourhood in post-war Britain. The area encompassed by Oxford Street, Charing Cross Road, Shaftesbury Avenue and Regent Street had long been a cosmopolitan enclave. The first Orthodox Church in Britain was built there in 1677 by refugees from the Ottoman Empire, who gave their name to nearby Greek Street. In 1681, the church was taken over by Huguenots, who had fled France to avoid persecution for their Protestant faith. These highly skilled silk weavers came to dominate the community as Soho transitioned from fields into a densely packed urban area. By 1739, Scots writer William Maitland observed, 'Many parts of this parish so greatly abound with French that it is an easy matter for a stranger to imagine himself in France.'

This Francophone enclave made Soho the obvious destination for those seeking to escape the terror of the French Revolution, and throughout the nineteenth century refugees from political upheavals on the Continent made their home in the area. During this period, Britain had no restrictions on immigration and the bohemian milieu of Soho made newcomers less conspicuous. Karl Marx and his family arrived in 1850, sharing a flat on Dean Street with some Italian teachers. An agent of the Prussian secret service who kept Marx under surveillance provides us with one of the few contemporary descriptions of a Soho dwelling: 'Marx lives in one of the worst, therefore one of the cheapest quarters of London. He occupies two rooms. The room looking out on the street is the parlour and the bedroom is at the back. There is not one clean or decent piece of furniture in either room but everything is broken, tattered and torn, with thick dust over everything and the greatest untidiness everywhere . . .'

Though the exiles of Soho were poor, they were industrious. Many were artisans – instrument makers, cobblers, watchmakers – and at the centre of their cultural lives were the restaurants that offered their native cuisine and acted as ad hoc community centres. Wherever immigrants lived in London, they headed to Soho at the weekend to enjoy their favourite dishes and catch up on the gossip from home. In the 1930s, eroticism was added to the menu when the first nude revue opened at the Windmill Theatre just off Piccadilly Circus, enhancing Soho's reputation as the red-light district of London. It was, declared the critic Ian Nairn, the free port that every city must have.

When the French pioneers of the moving image, the Pathé brothers, were looking to open a London office in 1910, Soho was the obvious choice. From their base in Wardour Street, they produced the cinema newsreels that accompanied movies until television news rendered them obsolete in 1970. In 1955, Pathé offered the British people a window into the diversity of the district in a two-minute newsreel entitled 'Soho Goes Gay'. In commentary laced with the arch tones sometimes employed by newsreels when dealing with social issues, the film begins with the words 'All the world lives in Soho . . .' and, over footage of flamenco dancers, 'even some English.' The subject of the film is the Soho Fair, an annual carnival bringing all of the communities of Soho out onto the streets, an event that local characters wouldn't miss 'for all of the goulash in Greek Street'.

The camera seeks out the exotic and the bizarre. Two men in Gypsy costume serenade passers-by; a Messerschmitt three-wheeled bubble car, painted in harlequinades, is seen with a Guardsman, wearing busby and tunic but no trousers, riding on the back; a line of scantily clad dancing girls appear right on cue as the narrator muses about what it is that draws people to Soho – 'It must be the food . . .' – cut to girls – 'or something.'

The wry commentary continues to draw attention to the foreign nature of Soho. When an Englishman wins the waiters' race, the narrator asks, 'Doesn't tradition mean anything?' Later, over footage of the carnival parade, we're told that 'if there's any nationality not represented, then Soho must be slipping'. The short clip concludes with the observation that, in Soho, 'you meet someone different every few yards', although the narrator can't resist adding, over a glimpse of some morris men dancing in the parade, 'even including some English'.

With its relaxed attitudes towards race, gender and sexuality, Soho in the 50s already looked and sounded like the multicultural London of the twenty-first century. In the drab and dowdy years of food shortages that followed the war, the most common place to find a bottle of olive oil in Britain would be at the chemist, where it was sold as an earwax softener. The idea that you could use it for cooking would have come as a surprise to a British public who had only recently been introduced to the bland delights of the fish finger. Those willing to explore the restaurants and delicatessens of Soho were offered a spicy cornucopia for the palate. It was already the only square mile in the country where coffee was more popular than tea.

———

During the Second World War, shortages of beans led to coffee being mixed with chicory and acorns to make supplies go further. Instant coffee was available in the 50s, but the adulterated version remained popular. The best-selling brand of coffee essence, Camp, came in a slim bottle, its label depicting a soldier in full Highland uniform sitting outside his tent in some far-flung corner of the Empire, where his faithful Sikh servant waits to serve him tiffin. A sweet, dark liquid that contained 4 per cent caffeine-free coffee essence and 26 per cent chicory, Camp Coffee was mixed with hot milk, in a similar manner to cocoa or Ovaltine, to make a soothing beverage.

In 1946, an Italian engineer named Achille Gaggia patented a new machine that used steam pressure to force hot water through ground coffee beans. Espresso machines had been around since the turn of the century, but relied on heating the water to very high temperatures in order to maintain pressure, a process that made the coffee taste bitter. Gaggia's machine used manually operated levers to create pressure, which meant that he could keep the water just below boiling point, resulting in a flavour that was much stronger yet less bitter.

Pino Risorvato, a dental equipment salesman from Milan, was related by marriage to a director of the Gaggia company. When travelling around Britain in the early 50s, hawking his wares, he was appalled by the dire quality of the coffee he was served. Sensing a gap in the market, he smuggled several Gaggia lever machines into the country via Ireland to avoid import controls and set up office in the heart of the Italian community in Soho, inviting restaurant owners to sample this new technology. To his dismay, the catering industry was singularly unimpressed, believing there was no market for frothy coffee.

Undeterred, he went into partnership with Scotsman Maurice Ross, who, like Risorvato, had no previous experience in catering. Together, they set about converting a bombed-out laundry at 29 Frith Street into Britain's first modern espresso cafe, the Moka Bar, named after the Arabian port of Mocha, where coffee first came to the attention of

European traders on the East India route in the seventeenth century. Seeking to create a continental ambience a million miles from the stewed atmosphere of the Lyons Corner House chain, they employed architect Geoffrey Crockett to design a contemporary interior. He covered the surfaces in Formica, a hard-wearing, wipe-clean plastic laminate introduced to Britain from America in 1947.

Soho already had a proven market for coffee. Just along Frith Street, the Bar Italia had been operating as a traditional Italian cafe since 1949, while the Algerian Coffee Shop just around the corner in Brewer Street had been serving customers since 1887. But the Moka was something altogether different, a stylish temple to modernism, a three-lever Gaggia machine its gilded altarpiece. Opened in April 1953 by Italian film star Gina Lollobrigida, it was soon selling a hundred thousand cups of cappuccino a year.

As Lonnie Donegan entered the *Record Mirror* charts with 'Rock Island Line' in the last week of 1955, the BBC broadcast a talk about the espresso cafes of London on its highbrow Third Programme. In *The Fall of the Hot Dog Bar*, writer John Pearson recognised that the introduction of the espresso machine had produced a 'strange social ferment'. The coffee bar exactly suited the mood of the post-war English youngster and its success represented a shift in teenage taste away from the US towards continental Europe: 'a triumph of bamboo over chrome, of coffee over Coke, of *mañana* over the hustle and ruthless competitiveness of the hot-dog bar'.

Look back to any evening in London before 1952, Pearson observed, and remember how there were very few places where young people looking for a cheap night could congregate. This was the true revolution that Pino Risorvato wrought: he created a new social space that was open to people of all classes and ages. There was none of the formality of the restaurant, nor the age restrictions of public houses. And while strict licensing laws kept pub opening hours tightly controlled, the espresso bars stayed open till very late, even on a Sunday. For the price of a few cups of coffee, teenagers could sit and socialise all night long.

The American novelist and war correspondent Martha Gellhorn toured the espresso bars of London for an article that appeared in the May 1956 issue of *Encounter* magazine. She was struck by the diversity of the young clientele she found. At the Moka, an accordion player of North African appearance was surrounded by a group of young people 'singing easily, loudly, all together, happily of amore. The boy at the espresso machine sang too.' Further along Frith Street, Gellhorn found the Grenada, a cafe frequented by 'negroes', where she saw black and white couples dancing to jazz in the basement as three young Greeks 'with lines of thought and suffering between their brows' disputed the issues of the day at a nearby table. Later, she was very taken with a young woman who she describes as 'a beauty . . . impossible to place, Chinese-Javanese-Siamese . . . telling a story to her friend, a girl who might have been Spanish-Arab-Cuban, some combination like that and to a boy of unknown nationality'.

It was from this milieu of teenage cross-pollination that skiffle emerged as a sub-genre in its own right. On 22 August 1955, the Club Calendar page of *Melody Maker* announced the birth of a new kind of venue: 'Skiffle and Blues: opening 1st September featuring Ken Colyer, Bob Watson's Skiffle Group and guests. Round House, Wardour Street. 8–10.30. Admission 2/-. Free membership opening night'.

Bob Watson was a twenty-year-old trad jazz fan from Hayes in Middlesex who had been following Ken Colyer since seeing him with the Crane River Band in the hut beside the White Hart in Cranford. He'd pestered Lonnie Donegan into giving him guitar lessons and was a regular visitor to Alexis Korner's house in Notting Hill, where he learned about the blues. A close friend of Dickie Bishop, Bob even turned up singing backing vocals on Donegan's *Backstairs Session*

EP. Together with bass player Adrian Brand, another Crane River devotee, he got a gig playing interval spots at the Fox and Goose pub in Ealing, west London, where Steve Lane's Southern Stompers had a Friday-night residency. Lane was a follower of the Ken Colyer school of trad jazz, so was only too happy to let some kids with guitars get up and play a few blues songs while he went to the bar. He didn't even mind if his banjo player, Cyril Davies, sometimes sat in with them.

Davies was a panel beater by trade, a stocky, balding man who looked older than his twenty-three years. He ran his own business in south Harrow, hammering car bodywork back into shape after collisions. Hailing from Uxbridge in north-west London, he was a big fan of Lead Belly and his metal-bashing day job gave him the muscular tone necessary to play twelve-string guitar in the style of his hero. He'd been performing songs like 'Frankie and Johnny', 'On a Christmas Day' and 'Rock Island Line' whenever the Stompers took a break, so when Watson and Brand turned up wanting to play some blues numbers, Davies was a natural fit.

Like Lead Belly, Cyril Davies was a larger-than-life figure, a man who looked like a working-class bruiser yet became possessed by the spirit of the blues when he sang, inhabiting the material in a way that electrified audiences in the heads-down, no-nonsense jazz scene. Wherever the Bob Watson Skiffle Band played in west London, they drew enthusiastic crowds wanting to hear more blues-based music. It was this reaction that inspired them to conceive of a club where the skiffle sessions weren't merely a short spot in an evening of trad jazz, but also an opportunity for audiences to hear a different kind of music that had hitherto been relegated to the fringes.

In post-war Britain, the only performers to be found using guitars to accompany themselves were outsiders – blues men, calypsonians, cowboys riding the range. Some jazz bands contained guitarists, but they were sat at the back in the rhythm section. Watson, Davies and

Brand set out to challenge that by declaring that you could have a whole night dedicated to guitar-based music. With Slim Whitman and the other singing cowboys dominating the charts throughout the summer of 1955, it seemed like an idea whose time had come. And there was only one place where they could open such a venue: Soho – the centre of what then passed for Britain's underground music scene.

Brewer Street takes its name from the brewhouses built there in the late 1660s. At the junction with Wardour Street, on a plot once known as Knave's Acre, stood the Blue Cross tavern, renamed the Round House in 1862. Rebuilt thirty years later, it currently hosts the O Bar, but, at the corner entrance, the building's earlier designation can still be seen in the ornate Victorian plasterwork above the door. Watson, Davies and Brand approached the landlord, an Irishman, about the possibility of hosting a Thursday-night club in his spacious upstairs function room. He was happy to oblige, telling them that 'so long as you don't have too much trouble, I don't mind what you do up there'.

It is somewhat fitting that the opening night of the first-ever skiffle club should have been graced by the man who'd started it all, Ken Colyer. However, it was Bob Watson's Skiffle Group that held the whole thing together, playing a set to kick the evening off, then backing up whoever came through the door wanting to sing the blues. Watson, having been tutored by Lonnie Donegan, played a Gibson Kalamazoo guitar that had previously belonged to his mentor. Adrian Brand had learned double bass from Jim Bray of the Chris Barber Band. And with his custom-built Grimshaw twelve-string, Cyril Davies was a force of nature, channelling Lead Belly and improvising his way to becoming one of Britain's earthiest harmonica players.

'Although it became known as skiffle and became very popular as that, to me and one or two others it was always about the blues,' says Bob Watson. 'I mean, Cyril Davies was a great bloke for the blues and this sort of thing and didn't really like the term "skiffle", he didn't think of what we were doing as skiffle.'

They may have thought they were playing the blues, but they did not dare call themselves bluesmen, for, in mid-50s Britain, the received wisdom in jazz-loving circles was that the blues was a music that could only be played by old black guys from America. Even someone who sweated all day beating panels over an anvil would be met with scorn should he claim to be singing the blues. Skiffle provided a way around this contextual dilemma for Britons who wanted to play American roots music at a time when their contemporaries in the US were showing little interest in this old material. White American teenagers wanted to hear the new sounds of rock 'n' roll, while the urban black population didn't want to listen to the blues songs their grandparents used to sing, music that reminded them of slavery and degradation. Although its popularisers looked earnestly to the US for inspiration, skiffle in 1955 was an indigenous sub-genre of roots music that was only played by young white guys from Britain.

Having run his own business, Cyril Davies was the organising force behind the club, dealing with the money and administration. It was he who placed the weekly ads in *Melody Maker*. Sometimes, he let his enthusiasm for the blues get the better of him and the name of the event listed in the Club Calendar subtly changed to become the Blues and Skiffle Club for a couple of weeks. However, it was soon clear to the three would-be bluesmen that it was skiffle that was drawing the crowds. By the end of the year, the place was packed every week with teenagers and twenty-something students desperate to hear the new sound. The pioneering spirit of the Round House sessions was underscored when adverts proclaiming it to be 'Europe's Only Skiffle and Blues Club' appeared in *Melody Maker*.

Thursday nights at the Round House were a magnet for kids who were already tuned in to the fledgling guitar-led scene. Born in 1939,

Ron Gould grew up in the Ship public house on New Cavendish Street, halfway between Soho and Fitzrovia. Being in the same trade, most of the club owners in the area knew Ron's father, so Ron was able to gain entrance to watch jazz bands from an early age, first seeing Ken Colyer at Cy Laurie's Club in the basement of Mac's Rehearsal Rooms in Windmill Street. He was an avid attendee of the record recitals run by Doug Dobell, who introduced him to the music of people like Herman Chittison, a piano player from New York who, it was said, smoked a meerschaum pipe filled with pot.

In 1955, Ron had begun playing washboard with a bunch of friends, busking in a derelict space caused by bomb damage next to the Admiral Duncan pub in Old Compton Street. His father was unimpressed by his son's sudden transformation into a musician. 'I was going out to play with a skiffle group, carrying a washboard, and as I passed through the bar of my dad's pub, he said to assembled patrons, "Look at him, he's going out to play with a band that uses scrubbing boards and God knows what! Call that a band?" When I came back a few days later and showed him a record and said, "Look at that, Dad, it says 'Bill Colyer – washboard'," my old man looked at me and said, "Yeah, but that's a real bloody musical washboard."'

Ron revelled in the fact that his parents didn't like the music he was playing. 'The attraction of skiffle was that it represented a rebellion against your parents and what they stood for. There was rock 'n' roll, but there were very few records coming over from America, and you couldn't hear much of that music anyway because it wasn't on the radio, but you could hear skiffle because it was being played in the street. There was a feeling that this was us; whatever they wanted to put on, we're doing this for ourselves. It was anti-commercial. We're going to play our music and sod all the rest. Skifflers were often heard to say that "I've got more in common with a black cotton picker than I have with my dad."'

Ron began attending the Sunday-afternoon sit-in sessions at Cy Laurie's. Bill Brunskill, now recovered from having his band stolen from under him by Lonnie Donegan, invited anyone who fancied a go to sit in with his jazz players. Encouraged by the band's guitarist, Ron had a go on the bass. 'Diz Disley said to me, "Can you play bass?" I said no. He said, "Well, give it a go." You just started playing! The idea that you could just pick up an instrument and play was in the air.'

Ron worked in a radio shop just along from the Round House, so was a regular at the Skiffle and Blues Club, sometimes performing a song or two with his band, the Southern Skiffle Group. Their repertoire came mostly from Woody Guthrie, Lead Belly, the Carter Family and Jimmie Rodgers. 'People who didn't know considered skiffle to be cowboy music because of the guitar we all saw in the films, stuff like Roy Rogers at Saturday-morning pictures. We were brought up on singing cowboys. That sounded like skiffle, so it was something we were all familiar with.'

Bob Watson estimates that the audiences at the Round House were mostly between the ages of sixteen and twenty-four. They would be dressed in the standard student garb of the moment, the duffel coat, which took its name from the Belgian town of Duffel, famous for producing a thick woollen material in the Middle Ages. The British duffel coat, designed for use by the Royal Navy during the First World War, had a voluminous hood, tartan wool lining and horn toggle fasteners that allowed the user to do up the coat while wearing thick gloves. It was a communal garment, left hanging on pegs for sailors to wear whenever they went on deck in inclement conditions. Thousands were produced during the Second World War as this utilitarian overcoat spread beyond the navy to all those in uniform.

With the outbreak of the Korean War in 1950, the duffel coat was once again popular with British troops facing the harsh Korean winter, but when the conflict ended three years later, the British

A session at the Round House Skiffle and Blues Club, Soho, 1956: Jack Elliot (*left*) sings with Cyril Smith (*right*), while Terry Plant plays bass and Big Bill Broonzy watches from the front row

government was left with a problem. Almost all of its overseas postings were now in tropical climes where there was no need for duffel coats, so, in 1954, they sold their stock to army surplus dealers. Not only were they warm and affordable, but teenagers found them attractive because they flew in the face of the fashionable styles of the day. At a time when even manual labourers wore a tie to work, the duffel coat divided the would-be beatniks from the squares, although among jazz fans this was a much-contested line.

'The skifflers and the trad fans wore army surplus duffel coats,' recalls Ron Gould. 'The people who went to Club 11 to hear Ronnie Scott and Benny Green, they wore Italian suits from Cecil Gee's in Charing Cross Road. They were modernists.' However, it wasn't just duffel-coated students who were drawn to the Thursday-night sessions at the Round House. Europe's first skiffle club also flushed out some fellow travellers.

————

Hylda Sims was given her first guitar in 1949 by Ivor Cutler, the Scottish humorist. 'It wasn't a very good instrument, but he taught me how to play three chords so I could sing the "Skye Boat Song".'

She was born in 1932 to parents who travelled from town to town in a wooden caravan, setting up pitch at markets the length and breadth of Britain. Her father was a 'crocus' – a hawker of self-concocted herbal remedies. Both parents were communists, Thomas Sims being involved with the Plebs League, founded in 1908 to educate adult workers in the theories of Marxist political economy. He later became a founding member of the Communist Party of Great Britain.

In line with her parents' anti-authoritarian views, Hylda was sent to the progressive Summerhill School during the Second World War. 'It was a wonderful place,' she recalls. 'Lessons were optional and activities were governed by meetings in which everyone had one vote each, from the youngest student to the oldest teacher.' Hylda left Summerhill for ballet school in London and by the age of fifteen was living alone in a flat in Swiss Cottage. Looking to meet people her age in an atmosphere that reminded her of home, she joined the Young Communist League. It was through her left-wing connections that she came across the London Youth Choir, founded in 1951 by John Hasted, a thirty-year-old Marxist and lecturer in atomic physics at University College London.

In 1949, Hasted had travelled to Yugoslavia to join volunteers from many western countries who took part in the building of the first proper road to link the capital, Belgrade, and the second city, Zagreb. There was very little contact across the Iron Curtain in the late 40s, but Yugoslavia, having recently broken with Stalin, was the first socialist country to open its doors to westerners. To build on the spirit of fraternity, a World Festival of Youth was organised in East Berlin in 1951, under the slogan 'For Peace and Friendship – Against Nuclear Weapons'. Hasted formed the London Youth Choir specifically to attend the event and he led them to subsequent festivals across Eastern Europe.

By the time she turned twenty-one, Hylda Sims had travelled with the choir to Budapest, Bucharest and Warsaw. As well as singing at the many left-wing events at which the choir performed, she was also taking her acoustic guitar into coffee shops in central London. 'They would let you sit there for hours and play the guitar. They even encouraged you to do it as it fetched in the punters.' A favourite haunt was the Nucleus Coffee Bar in Covent Garden, where a circle of strummers was already established. 'I'd take out my guitar, struggle to put it in tune and take my turn to sing. The songs passed around were a hotchpotch taken from black and white singers across the Atlantic. Josh White, Burl Ives, Woody Guthrie, Harry Belafonte, Lead Belly. We sang country songs, love songs, dustbowl ballads, calypsos, chorus songs, work songs.'

With long black hair in a ponytail, calf-length dirndl skirt and black top nipped tightly at the waist by a wide canvas belt with a big buckle, Sims affected the beatnik style, the final touch being her long green cigarette holder. The fact that she worked in the left-wing Collets bookshop and jazz record store in Charing Cross Road only added to her mystique.

In 1954, she took modernist painter Russell Quay as her lover.* She

---

* Quay is pronounced to rhyme with 'sway' rather than 'key'. This caused some confusion, so Russell added an 'e' to his surname during his skiffle years, to help with the pronunciation. For expediency's sake, I will be sticking to his proper surname.

first encountered this gaunt, red-bearded character singing music-hall songs at a party in south London, playing a four-stringed guitar and a tin kazoo.

Born in Beckenham, Kent, in 1920, Quay had had a chaotic home life. Following the death of his mother by suicide, he had run away from home aged fifteen with his younger brother, David. The two of them became travelling buskers, playing on the streets and in any pub that would have them, once roaming as far north as Yorkshire before being brought home by the police. Always artistically talented, Quay eventually got a job as a commercial artist working for the Victoria Wine Company in the East End of London. Seeing Oswald Mosley's Blackshirts marching through the area turned him into an ardent anti-fascist, and when war broke out in 1939, both he and his brother volunteered for the RAF.

David became a pilot, while Russell signed up as a rear gunner in a Lancaster bomber. Isolated for the duration of the flight, squeezed into a space too small to contain their parachutes, 'Tail-end Charlies' had the lowest survival rate of any member of a bomber crew. He still found time to paint, but his war work was lost when the ship he was travelling in was sunk on the Malta convoys.

When the war ended, Quay found solace in his painting, returning to Beckenham to attend the art college. By 1950, he was thirty years old, living a bohemian lifestyle in London that focused on art and music. An air of Augustus John-like chaos followed him around as he left wives and girlfriends in his wake. An imposing character, he performed cockney songs and Edwardian parlour ditties, accompanying himself on cuatro* and kazoo. His painting had an expressionistic style and he specialised in portraits of blues singers like Big Bill Broonzy and Pearl Bailey.

* Smaller than a guitar but larger than a ukelele, the cuatro is a four-stringed South American instrument that takes its name from the Spanish word for four.

Soon Sims and Quay, twelve years her senior, were living together in his terraced house in Waterloo. The place was crumbling and had no bathroom, damp on the walls and a lodger with a pet monkey. It was the ideal abode for a bunch of bohemians. The capuchin monkey was named Saki, and its owner turned out to be someone that Hylda recognised as one of the lads who hung around the jazz basement at Collets record shop.

The lodger was John Pilgrim, a former British Army deserter from Barnes. He'd begun playing washboard after seeing Beryl Bryden scraping up a storm at a lunchtime gig at the Regent Street Polytechnic and had been playing a few gigs with Quay. Sims joined them with her guitar, and when an architectural student named John Lapthorne came to stay, he was recruited into the ensemble. Lapthorne played one of the very first tub basses on the scene, made from a big cheese barrel, a broomstick and a length of twine. Soon the four friends were busking under the railway arches in Villiers Street, below Charing Cross Station, and calling themselves the City Ramblers. One night, to their amusement, two city gents responded to their playing by laying down their brollies in the shape of a cross and improvising a Highland sword dance, waving their bowler hats in the air.

The City Ramblers differed from the Colyer, Donegan and Watson groups in that they had not been formed as part of a trad band. As well as the usual jazz and blues numbers, their repertoire also included traditional British folk songs, comedy numbers from the halls and left-wing anthems that Sims had learned from her London Youth Choir days.

As autumn turned to winter, the house in Waterloo was condemned for demolition. Quay, looking for an artist's studio in which to work, found the ideal place just along from South Kensington Tube station. Lanning Roper, a landscape gardener of some renown, grew up in

Some called it 'spasm'. The City Ramblers, publicity shot, 1958: (*standing, left to right*) Jimmie MacGregor, Bobby Taylor (playing a 'blue blower'), Russell Quay, Vic Pitt and Eric Bunyan; (*seated*) Hylda Sims and Shirley Bland

America but had a cut-glass English accent. Gardening critic for the *Sunday Times*, he lived in a large house in Pelham Road, SW19, with a spacious studio flat in his garden. 'The place had previously been rented by a sculptor who undertook commissions from obscure Third World dictators with monumental ambitions,' remembers Sims. 'One such enormous figure still presided in the studio, three times life size, one arm raised as if to bless. We never discovered the name of the subject, nor of the sculptor for that matter.'

Having gained a following on the street and in the cafes where they played, the City Ramblers decided to host a regular musical evening at their new home. With a small balcony at one end and a high, windowed ceiling, the studio on Pelham Street made an ideal venue. 'It was a proper club,' says Sims. 'We went out and bought a load of folding seats and charged people for entry.' There was no announcement in *Melody Maker* – the whole endeavour relied on word of mouth – but in the last weeks of 1955, under the name Studio Skiffle, London gained its second club devoted to guitar-led music.

Flyer announcing the opening of Studio Skiffle, April 1956

12

RED SCARE REFUGEES

The first singles chart of 1956 that appeared in the *New Musical Express* confirmed the continuing dominance of Bill Haley and His Comets. 'Rock Around the Clock' had been in the Top Ten since mid-October, and now it was back at number one for the second time, having seen off a seasonal challenge from Dickie Valentine's 'Christmas Alphabet'. As the Brylcreemed British crooner plummeted down to number nine, Haley's follow-up single, 'Rock a-Beatin' Boogie', leapt from twenty-one to five, one place ahead of Alma Cogan's saccharine-soppy Latin novelty number 'Never Do a Tango with an Eskimo' (if you do, you'll end up with a freeze-up, according to its author, English songwriter Tommie Connor, who also penned 'I Saw Mommy Kissing Santa Claus').

As the festive-themed songs began to come down with the Christmas decorations, dust-covered cowboys from way out west rode into the charts. 'The Ballad of Davy Crockett' by Bill Hayes entered at number thirteen, while 'Sixteen Tons' by Tennessee Ernie Ford debuted at eighteen. Galloping along with them was a third hombre, toting a guitar and singing about riding on the railroad: Lonnie Donegan appeared in the charts at number seventeen with 'Rock Island Line'.

Two weeks later, he was in the Top Ten, telling the *NME* that, despite this sudden success, he had no intention of leaving his secure job in the rhythm section of the Chris Barber Jazz Band. If anything, he sounded rather embarrassed that Decca had released the song.

'I don't think it's a particularly good recording,' he said somewhat scornfully, before adding, 'I even asked to have it withdrawn when I first heard it.'

Donegan clearly had yet to grasp what was happening to him. On the same page as his interview, Starpic Studios were offering super-glossy photos of the latest stars for just 1/6 each. Top of the list was Tony Curtis – 'a thrilling new pose'. Straight in at number two – just above Hollywood starlet Shelley Winters – was Lonnie Donegan, 'a great shot of the sensational singer of "Rock Island Line"'. Had any trad sideman ever been given the glossy Starpic treatment? Was Donegan even a jazz musician any more?

Decca seemed to think so. The word 'Jazz' appeared twice, either side of the hole, in his 10" 78 rpm hit single. Yet the record was credited to a skiffle band, while the song came from the repertoire of a blues singer. The B side was even older. 'John Henry' tells the story of a steel-driving man who labours on the railroads. In one of the greatest of all American folk songs, when a steam-driven hammer is brought in to replace him, he challenges it to a contest. John Henry cuts more rock than the machine, but dies from the effort.

So jazz, skiffle, blues or folk? What kind of music was this and how did it get into the pop charts? There simply weren't enough fans of these relatively obscure styles to propel a single into the Top Ten. Some other forces must have been in play.

Was it the song itself that captured the imagination of the public? Having just been enchanted by the prospect of doing a tango with an Eskimo (or not, as the case may be), were record buyers taken by the notion of a thrilling ride on the Rock Island Line? Probably not. George Melly had recorded the song with barrelhouse piano accompaniment in 1951 but failed to catch the attention of record buyers.

The first chart of 1956 was full of highly polished pop. Most of the songs were string-drenched ballads and even the so-called hillbilly singers offered slick recordings backed by players who were masters of their craft. Bill Haley may have been the new sensation, but his records were crisp and clean. In such company, 'Rock Island Line' sounded raw. Lacking the metronomic time necessary for ballroom dancing, Lonnie Donegan's Skiffle Group threw a spanner in the works of mum-and-dad music by changing tempo, kicking up through the gears until their enthusiasm ran away with them. These cats were gone.

To young British listeners, whose cultural tastes had long been mediated by the beige instincts of the BBC, such musical mischief was infatuating. Where did it come from, this exciting sound? The answer knocked them for six. Used to hearing a mixture of sugary novelty songs, ersatz pop and white-bread rhythm and blues from their native artists, many had assumed Lonnie Donegan to be American. When news got round that he was born in Glasgow and had lived most of his life in the eastern suburbs of London, many teenagers experienced an epiphany that would change their lives. For those who were there in January 1956, the name of the first British artist to get into the charts singing and playing a guitar is as evocative to them as the name of the first man on the moon is for the generation that followed.

Lonnie Donegan broke the fourth wall of Britain's pop culture, except rather than making the audience feel that the performer was talking to them personally, his suburban background made it possible for working-class British teens to suddenly imagine themselves stepping out of the audience and into the pop pantheon. Up until this moment, most believed you had to be a trained musician to play an instrument and that everything cool and exotic in popular culture came from America. Now something sprang from the streets they walked, with an energy that threatened to upset the drab conformity of post-war Britain. A folk song played at a rock 'n' roll tempo, on instruments you could find in your home, 'Rock Island Line' took things back to basics and then made them all sound brand new, British and brash.

———

It wasn't only the nation's youth who were intrigued to find a Lead Belly song in the Top Ten. The American song collector Alan Lomax, who with his father John had been responsible for discovering Lead Belly singing in Angola Penitentiary some twenty years earlier, was living in London at the time and would certainly have pricked up his ears to hear 'Rock Island Line' on the radio.

Born in Mississippi in 1867, Lomax senior was very much an academic when it came to song collecting. His son Alan, born in 1915, had the energy of the Machine Age about him, always looking for new technological methods to record material. Both were respected folklorists, but Alan always sought out the political context that inspired the song. For him, folk music was the unedited voice of the people and he did everything in his power to amplify the messages it contained.

In 1937, Alan Lomax, aged twenty-one, was given the first paid position at the Archive of American Folk Song at the Library of Congress in Washington, DC. The money was lousy, a little over $30 a week, but the very fact that the government was willing to pay for the people's songs to be collected and published marked a significant watershed in American political culture.

This change in attitude was thanks in great part to Franklin D. Roosevelt, who had been elected president in 1933, with the US in the grip of the Great Depression. In his inaugural address, Roosevelt made it clear who he thought was culpable and outlined how he intended to put things right: 'The money changers have fled from their high seats in the temple of our civilisation. We may now restore that temple to the ancient truths. The measure of the restoration lies in the extent to which we apply social values more noble than mere monetary profit.'

Key among these social values was culture. 'The American Dream', said Roosevelt, 'was the promise not only of economic and social justice but also of cultural enrichment.' When the Works Progress Administration was set up to employ people in the creation of public works, it wasn't only infrastructure projects that were funded. As part of Roosevelt's New Deal programme, $27 million was spent on the employment of artists, musicians, actors, writers and historians under a WPA programme known as Federal Project Number One.

Beginning in July 1935, Federal One had five components: the Federal Art Project, the Federal Music Project, the Federal Theatre Project, the Federal Writers Project and the Historical Records Survey. In the spirit of the age, the work they produced tended to glorify the strength, craft and ingenuity of American labour. Federal One money allowed Alan Lomax to organise concerts by Aunt Molly Jackson, a singer of union songs from Harlan County, Kentucky. He used the funding to record long interviews with the great Creole pianist and composer Jelly Roll Morton. He was able to hire the nineteen-year-old activist and banjo player Pete Seeger to be his assistant. And in March 1940, Lomax coaxed a recalcitrant Woody Guthrie into the Library of Congress studio to make his first recordings. The only drawback to receiving public money was that it brought his work under political scrutiny.

When the US was drawn into the Second World War following Japan's surprise attack on Pearl Harbor in December 1941, an atmosphere of paranoia descended on Washington. Such was the fear of Japanese invasion that Congress passed a series of laws depriving American citizens of Japanese descent of their constitutional right to due process. Almost all the Japanese American population, around 120,000 people, were forcibly removed from their homes on the west coast and interned in military camps during the spring of 1942.

Around the same time, Alan Lomax was asked to come to FBI headquarters in Washington for what he assumed was a routine matter of increased wartime security. Instead, after being put under oath, he was interrogated about his political beliefs, particularly with regard to his relationship with the Communist Party. It was the beginning of a dark period in American history, when anyone who spoke out about inequality, racism or workers' rights could find themselves branded a traitor. Lomax was angered by the FBI's insinuations, but he didn't let them deter him from promoting the people's music. However, when the war ended and the Soviet Union emerged as America's rival for global hegemony, those perceived to be encouraging left-wing views in the arts came under further suspicion.

The House Un-American Activities Committee was set up to investigate subversion or propaganda that attacked or criticised 'the form of government guaranteed by the US constitution'. In 1947, the committee opened hearings into alleged communist influence in Hollywood. As a result, some three hundred artists were blacklisted by the film industry. In June 1950, the right-wing magazine *Counterattack* published a pamphlet entitled *Red Channels: The Report of Communist Influence in Radio and Television*, listing 151 figures in the entertainment world who, it alleged, were subversives. Among those on the list were Leonard Bernstein, Dashiell Hammett, Yip Harburg, Gypsy Rose Lee, Arthur Miller, Dorothy Parker, Pete Seeger, Orson Welles and Alan Lomax.

When Congress began preparing the McCarran Act, a law that would require any citizen suspected of subversive activities to register with the government which also contained provisions to prevent them from leaving the country, the atmosphere in which Lomax worked became decidedly chilly. Speaking at the Midcentury International Folklore Conference at Indiana University in the summer of 1950, Lomax put forward the idea of a series of albums that would record the ethnic music of the world. When Columbia Records offered to fund the project, Lomax took the opportunity to leave the country, sailing for Europe on 24 September 1950. He always denied that he had left to avoid being blacklisted, but in notes he made during his Atlantic crossing he bid farewell to America and his family, declaring, 'No more fear for me now.'

Lomax found a welcome in England, where his reputation as a song collector was well known. The United States Information Service in Grosvenor Square had a record library, open to public access, that contained everything released by the Library of Congress, including Lomax's field recordings of blues singers. Ron Gould recalls he'd often ask to hear a particular record, only to be told that it had been taken out by a Mr Tony Donegan and never returned.*

Lomax traversed western Europe, recording folk artists and scouring national sound archives, seeking material for Columbia's *World Library of Folk and Primitive Music* project. He had imagined it would take about a year to complete, but it was in fact to become his life's work.

By late 1955, he was living in London, picking up what work he could as a freelance writer and broadcaster between forays recording folk music around Britain and Ireland. When his plans for a children's television play based on the songs of Woody Guthrie and others fell through, he took the idea to Joan Littlewood, director of the Theatre Workshop, and together they turned his script

---

* Lonnie was unrepentant, admitting years later that he'd stolen a copy of Muddy Waters' plantation recordings that Lomax had cut in 1941. 'I borrowed it and never took it back. I told them I'd lost it and paid the fine . . . quite happily.' The fact that he'd deprived blues fans like Ron Gould of access to Muddy's first recordings never seemed to have troubled his conscience.

into a western-themed Christmas pantomime at the Theatre Royal, Stratford East.

Based on American folk songs, *The Big Rock Candy Mountain* required someone to play the role of the Cowboy, who sat at the side of the stage, singing the songs that moved the plot along. For this role, Lomax was able to call upon an acquaintance who had recently arrived from New York, Jack (later Ramblin' Jack) Elliott. To those who encountered him on the streets of London, Elliott was the epitome of the cowboy singer: Stetson hat, lumberjack shirt, Levi jeans and western boots, carrying an acoustic guitar. And the songs he sang projected the image of a life spent drifting around the States, picking up tunes and guitar licks as he went. For audiences who had never seen a pair of Levi's, nor heard anyone play guitar in the style of Mother Maybelle Carter, Jack Elliott was the real deal. The truth was a little more prosaic.

The son of a doctor and an elementary school teacher, Elliott Adnopoz had been born in Brooklyn in 1931. When he was nine years old, his parents took him to the World Championship Rodeo, held annually in New York's Madison Square Gardens. Amid all the bronco busting, steer roping and trick riding, the highlight was a performance by Gene Autry, America's top singing cowboy, who had starred in six movies in 1940 alone. After dismounting from his trusty steed, Champion, Autry sang his signature tune, 'Back in the Saddle Again'. By the end of the evening, young Elliott had abandoned any thoughts of becoming a doctor like his father. At the age of fifteen he ran away from home to join a travelling rodeo. His parents found him and brought him home, but not before he'd been introduced to the art of storytelling and folk singing by a rodeo clown named Brahma Rogers.

When he got back to Brooklyn, Elliott, with the help of a cowboy songbook, taught himself to play guitar and was soon spending his Sunday afternoons in Greenwich Village, where fans of 'hillbilly' music would gather to play songs on guitars, fiddles, banjos and dulcimers. It was in this milieu that he was introduced not only to the music of Woody Guthrie, but to the man himself.

Suffering from the onset of the debilitating Huntington's Disease that would eventually kill him, Guthrie hadn't been in a recording studio for four years when Adnopoz first met him in 1951. By then, the nineteen-year-old was calling himself Jack Elliott and had just hitch-hiked home from a trip to the west coast, singing Woody's songs at every stop on the way. Guthrie must have seen something of himself in the youngster, because Jack was soon living at Woody's house on Mermaid Avenue, sleeping on the couch, part babysitter, part apprentice.

The arrival of Jack Elliott gave Guthrie a chance to secure his legacy. As his condition worsened, he revealed all of his songs, stories and playing techniques to Elliott, who was only too eager to learn everything he could about the life that Guthrie had led. There was no formal teaching as such, but by watching and listening intently to what Guthrie was doing and saying, Elliott perfected all of his mannerisms, both musical and verbal.

Elliott would never become a great songwriter like his hero, but his skill lay in his ability to evoke the spirit of the songs he performed, his laconic introductions giving the impression that you were listening to him while sitting around a campfire on some cattle drive in the Old West. Crucially, he'd also gleaned Guthrie's ability to pick up a guitar and sing for his supper without any hint of embarrassment, a skill that would stand him in good stead when he arrived in England in September 1955.

Elliott had made a lot of contacts as Guthrie's apprentice, but he had no career to speak of, relying on busking and the occasional gig for his income as he rambled around the US in the early 1950s. His trip to Europe was instigated by June Hammerstein, an aspiring actor he'd met in Topanga Canyon. Jack was smitten and June agreed to marry him if he would take her to Europe. She figured that if he could earn some money busking over here, he'd surely be able to earn some money busking over there.

With impeccable timing, the couple arrived in London at the height of the singing cowboy craze and Elliott soon found himself in demand. His first port of call was Alan Lomax, who had been one of Woody Guthrie's earliest champions. By late 1955, the Dust Bowl Balladeer who had charmed Lomax in 1940 was a shadow of his former self, hospitalised with the incurable genetic disorder that affected his muscle co-ordination and mental function. Guthrie's visible decline greatly distressed his friends. Powerless to help the man, they each did what they could to ensure that his music would live on. Jack Elliott, seen as Guthrie's protégé, would be a key figure in this movement until Bob Dylan took the baton from him in 1961.

Jamming at the 44 Club, 1956: (*front row, left to right*) Russell Quay, Hylda Sims and Jack Elliott; John Hasted plays banjo behind Quay

Lomax introduced Elliott to Bill Leader, who ran Topic Records, a tiny independent label that had begun life in 1939 as the record label of the Workers' Music Association, the cultural arm of the Communist Party of Great Britain. Distributing its records by mail order, the label believed that music was a weapon to be utilised in the class struggle and featured artists such as A. L. Lloyd and Ewan MacColl. Although Topic had never released a long-playing record, Lomax convinced Leader to make an album of Jack Elliott singing the songs of Woody Guthrie. Recorded in October 1955 in the living room of Ewan MacColl's mother's house in Devon, the six-track *Woody Guthrie's Blues* was Elliott's first record and the only one to be released on an 8" disc.

In November, Elliott made a huge impression on music journalist Brian Nicholls, who ran into him at one of the National Jazz Federation's monthly 'New Orleans Encore' concerts at the Royal Festival Hall. 'We met a most intriguing character at the beginning of the month,' Nicholls told the readers of *Jazz Journal*, 'a real character, not one of the pseudo Bohemians one meets around town nowadays. We came across him quite by chance, singing folk blues and hillbillies. He certainly had the authentic touch, both in the material he was singing and in his appearance – a sort of non-dude cowboy outfit. The audience loved it and he certainly brought a fresh touch to the Recital Room.'

Jack's role as the Cowboy in *The Big Rock Candy Mountain* garnered even greater praise. On 28 December, *The Times* contained a round-up of the Christmas pantomimes running in the London suburbs. There was praise for Dick Emery in *Aladdin* at the Golders Green Hippodrome, *Puss in Boots* was deemed sophisticated in Wimbledon, Arthur Askey shone in Streatham's *Babes in the Wood*, and the Widow Twankey had a 'blancmange-like resemblance to the Prince Regent' in *Aladdin* at the Chiswick Empire. However, the review of *The Big*

Rock Candy Mountain at the Theatre Royal, Stratford East, was of a different magnitude altogether. Within the first paragraph, the pantomime was compared favourably with *Waiting for Godot*. The set has a 'primeval quality', the writer tells us, and the characters dream of escaping from what they love, Mother Nature. The whole thing 'recalls the legend of the two tramps in Mr Samuel Beckett's play'. Such high praise was somewhat tempered by the fact that the review was written by one Alan Lomax.

For his next project, Lomax was involved in a TV production of *The Dark of the Moon*, a play set in the Appalachian Mountains concerning two bewitched lovers. Based loosely on the folk song 'Barbara Allen', it had been a huge success on Broadway in the mid-40s and was now to be broadcast live in the London area as part of the ITV Television Playhouse series on 5 April 1956, starring Vivian Matalon, Paddy Webster and George Margo. In need of someone to play authentic Appalachian folk music, Lomax called on an old family friend who he knew was travelling in Europe at the time.

Peggy Seeger was the nineteen-year-old banjo-playing daughter of Charles Seeger, a pioneering ethno-musicologist and song collector, and Ruth Crawford, a composer and folklorist. Both had worked with Lomax and his father, John, at the Library of Congress in the 1930s. Peggy had grown up surrounded by folk music. Her parents' house in Chevy Chase was always full of musicians – her half-brother Pete would come by and play banjo for her and her brother Mike when they were children; Lead Belly was a frequent visitor, as was Woody Guthrie; even the housemaid, Elizabeth Cotten, was a folk artist of considerable talent.

By the early 1950s, the McCarthyite witch-hunts had cast their shadow over the family. Pete Seeger was named in the *Red Channels* list of subversives, leading to his band, the Weavers, being blacklisted. Charles Seeger, who had been music critic for the communist

Daily Worker in the 1930s, had the renewal of his passport turned down on the grounds that he was 'a person supporting Communist movements'. Undeterred by such blatant Red-baiting, Peggy went to Radcliffe College in Cambridge, Massachusetts, to study Russian. Following the death of her mother and her father's subsequent remarriage, she was sent to Leiden in Holland to study for a year, by coincidence crossing the Atlantic on the same ship as Jack and June Elliott, the Holland America liner MS *Maasdam*.

Peggy was lodging with her eldest half-brother, Charles, but after falling out with her sister-in-law, she took her banjo and a knapsack and hit the road. 'Around Christmastime 1955 I was picked up by a Catholic priest who saw the guitar and said, "I'm taking a travelling troupe of theatre performers to East Berlin. Would you like to come?" Well, I was a yes-girl and I said yes, definitely. So we picked up thirteen refugees who were fleeing communism. We brought them back to Belgium, where I was their little mother for three months. We had a tiny little two-up, two-down, and the priest started to convert me to Catholicism.'

Some friends became worried about the tone of Seeger's letters, so they came to rescue her. 'They found me at the table saying my rosary and they said, "We're leaving tomorrow." They had a little Fiat and took me to Denmark.' She was staying in a youth hostel in Copenhagen when a call came through from Alan Lomax in London. 'He said there's a television programme, they're doing *Dark of the Moon*, they're on budget and they need a female who plays the banjo and, well, Alan Lomax had been in my life ever since I could remember, so that's how I first came to England.'

'Rock Island Line' was still in the Top Twenty when Lomax met a thin and dishevelled Peggy Seeger at Waterloo Station on 25 March. Decca Records had a substantial hit on their hands but were unable to follow it up. They had failed to sign the Chris Barber Jazz Band to a formal record deal, preferring to pay the musicians a session fee of £75, which they split six ways, Lonnie picking up an additional fee of £3 10s. for his vocal performance on the skiffle tracks. Though his record sold over a million copies, under this deal Donegan never received a penny in royalties from the label.

Without an artist under contract, Decca were stymied. If anyone had been paying even scant attention, they might have realised that they had more material by the Lonnie Donegan Skiffle Group in their vaults – the versions of 'Nobody's Child' and 'Wabash Cannonball' that had been recorded during the *New Orleans Joys* session some twenty months before. Instead, they decided to release a couple of live tracks from a Chris Barber Jazz Band concert at the Royal Festival Hall in October 1954.

Decca must have been desperate, because the A side, 'Diggin' My Potatoes', was never going to get any airplay in mid-50s Britain. The song, written and originally recorded by Washboard Sam, uses euphemisms to tell the tale of a faithless wife discovered by her husband fellating another man. Not really the sort of thing you'd hear on *Housewives' Choice*. It sank without trace, but not before being savaged in *Jazz Journal*, whose reviewer dismissed it as suffering badly in comparison to Lead Belly's version.

What *Jazz Journal* failed to grasp was that the majority of teenagers who put 'Rock Island Line' into the charts weren't using Lead Belly as their main reference point. To them, Lonnie Donegan was competing with the new generation of young, guitar-toting rockers coming out of the US, the latest of whom featured in an advert that ran alongside the Top Twenty in the NME during the week that Peggy Seeger arrived in Britain. Heralding the first UK release by the man the ad calls 'The King of Western Bop', the copy introduces Elvis Presley to British record buyers.

'Take a dash of Johnnie Ray, add a sprinkling of Billy Daniels and what have you got? Elvis Presley, whom American teenagers are calling the King of Western Bop. He's twenty, single, scorns Western kit for snazzy, jazzy outfits. Now he bids emotionally for recognition in Britain with "I Was the One" and "Heartbreak Hotel".'

Snazzy? Jazzy? What kind of singing cowboy was this?

13

SKIFFLE ARTIFICIAL

Although it had emerged from their scene, skiffle was never going to be welcomed by the hardcore fans of trad jazz. They took great pride in adhering to what they perceived to be the tenets of New Orleans style and were dismissive of anything that smacked of commerciality. The popular success of 'Rock Island Line' and the elevation of Lonnie Donegan – one of their own – to the pop charts only served to exacerbate their prejudices. In April 1956, *Jazz Journal* gave Graham Boatfield a whole page in which to vent his spleen in an article entitled 'Skiffle Artificial'.

'The fact that records by English "skiffle" groups, so-called, are popular enough to merit performance on BBC request programmes', Boatfield declared, 'makes it necessary for us to look more closely at this phenomenon.' Clearly, he felt these kids demanding to hear skiffle on the radio didn't know what they were doing. After stating that he finds the experience of listening to skiffle 'painful in the extreme', he dismisses Ken Colyer's group as sounding like 'a bankrupt pier-show of black-faced minstrels'. Lonnie Donegan fares even worse, Boatfield deriding his records as giving the impression of 'a number of intoxicated hillbillies returning from some over-lengthy orgy'. He goes on to outline an argument that would find a pernicious echo in some purist quarters of the 60s folk revival, namely the notion that you shouldn't sing songs that don't come from your own local traditions. 'London voices, probably best naturally employed in singing "Knees Up Mother Brown" are not quite happy singing "Midnight Special".'

At a time when vintage jazz records were hard to come by in the UK, trad jazz critics took on the role of a priesthood, custodians and defenders of a high musical culture that could be enjoyed by mere mortals, but not fully appreciated without priestly intercession. Yet Boatfield was right to be concerned. Within a decade, those kids who were requesting skiffle on the BBC would come to dominate the airwaves and consign trad jazz to the margins.

Not every music journalist was as snotty about skiffle. *Music Mirror* covered jazz from the more popular end. Among the reviews and interviews, it carried articles that explained how to get the best from the newfangled hi-fi equipment that was coming onto the market (the answer was to build it yourself). Other pieces explained the difference between Dixieland jazz and the New Orleans variety, something that would never need to be explained to the more highbrow readers of *Jazz Journal*.

In February 1956, *Music Mirror* ran a substantial article about skiffle, written and illustrated by Paul Oliver, a twenty-eight-year-old art teacher at Harrow County School for Boys, in the north-western suburbs of London. Oliver would go on to become a leading authority on the blues and his obvious enthusiasm for African American music is tangible in everything he wrote. Rather than dismiss skiffle as disrespectful and derivative, he saw the sudden popularity of 'Rock Island Line' as an opportunity to introduce young listeners to the blues.

He begins by correctly identifying skiffle as 'a phenomenon almost exclusively of the British jazz world'. Recognising that there have been American artists who have used the word, he goes on to observe that 'one can look in vain in the American jazz magazines for the equivalent of "Europe's only Skiffle & Blues Club". The American jazz club or concert does not feature a "skiffle session" halfway through the programme, but the time appears to be fast approaching

191

when the popularity of a jazz club will largely depend on the inclusion of a "Skiffle Group". Turning to the standard histories of jazz and their derivatives is unlikely to help one understand the meaning of this branch of jazz, for neither the music nor even the word "skiffle" appears in any of them.'

Like a good teacher, Oliver explores the way that the term 'skiffle' was used during the 1920s and 30s, noting that it was never attached to any combination of musicians that resembled Lonnie Donegan's Skiffle Group. Furthermore, he finds it doubtful if terms such as 'skiffle music' were ever in use in the African American community, as the music was simply a part of their social environment and didn't require a specific label to identify it.

'It is only now, when jazz has become a self-conscious minor art form with exponents rather touchy about any disrespect for it, that labels and classifications become necessary. So the "skiffle band" has been born: not to provide background music to an uninhibited party, but as a specially featured instrumental group which has a faint link with the "jook bands" of Mississippi in its constitution, but includes in its repertoire folk songs, work songs, spirituals, gospel songs and the blues of the American Negro, with white folk tunes and hobo songs added for good measure.'

It's clear from this article that Paul Oliver knows exactly what he is listening to, and although he repeats many of Graham Boatfield's criticisms of Colyer's and Donegan's recordings, there is no condescension in his comments. Rather, he sees the popularity of skiffle as a means to an end: skiffle groups 'have inspired in many jazz enthusiasts an interest and an appetite for the more primitive and most authentic of American musical forms. It is up to the record companies now to meet this interest and potential market to the benefit of themselves, collectors – and the skiffle groups.'

The success of 'Rock Island Line' meant Donegan was suddenly in demand as a solo performer. When playing with the Barber band, his lack of musical training was no hindrance, as most trad jazzers played by ear. Artists booked to sing on Cyril Stapleton's popular radio show, however, were expected to turn up with the sheet music of their big hit so that the BBC Show Band could reproduce the arrangement heard on record. Donegan had no such thing and when asked to write out a simple chart for the musicians to follow, he had to admit that he couldn't read music.

His embarrassment was saved by the band's guitarist, who stepped in to help out. Bert Weedon had been playing guitar since before the war and would later gain fame and fortune selling his *Play in a Day* guitar tutorial to a generation of kids inspired by Lonnie Donegan. He recognised that skiffle marked a sea change in the way people would think of the guitarist. 'Congratulations,' he told Donegan. 'You're the first man to have made any money out of the guitar. Bloody well done!'

Donegan's sudden success kept him busy in the recording studio, cutting three tracks on 11 January 1956 for a new EP entitled *Skiffle Session*, with a band that featured Dickie Bishop on vocals and guitar, Chris Barber on bass and Ron Bowden on drums. The session was supervised by Denis Preston, who had been smart enough to sign Donegan to a personal contract when he cut the *Backstairs Session* EP for Polygon Records' Jazz Today imprint the previous summer. Since then, the label had undergone a significant expansion that would make it one of the major players in the following decade.

Pye Ltd had been manufacturing radio equipment in Cambridge since 1896. Their technical prowess was such that they provided the wireless receivers for the first radio broadcasts made by the BBC in 1922. In the years since the war, they had become the premier provider of radio equipment in the UK. In 1953, they were approached by Nixa Records, an independent label that specialised in European pop. Having recently expanded their business to include classical music, Nixa were looking for a partner to provide funds for expansion, and in 1953 Pye bought a controlling share of the business to create the Pye Nixa label.

Around the same time, Polygon Records finally managed to chart one of Petula Clark's singles, at the eighteenth attempt. 'The Little Shoemaker' reached number seven, but as often happens, this success only served to illustrate the limitations of Polygon's independent operations. Clark released another eight singles in the following two years, but none matched the success of 'The Little Shoemaker'. The owners of the label, Clark's father Leslie and her producer, Alan A. Freeman, decided they needed to be part of a larger operation, and in 1955 they joined forces with Pye Nixa. Petula Clark's next single, 'Suddenly There's a Valley', reached the Top Ten, beginning a decade of success for the artist.

As part of the Polygon deal, Pye Nixa acquired the rights to Denis Preston's Jazz Today imprint, which included the Chris Barber Jazz Band and their banjo player, Lonnie Donegan. Whether Pye were aware that the trad jazz banjo player they now had under contract would go on to become one of the label's top-selling artists is questionable. When Jim Irvin was compiling the sleeve notes for a Pye Records retrospective, a former employee confided that it was an enormous stroke of luck that Donegan ended up on their roster.

Such was the career of Lonnie Donegan. No record company A & R man had come to him offering a lucrative contract to record some of that amazing skiffle music because they believed it would be huge. He'd accidentally recorded a hit single and now had been inadvertently signed up by a major record label. After years of plunking away in the back rooms of pubs up and down the country, he'd become an overnight sensation and everybody wanted to hear what he was going to do next.

The first Lonnie Donegan record to appear on the Pye Nixa label was a reissue of the *Backstairs Session* EP, rushed out in February 1956. It featured the same picture sleeve as the version put out some five months before, but the words 'Jazz Today' had been replaced by the Nixa logo. This subtle shift failed to entice the public and, like Decca's attempt to cash in on Donegan's sudden success, the record didn't chart.

This appears to have spooked the label as they put the planned *Skiffle Session* EP on hold. Someone decided that the best way to follow 'Rock Island Line' was with another song from Lead Belly's repertoire that began with a spoken introduction. Thus Donegan's next single began, 'Now this here's a story about a racehorse called Stewball. Now Stewball was born down in California and when I was down there the other day, the jockeys was telling me they don't think it's an ordinary horse at all, in fact they all say it blew there in a storm.' No ordinary horse is right: when Donegan recorded that introduction, Stewball was already over two hundred years old.

Long before the pop single was invented, songwriters hit on a way of making money by printing topical lyrics to familiar tunes and selling them on the streets. Funny, ribald, satirical, political, these broadside ballads were hugely popular in late-eighteenth- and early-nineteenth-century England, part of an anarchic literary subculture that thrived in the years before the Industrial Revolution.

During the 1840s, when millions were leaving Britain and Ireland for America, Henry Mayhew studied the working lives of the lower classes of London in a series of newspaper articles. In *London Labour and the London Poor*, published in 1851, he described the various hawkers selling printed ballads on the streets of the city. There were 'long song sellers', who sold sheets three feet long, with songs printed in three columns, crying, 'Three yards for a penny'; pinners-up, who displayed their wares pinned to a wall; and, most numerous of all, the chaunters, who sang the ballads they were selling. Mayhew noted that this latter group often sang political or sporting songs, sometimes referring to events that had happened that very day.

Later English Broadside Ballads, published in 1975, contains a song entitled 'Scew Ball', which begins:

> *Come gentleman sportsman I pray listen all*
> *I will sing you a song in praise of Scew Ball*
> *And how he came over you shall understand*
> *It was by Squire Merwin, the pearl of our land*
> *And of his late actions that I've heard before*
> *He was lately challeng'd by one Sir Ralph Gore*
> *For five hundred guineas on the plains of Kildare*
> *To run with Miss Sportly, that charming grey mare.*

Over eleven verses, the ballad tells the story of a racehorse that converses with its owner, telling him to venture thousands of pounds in wagers, for he will definitely win the race. While the talking horse is clearly poetic licence, the song is based on historical events.

'Skewbald' is an old English word describing horses of a chestnut or bay colour which also have white patches in their coat, and records show that a horse of that name began racing in England in 1743. Merwin and Gore were well-known figures in Irish society and both served as president of the Irish Jockey Club. In 1752, the *London Evening Post* carried the following report: 'On Monday last the Races began at the Curragh of Kildare, when the grand match for £300 between Sir Ralph Gore's Grey Mare and Arthur Mervin Esqr.'s horse, Scuball, was run which was won with great ease by the latter.'

By 1829, Scewball's fame had crossed the Atlantic, with printed copies of the ballad appearing in US cities. Slaves working on the plantations created their own version, relocating the story to their own locale and changing the horse's name to Stewball. In 1934, John and Alan Lomax, collecting prison songs in the southern states, found 'it is the most widely known of the chain-gang songs in the states we visited and by far the most constant as to tune and words'.

Lead Belly recorded 'Stewball' in New York City in 1946, backed by Woody Guthrie and Cisco Houston, performing the song as it would have been heard on the prison farm, call-and-response style. It was this version that provided the template for Donegan's take on the song, and given that his mother came from Ireland, Lonnie could make some ancestral claim to it.

Still a member of the Chris Barber Jazz Band when he recorded 'Stewball' on 20 February 1956, Donegan called upon his bandmates to back him in the studio. Barber once again picked up the double bass, Dickie Bishop played guitar and sang back-up, with Ron Bowden on drums.

'Stewball' begins with a jaunty rhythm, gaining in intensity as the song progresses. As with 'Rock Island Line', the guitars are strummed frantically while the bass provides the musicality. The addition of drums was the first clear sign that Donegan wasn't a purist like Colyer. Lead Belly never used a drummer, nor did Woody Guthrie, but if Donegan wanted to compete in the pop charts, he needed the sonic attack that a full drum kit can provide.

For Ron Bowden, that transition was a breeze. 'It was terrific being on those records. I can't remember any hassle about the session at all. My part certainly was very straightforward, but Lonnie gave his all, all the time. He worked bloody hard when he was on stage and he was always pushing the tempos.'

For the flip side, Chris Barber suggested 'Long Gone Lost John', originally recorded in 1928 for Paramount by Papa Charlie Jackson. Born in New Orleans in 1887, Jackson was the first self-accompanied blues musician to release a record. As Donegan explains in the now standard spoken intro, this here's the story of an escaped convict. Donegan shortened the title to 'Lost John', extended the refrain and added a couplet to the end of the song that said much about his cheeky self-confidence: 'If anybody asks you who sung the song, tell 'em Lonnie Donegan was here and gone.'

'Stewball' was released in April 1956 and was recognised by most reviewers as a worthy follow-up to 'Rock Island Line'. The jazz critics were still baffled at Donegan's success. James Asman declared that 'as a jazz record, it can only be described as phoney'. However, he did have an inkling that there was something going on here, something different from that which had come before. 'I suspect that this is really a hardworking attempt to recapture the vast record buying public which rushed to the shops for the accidental Decca recording. One must, after all, remember that Donegan is now quite a remarkable figure in the popular field. Tin Pan Alley frankly admits its ignorance to the causes which threw an obscure guitar player in what was originally an amateur revivalist jazz band into the Hit Parade. The ones I talked to last week were completely baffled about the whole business.'

The manner in which Asman refers to 'Rock Island Line' as 'the accidental Decca recording' is a measure of the shockwave that followed Donegan's initial entry into the Top Ten. No wonder Tin Pan Alley was baffled. They ran the UK pop industry on the basis that whatever was a hit in the US was likely to be popular in the UK. By paying close attention to the *Billboard* charts, labels could record versions of American hits by UK artists and get the song in the shops before the original was released here. A huge amount of time and effort went into choosing and promoting the right song, yet along comes this guitar-strumming upstart who picks some obscure folk song from the repertoire of a dead blues singer, and before anyone can say 'Never tango with an Eskimo', he's storming up the charts.

If Tin Pan Alley was stunned by Donegan's success, what happened next was unprecedented. 'Rock Island Line' had been released in America on 6 March, on Decca's US subsidiary London Records. Ten days later, the *NME* was declaring that Donegan's single, 'already one of the most astonishing phenomena that 1956 is likely to produce . . . looks like becoming a quick fire sensation in the USA'. The report went on to say that the single had received a tremendous reception from American DJs, selling over two hundred thousand records in the days since its release. A few weeks later, in one of the most audacious examples of selling coals to Newcastle, the *NME* pop charts page showed 'Rock Island Line' entering the US Top Fifteen at number twelve, just as 'Stewball' was released in the UK.

The British music industry may have been bemused, but their American counterparts knew a hit when they heard one. Without waiting to discover what it all meant, they moved quickly to grab a slice of the action. When 'Rock Island Line' entered the *Billboard* charts, Mercury Records already had a copycat version in the shops, sung by Len Dreslar. A week later, there were a further four available. Don Cornell, a thirty-five-year-old nightclub singer, cut the song for Coral; Epic released a version by Jimmy Gavin; Merrill Moore, a boogie-woogie country pianist, released an up-tempo version for Capitol; and a nineteen-year-old crooner from the Bronx named Bobby Darin made 'Rock Island Line' his debut single. This fevered competition led London Records to place a half-page advert in *Billboard* declaring that Lonnie's was 'the original and hottest record in America'. It didn't deter the imitators one bit.

As the song climbed the charts, yet more versions appeared, all clamouring for a slice of Donegan's success. Grandpa Jones, a forty-three-year-old banjo player who appeared in character as an aged old-time musician, released the song on King Records, while Jimmy Work, a cowboy singer in the style of Lefty Frizzell, recorded a version for

Dot. Rod McKuen, a poet, songwriter and author who would go on to translate the work of Jacques Brel and write songs for Frank Sinatra and Barbra Streisand, made his recording debut with a version of the song, backed by Rock Murphy and His Rockets.

What is notable about these covers is that all of them repeat Lonnie Donegan's story about the tollgate outside New Orleans. None have taken their cue from Lead Belly nor gone back to the Library of Congress recordings to hear how it was originally sung by Kelly Pace on the Cummins State Farm. Even Johnny Cash, who opened his first album for Sun Records with 'Rock Island Line', repeats Donegan's intro. Twenty years later at the London Palladium, Cash introduced the song by calling on Lonnie, who was in the audience, to stand up and take a bow. The Man in Black claimed to have recorded his version before Donegan's, 'but I guess we didn't get it played on the right stations'. In fact, it wasn't until 13 July 1957 that Cash recorded 'Rock Island Line' at the Sun Studios in Memphis, over a year after Donegan was in the US Top Ten.

The most intriguing version was released by Stan Freberg 'and His Sniffle Group'. Freberg was a thirty-year-old satirist who had his own radio show. In the early 50s, he made a career out of poking fun at the hits of the day. His take on 'Rock Island Line' also utilises Lonnie's spoken introduction, to great comic effect. The fact that Freberg coupled his version with a parody of 'Heartbreak Hotel' by Elvis Presley says something about the way that Donegan was perceived in the US.

Of these cover versions, only Don Cornell's made it into the *Billboard* charts, climbing no higher than fifty-nine. Born Luigi Francisco Varlaro in 1919, Cornell happened to be touring on the British variety circuit as 'Rock Island Line' began ascending the American charts. Looking to get some free publicity, Cornell's manager, the New York impresario Manny Greenfield, concocted stories about the fierce competition between the two versions of the song in the US charts. It was nonsense, of course, but it generated welcome headlines. 'Don and Donegan are fighting out a record battle over "Rock Island Line",' claimed the *NME* on 16 March.

No doubt seeking to stoke up this 'rivalry', Greenfield invited Donegan to the opening night of Cornell's week at the Finsbury Park Empire. At the after-show reception, Greenfield was astonished to find that Donegan didn't have any representation in the US. Why would he? He was still technically employed as the banjo player in the Chris Barber Jazz Band. 'How would you like to go to America?' asked Greenfield. 'Who is going to pay the air fare?' countered Donegan warily. 'Oh, don't worry about that, I'll sort it out . . . just sign here.'

What could Lonnie do? His song was storming up the US charts and now he was being offered the chance to visit the land of his musical heroes. 'So I signed a contract for American representation, not knowing what the hell it was. Then I went to Chris, who said it was okay, they would get Dickie Bishop to play banjo in the band for a couple of weeks, until I got back.'

Donegan's timing could not have been better. Just six months earlier, the American Federation of Musicians had finally reached an agreement with the Musicians' Union to bring to an end the twenty-year embargo on British musicians touring in the US. After intense lobbying by American bandleader Stan Kenton and British counterpart Ted Heath, AFM president James Petrillo agreed to a reciprocal exchange, provided each band only performed full concerts – no club dates nor radio or TV appearances were allowed. Even with these restrictions, this was a victory for the MU, who had been pushing for such a deal since the early 50s. Although initially adopted for a trial period, the reciprocal arrangement, whereby a band wishing to tour the US could only do so if a similar American outfit toured the UK and vice versa, remained in place well into the 1980s.

For British fans of popular music, the news that they would at last be able to see their heroes perform live was cause for celebration. To get some sense of how the average jazz fan must have felt during the two long decades that the ban remained in place, imagine what it would have been like if no American artists had performed in Britain from the time of the skiffle craze to the rise of punk rock, and no British artist had been allowed to tour the US for the same period. No Beatles at Shea Stadium, nor Rolling Stones at Altamont. Jimi Hendrix would never have emerged from the London clubs nor Dylan been heckled at the Manchester Free Trade Hall. With the lifting of this cultural embargo, it felt like jazz had finally been taken off the ration.

Stan Kenton's West Coast modern swing orchestra were greeted like heroes when they arrived to tour the UK in March 1956, and the music papers were abuzz with rumours of other tours being planned. On 4 May, the *NME* reported that Louis Armstrong had secured an exchange with Freddy Randall's trad band, who, it reported, would be joining a rock 'n' roll package tour through the American south headlined by Bill Haley and His Comets. On the same page it was revealed that negotiations were under way to bring a young singer whom the headline referred to as 'Elvin Presley' to the UK. Good luck with that.

A week later, the *NME* informed its readers that Lonnie Donegan would be leaving for the US on the following Monday, heading for New York and a spot on Perry Como's TV show, followed by a trip to Cleveland, then considered the rock 'n' roll capital of America thanks to the work of DJs such as Alan Freed and Bill Randle. The report also broke the news that Donegan had parted company with the Chris Barber Jazz Band.

It was a big call for the banjo player from East Ham. In March 1955, he had married Maureen Tyler. When 'Rock Island Line' took off, the couple were expecting their first child, so Donegan asked his boss for a rise. Barber ran the band as a co-operative – everyone got an equal share of the profits – but Donegan felt this just wasn't fair. Now their audience was full of his fans, paying to hear him sing his hit. Barber stuck to his guns, advising Donegan to think about his long-term security: 'Jazz is your bread and butter. Skiffle is just the jam.'

With singles in the Top Ten on both sides of the Atlantic, Donegan knew which side his bread was buttered. He left for America on 14 May 1956, just a month after the birth of his daughter, Fiona.

14

THE ADVENTURES OF AN IRISH HILLBILLY

A four-engine propeller aircraft flying the London-to-New York route in the mid-50s could take fourteen hours to cross the Atlantic, with refuelling stops at Prestwick in Scotland, Keflavík in Iceland and Gander in Newfoundland, giving Lonnie Donegan plenty of time to consider how American audiences might react to skiffle. In his initial US publicity, Donegan was labelled the 'the Irish Hillbilly'. This was a complete misnomer – 'the Scottish Cockney' would have been a fairer reflection of his roots – but the term linked him in the minds of the record-buying public to another guitar-strumming young artist who had just scored his first number one single.

Coming from poor white southern stock, Elvis Presley was referred to in early articles as 'the Hillbilly Cat'. It was a fitting term. 'Hillbilly' suggested the old-time music much loved in Tennessee, where he was based, while 'Cat' implied a cool appreciation of black rhythm and blues. The label was borne out by the choice of songs that Elvis had cut for Sun Records – a mixture of bluegrass numbers like 'Blue Moon of Kentucky' and souped-up R & B romps such as 'That's All Right'. Like 'The King of Western Bop' and 'The Memphis Flash', these labels were conjured up by middle-aged music journalists trying to make sense of a new phenomenon. Sixty years after the event, the settled term for the music that Elvis was playing while he was at Sun Records is rockabilly.

In *Go Cat Go!*, his 1998 study of rockabilly music and its makers, author Craig Morrison produces a handy list of attributes that he believes helps to define the genre. It's worth examining, if only for the fact that skiffle and rockabilly, exact contemporaries, had many features in common. His first criterion is that there should be an obvious Elvis Presley influence. Given that 'Rock Island Line' was recorded just a week later than Presley's debut single, one can't claim that Lonnie was looking to Elvis, but the King influenced many of the skifflers who followed in his wake.

Morrison believes that rockabilly performers should have a country music background and an awareness of the blues, and while it would be hard for British musicians to be as steeped in country as their American counterparts, Donegan, Dickie Bishop and Johnny Duncan all shared an appreciation of the old-time hillbilly music. The identifiable country and rhythm and blues inflections that Morrison cites were also present in skiffle, as were the blues structures that he highlights. Any band that numbered Ken Colyer, Lonnie Donegan and Alexis Korner among its members, as the original Colyer Skiffle Band did, was bound to contain those ingredients.

The next three items on Morrison's list were all part and parcel of Lonnie Donegan's style, attributes he passed on to his followers: strong rhythm and beat; emotion and feeling; a wild or extreme vocal style. Upright bass, especially if played in a slapped manner, was common to both rockabilly and skiffle, the percussive slap necessary as both Elvis and Lonnie had initially fronted trios without a drummer.

Moderate or fast tempo is another of Morrison's criteria for rockabilly that is also a key aspect of skiffle. His narrow dating of rockabilly to the three-year period of 1954–6 echoes skiffle's own window of success in the years 1956 to 1958. He also decrees that rockabilly must have southern origins. Is it stretching things a little to argue that skiffle emerged in the south-east of England?

That final point aside, out of the dozen rockabilly criteria that Morrison cites, only one is inapplicable to skiffle: use of echo effect.

Such embellishments were available in Britain – producer Joe Meek, then a jobbing engineer, used echo on Humphrey Lyttelton's 1956 single 'Bad Penny Blues' – but skifflers sought authenticity and echo sounded too much like a gimmick.

Interestingly, Morrison's list of things that were a sure sign that a record was *not* rockabilly also apply to skiffle and are most helpful in identifying the pseudo-skiffle records that appeared on the market in the wake of Donegan's success: obvious commercial intent; condescendingly juvenile lyrics; chorus groups, especially female; harmony singing; bland or uninvolved singing; saxophone; electric bass; piano, unless it is Jerry Lee Lewis; weak rhythm; black performers; slower tempos; every year later than 1957.

In early 1956, Elvis Presley and Lonnie Donegan had astounded the musical establishments in their respective countries by appearing, as if from nowhere, in the Top Ten. 'Heartbreak Hotel' and 'Rock Island Line' sounded like they came from an altogether different planet to the sugar-coated pop music of the day. In the UK, the two were perceived as rivals, and the British music papers, while somewhat sceptical of Donegan's talents, felt they should get behind their boy, if only for patriotic reasons.

Just before Donegan left for the US, *Record Mirror* ran a full-page story to highlight the fact that, while Lonnie was a hit in America, Elvis Presley, whose first UK single had been released a week or two before, was failing to catch on over here. To rub in their sense of superiority, they ran a headline that parodied those beloved of US trade paper *Variety*: 'Donegan Socko in States But Limeys May Say Nix on Elvis'.

Much of the British resistance to the newcomer was voiced by fans of Johnnie Ray, who felt that Elvis was a poor imitation of their idol. 'How can Elvis Presley have the nerve to come into show business with no original ideas?' raged Judith Marks from Edgware,

Middlesex, in the *NME*. 'He sings like JR, he stands like JR, but he can't copy JR's showmanship and sincerity.'

It would not be long before Elvis won over British record buyers, his macho swagger proving popular with young men in a way that Johnnie Ray's tear-stained pleading never could. Meanwhile, Lonnie Donegan wasn't quite as 'Socko in the States' as the *NME* had claimed. While sales of 'Rock Island Line' had taken him to a peak of number eight in mid-April, plays on radio and jukeboxes kept the single in the *Billboard* Top Twenty until he arrived in New York.

———

When Lonnie Donegan set foot in the States, Joe Boyd was a fourteen-year-old from New Jersey attending school in Connecticut and listening to Top Forty radio stations such as WINS New York and WPRO from nearby Providence, Rhode Island. In the 60s, Boyd would relocate to England, going on to work as a record producer for artists such as Pink Floyd, Nick Drake, Fairport Convention, REM and myself, but in the spring of 1956, he was intrigued to hear 'Rock Island Line' on pop radio. While happy to dance to Chuck Berry and Fats Domino along with his teenage contemporaries, Boyd was more interested in old blues and jazz records. As the owner of a red vinyl copy of Stinson Records' *Lead Belly Memorial Album, Volume Two*, he was already familiar with 'Rock Island Line'.

'I had a bad attitude about white blues singers, but there was something about Donegan's nasal voice and British accent that made it sound almost as exotic as the Lead Belly version.' Boyd felt that the popular folk music of the period was devoid of real feeling. 'American folk singers mostly sang corny harmonies. Lonnie's attitude and strangely authentic sound was startling and refreshing. I was intrigued by the unselfconsciousness of his performance. I bought his LP and liked almost all the tracks. And when I heard where he was from, it helped fuel a desire to go to England.'

Boyd liked the way that Donegan inhabited the song, resisting the temptation to imitate Lead Belly. 'Outsiders often have a more interesting take on a music than the middle class from the same culture. American artists had too many racial complexes to be that straightforward. It wasn't until Dylan and a few of the Boston folkies like Eric von Schmidt and Geoff Muldaur that I heard white people singing black music in such an appealing way. I think it's safe to say that from 1956 until about 1962, I resisted most white folk singers, except Lonnie Donegan.'

Other teenagers across the States were listening in too. In Queens, the first record Art Garfunkel ever bought with his own money was Donegan's 'Rock Island Line'. A seventeen-year-old Phil Spector performed Lonnie's song – the first thing he learned to play on guitar – at his high-school talent contest in Fairfax, California. Down in New Orleans, Malcolm 'Mac' Rebennack, serving an apprenticeship with Professor Longhair that would later gain him the title Dr John, remembers being inspired by Lonnie's hit. And Buddy Holly, whose band had already opened for Elvis and Bill Haley in his home town of Lubbock, Texas, was so impressed with 'Rock Island Line' that he immediately incorporated it into his set. His drummer, Jerry Allison, later said, 'We thought it was a rock 'n' roll record.'

The Perry Como Show was the highest rated TV show on the NBC network in 1956, regularly reaching 12 million viewers. Donegan, who'd never appeared on TV before, was thrown in at the deep end on his arrival. Having left the Chris Barber band and with no musicians of his own, he faced being accompanied by the house band wherever he was playing in the US. That was no great challenge – by upping the tempo of his guitar playing, he was usually able to drive 'Rock Island Line' to a rousing conclusion. But when he turned up for rehearsals at NBC, the show's producers dropped a bombshell. The American Federation of Musicians had refused to grant him permission to play the guitar. The AFM/MU embargo may have ended, but there were still a few bumps in the road that needed to be ironed out. In the UK, this wouldn't have been an issue. There simply weren't enough guitar-playing singers for the Musicians' Union to be concerned about, so when an artist like Slim Whitman toured, the union had no qualms about letting him play his instrument. The scene in the US was different. The popularity of guitar players was putting the big bands out of business. The AFM weren't going to let some guy from England cause problems for their members.

Donegan was stunned. Here he was, about to make the biggest appearance of his career, and they weren't even going to let him play guitar. 'I feel naked without it,' he complained. 'Take away my guitar and I don't know what to do with my arms.' For the show, he was backed by a trio of guitar, bass and drums that included Al Caiola, who would go on to play the distinctive acoustic guitar riff that introduces 'Mrs Robinson'. 'They were sensational musicians and really wanted to help,' recalled Donegan, 'but they read my songs as country and western. They weren't familiar with this strange music we called skiffle and just had to busk it, which was very difficult as I tend to speed up and get frantic.'

Perry Como's star guest that Saturday night was Hollywood actor Ronald Reagan. The format of the show required Donegan to join Como and Reagan in stilted comedy sketches. The man who would go on to become the fortieth president of the United States appeared baffled by his encounter with the King of Skiffle, asking a question that may have been repeated in a number of households across America that tuned into *The Perry Como Show* that evening: 'What is a Lonnie Donegan?'

The following day, Lonnie flew to Cleveland to appear on *The Bill*

Randle Show, broadcast live on WEWS-TV every Sunday night. Randle was a hugely influential DJ who did much to introduce northern audiences to rockabilly. When Elvis Presley made his first TV appearance in January 1956 on the Dorsey Brothers' *Stage Show*, the compère, fifty-year-old Tommy Dorsey, called on Bill Randle, twenty years his junior, to introduce Presley, the old bandleader seemingly fearful of taking the responsibility for unleashing the Memphis Flash into the living rooms of middle America.

Randle had cut his teeth in Detroit during the late 40s as host of a radio show called *The Interracial Goodwill Hour*, aimed at introducing black artists to white audiences. Randle continued in this vein after moving to Cleveland, promoting concerts at which black and white artists appeared on the same bill. The city had been a hotbed for rock 'n' roll since local DJ Alan Freed began popularising the term on his show. Such was the appetite for rock 'n' roll that Elvis Presley had played his first gig north of the Mason–Dixon Line in the city's Circle Theater in February 1955.*

For his performance on *The Bill Randle Show*, Lonnie was backed by the Jonah Jones Quartet, led by a forty-seven-year-old jazz trumpeter from Louisville, Kentucky. Featuring piano, bass and drums, the quartet were quite at home playing the boogie-woogie and jump blues that had inspired so many of the early rock 'n' rollers, making it much

---

* Eight months later, Presley returned to play a show organised by Randle at the Brooklyn High School in Cleveland's south-western suburbs, a gig that some Elvis scholars cite as a catalyst for his meteoric rise to fame. Randle was being filmed for a documentary entitled *The Pied Piper of Cleveland: A Day in the Life of a Famous Disc Jockey* and, sensing that Presley was on the verge of becoming a national sensation, he had them film Elvis, backed by Scotty Moore and Bill Black, as he whipped the crowd of high-school teens into a frenzy with 'Mystery Train', 'That's All Right', 'Blue Moon of Kentucky' and 'Good Rockin' Tonight'. Randle mentioned the film when introducing Presley on the Dorsey Brothers' show, yet it never saw the light of day. Rumours abound as to why the film was never released. Some even question its existence. *The Pied Piper of Cleveland* has become something of a holy grail for Elvis fans.

easier for Donegan to sing in his own loose style. The next day, they backed him again at a benefit concert for the Girl Scouts of America.

Returning to New York, Donegan took up a two-week engagement at the Town and Country Club, on Flatbush Avenue, where artists such as Judy Garland, Harry Belafonte, Tony Bennett and Sophie Tucker were regular attractions. The owner, Ben Maksik, liked to promote the club as the 'Copacabana of Brooklyn' and it had a Las Vegas feel, from the modern-art decor right down to the mob connections. During the mid-50s, Bill Graham, who would go on to find success as a promoter of rock concerts, waited tables there. He described Maksik as 'a wiry guy with that intense Murder, Inc. face . . . always had six or eight half-dollars in his hand, like Captain Queeg's ball-bearings in *The Caine Mutiny*. His wife Doris dressed like she was sixteen years old and the party they were having was for her. Like that year's version of a Barbie Doll. She was at least forty years old.'

Refused permission to play his guitar, Donegan had to find a guitarist familiar with blues and American folk music who could accompany him for the two-week run. Someone came up with the idea of hiring Fred Hellerman, which, on paper, made total sense. Twenty-nine-year-old Hellerman had been a member of the Weavers, America's premier folk band until they were blacklisted in the early 50s for their left-wing views. The group had disbanded and Hellerman found work as a record producer, arranger and publisher. Fred took the gig but came to regret it. He knew Lead Belly, and had a huge respect for him and his songs – he'd even sung at Huddie's funeral. He was a close friend of Woody Guthrie, too. He didn't appreciate what this Brit upstart was doing to their material: messing with the lyrics, rocking it up, ignoring the context. He didn't much care for the audiences Donegan drew either, kids with no appreciation of roots music who saw him as one of those flashy guys with a guitar promising a break with the past.

'They were not a folk music crowd,' Hellerman recalled of the teen-agers who came to see Donegan at the Town and Country. 'They were less primed than the audiences who came to see the Weavers. They just listened, they didn't join in.' As for Donegan, 'He had little sense of what these songs meant. He was looking for a pop audience and doing it very badly.' Lonnie may have been selling coals to Newcastle when he got American teenagers to buy 'Rock Island Line', but in Fred Hellerman he found himself confronted by a local collier who didn't take kindly to seeing his wares being hawked in such a trashy manner each night.

There were others who also questioned Donegan's intentions in recording old blues songs. On 9 July 1956, *Billboard* reported that NBC's National Radio Fan Club had initially refused to play his new single, 'Lost John', on the grounds that his delivery of the lyr-ics amounted to racial stereotyping. Under the headline 'Intent Saves Donegan Disc', the report went on to explain that producer Parker Gibbs was able to convince the network's censorship department 'that the English singer is on the level and not doing an Amos 'n' Andy'. The story was deemed serious enough to merit appearing on the front page.*

Hellerman declined the opportunity to accompany Donegan on a ten-week tour of the States that saw him playing on a rock 'n' roll package show with artists such as Chuck Berry, Frankie Lymon and the Teenagers and Clyde McPhatter. By this time, Lonnie had received permission to play his guitar but he still had a mountain to climb. 'All the coloured acts were backed by an orchestra but I had no

---

* *Amos 'n' Andy* was the title of a radio comedy that ran from 1928 to 1955, con-cerning the adventures of two poor, uneducated African Americans who had left the south to seek work in New York. Written and performed by two white actors, it took its cues from the minstrel tradition, relying on negative racial stereotypes for comedic effect. Donegan's spoken introduction to 'Lost John' was his respect-ful homage to Lead Belly, but, in his attempt to imitate his hero's delivery, he had unwittingly strayed into a racial minefield. Fortunately for him, cooler heads prevailed and the people at NBC recognised his sincerity.

A poster for Lonnie Donegan's June 1956 gig in Cleveland, Ohio

parts [for the musicians to play] as I'd come from a jazz band. I was alone with a little Martin guitar.' The show was run as a continuous revue, doors opening at 11.15 a.m., five performances each day, with Donegan singing 'Rock Island Line' and 'Lost John'. 'It was ridiculous, I felt like a human sacrifice.'

During a five-day stint at the Fox Theatre in Detroit, Donegan finally found some kindred spirits. Also on the bill were the Rock 'n'

Roll Trio, a rockabilly band from Memphis. Led by Johnny Burnette, they are now considered the only real rivals to Elvis Presley during his Sun Records days. Johnny played guitar and sang with a holler and a growl, his brother Dorsey played bass and the line-up was completed by Paul Burlison, the king of the rockabilly guitarists. Their performance consisted of a three- or four-song set, usually containing their one regional hit, 'Tear It Up', along with 'Your Baby Blue Eyes', 'Tutti Frutti' and 'Train Kept a-Rollin'', which featured Burlison's trademark lick – playing a solo by plucking both the highest and lowest strings at the same fret.

On the second day of the show, Johnny Burnette approached Donegan. 'We love what you're doing, man. Can we come out and play with you?' Ever conscious of the bottom line, Donegan told him it was a great idea but he couldn't afford to pay them. 'Who said anything about money?' replied Burnette. 'Man, we just want to play with you.' Donegan was flattered. 'I said, "Great," and from then on, they were my backing group. Dorsey Burnette played slap bass and Paul Burlison played like Elvis's guitarist, Scotty Moore, and Johnny slashed the guitar like me and sang like a cross between me and Elvis. We enjoyed ourselves after that.'

During that week in Detroit, skiffle and rockabilly met on equal terms and were amazed to discover that, although they were born on opposite sides of the ocean, they were so alike as to be brothers. When Donegan finished his first round of touring, he flew Maureen out to the States and together they visited Johnny and Dorsey Burnette in Memphis. They were taken on a fishing trip, held a midnight barbecue where guitars were pulled out and songs sung, and Johnny even took Lonnie to meet his old pal, Elvis, who, sadly, was out of town. After Memphis, the Donegans made a pilgrimage to New Orleans, seeking out the old-style jazz still played in the French Quarter.

His American manager, Manny Greenfield, wanted Donegan to

214

join another ten-week package tour, but he had had about as much as he could take of the five-shows-a-day treadmill. In comparison with the UK – a country which, at the time, had one radio station and two TV channels – the promotional demands of US television and radio were exhausting. Having begun by chatting with the future president of the USA, Donegan had ended up being introduced by a ventriloquist's dummy named Knucklehead on a Saturday-morning kids programme hosted by Paul Winchell, a popular act who, in another life, would provide the voice of Tigger in Walt Disney's *Winnie the Pooh*. It was all too much. And anyway, his British management were desperate for him to come home. 'Lost John' was headed for the top of the singles charts.

15

YOUTH IN REVOLT

'A family with the wrong members in control – that, perhaps, is as near as one can come to describing England in a phrase.' So said George Orwell in 1940, and anyone who grew up in the decade that followed the war would recognise his characterisation of a country where 'the young are generally thwarted and most of the power is in the hands of irresponsible uncles and bed-ridden aunts'.

Since the early 50s, cultural forces had been trying to break out of the shadow cast by the Second World War. While the nation suffered rationing on a scale not experienced even during wartime, an exhibition was staged in London that looked towards a bright future in which technology solved the great societal problems of the day. The Festival of Britain was held on the site of a demolished jam factory near Waterloo Station. A series of modernist buildings was constructed on the south bank of the Thames – the Royal Festival Hall among them – to give visitors a vision of how the city might be rebuilt following the destruction wrought by the war. The centrepiece of the exhibition was the Skylon, a vertical steel cylinder, 250 feet high, shaped like a very thin cigar and suspended 50 feet above ground level by cables slung between three angled uprights. From a distance, it gave the impression of a rocket that had just taken off.

Eight and a half million people visited the Festival site over the summer of 1951, keen to see what the future might hold. Shortly after the exhibition closed, however, there was a change of government and the incoming Conservative prime minister was less than enamoured with futuristic idealism. On Winston Churchill's orders, the Skylon was torn down and sold off for scrap. Having succumbed to TB eighteen months before, Orwell sadly wasn't around to see his metaphor borne out.

For those whose youth had been disrupted by the war, there was an expectation that once hostilities had ended, popular culture would simply pick up again where it had left off. Spike Milligan, born in 1918, recalled how, as a teenager in the 1930s, he revelled in jazz and swing. The pop music of the day was provided by Irving Berlin, Cole Porter and Hoagy Carmichael, while George Raft, Betty Grable and the Marx Brothers ruled at the local cinema. When he was demobbed from the army in 1945, Milligan pulled his old suit out of mothballs and went back to the Palais de Danse to pick up where he had left off. Slowly it dawned on him that the Marx Brothers weren't making so many movies, that Max Miller was being replaced by Max Bygraves and that the big band sound was being challenged by modernists like Charlie Parker and Dizzy Gillespie. There would be no going back to the past.

As chief instigator and main writer of *The Goon Show*, which ran on the BBC Home Service from 1951, Milligan made clear to his young audience that he too knew the wrong members of the family were in charge. Week after week, he and his fellow Goons dragged the irresponsible uncle, the bed-ridden aunt and their stuffy contemporaries through an anarchic half-hour of radio comedy that was the first clear example of the contempt for authority that would come to dominate British youth culture in the 1960s.

Terence Rattigan, the most successful English playwright of the period, once claimed that, when writing, he had in mind a particular kind of theatregoer that he referred to as 'Aunt Edna', a 'respectable, middle-class, middle-aged, maiden lady'. (Whether or not this imaginary aunt was bed-ridden was never made clear.) Rattigan's refined dramas mostly occurred in the sedate world of the English upper middle class, where emotions were always understated and upper lips were kept stiff. In the spring of 1956, he was at the height of his powers, putting the finishing touches to the screenplay of *The Prince and the Showgirl*, a movie based on his 1953 play *The Sleeping Prince*, to be filmed at Pinewood Studios with Laurence Olivier and Marilyn Monroe in the title roles. He also had two successful plays running in the West End: *The Deep Blue Sea*, concerning the strained relationship between a drunk Battle of Britain pilot and the ex-wife of a High Court judge; and *Separate Tables*, which featured a repressed homosexual army major and a politician who had been jailed for beating his wife. Only Establishment figures, it seemed, had emotional lives worthy of examination.

Dissenting voices were occasionally heard. Samuel Beckett's play *Waiting for Godot*, which opened in London in August 1955, had shocked many theatregoers with its existentialist absurdity, but its target was as obscure as its meaning. Unable to grasp what was going on, middlebrow audiences were able to dismiss it as pretentious nonsense. However, in May 1956, a play opened at the Royal Court which made Rattigan seem suddenly old-fashioned. *Look Back in Anger* was the work of a twenty-five-year-old jobbing actor named John Osborne, who claimed to have written the play over seventeen days while sitting in a deck chair on Morecambe Pier, where he was appearing in *Seagulls Over Sorrento*.

The action takes place in a one-room attic flat in the Midlands, where Jimmy Porter, a working-class twenty-five-year-old with a degree from the wrong sort of university, vents his anger at the suffocating power of the Establishment, the passivity of his wife – calmly ironing while he rages against injustice – and his own sense of alienation. Porter expresses his rebellious streak by playing jazz trumpet, and it would not be stretching things to imagine him stood at the back of a Chris Barber gig, nursing a pint of Merrydown cider and tapping his foot while Lonnie Donegan, another working-class twenty-five-year-old, rattled through 'Midnight Special'.

Osborne's play was highly autobiographical – when his recently divorced first wife saw the opening scene, she thought, 'Oh no! Not the ironing board' – but the chord he struck resonated with an entire generation. The 1944 Education Act had opened the grammar schools to bright working-class students, which in turn led to greater demand for university places. Encouraged to go for the glittering prize of a degree, many state-educated graduates found that, despite their qualifications, the Establishment maintained a class ceiling that made sure only the right kind of people prospered. Too young to have fought in the war, but too old to have experienced the invention of the teenager, Osborne and his contemporaries felt trapped in a world where all of their elders retained military rank – Jimmy's father-in-law is called Colonel Redfern – while every sixteen-year-old seemed to be earning more than they did.

Look Back in Anger was a howl of rage from a generation that felt out of time. Articulate, yet frustrated by their inability to get a response from an apathetic world, they resorted to lashing out at everyone and everything. Marlon Brando expressed this same existential angst in *The Wild One* in 1953, when his character, Johnny, was asked what he was rebelling against. 'Whaddaya got?' he laconically replied. Jimmy Porter's plea for understanding is expressed with less of a cool shrug, yet it still provided a call to arms for anyone under the age of thirty who had to endure the dreary, parsimonious atmosphere of an English Sunday afternoon in the 50s: 'How I long for a little ordinary enthusiasm,' he wailed. 'Just enthusiasm – that's all.'

London's middle-aged theatre critics were contemptuous of the vagueness of Osborne's Weltschmerz, with the *Daily Mail* complaining that, while Jimmy Porter has 'a bitterness that produces a fine flow of savage talk, it is basically a bore because its reasons are never explained'. The *Evening Standard* dismissed the play as 'self-pitying drivel'. Among the brickbats, the *New Statesman*'s critic was percipient enough to observe that 'if you are young, [the play] will speak for you. If you are middle-aged, it will tell you what the young are feeling.' The most positive response, however, came from twenty-nine-year-old Kenneth Tynan, whose review for the *Observer* sealed his reputation as the most challenging theatre critic in Britain.

The piece took its title, 'Jimmy Porter, Prince of Scum', from a comment by the eighty-two-year-old writer Somerset Maugham, who had dismissed state-educated university students as 'scum'. Tynan advised anyone sharing that verdict to stay away from *Look Back in Anger* as it was 'all scum and a mile wide'. He compared Jimmy Porter to Hamlet and sought to silence those critics who carped about him being nothing more than a tiresome whinger. 'I agree that *Look Back in Anger* is likely to remain a minority taste. What matters, however, is the size of the minority. I estimate it at roughly 6,733,000, which is the number of people in this country between the ages of twenty and thirty. And this figure will doubtless be swelled by refugees from other age-groups curious to know what the contemporary young pup is thinking and feeling. I doubt if I could love anyone who did not wish to see *Look Back in Anger*. It is the best young play of its decade.'

Around the time the play opened, American playwright Arthur Miller visited London, where his new wife, Marilyn Monroe, was working on *The Prince and the Showgirl* with Laurence Olivier. When Miller asked to see *Look Back in Anger*, Olivier tried to dissuade him. 'It's just a travesty of England, a lot of bitter rattling on about conditions.' Miller got the impression that the play had somehow offended Olivier's sense of patriotism. Miller insisted they attend and later wrote that it gave him his first look at 'an England of outsiders like myself, who ironed their own shirts and knew about the great only from newspapers'.

When Olivier and Miller were invited backstage to meet Osborne, the American playwright was astonished to find that the great English actor had completely changed his mind. 'I overheard, with some incredulity, Olivier asking the pallid Osborne – then a young guy with a shock of uncombed hair and a look on his face of having awakened twenty minutes earlier – "Do you suppose you could write something for me?" in his most smiling tones, which could have convinced you to buy a car with no wheels for twenty thousand dollars.' Olivier's tour de force as washed-up music-hall star Archie Rice in Osborne's next play, *The Entertainer*, would give the fifty-year-old actor's career a new lease of life.

For all the furore that Osborne caused in London's theatrical circles, ticket sales for *Look Back in Anger* were unspectacular until a twenty-five-minute excerpt from the play was broadcast live on TV by the BBC in October 1956. Soon the term 'Angry Young Men' was being applied to the work of an emerging but unconnected group of British playwrights and authors whose work challenged the status quo by telling stories from a working-class perspective.

In 1958, Alan Sillitoe, a twenty-nine-year-old former factory worker from Nottingham, produced *Saturday Night and Sunday Morning*, a novel tapping into a deadening sense of disillusionment that many young people felt in post-war Britain. Shelagh Delaney was only nineteen when she wrote *A Taste of Honey* in 1957, determined to challenge what she saw as the stereotypical portrayal of northern working-class life. The proponents of Free Cinema were among those who responded to this trend. Karel Reisz's first feature film was an adaptation of *Saturday Night and Sunday Morning*, while Tony Richardson directed the film versions of both *Look Back in Anger* and *A Taste of Honey*.

It wasn't only the literary world that was trying to start a fire under the older generation. Since 1952, a group of artists, architects and critics had been meeting informally at the Institute of Contemporary Art in London to discuss how they might make art that reflected new technologies and the mass production of culture. They were drawn to images from movie posters, comic books, pulp fiction and magazine adverts, especially those that promised a better life through modern appliances. Utilising these 'found images' from outside of the art world to create vivid collages, the Independent Group, as they called themselves, introduced popular culture into what was, until then, the highly refined space of the art gallery.

In August 1956, the group staged an event at the Whitechapel Art Gallery in east London entitled *This Is Tomorrow*. More of an installation than an exhibition, a jukebox played continuously while visitors walked through a series of environments that confronted them with garishly enlarged, oddly juxtaposed images. The thirty-eight artists who contributed to the works were split into twelve multidisciplinary groups that each collaborated to create their own idea of contemporary art. Group Two, consisting of painter and collage artist Richard Hamilton, architect and designer John Voelcker and artist and sociologist John McHale, opted to create a 'fun house' of modernity which ultimately stole the show. The structure was designed by Voelcker and contained many examples of Hamilton's signature Bauhaus-inspired technique of scaled-up imagery. The entrance was guarded by an enlarged newsprint picture of the head of Marshal Tito, the Yugoslavian dictator, his face covered with exhortations to 'Look! Feel! Smell! Listen! Think Think Think!' A set of Marcel Duchamp's roto-reliefs spun alongside op art dazzle panels, while a jukebox played in front of a massive mural containing gaudy images from recent Cinemascope movies.

The most eye-catching imagery came in the shape of a twelve-foot-high reproduction of the poster for the newly released film *Forbidden Planet*, showing Robbie the Robot carrying the limp, scantily clad body of Anne Francis. This was juxtaposed with a life-size paint-ing of Marilyn Monroe, holding down her white skirt in the iconic updraught scene from *The Seven Year Itch*, which had been in British cinemas just a year before. The assemblage was completed by a five-foot-tall inflatable Guinness bottle. With this vivid combination of sci-fi, sex and booze, Hamilton had captured what was on the mind of almost every young male in the land, desperate to escape the gloomy parameters of post-war Britain.

However, the most influential image from the exhibition didn't appear on the walls of the Whitechapel Art Gallery. Compared to the scale of his other works in the 'fun house', Richard Hamilton's collage *Just What Is It That Makes Today's Homes So Different, So Appealing?* was tiny, just ten inches square, and only appeared in the exhibition catalogue, yet it was destined to become one of the defin-ing images of twentieth-century art. Hamilton cut pictures from con-temporary magazines brought back from the US by John McHale to create a colourful modern living-room scene. On the left, a woman hoovers her way up a long staircase, while to her right a cinema awning advertising *The Jazz Singer* is visible through large win-dows. In the centre, a lampshade is decorated with a mock-heraldic shield containing a crown, three lions and the word 'Ford', the hood emblem for the car company's 1950–1 models. The front cover of teen comic *Young Romance* dominates the back wall, hung in a thin black frame, as the past looks down disapprovingly in the shape of a small nineteenth-century photographic portrait of a stern-faced man. A TV in the right-hand corner shows a woman on the telephone, while a big can of ham dwarfs the coffee table it stands on. On the sofa, a female burlesque performer sits, naked except for sun hat and nipple covers, and a reel-to-reel tape recorder sits in the lower foreground.

The main focus of the image is a male body builder, muscles flexed, who stares out from the picture wearing white briefs. Like the

portraits of merchants depicted in all their finery by the Flemish masters of the seventeenth century, this is an image of male status. The
domestic appliances at his feet may look dated now, but in 1956 they
were cutting-edge and the He-Man is the master of them all. His viril-
ity is underlined by the giant Tootsie Pop lolly that he is holding in a
phallic position across his groin.

By drawing the eye to the word 'POP' on the lolly wrapper,
Hamilton was helping to define a new genre: Pop Art. Writing to
would-be collaborators in January 1957, he laid out what he believed
to be the characteristics of this new movement:

Pop Art is:
Popular (designed for a mass audience)
Transient (short-term solution)
Expendable (easily-forgotten)
Low cost
Mass produced
Young (aimed at youth)
Witty
Sexy
Gimmicky
Glamorous
Big Business

While academics argue about who first came up with the term
'Pop Art', most recognise that *Just What Is It . . .* was the first work
to crystallise the idea in the mind of the wider public. That such
an Americanised art would emerge in post-war Britain should be
no surprise. Artists working in the US sought to draw attention to
everyday objects that most Americans would be familiar with, like
Andy Warhol's soup cans. For those who saw his work in New York

galleries, Warhol's gaudy screen prints of Marilyn Monroe merely underscored how Hollywood had come to represent America to the world. In post-war England, however, Marilyn was a seductive siren, threatening to lure British culture into shallow waters from which it might never escape.

Seen through British eyes in the summer of 1956, *Just What Is It . . .* promised a future that was full of exciting new gadgets and attractive people, yet the overall effect was a trashy aesthetic at odds with the cosy conformity which often passed for, if not happiness, then at least contentment in the British advertising that was the equivalent of Hamilton's American source material. Our housewives were depicted as homely, while theirs looked inviting; our cars had matronly curves, while US autos displayed futuristic fins; and where our businesses stressed their traditional methods, corporate America seems to be not only looking to the future but actively creating it.

On 18 June 1956, while Lonnie Donegan was playing his five-night stand in Detroit backed by the Rock 'n' Roll Trio, *Time* magazine devoted a page to rock 'n' roll, declaring that 'it does for music what a motorcycle club at full throttle does for a quiet Sunday afternoon'. Among the advertisers in that particular issue were Norton Abrasives, whose two-page ad was captioned 'A Job That Reaches from Death Valley to Outer Space'; the Continental Can Company, who boldly claimed to 'open another door on the future of packaging'; and Moraine Products, whose ad for engine bearings depicts a four-lane highway teeming with fast, finned cars. No British ad agency of the time could give such a futuristic dynamic to tin cans, ball bearings and abrasives.

In later years, Hamilton recalled that when the trunk of ephemera that John McHale had collected while studying at the Yale School of Fine Art arrived in the UK – the raw material from which they would construct their exhibit – he and the other members of the group found a collection of Elvis Presley singles interleaved with copies of *Mad* magazine and were initially unsure if they had just been put in to keep the records from breaking or if they too were part of the treasure. This was culture as cargo cult: young people in the UK waiting for the latest new sounds, images, media or ideas to come from America and grabbing hold of them with both hands, even if they were only packaging.

One of the most vital manifestations of this anti-authoritarian youth culture was the 1955 movie *Blackboard Jungle*, which had drawn huge audiences of teenagers on both sides of the Atlantic. Now, a year later, realising that young people had more spending power than ever before, movie-makers in Hollywood and London were quick to exploit this new market. First out of the traps in the UK was the British production *It's Great to Be Young*, which went on general release in May 1956. Following on from his starring role in the most popular British war movie of 1955, *The Colditz Story*, John Mills plays Mr Dingle, the music master at a suburban grammar school, who encourages his pupils to form a jazz band.

When the crabby old headmaster fires Dingle for inciting enjoyment, the pupils go on strike until he is reinstated. With all of the kids wearing blazers and ties, while the teachers sport black gowns over their suits, this was a million miles from the leather jackets and tight skirts of *Blackboard Jungle*. The screenplay was by Ted Willis, creator of *Dixon of Dock Green*, the dialogue was painfully polite and the musical numbers string-drenched and sexless. Humphrey Lyttelton provided the jazz, but the overall effect wouldn't have upset Terence Rattigan's Aunt Edna. 'The first thing that strikes one about this film', said the bowtie-wearing critic from Pathé News, 'is that it features a bunch of youngsters who are not crazy, mixed-up kids. The kids in *It's Great to Be Young* are only crazy in the riotous sense. That's what makes it so refreshing.' That patronising attitude would turn sour within weeks, when riotous kids were suddenly seen as anything but 'refreshing'.

America's attempt to cash in on the success of *Blackboard Jungle* reached these shores in the form of *Rock Around the Clock*, which opened at the Pavilion Theatre in London on the last weekend of July 1956. But rather than seeking to emulate the menace and drama of its inspiration, its makers simply lifted the thing that most attracted teenage audiences – the music – and built a flimsy script around seventeen pop songs. Tony Martinez and his band play three Latin numbers, African American vocal group the Platters sing two of their great doo-wop ballads, and Freddie Bell and the Bellboys perform their hit 'Giddy Up a Ding Dong'. The stars of the show are Bill Haley and His Comets, who perform no fewer than nine songs, among them 'See You Later Alligator', 'Rock-a-Beatin' Boogie' and the eponymous 'Rock Around the Clock', which both opens and closes the movie.

The storyline concerns a promoter who, realising that the big-band sound is passé, books himself into a hotel in a little town in Maine, where he discovers Haley and the Comets performing at the local hop. He then spends the rest of the movie trying to make them successful and so win the hand of the cute girl who runs the hotel. As feeble in its own way as the plot for *It's Great to Be Young*, *Rock Around the Clock* is completely reliant on the music to pull it through. There are no strong teen characters as in *Blackboard Jungle* or *Rebel Without a Cause* – the kids in the movie are peripheral to the story. Haley and his band play with vigour, but, from a teenager's perspective, they look more like your uncles than your mates.

Haley might be playing the new music, but he's showing his roots. The Comets' line-up includes a lap steel guitar, a remnant from his days as a cowboy singer, and at one point the keyboard player straps on an accordion. This isn't the result of a musical alchemy conjured up in Sun Studios by excited southern teenagers. When it was matched to the edgy images of *Blackboard Jungle*, 'Rock Around the Clock' had the shock of the new. Seeing Haley and the Comets perform in this movie serves only to remind us that, for all its revolutionary verve, the song was originally written as a novelty foxtrot by Max C. Freedman, a Tin Pan Alley songwriter born in 1893.

British teenagers weren't aware of this back in 1956. They'd never seen a real rock 'n' roll band before. Maybe they all featured accordion players? Most were more interested in how American teenagers behaved when listening to the new music – how they danced, what they wore, how they did their hair. None of this information was available from the adult-dominated media of the day. Just to get a glimpse into that world was magical. And the music, so fast! And loud! In most towns in the UK, the sound system in the cinema, though primitive, was bigger than any you might find in a domestic setting or at a concert hall. It had been designed to carry the most intimate sounds of romance and the tumult of war. When Bill Haley came blasting out of the speakers at full volume, it was the closest any of those British kids had ever been to a rock 'n' roll gig, so they did what came naturally.

Jack Good, who would do much to popularise rock 'n' roll in Britain as producer of pioneering pop TV such as *Six-Five Special* and *Oh Boy!*, witnessed the phenomenon first hand at a screening of *Rock Around the Clock*. 'Bill Haley shouted out, "On your marks. Get set. Now ready. Go! Everybody razzle-dazzle!" and with one accord, the audience leapt to its feet and started bopping about in a way I had never in my life seen before! I was looking at the screen and then the audience, back and forth, as though I were at Wimbledon. I was totally bowled over by the simple display of animal force and energy – and I loved it.'

Youthful exuberance was tolerated by the irresponsible uncles and bed-ridden aunts, so long as everyone calmed down and went home when they were told. But these dancing teens were no longer the fun-loving rascals of *It's Great to Be Young*. Dancing in the dark to 'Rock Around the Clock' cranked up real loud, they felt like the crazy mixed-up kids from *Blackboard Jungle*, and all they desired was a confrontation with an angry authority figure to make their fantasies complete. It wasn't long before they got what they wanted.

'Teddy Boys Jive Brings Police', reported the *Daily Mail* on 27 August 1956. 'Sixty teddy boys danced in the aisles during last night's showing of the new American jive film *Rock Around the Clock* at the Shepherd's Bush Gaumont. They then picked up the protesting cinema manager and carried him into the foyer. Police restored order.'

In the following week, this unruly behaviour followed the movie out into the London suburbs. '14 Held in Rock and Roll Riot', read a headline on the front page of the *Daily Mail* on 3 September. Police were called to disturbances in Twickenham, Chadwell Heath, Dagenham and West Ham. The next day saw the trouble reach the north, with the *Manchester Guardian* reporting that seats had been smashed and torn, light bulbs shattered and fire hoses turned on at a cinema in Burnley where *Rock Around the Clock* was playing. Surveying the damage, the manager, Mr William Howarth, said, 'I'm surprised and a little shocked. I know this kind of thing has been going on in some cities, but I never expected it to happen in a provincial town like Burnley.'

It wasn't only Mr Howarth who was shocked. This was a totally new phenomenon. The authorities were used to dealing with pop-crazed crowds – thousands had gathered to mob Johnnie Ray – but up until now they had been female. Boys were expected to line up in an orderly fashion for conscription, not jive in the cinemas and smash up the seats. As ever, the *Daily Mail* knew where to point the finger of blame: '[Rock 'n' roll] is deplorable. It is tribal. And it's from America. It follows rag-time, blues, Dixie, jazz, hot cha-cha and boogie-woogie, which surely originated in the jungle. We sometimes wonder if this is the Negro's revenge.'

The next weekend only brought more trouble. 'Rock'n'roll Terrorises a City', screamed the *Mail* on Monday 10 September. Having been prohibited from dancing in a Manchester cinema by police who ejected anyone who clapped or stamped their feet, 'rhythm crazed teenagers jammed the roads by throwing fireworks and jiving in the city centre's main streets'. The *Manchester Guardian* headlined the same story with a little less of the *Mail*'s sensationalism – 'More Scuffles with Police After Rock'n'Roll Film: Ejections from Cinema Taken Unkindly'.

It was beginning to dawn on the authorities that the teenagers were revelling in their sudden notoriety. 'Opposite the cinema in the early evening was a newspaper bill, "Manchester Rock'n'roll Rioting: Police Act",' the *Guardian* journalist noted. 'I watched three teddy boys stand before the bill like film stars examining photographs of themselves and shouting, "That's us, brother. That's us."' The article pointed out that other cinemas in Manchester had shown the movie for a week with only a little 'audience participation'. Maybe it was the lurid headlines that had stirred up copy-cat trouble?

When fourteen defendants, ten of them juveniles, appeared before the magistrate following the Manchester disturbances, one seventeen-year-old youth complained that when he had seen the film on the first Sunday it was shown, there had been no 'larking about'. The trouble spread, he claimed, when the newspapers started reporting it. Levying fines on ten of the participants, the stipendiary magistrate, Mr F. Bancroft Turner, lamented that 'it would have been much better if the police had been allowed to deal with you in a way which would have given you real cause to rock and roll around a bit'.

In an effort to analyse what was going on, the *Daily Express* sent a team of journalists and a Harley Street psychiatrist to view *Rock*

Around the Clock. Under the banner headline 'This Crazy Summer's Weirdest Craze', and amid the usual dismissive jibes about 'jungle music' and 'maladjusted, primitive people', George Gale made an astute observation when he commented that the film 'wouldn't raise the temperature of wintering Eskimos more than half a degree centigrade'. Surprisingly, these 'experts' came out five to one against banning the film.

The *Express* also took the trouble to interview two 'rock 'n' rollers' who had been fined following disturbances at a cinema in Peckham. Tony Scullion, aged twenty-one, recalled that 'when they got to "See You Later, Alligator" I just signalled to the boys and we went out in the aisles. After that, I didn't hear much music. We were jiving and stomping – even when they cut the film.' Kenneth Gear, aged eighteen, explained why things boiled over: 'We couldn't dance properly inside the cinema so we went on dancing when we got outside. There must have been four or five hundred of us in the street. I've never felt so excited in my life.'

My mother's youngest sister, Christine D'Urso, was a teenager living in Harold Hill in Essex in 1956 and spent weekends jiving to Bill Haley and Elvis Presley at a local dance hop called the Shack. With her then boyfriend, now husband, Dave Mutton, she went to see *Rock Around the Clock* at the Gaumont in Romford during the first week of release. 'We queued up to get in and there was a bloody riot,' recalls Dave. 'The film was on and everybody was jiving in the aisles and then some idiot turned the fire hose on us. They pulled it out of the wall and just let it go. Everyone was diving for cover.'

The phenomenon reached its peak on Tuesday 11 September, two days after the disturbances in Manchester, when a mob of over a thousand youths jived in the streets of the south London district of Elephant and Castle. Trouble began at around 10.40 p.m., following the final screening of *Rock Around the Clock* at the Trocadero Cinema in the New Kent Road. According to the *Daily Mail*, three hundred police officers were required to quell the riotous behaviour. *The Times* reported that bottles and fireworks were thrown and four shop windows smashed. It was claimed that jiving teenagers held up the traffic on nearby Tower Bridge.

In just ten days, boisterous teenagers had brought rock 'n' roll to the attention of an outraged general public. Following the widely reported disturbances in Manchester and south London, the authorities began to fight back. Across the UK, dozens of town councils banned *Rock Around the Clock* from being screened, seeing it as a threat to public order. A more common tactic was to remove the film from screens on Sundays. It was felt that on Saturdays, the rowdy element tended to gravitate towards football matches and dancehalls, whereas on Sunday night, there was nowhere else for them to go except to the picture house. Mr R. C. Wetherill, general manager of the Gaiety Cinema in Manchester, where unrest had broken out the previous Sunday, seemed unperturbed by the trouble caused by the film, telling the *Manchester Guardian* that he had booked *Rock Around the Clock* for the next three weeks. 'Even without Sunday, it's the best business we've had for five years.'

The Cinema Exhibitors' Association, whose profits had been dented by the introduction of a second, commercial TV channel in 1955, protested that the trouble had been stirred up by the papers. 'The press have offered a challenge to the teddy boys by the publicity they are giving them,' complained Mr A. Rockett.

Now that rock 'n' roll was in the public consciousness, the newspapers sought to undermine its popularity among teenagers by involving Establishment figures. Reports began to appear about aristocrats dancing to Bill Haley. Sir Malcolm Sargent made reference to 'roll and rock' while conducting at the Last Night of the Proms, and it was claimed that the Queen had asked for *Rock Around the Clock* to

Teenagers dancing outside the Gaiety Cinema following a showing of *Rock Around the Clock*, Manchester, 21 September 1956

be shown to the royal family while they holidayed at Balmoral. An editorial in *The Times* tried to offer some perspective: 'Much of the hooliganism has drawn strength from an atmosphere not unlike that which rouses undergraduates after bump suppers and others on Guy Fawkes night. This is not to excuse some of the recent incidents, but merely to suggest that too much can be made of them.'

To reassure the British public that they were not alone in being confronted by jiving youths, reports began to appear of rock 'n' roll-related disturbances in other countries. Singapore banned *Rock Around the Clock* on the grounds that it debased true Chinese culture. Six hundred Norwegian youths clashed with baton-wielding police when the film was shown in Oslo. It led to divisions between Sikhs and Muslims in a Bombay cinema. 'Rowdyism' was reported at screenings in the West German city of Duisberg, where the police dismissed the teenagers as *'die Halbstarken'* – literally, the half-strongs, or hooligans. The *Manchester Guardian* noted that parents in America had 'rejoiced when they learned that teenagers in Manchester had wrecked a cinema under the inspiring influence of "Rock Around the Clock" . . . We are all in the same boat it is gladly believed. Not only American kids are crazy.'

A new generation had announced its arrival with a bang, the first explosion of a pop culture that would hold sway for the next sixty years – not that anyone realised this at the time. D. W. Brogan, a Scottish academic born in 1900, concluded an article in the *Manchester Guardian* on 'the rationale of rock 'n' roll' by championing the songs of his own youth: 'We sang "Tea for Two" and "Avalon" and in Boston they have revived "Does Your Mother Know You're Out, Cecilia?" Who will sing "Blue Suede Shoes" ten years from now?'

16

THE PEOPLE'S MUSIC

In his inaugural address to the English Folk Song Society, delivered in 1899, Sir Hubert Parry issued a stark warning: 'There is an enemy at the doors of folk music which is driving it out, namely, the common popular songs of the day; and this enemy is one of the most repulsive and most insidious. If one thinks of the outer circumference of our terribly overgrown towns where the jerry-builder holds sway; where one sees all around the tawdriness of sham jewellery and shoddy clothes, pawnshops and gin-palaces; where stale fish and the miserable piles of Covent Garden refuse which pass for vegetables are offered for food – all such things suggest to one's mind the boundless regions of sham.'

Parry, who seventeen years later would compose the musical setting for William Blake's 'Jerusalem', was in no doubt as to who was to blame for this attack on the nation's folk music. 'It is for the people who live in these unhealthy regions – people who for the most part have the most false ideals or none at all – who are always struggling for existence, who think that the commonest rowdyism is the highest expression of the human condition; it is for them that the modern popular music is made, and it is made with a commercial intention out of snippets of musical slang. And it is this product that will drive out folk music if we do not save it.'

For the next fifty years, the English Folk Song Society did much to fence folk music off from the 'rowdy' people of the 'unhealthy regions', formalising it for performance on piano by the upper middle class. Despite this, some of the great unwashed were able to hold on to their own traditions without needing academics or knights of the realm to explain it to them. In rural inns up and down the land, old-timers sang the songs of their ancestors, unaccompanied save for the harmonising voices of kith and kin.

In 1944, a book appeared that challenged Parry's definition of folk music head on. The author was a self-taught folklorist from Wandsworth, south London, named Albert Lancaster Lloyd. Born in 1908, Bert Lloyd had travelled the world, collecting songs while he worked as a sheep shearer in Australia and later as a crew member on a whaler off the coast of Antarctica. *The Singing Englishman* was the first general book on the subject since Cecil Sharp published *English Folk Song: Some Conclusions* in 1907.

Lloyd, who had joined the Communist Party in 1934, spent years researching his songs in the British Library, but this was not an academic work. Rather, his book was a polemic aimed at wrenching the English folk song out of the hands of Parry and Sharp and giving it back to those who created it – the working people of England. 'What we nowadays call English folksong is something that came out of social upheaval,' he declared. 'That is no random remark, but a statement of what happened in history. It grew up with a class just establishing itself in society with sticks, if necessary, and rusty swords and bows discoloured with smoke and age. While that class flourished, the folksong flourished, too, through all the changing circumstances that the lowborn lived in from the Middle Ages to the Industrial Revolution. And when that class declined, the folksong withered away and died.'

Lloyd's Marxist analysis of the English folk song was not to everybody's taste, but *The Singing Englishman* marked the point at which the seeds of the second English folk revival (following on from the first one led by Sir Hubert Parry and friends) were sown. The book was published by the Workers' Music Association, in which Lloyd took an active role, as well as penning articles on folk music for the *Daily Worker*. In 1950, he formed a singing group called the Ramblers with fellow communist John Hasted, the physics professor who led the London Youth Choir. Inspired by the recordings of the Almanac Singers, a New York-based collection of left-wing musicians formed by Pete Seeger in 1940, they got together with Jean Butler, an American banjo player who had shared stages with the Almanacs at union rallies in the US. The quartet was completed by guitarist Neste Revald.

At political meetings in the UK, music was generally provided by choirs of activists, brass bands from collieries or the occasional trad jazz ensemble. At one of the Ramblers' first appearances, a rally for the Clerical Workers' Union addressed by Clement Attlee, the sight of guitars and banjos on the platform took many by surprise, but the crowd, who had been hostile to the Labour leader, were won over by the group's enthusiastic performance. The Ramblers ran out of steam before they had time to make any recordings, but they were the first British group inspired by the topical song movement that had flourished in the United States under the tutelage of Pete Seeger and Alan Lomax.

In the early 50s, Lomax – based in London while making field recordings for his Columbia Records *World Library of Folk and Primitive Music* project – was looking to complete his collection of English folk songs with some industrial and urban ballads. He was directed to seek out Lloyd for examples of the former and Ewan MacColl for the latter. Born Jimmy Miller in Salford in 1915, MacColl had changed his name after deserting from the British Army in 1945 and told people he came from Auchterarder in Scotland. In fact, it was his parents who hailed from north of the border, but their strong emotional connection with their homeland, coupled with the accident of being born on Burns Night, reinforced MacColl's Scottish identity.

A member of the Communist Party since the 30s, MacColl had

been involved in agit-prop, both as a performer and writer, cutting his teeth on the streets of Manchester with a theatre group known as the Red Megaphones. He wrote plays, sketches, skits and radio programmes, and if a song were needed in the production, he'd write one of those too. When Lomax introduced him to Bert Lloyd, MacColl was working with Joan Littlewood at the Theatre Workshop, performing polemical theatre in schools, factories and village halls. He was familiar with Lloyd's name, having read his translation of Federico García Lorca's *Lament for the Death of a Bullfighter and Other Poems*, published in 1937.*

At the time they met, Lloyd was collecting material for his anthology of industrial folksongs, *Come All Ye Bold Miners*. His enthusiasm for the subject helped MacColl to understand that, beyond the sanitised vision of a pastoral past peddled by the English Folk Song Society, there was a vibrant tradition of radical ballads and shanties that represented the unedited voices of the working people.

Soon the two were collaborating on radio programmes for the BBC. *Ballads and Blues* was a six-part series broadcast in the spring of 1953, the aim of which was to illustrate themes and tones that were common to both the industrial ballads of the British Isles and the blues and work songs of the United States. The series featured American artists such as Big Bill Broonzy and Appalachian dulcimer player Jean Ritchie, alongside Irish piper Seamus Ennis and Scottish folk singer Isla Cameron. MacColl and Lloyd also weighed in with songs on different weekly themes. Some blues numbers were traced back to their roots in British traditional songs, while the experiences expressed in lyrics were found to be similar on both sides of the Atlantic. The message was clear: the people's music knew no boundaries, no borders; it belonged to everyone and no one.

---

* A skilled linguist, Lloyd also published a translation of Franz Kafka's *Metamorphosis* in the same year, the first time it had appeared in English.

LEWISHAM TOWN HALL
CATFORD

MONDAY, 10th OCTOBER, 1955
7.45 p.m.

Pete Payne (Payne's Music Shop)

presents

A Concert of

JAZZ
BALLADS
BLUES

with

KEN COLYER'S JAZZMEN
THE SKIFFLE GROUP
EWAN McCOLL & A. L. LLOYD

SOUVENIR PROGRAMME   Price - SIXPENCE

Jazz, Ballads and Blues at Lewisham Town Hall, 1955

On 5 July 1954, the *Daily Worker* organised a fundraising Ballads
and Blues concert at the Royal Festival Hall, where MacColl and
Lloyd presided over an event attended by over six hundred left-wing
music fans. Acts included Isla Cameron, the Irish traveller Margaret
Barry, who accompanied herself on banjo, and calypsonian Fitzroy
Coleman. The Ken Colyer Jazz Band were also on the bill and performed 'Take This Hammer', one of their skiffle songs, but whoever
covered the show for *Sing* magazine wasn't familiar enough with the
term to distinguish it from the rest of the jazz they played that night.

Sing had first appeared in May 1954, written, edited, produced
and distributed by John Hasted and Eric Winter, a left-wing journalist from Manchester. The pair had been inspired by *Sing Out!*, the
American topical song magazine founded in 1950. Costing a shilling,

Sing was another means by which Hasted sought to take on the mantle of the English Pete Seeger.

The impetus for the magazine seems to have been the United States' detonation of the first hydrogen bomb on 1 March 1954. To the surprise of its designers, the destructive power of the weapon was twice its expected yield, resulting in the contamination of over seven thousand square miles of the Pacific Ocean around Bikini Atoll. The suffering of those caught by the blast and fallout, on nearby islands and shipping, made it impossible for the US to keep the test a secret and the world was suddenly made aware of a weapon a thousand times more powerful than that which destroyed Hiroshima and Nagasaki in 1945. Within a month, Labour MP Fenner Brockway had formed the Hydrogen Bomb National Campaign Committee to oppose British plans to build such a weapon.

The first issue of *Sing* contained Leon Fung's calypso 'The Atom Bomb and the Hydrogen', as well as Hasted's own song 'Talking Rearmament'. With a readership of around a thousand, the magazine arrived just as the topical song movement in the UK was gaining ground. Hasted found that his forty-strong left-wing choir was beginning to fragment into smaller groups consisting of three or four singers with a guitar accompaniment. *Sing* fed this trend by providing new topical songs every few months. By November 1954, Hasted announced to his readers that 'Londoners can go and hear folk singers performing any Monday night at 8 by burrowing into "The Good Earth", a club situated well below 44 Gerrard Street, near Piccadilly. It is the first venture of this sort to be started in England and *Sing* wishes it every success.' The Good Earth was ahead of its time, but only just.

The foundations of what would develop into the second English folk revival were in place by 1954, but a key element was missing – a circuit of folk clubs. In September 1953, Peter Kennedy, folk collector and broadcaster and the man who had introduced Lloyd and MacColl to Alan Lomax, created an influential radio series that introduced the traditional musical styles of the British Isles to a new audience. *As I Roved Out* took its title from a song by Sarah Makem, the matriarch of a family of Irish folk musicians. The first programme, broadcast at 10 a.m. on a Sunday, came from Mrs Makem's kitchen in County Armagh, Northern Ireland, and featured two of the stalwarts from the *Ballads and Blues* series, Seamus Ennis and Isla Cameron.

Over the next six months, the programme followed a similar format. Folk singers and musicians were recorded in their natural environment – most often their home, sometimes the corner of a local inn – or else invited into the studio. *As I Roved Out* soon found a dedicated audience, many hearing their national folk music for the first time. The English Folk Song Society had merged with the English Folk Dance Society in 1932 to create the English Folk Dance and Song Society, and staged formal events at their London headquarters, Cecil Sharp House, but there was no circuit of folk clubs where audiences could gather to hear traditional music. If you didn't live in an area with a living folk tradition, you had to travel to experience folk music at first hand.

Shirley Collins discovered English folk music from the radio. Born in Hastings, Sussex, in 1935, and brought up in a communist household, she and her sister Dolly helped their mother sell copies of the *Daily Worker* on Saturday mornings and sang together at Labour Party socials in their mid-teens. Shirley wasn't a fan of early 50s pop music.

'It was all Vera Lynn and Ted Heath and his band, and I just wanted to jitterbug because it looked so good and it must have felt wonderful and it was a release, you know, it was freedom. You could wear ankle socks and be thrown over blokes' shoulders. I went on the pier at Hastings when I was fifteen or so because they had dances, and I used to go down there sometimes with Dolly, sometimes on my own, and I'd think, "Oh, I'll be able to find a partner I can dance with."

'My Aunt Grayson made me a special dress for me to go dancing. It was yellow seersucker with a bouffant skirt and she had also got a little black velvet jacket that she lent me to go in, and so I went down to the pier in my black and my yellow, but they were all old gits. There was nobody under the age of what seemed like sixty to me at the time. They were doing foxtrots and ballroom stuff and it wasn't sexy and it didn't feel like fun.'

Before she had a chance to be thrown over some bloke's shoulders, Shirley's head was turned by folk music. *Country Magazine* was a weekly programme on the BBC Home Service which featured some traditional music, but it was the arrival of *As I Roved Out* that sent her off to London to explore the folk song library at Cecil Sharp House. 'I wasn't running away from anything, I was running towards something. There was nowhere in Hastings to find out anything. My gran and grandad sang one or two songs and my aunt and my mum did, but all the songs that they sang, that I learnt from them, had come from Sharp's *English Folk Songs for Schools* [published in 1925] because that was being taught at the time, and thank God it was.'

After moving to London in late 1953 and finding employment in a bookshop, Collins spent as much time as she could researching folk songs. 'It was all so laborious. I didn't read music, they didn't have a photocopying machine, I just dotted down all the notes and the words, and when I'd got a little sheet of stuff I would go home to Hastings, where Dolly would play it on a piano for me.'

Collins was soon taking part in the singarounds organised by Peter Kennedy in the basement at Cecil Sharp House. She also joined a group of singers who met at John Hasted's study at University College in Gower Street. In 1955, as a member of the London Youth Choir, she attended the World Festival of Youth in Warsaw along with Hylda Sims.

'John Hasted was one of those co-ordinating people that could make things happen, but he was a funny mixture,' recalls Sims. 'He was Oxbridge, a distinguished scientist, lived with his wife in a pleasant house, had this astonishingly upper-middle-class life and accent – but then he had this other side, the choir and communism.'

A great admirer of Pete Seeger, Hasted had a gift for bringing people together, but, like Seeger, he came from a privileged, academic background. He and his middle-class friends desperately wanted to create a popular song movement of the kind that had emerged in the 40s in America, but they lacked a figure like Lead Belly or Woody Guthrie, someone from a working-class background whose earthy music could reach beyond their circle and connect with the masses. When 'Rock Island Line' came out of nowhere to race up the charts in early 1956, Hasted saw his chance. Sure, Lonnie Donegan wasn't a legendary figure like Woody Guthrie – how could he be? He was from East Ham. But on the back of his success a lot of people were able to build careers.

———

When punk rock exploded into Britain's national consciousness in December 1976, following the Sex Pistols' profanity-fuelled appearance on teatime TV, the shockwave that followed swept away a lot of old wood. Glam rock toppled from its platform boots and long-haired bands with flared trousers became passé overnight. However, once the music press had been scourged of its pomposity, it wasn't just spiky-haired kids playing furious and fast who thrived in the new harsh landscape – there was also space for older troupers who looked sharp. Elvis Costello had been playing around the fringes of the pub rock scene for years as Declan MacManus. With a new name, a skinny tie, an obscure 60s Fender guitar and a huge chip on his shoulder, he suddenly found that he fitted right in with the new dispensation. Likewise Ian Dury, one of life's magnificent mavericks. He was thirty-five when punk happened, the same age as Paul McCartney, but with a brilliant new band and a touch more menace in his voice, he was able to ride the wave of punk as if he were an angry nineteen-year-old.

Just as the Pistols had created a market for music with attitude, Lonnie Donegan's success gave kids an appetite for guitar music. Hasted and his little group had been working on the periphery, playing at rallies and on street corners for little reward. Suddenly, their style of music was in the charts. John Hasted realised that if he cut his cloth a little more like Donegan's, then he could gain himself an audience. So when The Good Earth moved out of 44 Gerrard Street to new premises in Mac's Rehearsal Studios near Piccadilly, he was quick to seize the moment.

On 3 April 1956, Hasted opened the Forty-four Skiffle and Folksong Club in the basement vacated by The Good Earth. The advert that appeared in the April/May edition of *Sing* had the word 'skiffle' in large letters, with the word 'folksong' in smaller type beneath. Like the blues fans down at the Round House, just two blocks away across Shaftesbury Avenue, Hasted realised that, if he wanted to create an audience for folk music, he needed to utilise the 's' word to get bums on seats.

The resident band at the Forty-four was nominally the John Hasted Skiffle and Folksong Group – the latest bunch of people he'd gathered together. Hasted led the band himself, playing twelve-string guitar and banjo. John Cole, a former human guinea pig for chemical warfare experiments, played harmonica, Paul Fineberg played clarinet, while the rhythm section consisted of Chaim Morris and Dennis Finn on double bass and washboard respectively.

The vocalists were a trio of strong singers. Shirley Collins and Judith Goldblum had been stalwarts of the London Youth Choir, while Redd Sullivan was a ginger-bearded merchant seaman who worked as a stoker. The contrast between the singing styles of Collins and Sullivan was stark. He was a blues shouter reminiscent of Lead Belly, while Collins, for all her love of the jitterbug, sang with the pure, unadorned voice of a lass from the Sussex Downs. Given that their repertoire contained a number of American folk songs that had emigrated from the British Isles, there were occasional disputes over which version of a song was the most appropriate to perform. Sullivan would want to sing it the way he heard it on a Library of Congress recording, while Collins would prefer the version she had discovered in Cecil Sharp House.

Just two weeks after Hasted opened the Forty-four, another skiffle club came into being, in the upstairs function room of the Princess Louise, a Victorian pub near Holborn Underground station, just a ten-minute walk from Soho.

The weekly club that Russell Quay and Hylda Sims had been running in the studio flat of Lanning Roper's South Kensington house had become popular among a group of bohemian friends who enjoyed guitar-based music. Jack Elliott played there so often he became a fixture, sleeping on the couch. However, this regularly rowdy bunch of beatniks weren't popular with the neighbours, so, following complaints, Roper threw them out. Undeterred, they simply transferred their studio club to the Princess Louise. In the same edition of *Sing* that had announced the Forty-four Club, an advert appeared declaring 'Monday Night is Studio Skiffle Night with the City Ramblers'. For anyone wondering what that might entail, visitors were promised 'work songs, ballads, blues, union songs and stomps'. Guests included Bert Lloyd, Margaret Barry and Michael Gorman, Jack Elliott, Cyril Davies, Redd Sullivan and the Ted Wood Skiffle Group. Nancy Whiskey performed during the intervals, singing folk songs from her native Scotland.

Bo Bo Buquet (*far left*) and Pete Maynard (*right*) of the
City Ramblers, Studio Skiffle, 1956

Born Anne Wilson in 1935, Nancy took her name from 'The Calton
Weaver',* with its chorus of 'Whisky, whisky, Nancy Whisky, whisky,
whisky Nancy-o.' She came to London to try her hand singing in the
clubs and cafes of Soho, recording a six-track album of traditional
folk songs for the Topic label, although this had not yet been released
when she took up residence at Studio Skiffle. When the City Ramblers
left to tour Europe in July 1956, it was Nancy who took over the running of the club.

* Calton, a village just outside of Glasgow, was the site of the earliest major
industrial dispute in Scotland's history when, in 1787, troops were sent in to sup-
press loom-breaking weavers who were agitating for higher pay.

A German jazz promoter had offered the group a series of European dates and, taken with the romance of travelling around the Continent playing in piazzas and platzes, the City Ramblers gathered up their instruments and headed for the Channel ports. Transport was a converted Chevrolet field ambulance that had seen service with the Canadian Army in the Second World War. Somehow, nine people squeezed into the vehicle, among them Jack and June Elliott, who seized on the opportunity to extend the scope of their European adventure.

The promoter turned out to be a heavy drinker who expected the group to play until 3 a.m., then sleep in the venue before moving on. The van was no more reliable, needing to be pushed to start and regularly breaking down. They found themselves playing to American troops in Frankfurt, Kaiserslautern and Heidelberg, while some staid German audiences were critical of their bohemian appearance.

Tensions among the travellers began to build. As the Suez Crisis turned from stand-off to confrontation, tub bass player Bo Bo Buquet (aka Tony Edwards) decided to head home. A naval reservist, he felt certain he would be called up for duty if the situation worsened. Pete Maynard, who had come along to drive the van and occasionally play the spoons, took over on bass.

Eventually, the gigs ran out and the promoter ran off, leaving the band stranded in Denmark. With help from the Danish Musicians' Union, they were able to get back to England, but not before stopping off in Brussels to play in a swish cabaret club.

The next artist to hasten through the door that Lonnie Donegan had opened was Ewan MacColl. MacColl was among those who were hired to make musical programmes by Granada when the independent TV company brought commercial television to north-west England in May 1956. He again teamed up with Alan Lomax to create a weekly folk music programme around a new ensemble who they

The Ramblers: (*standing, left to right*) Alan Lomax, Sandy Brown, Jim Bray
and Bryan Daley; (*sitting, left to right*) Peggy Seeger, Ewan MacColl and Shirley
Collins

hoped would grow to be the British equivalent of the Weavers, bringing a broad selection of roots music to a mass audience. The Ramblers
took their name from MacColl's first and, at that point, most famous
song, 'The Manchester Rambler', his account of the mass trespasses
on private land that took place in the early 1930s. These acts of civil
disobedience were led by the Young Communist League with the aim
of securing free access for all to England's moorland and mountains.

With a budget from Granada, MacColl and Lomax were able
to assemble a number of top session musicians to provide backing.
Clarinettist Bruce Turner and Jim Bray, Chris Barber's bass player,
provided the jazz element, while Nigerian-born Nat Atkin supplied
percussion. Shirley Collins, who, having been introduced to Alan
Lomax at a party at MacColl's house, was now romantically involved

with the American, was hired as a vocalist and the line-up was completed by Peggy Seeger on five-string banjo.

Shortly after arriving in London in March 1956, Peggy was performing in West End coffee bars, travelling from gig to gig on her motor scooter, banjo strapped on her back, guitar clenched between her knees. Occasionally she carried passengers. 'I lived in Highgate at the time, at Alan Lomax's house, and I got a scooter. He had to go into town and I'd only just learnt how to drive it, and he says, "I'll hop on the back of that, honey" – he always called me honey – and he probably weighed twice as much as I did. Neither of us had a helmet and I remember trying to manoeuvre this thing with this enormous weight behind me. I once went all the way to Scotland on that little scooter with a banjo and a guitar, knapsack and no visor, no helmet. Isn't that crazy?'

She had been welcomed into the London skiffle scene, playing spots at the Forty-four Club and Studio Skiffle. 'I joined in and was taken up with these wonderful people who welcomed an actual American, because the songs they were singing were American. I hadn't heard skiffle music in America – I had heard jug bands, I had heard the musical saw, I'd heard all manner of banjos, guitars, fiddle music from the time I was very little because my mother transcribed it from the Lomax recordings. I had the background and I also had a number of songs they didn't have, so I brought songs over.'

Peggy had also struck up a relationship with Ewan MacColl that would last a lifetime. Not a musician himself, MacColl relied on others for accompaniment and in the twenty-one-year-old with a broad knowledge of American folk music and a fine singing voice he had found his perfect partner. At the time, MacColl was still married to his second wife, Jean Newlove. The weekly trips to Manchester provided the space for his and Peggy's relationship to flourish.

The Ramblers was an apt name for a programme that never found a regular home in Granada's schedules. The new channel was trying out different formats, discovering as it went along what worked and what didn't. The first episode was broadcast on Tuesday 29 May at 10.30 p.m., in a fifteen-minute spot between a boxing match and the final news report before the channel closed down at 11 p.m. The *TV Times* promised 'a new adventure in music and song presented by Alan Lomax'.

Peggy Seeger recalls the format. 'It was a kind of farmyard. It had fences and it had a hay bale and they hadn't told anybody that Peggy Seeger gets terrible hay fever. We would lounge against the fences and there were boxes, kind of like crates, that we would sit on to play. Nat would do one of his African songs, Fitzroy would do a calypso, Ewan would sing one of his songs, like "Hard Case" or "Dirty Old Town", and Alan would write a script that was very corny.'

Like almost all of Granada's output at the time, *The Ramblers* went out live and no recordings of the show have emerged. The general feeling among those who were there is that the tone was overly earnest and that Lomax, with his gushing exhortations to the viewers at home to gather around the TV with their beer mugs and tea cups and come a-rambling around the world, was a rather hokey host.

The executives at Granada seem to have shared this view. For its second programme, *The Ramblers* was shifted to Monday. A week later, it had disappeared from the schedule altogether, only to re-appear on 18 June, trailed in the *TV Times* as 'a novel experiment in folk music by a new singing group created by Granada TV Network'. By the following Monday it was gone again. When it returned on 9 July, squeezed in between half an hour of Liberace and the news programme, Lomax and MacColl were highlighted in the preview.

Viewers lulled into the assumption that *The Ramblers* was a fortnightly feature would have been surprised to find it back the next week, described as 'an unusual programme bringing folk songs, ballads and skiffle music together'. However, anyone tuning in the following week found the 10.30 p.m. slot taken up by '*Let's Listen*: Granada invites viewers to listen to the conversation of the kind of people they would like to have in their own after-dinner discussion'. The Ramblers were gone, never to return, but not before they recorded a single for posterity.

'Hard Case' was a Ewan MacColl song about a convict's fear of being sent to Dartmoor Prison. Recorded by Alan Lomax and the Ramblers on 2 August 1956, it had the up-tempo energy of a skiffle song, but Sandy Brown's clarinet gave it a jazzy feel. The B side would go on to become one of MacColl's most famous songs, one he had first recorded for Topic in 1952. A grimy hymn to the industrial landscape of his Salford childhood, 'Dirty Old Town' began its life as a song to cover a scene change in one of MacColl's Theatre Workshop plays. On the Ramblers' record, John Cole's plangent harmonica picks out the tune, while Lomax plays a plodding guitar that would be better suited to a solemn cowboy ballad. While none of this detracts from MacColl's rich imagery, it's only when Peggy Seeger's willowy voice joins him in the later verses that the song comes alive. The group also recorded two songs written by Lomax during the 2 August session – 'Oh Lula' and 'Railroad Man' – both of which were subsequently released when the whole session was made available on a four-track EP on the Decca label in 1957.

The Ramblers had one last stab at hitching themselves to Lonnie Donegan's bandwagon, producing a songbook entitled *The Skiffle Album* and featuring eleven songs that had been performed on the Granada TV series. Along with the tracks from the EP, the collection consists mostly of traditional ballads from the British Isles. Lomax and MacColl make their intentions explicit in the foreword: 'Not so long ago, a guitarist was quite a rarity in London, and the singer of folk songs was even more unusual. Today, however, a great revival of folk songs and skiffle music has taken place in this country. The

Alan Lomax and the Ramblers' *Skiffle Album* songbook, 1957

British and American people, who were great song singers a few centuries ago, are apparently on their way to becoming performers and ballad makers again. The British skiffle movement is an important part of this whole picture. Alan Lomax and Ewan MacColl, both of whom were raised in their youth with ballads and folk songs, hope that skiffle and folk song singers everywhere will find more of their songs on their home ground and that is one of the reasons for the publication of this book.'

Fifty-odd years after Sir Hubert Parry had sought to save traditional music from the grubby hands of the masses, Lomax and

252

MacColl were actively trying to give the people back their songs. Parry could have been describing the kids who flocked to play skiffle when he dismissed those for whom 'the commonest rowdyism is the highest expression of the human condition'. The rowdy commoners were about to storm the barricades of British culture.

HERE'S THREE CHORDS

At the end of June 1956, just before the City Ramblers set off on their European jaunt, a new, young skiffle band made their first advertised appearance on the bill of the Monday-night Studio Skiffle sessions at the Princess Louise. The Vipers Skiffle Group took their name from an autobiographical novella published that summer. *Viper: Confessions of a Drug Addict* was a racy account of life in the Soho drug scene, written by Raymond Thorp 'in the vocabulary of those who have given their souls to marijuana'. 'Viper' was a jazz term for someone who smoked grass, and twenty-something Londoner Thorp sought to follow in the footsteps of Thomas De Quincey, founder of the tradition of addiction literature, who walked the streets of Soho in the early 1800s in search of a thrill.

While none of the Vipers were inclined to give their souls to marijuana, the name gave them a certain hip cachet amongst the beatniks and bohemians who hung around the late-night coffee bars in central London. The arrival of the Gaggia espresso machine seems to have drawn guitar players into the cafes. *Sunshine on Soho* ends its visit to the 1955 Soho Fair by dropping into Les Enfants Terribles in Dean Street, where a young man strumming a Spanish guitar sings *chanson* to a group of attentive French students. The spirit of the Left Bank permeated the Gyre and Gimble, a basement coffee bar at 31 John Adam Street, just a few hundred yards from the skifflers' favourite busking spot, underneath the arches of Charing Cross Station. As early as 1954, young people were gathering there to smoke Gauloises and

The Vipers Skiffle Group: (*left to right*) Johnny Booker, Wally Whyton, John Pilgrim, Freddy Lloyd and Tony Tolhurst

look cool. A few guitars strummed in a corner added to the ambience. Orlando's in Old Compton Street was actually an Italian delicatessen by day, but the presence of a Gaggia drew in the kids. As evening fell, the place was converted into a cafe, and musicians played among the salami hanging from the ceiling.

The Vipers were formed at the Breadbasket, a coffee shop along Cleveland Street in nearby Fitzrovia. Local lad Wally Whyton, born in 1929, worked at a West End advertising agency, but on weekends he was to be found playing his guitar at the Breadbasket. The cellar cafe, decorated with Spanish-themed murals of flamenco dancers and guitarists, was a magnet for those eager to test out the three chords they'd just learned from listening to Lonnie Donegan. Ron Gould played tea-chest bass with the house band for a while and a young merchant seaman named Tommy Hicks would sit in on guitar when he was on shore leave.

By the spring of 1956, Whyton had formed a duo with Johnny Booker, who'd picked up the rudiments of guitar playing while hanging out with Diz Disley at the Gyre and Gimble. He brought another G & G regular to join the band. Jean Van den Bosch had all the accoutrements of a genuine bohemian: exotic name, goatee beard, deep baritone voice and acoustic guitar. In fact, he was a product of the English public-school system, working by day as a wire salesman. By spring 1956, augmented by various friends, the Vipers were playing regular if informal gigs at the Gyre and Gimble and the Breadbasket.

On 14 July, the band were among those thronging the streets of Soho for the annual festival of food, drink and song that was the Soho Fair. Aiming to busk on some busy street corner, they bumped into John Hasted and Redd Sullivan from the Forty-four Skiffle Club. The parade of floats that snaked through the streets was beginning to move off when Hasted encouraged them to bring their instruments and climb up onto a flatbed lorry that he intended to tag onto the end of the parade.

The object may have been to promote the Forty-four, or perhaps to spread the word about one of Hasted's left-wing causes, but for the next hour or so the Vipers found themselves backing the stentorian figure of Redd Sullivan as he belted out the same song over and over again. 'Sail Away, Ladies' had been popular with Appalachian fiddlers since the mid-nineteenth century, although there is some debate about whether the song began life as a sea shanty. The construction of the chorus suggests that it may have originally been sung as call and response: when hauling ropes, the shantyman would sing 'Don't she rock?', while the crew sang 'Die-dee-o' as they pulled together. Sullivan, having been a merchant seaman, was fond of shanties, and there is every reason to suppose the song was in his vast repertoire. Whether he picked up 'Sail Away, Ladies' from his days at sea or from the 1927 recording by Uncle Dave Macon and His Fruit Jar Drinkers is a moot point, but its catchy chorus made it an ideal soundtrack for the bustling energy of the Soho Fair.

When the parade came to a halt in Old Compton Street, the Vipers found themselves outside the 2 I's, one of the numerous coffee bars in the area, but not one they'd ever frequented. In need of refreshment, they jumped down from Hasted's red lorry in search of some caffeine. While waiting to be served, they couldn't help but succumb to the infectious earworm of 'Sail Away, Ladies'. When someone changed the words of the chorus to 'Don't you rock me, daddy-o', they all laughed and joined in, singing raucously while the owner prepared their coffees. Had they misheard what Redd Sullivan was singing or

Outside 2 I's, Soho: (*far left to right*) Chas McDevitt, Vince Taylor and Tony Sheridan (others unknown)

were they just riffing on a line from *Blackboard Jungle*? Either way, they'd just come up with the phrase that, in time, would define the generation gap in late 50s Britain.

The proprietor of the 2 I's was happy to have the band playing in his cafe. He'd been trying to draw customers in by employing singer Max Bard, whom Ron Gould recalls doing a kind of Burl Ives act in the cellar, but that wasn't bringing in the teenagers. These guys seemed to have that young sound, so as they finished up their coffees and headed back out into the rowdy rush of the Fair, he invited them to come back and play any time. They promised to return the following week.

The cafe at 59 Old Compton Street, almost on the corner of Wardour Street, took its name from the original owners, Persian businessmen Freddy and Sammy Irani. In April 1956, they leased the 2 I's to a pair of Australian wrestlers, Paul Lincoln, who wore a mask and fought under the name Dr Death, and 'Rebel' Ray Hunter, a giant of a man who would go on to be heavyweight champion of the British Empire.

The Vipers on stage at the 2 I's in 1956: (*left to right*) Tony Tolhurst, Jean Van den Bosch, Johnny Booker and Wally Whyton

They had arrived in England in 1951 and were soon busy both fighting and promoting bouts. They refurbished the cafe and, as the Irani brothers were their landlords, retained the name. The cellar was tiny, barely twelve feet wide and twenty feet long, but soon the Vipers were playing there regularly.

On 30 July, Lonnie Donegan, fresh from his US trip, came to see the Vipers perform at the Breadbasket. His agent, Lyn Dutton, had checked out the band a week earlier and decided to pass on representing them, but Donegan seemed taken with their performance, joining the group on stage for a couple of numbers. Since their experience at the Soho Fair, the Vipers had taken the bones of 'Sail Away, Ladies' and transformed it into a barnstorming number. Having written an entirely new set of lyrics, Wally Whyton and Johnny Booker had rechristened the song 'Don't You Rock Me Daddy-O' and it was going down a storm.

Donegan was so impressed with Booker's guitar playing and singing skills that he invited him to join the group he was putting together to record new material and undertake a British tour. Booker was unemployed at the time and, as the Vipers had no intention of turning pro, joining Donegan's band seemed like a way of making some money playing music. What could be better than that?

But Donegan wasn't only after a new singer/guitarist. At the first rehearsal session, he took Booker to one side and asked him about that new song the Vipers were playing at the Breadbasket. Booker taught the band 'Don't You Rock Me Daddy-O', and after they had run through it a few times, Lonnie declared that it was such a good song he intended not only to record it himself, but to take the copyright too. 'Don't worry,' he assured Booker. 'I'll take care of you.'

Johnny Booker was outraged and rightly so. He and Wally had been working on that song for weeks and now Donegan was going to steal it from them. If this was the price for being in his band, then Booker

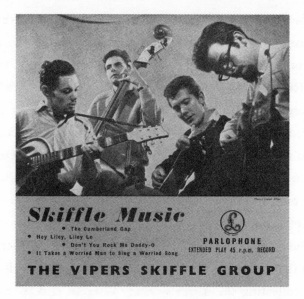

wanted nothing to do with it. He immediately contacted Whyton and together they set out to copyright the song themselves before Donegan could get his hands on it. They headed down to London's Tin Pan Alley, Denmark Street, where they sought out Gyre and Gimble regular Bill Varley, who along with Roy Tuvey ran a business cutting 78 rpm acetates from publishers' demo tapes. Varley took them to see Gerald Benson, who ran a little music publishing company a few doors away. He quickly drew up a contract and 'Don't You Rock Me Daddy-O' was published by the Benson Music Co., thwarting Donegan's plans.

Whatever sense of relief Johnny Booker got from preventing his song being stolen from under him must have been somewhat dented when he later found out that the writing credits had been given to Wally Whyton and Bill Varley. This sleight of hand wasn't uncommon in the early years of rock 'n' roll. Elvis Presley is credited along with Mae Axton and Thomas Durden as the writer of 'Heartbreak Hotel', yet he never made a contribution. One third of the publishing was given to him as an inducement to record the song.

This practice was even more prevalent on the skiffle scene as few British musicians knew who had originally written the old blues and folk songs that made up much of their repertoire. When Decca released 'Rock Island Line' in 1955, the songwriting credit on the label merely read 'Traditional', meaning that, as far as they were concerned, this was a folk song and the name of whoever wrote it was lost in the mists of time. It also meant that Decca were able to keep all the royalties derived from the songwriting and arranging. Just a few months later, when Decca reissued the song on 7" vinyl in the wake of Lonnie Donegan's success, the songwriting credit had been altered to read 'Traditional, arr. Donegan'. While Decca would still retain the royalties due to the unknown writer, Lonnie Donegan was now collecting the arranger's royalties (and why not? Decca had declined to pay him anything on the sales of 'Rock Island Line', a massive hit on both sides of the Atlantic). When they produced the sheet music anthology *Lonnie Donegan Album of Folk Songs* for two shillings and sixpence in late 1956, Essex Music came up with a new form of words that allowed them to claim all of the royalties for 'Rock Island Line': 'New Words and Music by Lonnie Donegan (based on a traditional theme)'.

But did Donegan really write new verses for the song and create a new arrangement? Wasn't his performance just a copy of Lead Belly's? Surely the King of the Twelve-String Guitar should get the songwriting credit under his real name, Huddie Ledbetter? However, if you look at copies of Lead Belly's records from the 1940s and 50s, 'Rock Island Line' is often credited to 'Huddie Ledbetter, John Lomax and Alan Lomax', which in itself is another publishing sleight of hand.

Lead Belly was in the employ of John Lomax in 1934, when he first heard Kelly Pace sing 'Rock Island Line'. Always on the look-out for new songs to add to his repertoire, he liked it so much that he dropped the verse that linked the song to Arkansas, kept the 'glory to God' verse, added a few more of his own, and developed the narrative that Donegan later repeated, the tale of how the train driver fooled the depot agent. Lead Belly didn't see this as stealing. It was how he composed many of his songs. He'd hear something he liked and adapt it to his style, adding lyrics to make it entertaining to his audience. Everyone who performed in the juke joints and dancehalls of Shreveport, where Huddie had learned his trade as a teenager, did the same. It was how songs were spread around back then, people picking them up and taking them as their own. In a culture where few people relied on sheet music, these songs belonged to everyone and each singer was free to add their own twist. Through this process, what we now call folk music was created.

This was the reason why Lead Belly was so valuable to John Lomax. His deep well of material, taken from many different styles and traditions, coupled with his ability to write his own topical material, gave Lomax great kudos among the small band of folk musicologists who were collecting songs in rural America during the early part of the twentieth century. When other academics gave lectures about Negro work songs, they had to rely on scratchy field recordings. John Lomax, however, could call on the real thing. Not only was Lead Belly one of America's greatest folk singers, he was also a convicted murderer, and Lomax traded heavily on this, sometimes requiring Lead Belly – his employee – to perform in striped prison clothes on the lecture tours they did together.

In 1936, Alan Lomax collaborated with his father on a book that told the story of this remarkable man. *Negro Folk Songs as Sung by Lead Belly* contained forty-eight numbers, with explanatory texts and sixty-four pages of biography. It was the first such book ever published about an American rural performer and, although it suffers today from Lead Belly's words being rendered in an excruciating

'Yas suh, Boss man' style, it sealed the Lomaxes' reputation as the nation's premier folk musicologists.

Lead Belly's songs, the mother lode of material that he had been carrying around with him for forty-odd years, were now being bought and sold, and as the inevitable invitations to record began flowing in, he discovered that he was no longer working in the folk tradition; he was now in the music business. When the record company enquired who owned these songs, the Lomaxes stepped forward. Perhaps they felt responsible for Huddie, concerned that he'd be ripped off if left to sign a publishing deal on his own. (And they had a point. An unscrupulous publisher would have had little compunction about not paying an African American his due in the 1930s.) Perhaps John Lomax felt that, as he'd had a hand in the discovery and promotion of these songs, he should get some credit. There was also the fact that Lead Belly had assigned all publication and other rights to the songs in the book to John and Alan Lomax for $250, just over $4,300 in today's money. Whatever the reason, 'Rock Island Line', along with a number of other Lead Belly songs, came to be credited to Ledbetter/J. Lomax/A. Lomax.

Yet surely if anyone deserved to have their name on the song it was Kelly Pace, the twenty-one-year-old convict serving his second jail term for burglary who led the group that performed the song to Lomax and Lead Belly at Cummins Farm that warm October day in 1934. However, just a week or so before, Lomax had recorded a similar version of 'Rock Island Line' at Tucker Prison, some fifty miles north of Cummins. The song was clearly in circulation among the prison population in Arkansas.

Far from being the author, Kelly Pace was an adapter, not that different in his motives from Lead Belly or Lonnie Donegan. If the song belonged to anyone, it was Clarence Wilson, the engine wiper in the Biddle Shops of the Rock Island Line in Little Rock. It was his performances of the song, as a member of the Rock Island Colored Booster Quartet in the late 1920s, that had made the song popular across southern Arkansas.

Nearly a century after the song was written, the writing credits are still a matter of some confusion. In 2015, the BBC broadcast a TV programme in which the comedian Frank Skinner looked at how popular entertainment had developed over the course of the twentieth century. In one episode, he got together with Lonnie Donegan's son Peter and skiffle great Chas McDevitt to perform 'Rock Island Line'. As they kicked into the first verse, a caption appeared on screen that summed up three generations of appropriation: 'Rock Island Line', it read, 'Written by Donegan/Ledbetter/Lomax/Lomax'.

———

Lonnie Donegan had returned home from his US tour on 22 July to find he was a sensation. 'Lost John' had peaked at number two in the charts, but even more astoundingly, his *Skiffle Session* EP had made it into the Top Twenty, the first time an extended-play record by a British artist had charted. Released as part of Denis Preston's jazz series, rechristened Nixa Jazz Today since the deal with Pye Records, the songs on *Skiffle Session* spoke of legendary figures from America's past.

The lead track, 'Railroad Bill', told the story of an African American outlaw, real name Morris Slater, who robbed trains and killed lawmen across the south in the 1890s. Alan Lomax recorded Hobart Smith singing the song in Saltville, Virginia, in 1942, which Donegan may have heard on the Library of Congress recordings held by the American embassy in Grosvenor Square. 'Stackalee' is a widely sung murder ballad concerning the killing of Billy Lyons by 'Stagger' Lee Shelton, in St Louis, Missouri, in 1895. 'The Ballad of

Jesse James' had been recorded by Woody Guthrie for Moe Asch in 1944, and the final track, 'Ol' Riley', came from Lead Belly's repertoire and concerned an escaped convict hunted by a bloodhound called Rattler.

When the tracks were recorded in early January 1956, Donegan was still a member of the Chris Barber Jazz Band and was backed by their skiffle group. The fact that Preston was happy to allow Dickie Bishop to sing lead on 'Stackalee' and 'Jesse James' is a mark of how Lonnie's rise to fame took even those involved in it by complete surprise.

Having handed Barber his notice before he left for America, Donegan returned home in need of a band. Barber's bass player, Mickey Ashman, jumped ship to join him and Monty Sunshine suggested former Christie Brothers drummer Nick Nicholls. When the band got together on 2 August to record Donegan's next single, Johnny Booker's no-show necessitated Denis Preston getting on the phone to Denny Wright, a thirty-two-year-old jazz-influenced guitarist who had set up London's first bebop club in Soho in 1945. Wright brought a new energy to the group, audible on one of the two tracks they recorded that day. 'Bring a Little Water, Sylvie' was a work song popularised by Lead Belly. Donegan used his trademark frenzied vocal style to ratchet up the tempo of the song, calling to Denny Wright to play a solo as the tune gained momentum. The B side was an amble through Woody Guthrie's 'Dead or Alive'.

The new Lonnie Donegan Skiffle Group made its debut at the Blackpool Palace on 19 August 1956 and three days later recorded their debut album, *Lonnie Donegan Showcase*. The week ended with a sold-out show at the Stoll Theatre in London, where the *NME* reported that 'fans stamped and whistled, cheered and chanted for minutes on end after the final curtain was rung down'. Seeing the excitement that Donegan generated, Val Parnell, managing director

of the Moss Empires variety circuit, booked the band for a fourteen-week tour.

Variety had its roots in the music halls that had emerged as the main provider of mass entertainment in the mid-nineteenth century. The halls were boisterous places, where performers sang risqué songs and told bawdy jokes. By the early twentieth century, the music-hall greats were dying off and their place taken by a new kind of act, one that a man could bring his wife or girlfriend to see without the possibility of causing embarrassment. Variety produced its fair share of comedians and singers who revelled in the kind of smutty double entendres loved by British audiences, but overall, the atmosphere was less rowdy than the beery music halls of old.

Establishing itself as the staple family entertainment, with theatres in every major town, variety took its name from the mixed bag of acts that would perform for a week before moving on. For an artist looking to exploit their new-found popularity, it was literally the only show in town. The very few jazz clubs outside London were simply not big enough to accommodate a performer as popular as Donegan had become. The only national touring circuit open to the new breed of skiffle groups was variety.

Beginning in Nottingham on 10 September 1956, the Lonnie Donegan Skiffle Group played two shows a night, six nights a week across the UK, with week-long stands in Edinburgh, Glasgow, Birmingham, Sheffield, Newcastle, Manchester, Leeds, Liverpool, Sunderland, Hanley and Bradford. The bill consisted of a troupe of dancing girls, a ventriloquist, a trio of comedy acrobatic cyclists, two comedians, a calypso pianist, and Mundy & Earle, whose act was simply described as 'A Boy, a Girl and a Gramophone'. With shows at 6.20 and 8.35 p.m., acts were lucky to get five minutes of stage time. Top of the bill was Donegan – 'direct from his terrific American success' – and he had the luxury of a thirty-five-minute headline spot in which to lead his skiffle group through a set which included 'Wabash Cannonball', 'Lost John', 'Nobody's Child', 'I Shall Not Be Moved', 'Sylvie', 'Dead or Alive' and, of course, 'Rock Island Line'.

On 5 November, the tour reached the Liverpool Empire, whose neo-classical facade dominated the corner of Lime Street and London Road. Built in 1925, the theatre had seats for almost two and a half thousand people, and during the six-night run Donegan drew packed houses of skiffle fans, eager to witness this new music at first hand. Up until this point, there had been no rock 'n' roll tours. Bill Haley, who had kicked the whole thing off, was still four months away from his UK debut. Elvis Presley, who had set the UK charts alight, would never perform in Britain. Lonnie was the first to take the message to the provinces, to let loose all of the teenage energy that had been building up since they tore down the bunting after VE Day. As must have happened in cities up and down the country, the arrival of Lonnie Donegan and his Skiffle Group in Liverpool had a catalytic effect on those who saw him perform.

Lonnie Donegan plays Liverpool, November 1956

It wasn't just his fast and furious music that excited teenagers –
1956 had been a year full of exciting new music. What made Donegan
stand out for the kids who saw him on that first UK tour was the
fact that, unlike all of the other purveyors of the new sound, Lonnie
was British, just like them. Furthermore, his music was made from
everyday objects that you could find in your home – washboards, tea
chests, broom handles. Okay, you needed to find a guitar, but then
you only had to learn three chords to be able to play this skiffle music.

Put together, these were perhaps the two most liberating ideas ever to sweep through a generation of British teenagers: 1) you don't have to be a musician to make music; and 2) you don't have to be an American to play American songs.

Among those drawn to the Empire during Donegan's stay was thirteen-year-old George Harrison, who borrowed money from his parents so that he could attend every night. When he discovered that the star was staying in nearby Speke, the excited teen hammered on his door until Donegan came out and gave him an autograph. George had a school friend, fourteen-year-old Paul McCartney, who shared his love of the new music. Hoping to catch a glimpse of Lonnie, Paul took off from school in his lunch break and headed down to the Empire. He found Donegan at the stage door, surrounded by factory girls, writing a note to their employers explaining why they were late back to work. Suitably impressed, after getting an autograph for himself Paul bought a ticket for the show.

It is not recorded if the sixteen-year-old John Lennon saw Donegan at the Empire, though it's highly likely that he too was touched by the mania that gripped Liverpool's teenagers in that November week. John was already a rock 'n' roll wannabe, and had played his 78 of 'Rock Island Line' almost to destruction. Mark Lewisohn, perhaps the world's leading authority on the Beatles, states that Lennon began playing the guitar 'from approximately the last weeks of 1956'. That is, in the wake of Donegan's Liverpool appearance. Though memories are vague, those who were there also believe that John's idea of forming a skiffle group among his friends from Quarry Bank School who hung out together to listen to Lonnie Donegan records also occurred during this period. What is clear is that by the end of 1956, the Quarrymen Skiffle Group were getting together whenever they could, trying to work out how to play Lonnie Donegan's entire repertoire.

The Quarrymen, November 1957

Paul McCartney was similarly inspired. After seeing the show at the Liverpool Empire on 11 November, he asked his recently widowed father to buy him a guitar. His friend George already had one, and now the younger boy, whose first-ever purchase as a music fan was 'Rock Island Line', could teach him some chords.

Not everyone was as enthusiastic about skiffle as the teens who took Lonnie Donegan as their inspiration. For the older generation of skifflers who venerated musical authenticity, the popularity of what they considered to be their own little scene was met with dismay. Under the headline 'Skiffle or Piffle?', Alexis Korner penned a scathing attack in *Melody Maker* on the new music. Pointing to the 1945 piano recordings of Dan Burley and His Skiffle Boys, Korner asserted that skiffle cannot be sung, only played. He even went so far as to state that it was 'a private music' that should not be played in public. Harrumphing like a furious colonel from the pages of the

Daily Telegraph, he asserted that 'British skiffle is, most certainly, a commercial success, but musically it rarely exceeds the mediocre and is, in general, so abysmally low that it defies proper musical judgment'. Tell that to the teenagers in Liverpool, Judge Korner. The article contained a postscript from Ken Colyer, complaining that 'skiffle over here has not produced any worthwhile talent and that is a pity. There is no originality' (says the man who won't play with anyone who doesn't replicate the style of New Orleans jazzers from before 1910).

Having introduced skiffle to the British public, the purists were desperately trying to close the stable door on their precious find. But that horse had already bolted and now Lonnie Donegan, like a skiffling Paul Revere, was riding it from town to town, spreading the good news: a new dawn is breaking! Here's three chords: now form a group.

LONNIE OPENS THE DOOR

Ken Colyer can be forgiven his bitter comments in *Melody Maker*. His skiffle group released three singles in 1956, none of which managed to capture the energy that had made Lonnie Donegan's records so attractive to teenagers. Not that Colyer wanted the adulation that came with chart success. He had the doggedly anti-commercial attitude of a purist who wasn't interested in meeting his potential audience halfway.

Others in the trad jazz scene were not so squeamish. In the summer of 1956, Humphrey Lyttelton enjoyed six weeks in the charts with his instrumental number 'Bad Penny Blues'. It was the first time a trad jazz single had made it into the Top Twenty and the first hit single to be given the signature Joe Meek sound.

Born on the edge of the Forest of Dean in rural Gloucestershire in 1929, Meek came from a working-class agricultural background and, while he never shone at school, from an early age he showed an interest in radios and how they worked. In 1938, he asked Santa to bring him a copy of *The Practical Wireless Service Manual*, advertised as 'a Complete Work on the Testing of all Types of Wireless Receivers and the Remedying of Faults in Them'. A strange gift for a nine-year-old child perhaps, but his parents duly obliged and soon Joe was tinkering with all manner of broken and second-hand radios and gramophones in the garden shed. At the age of sixteen, he was supplying music for local dances and theatrical societies with a portable amplifier, and in 1946 he astounded locals by building a TV set. No one in the area actually possessed one of these things, yet here was this teenager, building one in his shed. His achievement was somewhat diminished by the fact that the BBC had yet to start broadcasting in the area, so all he could show people was a blank screen emitting white noise.

While many teenage boys of the period dreaded the prospect of being conscripted into Britain's armed forces, Joe saw the call-up as a way of getting his hands on some really powerful equipment. When the buff envelope arrived from the War Office in 1948, he volunteered for the RAF and was one of only two recruits out of two thousand who passed an exam to become a radar mechanic. Demobbed two years later, he used his new qualifications to get a job in the workshop of the Midlands Electricity Board in Gloucester. When not repairing televisions, he would be using company equipment to build tape recorders, which, with two massive speakers, he took out on the road as an early sound system, playing tracks he'd recorded from the radio. In 1953, he built his own disc cutter, which he used to produce recordings of local bands. Heading to London, he managed to wangle a job with the Independent Broadcasting Company, which ran Britain's leading recording studios.

Initially employed on the Radio Luxembourg Road Show, which saw him travelling around the UK, rigging and then recording a show in front of a live audience, before editing it down for broadcast, Meek began honing his studio skills. By the end of 1955, he was senior balance engineer at the IBC Studios in Portland Place, where independent record producer Denis Preston was making a name for himself in the jazz world.

In April 1956, Preston had a session booked with the Humphrey Lyttelton Band and called Meek in as engineer. As so often happened in these early days, serendipity played a part in the recording. The saxophone player, booked for another gig, had to leave early, so Preston asked the band to play some boogie-woogie. Fortunately, Lyttelton's piano player, Johnny Parker, specialised in the barrelhouse style of Dan Burley, and with time running out the band performed a number that they'd often jammed at the 100 Club called 'Bad Penny Blues'.

Lyttelton was about to go on vacation and, anxious to get away, didn't bother hanging around to hear the recording. As a result of this haste, he never got to approve the effects that Meek had applied. 'Had I not gone on holiday, had we all gathered around and listened to the playback, I would have had a fit,' he recalled. 'I would have said, "That's dreadful! You've over-recorded the drums and I don't want that. You've distorted the piano and I don't want that either."' Lyttelton, very much a product of the upper middle classes, expected the rude mechanicals to follow orders. 'The idea of a sound engineer not doing what you tell him, but actually twiddling the knobs and distorting things – that was a totally new world to me.'

Denis Preston saw it differently, recognising that Meek 'had a drum sound – that forwards drum sound which no other engineer at the time would have conceived of doing, with echo'. Meek had also heavily compressed the sound of the record, which made it leap out of the radio in a way unheard of in British recordings of the time.

———

If Ken Colyer was irked to have lost control of skiffle and Humph found he was no longer in charge of his sound, their frustration was as nothing compared to that of the denizens of Tin Pan Alley, who found that they had lost control of British pop music. For years they had found good-looking singers, groomed them, chosen their material and presented them, fully packaged, to an audience of predominantly adult record buyers.

Lonnie Donegan had blown a hole in that business model. Not only did he get his material for free from the blues and folk traditions, he'd also discovered a teenage market for British pop. But how could the music business get a slice of this action? The whole attraction of skiffle was that it wasn't polished and presentable. It was organic, both in the way it was performed and in the manner in which its popularity spread. If Tin Pan Alley wanted to tap into this new-found wellspring of teenage consumers, they needed someone from the skiffle scene who was pliable.

The straights knew they'd never find this willing soul among the hard core in Soho. Nobody at the Skiffle & Blues Club wanted to be the new Dickie Valentine; they were more interested in becoming Muddy Waters. The Studio Skiffle crowd would rather go busking around Europe than play ball with the business of show and everyone knew that the Forty-four Skiffle Club was a nest of communists.

In the autumn of 1956, the tabloid newspapers began to report on the new coffee bar scene, running picture spreads of teens jiving to washboard-playing bands. The audiences looked less hostile than the skiffle club crowd, their tastes seeming to lean a little more towards pop. As a result, some figures on the fringes of the music business began taking their cappuccinos with the kids and, although no one actually said, 'If I could find a skiffler who sang like Elvis Presley I could make a million,' that's more or less what they were all thinking.

On 16 September 1956, the front page of the *People*, one of Britain's biggest Sunday newspapers, carried 'exclusive pictures' of upper-class people dancing wildly to rock 'n' roll music. 'Now the Smart Set Are at It', claimed the headline. Young debutantes with double-barrelled names were said to have danced till dawn to 'Britain's top rock and roll guitarist'. Who was this kid?

Tommy Steele had been discovered in the 2 I's coffee bar after he leapt on stage during a skiffle session and sang a rock 'n' roll song.

That was enough to get him invited to play at the debs' party, which in turn led to a residency at the Stork Club. This upmarket West End nightspot, frequented by minor royalty, was soon generating more headlines for Steele. According to the *Daily Sketch*, the Duke of Kent thought Tommy was 'great, great, great'.

For the class-obsessed British press, a quote from the twenty-year-old duke endorsing rock 'n' roll was manna from heaven. The following weekend, Britain's other main Sunday tabloid, the *News of the World*, picked up the story, adding the Marquis of Milford Haven to the list of aristocrats in thrall to the blond-haired rocker. These were the days when an endorsement by the aristocracy still carried considerable cachet, especially among the broadcast media. Up until now, rock 'n' roll had been associated with riotous behaviour and condemned by the mainstream media. If Prince Edward of Kent, the Queen's cousin no less, was dancing to this music, then surely it was okay to play it on the BBC?

The papers provided a little biographical detail: Tommy Steele is nineteen years old, comes from Bermondsey in south London and, since leaving school, has been working as a 'bell hop' on transatlantic liners plying the London-to-New York route. When home on leave, he likes to bring his guitar into the coffee shops of Soho and sing a few songs. Inspired by seeing Elvis on TV when in New York, his speciality is rock 'n' roll.

The tabloid press seemed convinced that they had found the first home-grown rock 'n' roll star. What was special about Tommy Steele was his age. Other British artists had tried to jump aboard the rock 'n' roll bandwagon in 1956, but none had captured the imagination of the teen audience. Tony Crombie and the Rockets could lay claim to being the first British rock 'n' roll band with their single 'Teach You to Rock'. Having played around the scene for over a decade, respected jazz drummer Crombie went to see *Rock Around the Clock* and emerged a changed man. He convinced a gang of fellow jazz and swing players that, if they wanted to keep earning a living, then rock was the way forward. After they'd all duly traipsed along to see the movie, they formed a band that aped the Comets in style, sound and presentation. Born in 1925, Tony Crombie was the same age as Bill Haley and, in the fevered months after the emergence of Elvis Presley, there was no way he could compete with a nineteen-year-old guitar-playing Tommy Steele. But it wasn't only age that gave the Bermondsey boy his edge. He was also the beneficiary of the first rock 'n' roll hype ever perpetrated by Tin Pan Alley.

Tommy Hicks fitted right into the London skiffle scene. He loved playing guitar and his job as a merchant seaman gave him both an air of exotic wanderlust and access to plenty of American music. When on shore leave, he'd often end up at the Gyre and Gimble, and he'd add a little contemporary music to the folk blues and sea shanties that were most often heard there. When the weather warmed up, he'd join the gang who caught the 4.30 a.m. train down to Brighton, where they'd busk on the beaches all day.

Through Johnny Booker, who ran the G & G, Tommy was introduced to Wally Whyton and often sang at the Breadbasket with the crowd who would go on to coalesce as the Vipers. Another coffee-bar friend was Lionel Bart, a twenty-five-year-old member of the Communist Party who cut his teeth writing left-wing songs for the agit-prop productions of the Unity Theatre in London's East End. Lionel had recently branched out into light entertainment, selling a song to avuncular bandleader Billy Cotton. 'Oh for a Cup of Tea (Instead of a Cuppuchini!)' bemoaned the fact that it was becoming difficult to find a decent cuppa now that espresso had arrived. Bart, who along with his buddy Mike Pratt had redecorated the cellar of the 2 I's in return for a crate of beer and life membership, wasn't taking sides in this debate. He was just happy to have earned twenty-five guineas for one of his songs. It was the beginning of a very successful career.

Pratt, who would later gain fame as Jeff Randall in 60s detective series *Randall and Hopkirk (Deceased)*, was another G & G regular who played piano. Along with Wally Whyton on guitar and Johnny York on tea-chest bass, he was a member of the Cavemen, an ad hoc group of musicians who Tommy Hicks gathered together whenever he wanted to play some music at a party.

Over the summer of 1956, Tommy came and went, two weeks at sea, two weeks at home, living with his mum and dad on the south side of Tower Bridge. Starting in May, Elvis began lobbing singles into the UK Top Ten: 'Heartbreak Hotel', 'Blue Suede Shoes', 'Hound Dog'. This was music that spoke to Tommy, much more so than the songs that Lonnie Donegan was singing. With plenty of time to perfect his performances while at sea, when he came back to London that autumn all he wanted to do was play rock 'n' roll.

Tommy had an urge to write his own song and even had a title: 'Rock with the Caveman'. Lionel Bart wrote some lyrics that referenced the recently exposed Piltdown Man forgery, Mike Pratt added a few melodic touches and they performed the song at various parties and cafes around the West End. Hicks was preparing to return to his ship, the *Mauretania*, when he was approached by Dennis Grayman, a photographer who worked for the Moss Empires theatre chain. Grayman arranged for Tommy to audition for two big London agents, but neither showed any interest in this kid with the guitar.

Undeterred, Grayman eventually sought out Bill Varley and Roy Tuvey, who he knew had recently helped the Vipers secure a publishing deal for 'Don't You Rock Me Daddy-O'. Tuvey immediately saw the potential in Tommy Hicks and offered to manage him, bringing in agent Geoff Wright. By September, the Vipers had a residency at the 2 I's and Tuvey arranged for Tommy to play a guest spot with the band.

His aim was to recruit John Kennedy, a New Zealand-born PR man, to help promote their new client. The 2 I's wasn't Tommy's usual stomping ground, but since their appearance at the Fair, the Vipers had turned it into the happening place in Soho. The Gyre and Gimble was hipper, darker and had a more edgy clientele, but the brightly lit 2 I's drew the teenagers, and that was the audience everyone was looking for.

When the Vipers took a break, Tommy jumped up and played an energetic version of 'Rock with the Caveman', and Kennedy was hooked. When he offered to make Tommy a star, the incredulous teen asked him what he knew about show business. 'Absolutely nothing,' Kennedy replied. 'But what do you know about singing?'

What Kennedy did know about was publicity. If Tommy was to be a star, then he'd need a new name. Hicks just didn't sound rock 'n' roll enough. It was Tommy who suggested Steel, taking a cue from his grandfather, Thomas Stil Hicks. Someone at Decca Records later added the 'e'. Kennedy's next step was to create a fuss around his new charge. But how to do so without alienating the press and the BBC? September 1956 was the month of the *Rock Around the Clock* riots. For weeks the papers had been full of these terrible Teddy Boys tearing it up, and rock 'n' roll was getting all the blame.

Kennedy had a stroke of genius. He gathered together a bunch of teenage Soho showgirls and models and had them bring their boyfriends down to a private house in Wandsworth, where Tommy Steele and his band were having a party. After instructing the teenagers to give posh double-barrelled names if asked any questions by the press, he tipped off the *Sunday People* that the first society rock 'n' roll party was taking place and invited them to send a photographer along to capture the moment. The mixture of posh and pop was too much to resist for a newspaper notorious for salivating over any suggestion of transgressive behaviour. The following weekend, Tommy Steele was front-page news and, more importantly, rock 'n' roll gained a veneer of respectability from its association with the 'smart set'. Tin Pan Alley began to take note.

Decca Records signed Tommy that same week after Hugh Mendl saw him perform 'Rock with the Caveman' not in a Soho coffee bar, but in the toilets at Decca's West Hampstead Studio. Mendl, the man who'd supervised the recording of Lonnie Donegan's 'Rock Island Line', was so eager to hear Steele that he invited him to audition without first checking if any of the studios were free. Hence the performance in the gents, where the natural echo was ideal for rock 'n' roll.

Next in the queue for a slice of this new talent was Larry Parnes, a twenty-seven-year-old businessman who ran a women's clothing shop in Romford and fancied himself as an impresario. In 1955, he'd invested in a West End production called *Streets of Shame*, which was losing money until John Kennedy was hired as publicist. He promptly changed the name of the play to *Women of the Streets* and paid two actresses from the cast to stand outside the theatre impersonating prostitutes. They were all arrested, but the subsequent publicity turned the play into a success.

Kennedy recognised that Tuvey and Wright were just too small-time to handle the kind of career that he had in mind for Steele, so he brought Parnes in as co-manager. On 26 September, just ten days after he had first appeared in the *Sunday People*, Tommy, after consulting his mother, signed a management deal with Parnes and Kennedy which gave them 40 per cent of his earnings. Tuvey and Wright were out and Larry Parnes had secured the first in what would become a stable of British teen idols.

Although he'd come late to the Tommy Steele story, Larry Parnes quickly developed a reputation for creating stars. After being tipped off by Lionel Bart about a lad named Reg Smith singing rock 'n' roll at the Condor Club, Parnes got an address from the club's manager and drove down to the Smith family house in Greenwich with a contract for Reg already drawn up in the glove compartment of his pink-and-grey Vauxhall Cresta. Young Smith didn't take much convincing to sign up, but Parnes insisted that he change his name to something more suitable for a rock 'n' roll star. At six foot three inches tall, Reg Smith didn't much like having a daft-sounding moniker foisted on him, so Parnes offered to toss a coin. Reg called it wrong and in that instant became Marty Wilde.

By the end of the decade, Parnes was overseeing the careers of a number of English lads whom he'd rechristened in a similar way, Billy Fury, Johnny Gentle, Vince Eager, Dickie Pride, Duffy Power and Georgie Fame among them. Of all his artists, only Joe Brown resisted having his name changed, which is understandable given that Parnes wanted to call him Elmer Twitch.

Tommy Steele recorded 'Rock with the Caveman' on Monday 24 September 1956, backed by sidemen from the London jazz fraternity. Piano was provided by Dave Lee, from Johnny Dankworth's band, and Ronnie Scott played the tenor sax that drove the track along. It was released by Decca on 12 October, and three days later Tommy made his television debut on the BBC's stuffy *Off the Record* programme. The new commercial channel was quick to follow the BBC's lead, with Tommy appearing on Jack Jackson's eponymous Sunday-night show. With his single climbing the charts, John Kennedy must have felt he'd hit the jackpot.

But 'Caveman' stalled at number thirteen and the follow-up, 'Elevator Rock', failed to chart at all. Just as it looked like all their best efforts were about to unravel, Kennedy and Parnes came up with a classic Tin Pan Alley trick. Guy Mitchell was one of a number of American crooners who were fighting an increasingly futile battle against Elvis Presley at the top of the US charts. His song 'Singing the Blues' had taken the top spot from 'Love Me Tender' in early December and was about to be released in the UK.

Decca rushed Steele into the studio to record a rival version that, apart from Tommy's vocal slurring of the title à la Elvis, was so similar to the original that Mitchell quipped that his arranger deserved a credit on Steele's record. The two singles raced each other up the charts and Mitchell pipped Steele to number one, but at the crucial moment he suffered a distribution problem and Steele snatched the top spot from him. He only held it for a week, but it was enough for Tommy Steele to claim that he was the first rock 'n' roller to score a number one in the UK, albeit with a carbon copy of a crooner's ballad.

Steele ramped up his chart success with a variety tour, topping a bill that included comedians Mike and Bernie Winters and 'Thunderclap' Jones, 'the Welsh Wizard of the Keyboard', a kind of cut-price Jerry Lee Lewis from the Valleys. On the last night of a week-long stand at the Finsbury Park Empire, among the audience was another Jones who would create his own thunderclap in the 1970s. Having crossed London from Bromley with his father and his cousin Kristina, nine-year-old David Jones – later Bowie – was electrified by what he saw and heard that night, proclaiming that he wanted to be a rock 'n' roll singer like Tommy Steele. Look at those Cavemen go.

———

In the last week of December, Lonnie Donegan's first album entered the UK charts. This wasn't some thrown-together, here's-all-the-hits, cash-in-for-Christmas release. *Lonnie Donegan Showcase* featured none of the three Top Ten singles that Donegan had scored that year. Instead, the 10" vinyl album contained eight new recordings cut with his touring band in August.

The first and third tracks on the album, 'Wabash Cannonball' and 'Nobody's Child', had been recorded by Donegan, with Chris Barber on upright bass and Beryl Bryden on washboard, back in the summer of 1954, during the session that produced 'Rock Island Line'. Yet, despite his title as the King of Skiffle, Donegan had never again used a washboard on his records and the new album benefited from the driving rhythm of a full band. Charlie Patton's 1929 recording of 'I Shall Not Be Moved' may have been the source for Donegan's take on this old gospel song, although the overenthusiastic use of a tambourine makes his version sound like a singalong at the local Salvation Army hostel. Lead Belly is present, of course, 'I'm Alabamy Bound' being one of the many roots songs that Lonnie had borrowed from his material.

Donegan may have first heard 'Wreck of the Old 97' while he was stationed in Vienna, listening to the American Forces Network. This classic railroad song was a popular number among the bluegrass bands of the period. It told the story of Number 97, a fast mail service on the Southern Railway between Washington, DC and Atlanta, Georgia. On Sunday 27 September 1903, the train left Monroe, Virginia, an hour behind schedule. Desperate to make up time, the driver took the approach to the wooden trestle bridge across Stillhouse Creek, just outside of Danville, North Carolina, too fast. As a result, the engine and all five cars plunged seventy-five feet into the ravine below, killing nine people, including the train's crew. This ballad appeared shortly thereafter, borrowing its tune from Henry Clay Work's song 'The Ship That Never Return'd', first published in 1865.

The most powerful track on the album is the closing song, 'Frankie and Johnny'. Lonnie ramps up the emotions, seeming to tear the words out of himself, the terrible tale almost too much for him to bear. By the climax of the song, he's near-hysterical, exhibiting the loss of vocal control that would later become the hallmark of Joe Strummer's performances with the Clash. John Peel, aged seventeen when the album came out and no stranger to music that pushed the boundaries, credited Donegan's version of 'Frankie and Johnny' as being 'one of the most astonishing performances in all recorded music'.

Unlike any album released by a British artist before or since, *Lonnie Donegan Showcase* went into the singles chart, as if the music industry just didn't know what to do with him. The press seemed similarly unsure where skiffle belonged in the new dispensation. On 8 December, *Melody Maker* ran a feature entitled 'Rock 'n' Roll Pays Off'. Alongside pictures of Donegan and Tommy Steele, the paper declared, 'Critics may snarl, musicians may sneer, Variety artists may weep but the much-abused rock 'n' roll spells big business in Britain today.' The same paper ran a joint live review of Donegan and Steele under the headline 'Rock 'n' Roll (Or Was It Skiffle?) Comes to Town'.

Reporting from the Prince of Wales Theatre in London, where Donegan ended his amazing breakthrough year with an unprecedented three-week residency, Laurie Henshaw declared him to be the most uninhibited British singer he had yet seen. By contrast, Dick Hall, reviewing Tommy Steele, was unimpressed with what he saw at the Finsbury Park Empire. 'Thunderclap Jones pleased with his punchy playing – although his rendering of the Warsaw Concerto could be much shortened.' Steele, however, 'offered little in the way of musical entertainment. His voice was frequently out of tune. His intonation was also bad. Perhaps it would be kinder not to mention his guitar playing.' Tommy might have looked like a rocker, but it's clear that he was still skiffling his way through performances, despite the hype surrounding him.

The meteoric rise of Tommy Steele came towards the end of a year in which youth culture pushed its way into the public consciousness in post-war Britain. Up until then, developing a taste for the music and fashions of your parents had been a signpost on the road to maturity.

However, as the year drew to a close, even the headline writers of populist tabloids were raiding teen culture to report on world events. 'RAF Rock 'n' Roll 'Em Round the Clock' was the way the *Daily Sketch* chose to report the bombing of Egyptian air fields during the Suez Crisis.

At the start of 1956, Lonnie Donegan had stumbled through the door to chart success, carrying his acoustic guitar and singing American roots music. His success had legitimised the skiffle scene and made it possible for both the music industry and the public at large to conceive of a guitar-playing British singer. As the year ended, Tommy Steele, nurtured by the skiffle scene, had skipped through the door that Donegan had opened, carrying an electric guitar and playing the latest sounds from the US. Over the next twelve months, skiffle and rock 'n' roll would battle it out for the heart and soul of Britain's pop fans.

19

GOING SO FAST

Lonnie Donegan began 1957 on a wave of popularity. If the appearance of his debut album in the singles charts seemed incongruous, then Tin Pan Alley must have been dumbfounded when he came second in the *NME*'s annual popularity polls. Elvis had only managed third behind Frank Sinatra and Johnnie Ray in the American Male Singer category, but Lonnie snuck in between big-band leader Ted Heath and crooner Dickie Valentine, who took the title of Most Outstanding British Musical Personality.

It wasn't just Donegan who was suddenly outstandingly popular. The *Daily Herald* reported jam-packed crowds of 'duffel-coats and horsetails' gathering in Orlando's, Johnny Grant's deli/coffee bar just a few doors along Old Compton Street from the 2 I's. The article carried a picture of the Ghouls skiffle group performing among the salami and olive oil. Bearded boho Fath Maitland, the group's leader, explained how he and some friends had asked Grant if they could play in his shop for fun, only to find a few weeks later that they now needed a doorman to keep the crowd outside from blocking the pavement.

Despite complaining that all the songs sounded the same, the journalist reported that there were now four other skiffle bars in Old Compton Street alone, with about twenty in Soho and more further afield. Nineteen-year-old Joan Pike, who was taking the hat around for the Ghouls, told the *Herald* that the attraction of Orlando's was that it provided teenagers with 'a place of our own, where dreary, old middle-aged people in their thirties won't bother us'.

The Ghouls perform amid the salami at Orlando's

Ken Sykora, writing in *Music Mirror*, noted approvingly that the Ghouls were known to nip next door to the 2 I's and borrow a spare guitar string from the Vipers. The emergence of Tommy Steele from the skiffle scene and Donegan's continued success meant that doors began opening for skiffle groups, and the Vipers were among the first to benefit. Having passed on signing Tommy Steele, George Martin, the youngest record company executive in town, signed the Vipers to his Parlophone label in October 1956 and produced their debut single at Abbey Road.

Martin's genius was to resist bolstering the group's sound with professional sidemen from the swing bands that provided the pool of session musicians working on the pop records of the day. There were no jazzy guitar chords seeking to soften the sound for the Light Programme on the Vipers' records, just three fiercely strummed acoustics, backed by a rockabilly bass line and John Pilgrim's lap-played washboard. Martin created the first record to contain the real sound of skiffle, as heard in the basements and cafes of Soho. The Vipers were much admired by skiffle fans, not least because their no-frills approach to recording conveyed the idea that anybody could make this music.

Lonnie Donegan's success had catapulted him from the back of Chris Barber's Jazz Band to the top of the bill at ATV's prime-time variety show, *Sunday Night at the London Palladium*. He was seen on TV dressed in a dark suit and bow tie, playing his acoustic, but now backed by an electric guitarist and a jazz drummer. By contrast, the Vipers looked like they'd just been busking outside the Palladium. Twenty years before punk rock made a fetish of the DIY approach, the Vipers' authenticity endeared them to a generation of skiffle fans in their early teens.

Like Donegan, the Vipers plundered Lead Belly's repertoire for their first single. The A side was an up-tempo run through the old spiritual 'Ain't You Glad', backed with the African American work song 'Pick a Bale of Cotton'. The latter had first been recorded by John and Alan Lomax at Sugarland prison farm in December 1933, performed by a sixty-three-year-old inmate named James 'Iron Head' Baker, whose ability to both recall and improvise a vast number of songs led John Lomax to dub him a 'black Homer'.

The Vipers' debut single didn't trouble the charts, but in January 1957 they released a song that would come to define the skiffle movement. With its infectious chorus and call-and-response verses, 'Don't You Rock Me Daddy-O' had been transformed by George Martin from a sea shanty into a clarion call for the coming war of the generations.

Now that it had been commercially released, there was nothing to prohibit Lonnie Donegan recording his own version. Featuring a brief drum solo and a burst of jazzy lead guitar from Denny Wright, this was a polished pop song and duly rose to number four in the charts. The

Vipers' original, sounding, by contrast, like it was recorded in the invigorating confines of a crowded coffee bar, only managed to reach number ten, but this was enough to put them on the map. The second skiffle group to make the charts, they soon found themselves in great demand, following Donegan and their erstwhile bandmate Tommy Steele onto the variety circuit, where they were welcomed with open arms.

As the independent television network was becoming more populist in order to differentiate itself from the highbrow BBC, it naturally began to feature more variety comedians in its lighter programming. The effect was soon felt in the theatres. Why go out on a wet Wednesday to a draughty old music hall and pay to sit through a series of antiquated vaudeville acts when you could watch them all in the comfort of your own home for free? Desperately in need of new blood, the variety promoters grabbed skiffle with both hands.

The Vipers first trod the boards at the Prince of Wales Theatre, just off Piccadilly, where for two weeks they shared a spot just before the intermission with the Bob Cort Skiffle Group. Top of the bill was blonde bombshell and TV singing star Yana, a former hairdresser's assistant from Billericay in Essex whose real name was Pamela Guard. The rest of the bill was filled with the usual comics and animal acts, although history doesn't record whether Bob Hammond 'and his Feathered Friends' were the former or the latter. Being placed in the middle of the batting order allowed the skifflers to carry on with their regular gigs in the late-night cafes and clubs of the West End.

Around the same time that the Vipers were commencing their engagement at the Prince of Wales, the City Ramblers, returning from their European jaunt to find the skiffle craze in full swing, undertook a national variety tour under the banner 'It's (S)Cool for Cats'.* Promoter

---

* The bracketed 'S' of the title was probably there to stop Bernard Delfont from being sued by ITV, who in 1956 had launched a new music programme for teenagers called *Cool for Cats*.

(S)Cool for Cats. Skiffle on the variety circuit, 1957

Bernard Delfont was trying hard to draw the teenage audience into his theatres. The poster advertising the City Ramblers' week at the Sunderland Empire promised 'Skiffle', 'Rock 'n' Roll' and 'Boogie Woogie'. When the tour reached Hull in mid-March, it had become 'Britain's First Ever Rock 'n' Roll Tour'. In truth, it was just another variety bill, albeit one without any dog acts or trick cyclists: the Manton Brothers did the soft-shoe shuffle, Billy 'Uke' Scott strummed his ukelele and comic Andy Stewart was the MC. The only real hint of rock 'n' roll on the bill came from Little Abner, a singer and boogie-woogie

290

pianist in the style of Big Joe Turner, born Abner Kenon in Florida in 1917. As a subtle warning to those of a nervous disposition, Delfont made sure audiences realised that they were about to see a black man on stage by billing Little Abner as 'Harlem's Coloured King of Rock 'n' Roll'.

On 21 January, a new combo, the Chas McDevitt Skiffle Group and Nancy Whiskey, made their debut in variety at the Metropolitan in London's Edgware Road, on a bill which included three comedians, a juggling duo, a balancing act and the 3 Quavers, intriguingly described in the programme as 'instrumentally different'. McDevitt was born in Glasgow in 1934 and had been playing banjo with the Crane River Band, Ken Colyer's original outfit, recently re-formed with new members and performing regularly at Cy Laurie's. Chas led the breakdown group.

In late 1956, McDevitt's skiffle group entered a talent contest on Radio Luxembourg and came top for four weeks in a row. Nancy Whiskey, who had taken over running the folk and skiffle night at the Princess Louise while the City Ramblers were rambling across Europe, also appeared on the programme, and the group's manager duly took note. Bill Varley – he who had snaffled a co-writing credit on 'Don't You Rock Me Daddy-O' for simply introducing Wally Whyton to a publisher – understood that, if they were to make their mark, the McDevitt group needed a gimmick. And, in the exclusively male world of skiffle, what better gimmick than a girl singer?

McDevitt wasn't enamoured of the idea, feeling it suggested that Bill Varley had no confidence in the act, while Whiskey preferred to sing traditional Scottish songs. However, it was clear to everyone in the Soho scene that skiffle was taking off, so Whiskey agreed to join McDevitt's group for six months.

Their first joint recording was a song that McDevitt had originally heard performed by Peggy Seeger. As a result of her folk-infused upbringing and her time at university, Seeger's repertoire differed from those of performers on the London skiffle scene, who had mostly learned their material from commercial recordings. 'Both my brother Pete and I went and looked up songs when I was at Radcliffe, which was the female section of Harvard. I would go into the Harvard Library and get out all the old anthologies and I'd learn songs from them.'

However, one of the stand-out songs in her repertoire hadn't come from the anthologies compiled by her musicologist parents, nor from the library at Harvard. Seeger had learned 'Freight Train' from an African American woman who was housemaid at her family's Washington, DC residence. Born in North Carolina in 1895, Elizabeth Cotten was hired by the Seegers in 1945, after she found Peggy wandering alone in Woodward and Lothrop, Washington's largest department store, and returned her to her mother. 'Libba would have come probably when I was ten,' recalls Seeger, 'but it wasn't until I was about fourteen that I came into the kitchen and found her playing the guitar that always hung on the wall. Up until then, whenever you came in the kitchen she was ironing or she was cooking or she was putting dishes away or whatever.'

Cotten had played since childhood, initially mastering the banjo and then moving on to the guitar. Being left-handed, she developed her own distinctive picking style to allow her to play guitars strung for right-handed people. However, she had ceased playing after joining the church in the early 1920s. Working in a house full of musicians had encouraged her to pick up the instrument again, and she began entertaining the Seeger children with songs she'd played as a child, among them one she'd composed herself, 'Freight Train'. With its mournful lyrics concerning the killing of a friend, a hanging and a burial, it must have sounded like a classic American murder ballad when Peggy Seeger played it in the coffee bars and skiffle clubs of Soho. And in the febrile atmosphere that followed Lonnie Donegan's runaway success with what everyone assumed to be a traditional railroad song, it was only a matter of time before someone exploited Seeger's repertoire.

Denny Carter, one of the guitarists in the McDevitt group, told Pete Frame how he 'collected' it one evening at the Princess Louise. 'I've got a very good ear for a melody – once a song has been sung, I know it. So I concentrated on the tune, Chas noted the chord shapes and sequences, and the girlfriend scribbled the words down.'

Chas McDevitt had already recorded a version of 'Freight Train' in late 1956, before Nancy Whiskey came onboard. At Bill Varley's suggestion, they recut the song, playing the tune in double time. With Nancy's chirpy vocal and Chas whistling a harmony line between each verse, they transformed a dark tale of evil deeds into a catchy pop song.

'Freight Train' was released as a single in January 1957 and initially got little attention, but during March the band took part in an extensive tour of British theatres, opening for Slim Whitman. There were no variety artists on this bill, just Slim, the McDevitt Skiffle

Group and Nancy Whiskey, and Terry Lightfoot's Jazzmen, a blues-influenced trad band. This was enough to propel 'Freight Train' into the charts by mid-April, beginning a run of seventeen weeks that saw the single peak at number five.

They followed the Whitman tour by joining with Lightfoot again to open for American sensations Frankie Lymon and the Teenagers, touring on the back of their UK number one hit, 'Why Do Fools Fall in Love?'. Again, there were no cheesy variety artists to get in the way of the stars. This was a bill aimed exclusively at those under twenty: nothing but trad, skiffle and rock 'n' roll.

But the big sensation of early 1957 was the arrival from the US of Bill Haley and His Comets for their first UK tour. The *Daily Mirror* took a bunch of teenagers to Southampton to meet the band at the dockside and chartered a special train to take them to London, where fans thronged the station to see their hero. But what they saw puzzled them. In the flesh, Bill Haley was a portly, middle-aged father of five who looked more like one of the square teachers in *Blackboard Jungle* than one of the too-cool-for-school kids. He didn't seem to have realised that James Dean had reset the image of the teen idol as a potent mixture of moody, sexy and rebellious. Haley was none of these and, although the tour was a huge success, it all but killed his career.

Since 'Rock Around the Clock' reached number one in October 1955, Haley had scored nine Top Twenty hits in the UK; after his British tour, he didn't manage to get another single in the charts until March 1974 – ironically, a reissue of his original hit. For all the tumult he had caused, Bill Haley wasn't the King of Rock 'n' Roll after all. He was the herald, and 'Rock Around the Clock' the clarion call, alerting the first generation of British teenagers to the coming of the One True King, Elvis Presley.

Now that Tommy Steele had shown that English kids could play rock 'n' roll too, everyone wanted a piece of the action. Paul Lincoln, at the 2 I's, kept his ear out for another teenager who could sing like Elvis among the crowds who thronged to his cafe every night. Terry Williams, a seventeen-year-old from south London, had been singing rock 'n' roll songs in the boiler room of the HMV record plant where he worked. He liked the way the natural echo made his voice sound like Elvis. One night he took his guitar along to the 2 I's and asked if he could sing a song. His version of 'Poor Boy' from the soundtrack of Presley's first movie, *Love Me Tender*, so impressed Lincoln that he took Williams under his wing, changing his surname to Dene (after James Dean).

Quickly finding an agent for his new charge, Lincoln staged what may have been the first all-British teenage package show, at Romford Odeon, on the outskirts of London, on 31 March 1957. Terry Dene made his debut supporting the Chas McDevitt Skiffle Group and Nancy Whiskey, backed by rockers Rory Blackwell and the Blackjacks. Lincoln astutely used the popularity of skiffle to blood his would-be rock 'n' roll idol.

The fact that skiffle had crossed over into the mainstream was evidenced on Easter Monday 1957, when 'London's First Big Skiffle Session' was held at the Royal Festival Hall. The afternoon event featured a number of artists who had emerged from the jazz scene following the success of 'Rock Island Line'.

After Lonnie Donegan left the Chris Barber Jazz Band in May 1956, Barber had been wondering how to replace him, when, one night, Johnny Duncan walked into the 100 Club looking like a younger Lonnie and wearing almost exactly the same clothes. Johnny was born in Oliver Springs, Tennessee, in 1932 and had married an English girl while stationed in East Anglia with the US Air Force.[*] He played guitar and mandolin and sang in the high-pitched tones of

---

[*] Duncan's place and date of birth have both been disputed, however.

a traditional bluegrass singer. He was soon sharing vocal duties with Dickie Bishop in the Chris Barber Skiffle Group.

In September 1956, Denis Preston took them into the studio to record an EP for the Nixa Jazz Today series, with pleasing results. The closeness of the harmonies and Duncan's mandolin playing pushed the songs in the direction of bluegrass duos such as the Louvin Brothers and the Blue Sky Boys. It sounded great, but was it really skiffle? Barber didn't think so. He'd booked a tour with Big Bill Broonzy and Brother John Sellers and needed his skiffle group to sound more bluesy.

In February 1957, Duncan jumped ship before he was pushed. Having lost Bishop to Donegan's band some three months before, Barber, who had been midwife to the skiffle boom, decided not to replace either guitarist, quietly dropping the skiffle interludes in his set just as the craze was taking hold. However, his commitment to American roots music remained undimmed, and in the following decade he brought over the finest American blues musicians to tour with his band, acting as midwife again, this time to the blues boom of the early 1960s.

By the time of the Easter Monday Skiffle Session, Dickie Bishop had left Lonnie Donegan's Skiffle Group after just three weeks in the job and formed his own group, the Sidekicks. Another escapee from Donegan's band, guitarist Denny Wright, had joined Johnny Duncan and His Blue Grass Boys. Both groups were on the bill at the Festival Hall that afternoon, along with Bob Cort, a bald and bearded twenty-seven-year-old advertising man from Loughborough. Despite being also-rans in the skiffle craze, the Bob Cort Skiffle Group included key figures from the scene. Guitarist Ken Sykora would go on to host *Guitar Club* on the BBC Light Programme from July 1957, encouraging listeners to play in styles 'from Spanish to skiffle', and the washboard player was none other than Bill Colyer, the Godfather of Skiffle himself.

Bob Cort's claim to fame is that he recorded the original title song for *Six-Five Special*, but for my money his cover version of Chuck Berry's 'School Days' deserves recognition for sheer chutzpah alone. 'Hail, hail, skiffle and roll, deliver me from the days of old!' he cries, unconvincingly, while Ken Sykora fires off jazz runs on electric guitar. 'Long live skiffle and roll, the beat of the washboard loud and cold!' The kids weren't biting. Cort looked like an off-duty geography teacher and sang like one too.

Also on the bill were the Avon Cities Jazz Band, who, like the Colyer and Barber outfits, had their roots in the late 1940s. The band's clarinettist, Ray Bush, led the skiffle group that recorded eight tracks for Decca subsidiary label Tempo in June 1956. Hailing from Bristol, they differed from the standard skiffle group by featuring both banjo and mandolin.

Chas McDevitt, whose group were headliners that day, recalls the Avon Cities provided a much-needed rhythmic anchor during the final ensemble number, 'Momma Don't Allow'. After the sound of a dozen or so heavily strummed guitars and the metallic scrape of the half-dozen washboards involved in the encore had subsided, it was the Avon Cities who played a passable version of the National Anthem to close the event, something beyond the capabilities of many of the assembled skifflers.

———

In the spring of 1957, Chas McDevitt had emerged as the first real rival to Lonnie Donegan for the title of King of Skiffle. But while 'Freight Train' reached number five in the charts in April, the following month saw the first skiffle number one.

Cumberland Gap is the name of the only pass through the Cumberland Mountains, long known to Native Americans and discovered by European settlers in the 1670s. It provided a route through the Appalachians to Kentucky from Virginia, and the song of the same name is thought to have originated in the area around the end of the nineteenth century. The earliest recording of the song with lyrics, made by Gid Tanner and his Skillet Lickers in 1926, still evidenced its roots as a fiddle song, with Tanner throwing in the occasional stanza between longer instrumental passages. By the time Woody Guthrie recorded the song in 1944, the chorus declared that Cumberland Gap was seventeen miles from Middlesboro, Kentucky.

In early 1957, the Vipers got hold of the tune and declared that the distance to Middlesboro was in fact nineteen miles. The discrepancy may be down to how fast you're travelling – Lonnie Donegan's high-tempo version, released just after the Vipers' single, claimed the distance was only fifteen miles. Using his trademark runaway-train style of delivery and with his backing group frantically skipping between the two chords that make up the entire song, Donegan accelerated past the Vipers to score his first number one.

He followed it up with a live single taken from his week's residence at the London Palladium with the Platters. 'Gamblin' Man' offers some insight into the intensity with which Donegan performed during this period. The song begins with a slow introduction but soon takes up a relentless rhythm, which has Donegan gasping for air at the start of each line. Halfway through his voice pushes up a gear as the tempo of the song gathers. He calls up a guitar solo that threatens to run out of control, before returning to sing with raucous abandon. The audience go wild.

If Lonnie dipped into the repertoire of skiffle hero Woody Guthrie for this tour de force, the song he paired it with as a double A side was much more in the variety tradition. 'Puttin' on the Style', first recorded by Vernon Dalhart in 1926, is a sardonic commentary on the youthful fashions of the day. Donegan updated the lyrics and struck a chord not only with the teenagers in his audience, but also with the parents accompanying them to the Palladium show. Their teenage years had been lived during the Great Depression and the Second World War, when style had been on ration. Donegan, already pushing thirty and perhaps eyeing a potential audience of mums and dads beyond the skiffle craze, gave them a wink to let them know that he too looked askance at the fashions and fandom of the children they'd raised. The single duly went to number one, becoming both the first double A side to top the charts and the first live recording to do so.

Between these successive number ones, Donegan had returned to the States for a second tour. The reciprocal touring agreement between the UK Musicians' Union and the American Federation of Musicians required a like-for-like swap of artists, so when Bill Haley and His Comets were booked for their British tour, there was only one act who could be sent to America in exchange. But while Haley was met with adulation wherever he went, Lonnie found himself providing a half-time show for sports fans, performing on a nationwide tour by the Harlem Globetrotters. In basketball arenas with dreadful acoustic properties, Donegan played to ten thousand people buying popcorn, some of whom complained that the Globetrotters didn't have their usual comedian entertaining the crowds. The schedule was gruelling – nineteen cities in nineteen days, each of them hundreds of miles apart.

Donegan wasn't the only skiffler to visit the US in the summer of 1957. 'Freight Train' proved just as irresistible to Americans as it did to Britons. The Chas McDevitt Skiffle Group with Nancy Whiskey reached number forty in the *Billboard* charts in the second week of June. Fresh from a cross-Channel skiffle and rock day trip organised by Paul Lincoln and billed as 'The 2 I's Rock Across the Channel', Chas and Nancy found themselves performing on *The Ed Sullivan Show* in New York – fronting a group of US musicians insisted upon by the AFM, among them Hank Garland, who would later play on a string of Elvis Presley's singles, including '(Marie's the Name) His Latest Flame'. Without the necessary work permits, the only appearance they made was at Palisades Park, just across the Hudson from New York City, where they had to follow a guy who jumped off an eighty-foot tower into a pool of water – on a horse.

The success of 'Freight Train' in America caused the inevitable copycat versions to be released, just as Donegan had experienced with 'Rock Island Line'. But unlike Lonnie, the McDevitt Group was not able to hold off the competition, most notably from carrot-topped country crooner Rusty Draper, who reached number eleven with the song.

The song's popularity caused a good deal of consternation in the Seeger family, who were surprised to hear a song written by their sixty-two-year-old housemaid being played on the radio and TV, given the fact that she had no publishing deal with which to collect royalties. Their concerns grew when, on looking at the record label,

Ed Sullivan meets skiffle, New York, 1957: (*left to right*) Marc
Sharratt, Ed Sullivan, Nancy Whiskey and Chas McDevitt

they found the song was credited not to Elizabeth Cotten but to Paul
James and Fred Williams, a songwriting team from England.

This wasn't the first time British skifflers had run into trouble with
US publishers. Legend has it that Lonnie Donegan's American man-
ager, Manny Greenfield, went to see the boss of Folkways Records,
Moe Asch, to complain that one of Folkways' artists, a certain Mr
Lead Belly, was recording Lonnie's songs without permission or pay-
ment. Moe threatened to break the allegedly offending records over
Manny's head.

Pete Seeger led the campaign to get proper recognition and royalties
for Elizabeth Cotten and, in the ensuing litigation, it transpired that

the pair who claimed to have written the song, James and Williams, were none other than Chas McDevitt and his manager, Bill Varley, for whom purloining credits was becoming something of a habit. The case was eventually settled amicably out of court, and Elizabeth Cotten went on to record an album of original material in 1958, produced by Mike Seeger.

Problems with visas prevented the Chas McDevitt Skiffle Group from playing concerts in the US, but they returned home to a record-breaking tour of the Moss Empires variety circuit, during which their second single, 'Greenback Dollar', edged into the Top Thirty. By the time the tour ended, Nancy Whiskey felt she'd come to the end of her six-month commitment to skiffle and returned to singing traditional Scottish material, complaining to the music press that she never liked skiffle anyway.

20

THIS'LL MAKE YOU SKIFFLE

If the number of skiffle acts reaching the charts and crossing the Atlantic can be counted on the fingers of one hand, then those playing skiffle at grassroots level were legion. It is estimated that there were between thirty thousand and fifty thousand active skiffle groups at the height of the craze in 1957. 'Skiffle' guitars could be purchased by mail order for as little as £6 6/-. The difference between a regular guitar and a 'skiffle' model was never explained in the adverts, but if you couldn't afford the full price, the guitar would be mailed to you for five shillings up front (plus five shillings postage and packaging), to be followed thereafter by twenty-two fortnightly payments of six shillings and sixpence.

Ben Davis, managing director of one of Britain's biggest whole-sale and retail musical instrument firms, told the *News of the World* that demand for guitars had increased tenfold since September 1956. 'At Christmas people were walking around Charing Cross Road with bundles of notes in their hands looking for guitars. At the moment I have twenty thousand on order and wish I could get more. I estimate that this year over a quarter of a million will be imported into this country, compared with about six thousand in 1950.'

The craze reached far beyond the capital. Jim Reno, owner of Reno's music store in Manchester, one of the largest in the north of England, declared, 'I cannot cope with the demand for guitars, with young lads in here every day asking for them. One day last week I sold one hundred guitars.' Bell Music of Surbiton in Surrey offered a

'Skiffle Basselo', a cello-sized double bass with two strings, for just £3 down and twenty-four monthly payments. Hidden in the small print was the full price, twenty-nine guineas (£30 9s.) – an expensive piece of kit in 1957, when the average weekly take-home pay for a manual worker was just over £20.

For those not able to stretch to a basselo, John Hasted printed a handy guide to constructing your own tea-chest bass in the pages of *Sing* magazine. The same December 1956 issue carried an article entitled 'How to Build a Lagerphone'. An Australian invention – with, it was claimed, roots in medieval Turkey – the lagerphone consisted of three hundred lager bottle tops attached to a broom pole in such a way that they rattled when the bottom of the pole was bounced on the floor.

Hasted used his columns in *Sing* to defend skiffle from 'supercilious critics who clutter up the newspapers and magazines'. He argued that it was a people's music, with its own momentum, independent from the commerciality of the music business, and that playing guitar had empowered youth to find its voice. 'There must be over four hundred skiffle groups in London alone,' he reported with glee in spring 1957. 'Local competitions receive entries from about ten groups in every borough.'

Hasted also understood that, to overcome its limitations, skiffle had to progress beyond its original canon, presciently predicting how it would lead to the British blues boom. 'Unlike the older skiffle groups, the new ones make no distinction between a rock 'n' roll number and a folk song and I think this is only to be expected and is not a bad thing anyway. The groups will get very tired of the rock 'n' roll up-tempo twelve-bar and turn to the real blues if they've got it in them.' He also cautioned those who, gripped by the skiffle craze, looked to take the short cut to guitar playing. 'Don't take the easy way out with your guitar by fixing that German machine to the neck, to get the press button chords. Within a few months you'll find that it limits your style severely.' He was referring to an oblong contraption that clamped onto the fretboard of the guitar, near the headstock. On top were a series of buttons marked with the names of half a dozen guitar chords in the same key. When you pressed a particular button, felt pads would hold down the strings in the correct shape for the chord, allowing you to strum a song without learning how to actually play the guitar.

Others were not so enthusiastic about the rise of this do-it-yourself music. On 9 March 1957, *Melody Maker* put skiffle on trial: 'What IS skiffle? Is it a creative music, a menace or just a form of rock 'n' roll?' Chris Barber gave the purist's view: 'I regard skiffle as important only in so far as it relates to the origins of jazz.' Tommy Steele opined that, although he once played skiffle in coffee houses, what he was playing now was something else. 'People say skiffle appeals to the same audience as rock 'n' roll. That's not true. Skiffle is more intellectual.' Bill Colyer, now playing occasional washboard with the Bob Cort Group, pleaded guilty to giving skiffle its name, but warned the critics not to look down on the craze. 'It's well known that today skiffle sells to rock 'n' roll and Presley fans. That's no reason though for anyone to get smug and self-righteous.'

Unfortunately, *Melody Maker* journalist Bob Dawbarn's horse was far too high for him to hear Bill Colyer's words. 'Skiffle is the dreariest rubbish to be inflicted on the British public since the last rash of Al Jolson imitators,' he fumed, sounding like Tommy Steele's grandad. 'Let's face it, skiffle has as much to do with jazz as rock 'n' roll, Guy Lombardo and ballroom dancing. Like the other three, it is a bastardised, commercialised form of the real thing, watered down to suit the sickly, orange-juice tastes of musical illiterates.' Dawbarn was no doubt mumbling that last phrase under his breath five years later when, as editor of *Melody Maker*, he had Bob Dylan thrown out of the paper's office.

The summing up for the defence came from Lonnie Donegan: 'I did it from the beginning because I believed in it. Chris Barber, Ken Colyer and I forced it on the public in the face of early hostility. We felt that it illustrated the origins of jazz. None of us did it to make easy money.'

Since he had been crowned King of Skiffle, defensiveness had become a reflex action for Lonnie. Many of the jazzers who used to respect him during his Barber band days were bemused by his sudden elevation to matinee idol. *Melody Maker* itself wasn't sure how to handle him. One week he was on the front cover with banner headlines announcing his season at the London Palladium, then a few weeks later he found the paper accusing him of being conceited. 'It's all very well, some say, for a star to act like a star – but [Donegan] is a mere skiffler, a man swept to accidental fame by a teenage craze.'

The old sweats at *Melody Maker*, unsettled by a music industry increasingly dominated by teenage tastes, were constantly on the lookout for a new dance craze to come along and sweep skiffle and rock 'n' roll away. In the spring of 1957, calypso was hotly tipped as the next big thing and *MM* ran a full-page feature entitled 'Will Calypso Knock the Rock?' The article centred on the only artist who seemed able to resist the inexorable rise of Elvis Presley – Harry Belafonte, whose album *Calypso* had vied with Presley's eponymous debut for the number one position in the *Billboard* charts throughout 1956.

Teen magazines pitted them against one another, the King of Rock 'n' Roll vs the Calypso Champion. The subtext of this contest was the growing generation gap. Belafonte was a highly talented twenty-nine-year-old nightclub singer, his smooth delivery popular with fans of swing who had, since the war, been the taste-makers for the music industry. They had driven the mambo mania of 1955 and calypso looked a likely candidate to push rock 'n' roll back to the juke joints from which it had sprung. Elvis, aged just twenty-one, represented the teenagers and their burgeoning spending power. Among the predominantly album-buying adults, Belafonte won the popularity contest, spending more time at the top of the charts than his rival. However, it was in the crucial singles market that Elvis cleaned up. Belafonte scored a big hit with 'Day-O (The Banana Boat Song)', which reached number five in the US and two in the UK, but Presley's run of hit singles in 1956–7 made him unassailable. The failure of calypso to ride to the rescue seemed to rile Bob Dawbarn, who, looking for someone to take it out on, penned an eviscerating article for *Melody Maker* entitled 'Has Trad Jazz Had It?' (His answer? I bloody well hope so.)

Tommy Steele's assertion that skiffle was more intellectual than rock 'n' roll seemed to be borne out by an article that appeared in highbrow Sunday broadsheet the *Observer* in June 1957 under the title 'Skiffle Intelligentsia'. 'Hardly a week goes by without some denigration of skiffle in the musical magazines,' wrote Hugh Latimer. 'But skiffle refuses to die. A year ago there were only about twenty groups around London. Now there are nearer 400, with one to ten groups in every English-speaking centre from Glasgow to Cape Town. Sales of guitars have broken all records; shops in Surbiton display them hanging in rows like so many turkeys for Christmas. You can buy washboards, tea-chests, lagerphones, all the paraphernalia of a down-and-outs band. Skiffle has taken by storm the youth clubs and the public schools, and the Army has carried it to Germany. The remarkable thing is that in an age of high-fidelity sound, long players and tape recorders, the young should suddenly decide to make their own music.'

Latimer also proffered evidence that, far from resisting calypso, the skiffle kids were incorporating it into their DIY music along with all the other musical styles that got them dancing. 'The newer skiffle groups do not distinguish between skiffle and rock 'n' roll, submerging them all in the same breathless din; if a folksong or a calypso achieves commercial popularity, it goes into the repertory too.'

A month later, *The Times* suggested that skiffle might represent a new popular art among young people. Their correspondent astutely observed that music hall, the last great popular art to arise in England, had begun with 'amateur performers singing in modest public houses, conditions which one might, without exaggeration, compare to the sudden appearance of the skiffle singers in the cellarage of coffee bars'.

Fred (later Karl) Dallas attested to the energising effect the skiffle craze was having on the fledgling folk scene. 'For nearly a decade, my wife and I played and sang folk songs to small, select gatherings. But the "folk" didn't want to know. Now when my skiffle group plays in the open air at Walton Bridge on Sundays, we can hold crowds of over a hundred with the same songs we've been singing all these years.'

The popularity of skiffle as a national phenomenon had been heightened by the arrival in February 1957 of *Six-Five Special*, a TV pop programme aimed at teenagers, broadcast live by the BBC on Saturday evenings. BBC television had already dabbled in pop music, starting in January 1952 with *Hit Parade*, on which popular songs of the day were covered by artists such as Petula Clark and Dennis Lotis. This was followed in May 1955 by *Off the Record*, introduced by Jack Payne, who had served in the Flying Corps during the First World War and led the BBC Dance Band from the 1920s onward. Both shows were aimed at adult audiences, with Payne in particular resisting any move towards skiffle or rock 'n' roll. When Elvis arrived on the scene, Payne used his *Melody Maker* column to fulminate against the new movement. 'Are we to let youth become the sole judge of what constitutes good or bad entertainment? Are we to move towards a world in which the teenagers, dancing hysterically to the tune of the latest Pied Piper, will inflict mob rule on music?'

ITV's attempt to cater for the teenage audience, *Cool for Cats*, was a fifteen-minute show hosted by the avuncular Radio Luxembourg

DJ Kent Walton, who played popular records while a troupe of dancers interpreted them for viewers. It was broadcast twice weekly at 7.15 p.m., the earliest time slot available for young adults that wasn't part of children's programming.

Thanks to a broadcasting regulation known as the 'Toddler's Truce', both BBC TV and ITV left a gap in their schedules every night between 6 and 7 p.m., ostensibly to give parents the opportunity to usher their little ones off to bed. While this may have made sense within the public service ethic upheld by the BBC, for their commercial rivals it meant an hour of lost revenue. And when the independent channels began to struggle financially, the government moved to lift the restriction, much to the annoyance of the BBC, to whom the hour gap represented an opportunity to save costs.

The date agreed for the lifting of the Toddler's Truce was Saturday 16 February 1957, and the BBC chose to fill the new time slot with a show featuring live music aimed at a teenage audience. The programme was the brainchild of Jack Good, a twenty-five-year-old Oxford graduate who had been president of both the University Debating Society and the Balliol Dramatic Club. Since coming down to London, Good had acted on the West End stage and been part of a comedy duo telling gags between the nude tableaux at the Windmill Theatre in Soho. Finding the commercial pop of the day boring, he fell in love with rock 'n' roll after witnessing the frenzied dancing of the *Rock Around the Clock* audiences in a London cinema. By his own admission, he wasn't overly keen on the music, but he loved the sense of chaotic energy that it generated among the teenagers.

Good wanted to bring some of that energy to the TV screen and approached the BBC with a proposal for a rock 'n' roll show that would take the audience out of the stalls and place them between the cameras and the artists, giving the viewer the impression that they were watching a teenage party. Realising that they needed to provide something for the growing audience of young adults, the BBC agreed to let Good make six programmes. A number of titles were suggested, among them *Start the Night Right*, *Take It Easy*, *Don't Look Now*, *Hi There* and *Live It Up*, before the producers settled on one that reflected skiffle's obsession with trains: *Six-Five Special*.

The paternalistic BBC wouldn't give Good free rein with the content, insisting that anything aimed at young people should have some educational value. The resulting programme was a mixture of music and magazine, as variety performers shared the screen with boxers and features on outdoor pursuits followed *Blue Peter*-style demonstrations of how to make a handy item from a cardboard toilet-roll holder and some egg boxes.

Host Pete Murray kicked off the first programme, welcoming viewers aboard the Six-Five Special with some jive talking: 'We've got almost a hundred cats jumping here, some real cool characters to give us the gas, so just get with it and have a ball.' His co-presenter Jo Douglas, who along with Jack Good also produced the show, followed that by declaring, 'Well I'm just a square, it seems, but for all the other squares with us, roughly translated, what Peter Murray just said was, we've got some lively musicians and personalities mingling with us here, so just relax and catch the mood from us.'

While the screen was filled with young people, it still felt as if the mood was being dictated by the grown-ups. The closest thing to rock 'n' roll on the bill that first Saturday evening was the King Brothers, a doo-wop-style trio from Essex who had graduated from children's TV. Crooner Michael Holliday sang some big-band ballads and a sixty-five-year-old Ukrainian-born concert pianist named Leff Pouishnoff played selections from Beethoven and Chopin. Kenny Baker's jazz band opened and closed the show.

By week three, things had begun to change – Tommy Steele topped the bill. And the following week, Jack Good really got into his stride, producing a show that featured Steele, the Vipers and Big Bill Broonzy. With little competition from the other teenage pop programmes, *Six-Five Special* was soon drawing a regular 10 million viewers, but Good was hampered by his relatively skimpy budget – just £1,000 per show, much too low to attract big American artists – and the lack of genuine British rock 'n' rollers. As a result, the music featured on the show tended to be a mixture of pop ballads, trad jazz, skiffle and indigenous rock 'n' roll, with a sprinkling of classical music and calypso thrown in.

When Tommy Steele first appeared on the show on 2 March 1957, he found himself sharing the bill with a steel band, a classical guitarist and comedy duo Mike and Bernie Winters. Lonnie Donegan was a regular performer, as was Humphrey Lyttelton with his jazz band. Jack Good even managed to squeeze a member of the aristocracy onto the show in the shape of the fourth Earl of Wharncliffe – twenty-one-year-old Alan James Montagu-Stuart-Wortley-Mackenzie was only the drummer for the Johnny Lenniz Group, who appeared on the show on 27 April, yet his title merited a picture in the *Radio Times*.

Looking to generate excitement with limited resources, the producers took the programme out on the road, presenting live broadcasts from Scotland, Wales, the north, Paris and the NAAFI, a canteen for servicemen, in Plymouth. The most famous of these came on 16 November, when the programme took over the 2 I's coffee bar in Soho. The Chas McDevitt Skiffle Group with Shirley Douglas were featured, as were the Worried Men Skiffle Group, one of whom, singer Terry Nelhams, would top the charts two years later as Adam Faith.

Such was the lack of space, artists were thrown in to do their piece to camera, only to be ejected back out onto Old Compton Street once they had performed, where television vans blocked the road and the pavement was full of nervous young lads wearing make-up, trying to keep their quiffs intact for their spot on national TV. Terry

Dene was prominent among them, but the show also featured Larry Page, the Teenage Rage, who would go on to produce records by the Kinks and the Troggs in the mid-60s; Jim Dale, later an actor in the *Carry On* movies; and thirteen-year-old Laurie London, who, within six months, would find himself at the top of the US charts with a chirpy version of 'He's Got the Whole World in His Hands' and gain immortality in the opening sentence of Colin MacInnes's 1959 novel *Absolute Beginners*.

Despite the conditions, it was by all accounts great TV, but, as all of the *Six-Five Special* shows were broadcast live – including those filmed at its Lime Grove Studios home in west London – there is no surviving footage to confirm that Gilbert Harding, the fifty-year-old fuddy-duddy broadcaster, no doubt invited by Good to cast his irascible eye over proceedings, was referred to as 'Daddy-O' by Wee Willie Harris. The fact that the BBC never taped any episodes of *Six-Five Special* also deprives us of the sight of Harris, five foot two, red hair, oversize Teddy Boy drape, big bow tie, pink socks and massive crepe-soled creepers, singing his theme tune, 'Rockin' at the 2 I's', with Mike and Bernie Winters and the King Brothers.

If the chaotic broadcast from the 2 I's was Jack Good's finest hour, it was also his swansong. Within two months he'd jumped ship to ITV, leaving the programme in the hands of self-confessed 'off-duty Mozart fan' Dennis Main Wilson. Good re-emerged eight months later at the helm of *Oh Boy*, the rock 'n' roll show that he'd always wanted to make. Broadcasting in direct competition to *Six-Five Special*, he set the tone from the first show, which featured the TV debut of Cliff Richard, whose explosive performance of 'Move It' propelled him into the charts and caused the *Daily Mirror* to ask 'Is This Boy Too Sexy for Television?' The show was 100 per cent rock 'n' roll, no skiffle or trad, no comedians goofing around, no films about orienteering or how to apply make-up. The audience were missing too, sat back in the stalls (of the Hackney Empire in London's East End), although their screams of delight could be heard throughout the broadcast.*

Despite the loss of its founder, *Six-Five Special* continued to get good viewing figures and its first anniversary was celebrated by a front-page feature in *Melody Maker*. A month later, a movie spin-off was released, featuring performances from Lonnie Donegan, Dickie Valentine and the ever-present King Brothers, among others. The fact that there were no recognisable rock 'n' roll acts in the film reflected the problem *Six-Five Special* faced. Its commercial rival, *Oh Boy*, had both the budget and the format to attract British rockers. *Six-Five Special* – never sure if it was a teen pop show or a variety programme – just couldn't compete for the likes of Cliff Richard.

Instead, while *Oh Boy* became the nursery for Britain's would-be rock 'n' rollers, *Six-Five Special* embraced skiffle in the form of Stanley Dale's National Skiffle Contest. The skiffle contest was a phenomenon that harnessed the momentum of the craze, putting the spotlight on amateur players, most of whom were under twenty. The skifflers who enjoyed chart success in the 50s – Donegan, McDevitt, the Vipers – were all born in the 1930s and came out of the jazz clubs. The kids they inspired were almost all born in the 40s and got together in village halls, school gyms and scout huts. Too young to play in pubs and clubs and mostly living out in the provinces, their stage was the skiffle contest.

As many groups were formed from competitive cliques at school, the idea of competing against other skiffle outfits was part of their culture. For fourteen- and fifteen-year-old boys, skiffle had an even greater attraction than football. Sure, being in the school team might

---

* *Oh Boy* was Jack Good's masterpiece and its influence can be seen in the production values of 60s shows like *Ready, Steady, Go!* and *Top of the Pops*. Good went on to work in America, where he created *Shindig* for the ABC network in 1964.

impress your mates, but playing skiffle attracted girls, who, more than anything, wanted to jive to up-tempo music (often with each other, much to the chagrin of local lads).

The heats of the skiffle contest were held at the local cinema or variety theatre, with winners decided by the reaction of the crowd. Victory in the local heats would send groups through to semi-finals against outfits from around the country and success could bring national recognition – in November 1957, the BBC broadcast the finals of the World Skiffle Championship on prime-time TV as part of the popular ballroom dancing show *Come Dancing*. The *Daily Herald* newspaper offered a prize of £175 to the winners of national weekly skiffle contests held during the summer of 1957 at Butlin's holiday camps across the country, later claiming that around eight hundred groups had taken part.

Whit Monday, the public holiday that heralds the beginning of the summer season, had traditionally been the date on which the Round Table in Bury St Edmunds, a sleepy town in rural Suffolk, held their charity fete. In 1957, it fell on 10 June and they decided to hold a one-day national skiffle contest in conjunction with the International Jazz Club. Groups came from as far afield as Swansea and Glasgow, one determined bunch – the Skiffle Cats from Paddington – walking the seventy-five miles from London to Bury St Edmunds. Once the non-skifflers had been weeded out from the hundreds of groups that tried to enter, forty-four were chosen to participate. In the event, only thirty-four turned up, the outdoor venue and the classic British Bank Holiday downpour discouraging the more faint-hearted. Each group was given six minutes to perform two songs before the judging panel of Johnny Duncan, blues and skiffle authority Paul Oliver and jazz critic Graham Boatfield. There were prizes to be won and the promise that winners would be recorded by Esquire Records.

In an article for *Jazz Journal*, Boatfield described the groups as predominantly acoustic, with an average of three guitarists each. If he detected a unifying characteristic among the youths who gathered under the trees, trying to keep their instruments dry on that damp Bank Holiday, it was one of class. 'If one must categorise skiffle, it seems on this showing to be a very thriving music of young workers from the towns.'

Boatfield detected the 'pernicious influence' of Lonnie Donegan on the material chosen by performers, with some Elvis Presley thrown in for good measure. He even found some 'deep diggers looking for their own native folk music'. Sixty years later, his description of the crowd will resonate with anyone who has ever attended an English charity fete on a wet weekend: 'A surprisingly large crowd stood in the steady rain watching the performers, gently exuding a sort of damp uncon-cern and that inspired melancholy with which the Anglo-Saxons take their pleasures.' The fact that the MC was a young clergyman seals the scene.

Boatfield's main complaint was the paucity of original mater-ial. Again and again the same songs were thrashed out in the rain: 'Wabash Cannonball', 'Worried Man', 'Cumberland Gap' and the ubiquitous 'Don't You Rock Me Daddy-O'. 'After the tenth repeti-tion of any opus one's spirits flagged and it was refreshing to hear a few others which, if not original, at least showed some acquaintance with a wider field.' The youngest musician was just twelve years old.

Each group was given marks for style, originality, ease of perfor-mance and musical ability. Independently from these scores, points were awarded for original compositions, of which more than a dozen were performed. The eventual winners – 'not difficult to spot, but it took a long time to get there', lamented Boatfield – were the 2.19 Skiffle Group from Gillingham, Kent, who doubtless impressed the old jazz journalist by taking their name from Louis Armstrong's '2.19 Blues'. Second came the Station Skiffle Group from Fulham, and in third place were the winners of the All Scottish Skiffle Contest, the Delta Skiffle Group.

Yet as the damp crowds dispersed at the end of a long day's skiffling, spirits among some of the victors were even damper. Having made a 750-mile round trip from Glasgow – in a Britain that had yet to build any motorways – the Deltas were angry that, despite the advert for the contest promising cups and cash prizes, they were given just £5 and no trophy for coming third. Promised a gig in London to tie in with their Esquire recording session, all they received was £1 between them and their train fare home to Glasgow. And although an album featuring all three bands duly appeared on Esquire Records, in hindsight the impartiality of the organisers is put into question by the fact that, before the contest was held, the 2.19 Skiffle Group had already released two EPs on the Esquire label.

The skiffle contests were run almost entirely on enthusiasm, and it wasn't long before someone hit on a way to make money from the phenomenon. Stanley Dale, a middle-aged variety promoter and manager of the Vipers, shrewdly noted that, if a contest was judged

on audience reaction alone, then competing groups would be likely to bring as many people as possible to the gig, in the hope of getting the loudest applause. In August 1957, Dale sent the Vipers out as headliners on a traditional variety tour billed as 'The Great National Skiffle Contest'. Just before the interval, following the usual selection of variety acts, four skiffle bands would compete for a place in the final at the end of the week-long residency, the winners receiving cash prizes and the promise of an appearance in a big championship show 'sometime in 1958'. When the Vipers closed the evening with their three guitars, washboard and bass, they were more or less guaranteed a packed house of enthusiastic skiffle fans – the most ardent of whom would all come back on Saturday for the 'finals'.

Despite the obviously exploitative nature of the whole enterprise, the popularity of playing skiffle in front of an audience was so attractive to young groups that Dale was able to run the tour all the way to the spring of 1958. During the one-week stand at the Finsbury Park Empire, fifty amateur skiffle groups performed, with twenty-eight others being invited to participate in later local contests. In his most audacious move, Dale booked Barking Odeon for what Fraser White, writing in the *Weekly Sporting Review & Show Business*, described as 'the cheapest Sunday concert that has ever been known in London' – cheap for the promoter, that is. Such was the popularity of skiffle in the working-class suburbs of the outer East End that Dale – dispensing with the entire variety bill for this one show, and retaining only the contest's MC, Jim Dale (no relation) – was able to find four dozen eager skiffle groups to fill the stage. White was beside himself with admiration. 'On the bill was only one paid artist . . . Jim Dale. The rest of the bill, in both houses, was made up of 48 unpaid skiffle groups who clamoured at the door to make money for Stanley Dale. All the know-alls said he's nuts. He'll lose a packet. But they were wrong. Dale gained a packet – a packet of five hundred crisp one-pound notes, which was the clear profit he carried away from one night at Barking!'

The contest was won by the Saxons, who, in keeping with what seemed to be a trend among amateur skiffle bands, took their name from an aspect of local history, in their case the founding of Barking Abbey in AD 666 by Erkenwald, the Saxon bishop of London. That a local band should win might seem obvious, given that they could rely on supporters to turn up on the night, but some background to their brief career offers an insight into what was a flourishing amateur skiffle scene.

The Saxons were comprised of Keith Jacks, eighteen years old, on banjo and guitar; Denis McBride, seventeen, on banjo; Michael Platt, sixteen, on guitar; David Bruce, sixteen, guitar; Alan Taylor, seventeen, on washboard; and Thomas Clatworthy, eighteen, on tub bass. They were all members of the youth club that met at St Thomas's Church on the Becontree Estate, the largest housing project in Europe, constructed between the two world wars. The local paper described them as by far the best group in the competition, a view supported by the fact that they had won first place in a similar contest held at the Gaumont on Dagenham Heathway just a week before, first place in a contest in Holborn, and had triumphed in the Southern England finals of the World Skiffle Contest that had aired on BBC TV's *Come Dancing*. A report in the local paper noted that these busy boys were also making frequent appearances at the Skiffle Cellar in Soho.

By February 1958, Stanley Dale's National Skiffle Contest had turned into Groundhog Day. The same lame comedians telling the same tired jokes, dozens of skiffle bands thrashing out their own frenzied version of 'Don't You Rock Me Daddy-O', and the Vipers themselves locked into a straitjacket of a seventeen-minute set, twice a night, every night. And the tour just kept on rolling, with no real end in sight. Every time they pulled in to a new town, a crowd of local skifflers appeared, eager for their moment in the spotlight.

Dale had one final trick up his sleeve. In January, he announced that the final rounds of his National Skiffle Contest would be broadcast live on TV. The first heat took place on *Six-Five Special* on Saturday 1 February, with viewers being encouraged to send in postcards in support of the contesting groups. By the time that the Saxons appeared on the programme on 26 April 1958, *Six-Five Special* had given up any pretence of being a rock 'n' roll show. The main act that Saturday was Ronnie Aldrich and the Squadronaires, a big band of former RAF musicians. Mick Mulligan's trad jazz band had a spot, as did the Lana Sisters, a vocal trio that included one Mary O'Brien, later to find fame as Dusty Springfield. The only teenage music on the show was provided by the skiffle contest.

The Saxons defeated the Sinners from Newcastle and went through

The Saxons rehearse for their *Six-Five Special* appearance at St Thomas Youth Club, Dagenham, July 1956

to the second of three semi-finals on 19 July, where the middle-aged, middle-of-the-road Ted Heath Band was top of the bill. The boys from Barking performed their version of 'I'm Satisfied', which had been the B side of the Chas McDevitt Skiffle Group's third single, 'Greenback Dollar'. One of their opponents that evening was the Station Skiffle Group from west London, who had come second at the wet Whit Monday contest in Bury St Edmunds a year before. Both they and the Moonshiners from Sheffield performed songs from Lonnie Donegan's repertoire, 'Tom Dooley' and 'The Grand Coulee Dam' respectively. Again the Saxons were victorious and made it through to the final.

Broadcast on 23 August, almost a year to the day after Stanley Dale had first sent the Vipers out on the road with the National Skiffle Contest, the finals were won by the Woodlanders from Plymouth, with the Saxons coming a close second. Derek Mason, who played washboard for the Station Skiffle Group, later commented that 'we felt that was an injustice as [the Saxons] were by far the better of the three finalists'.

The skiffle contests blooded a new generation of amateur musicians who were able to get a shot at national recognition without having to surrender their personalities to the demands of music business impresarios such as Larry Parnes who would single out a boy, change his name and hairstyle, provide his clothes and tell him what to say. The skiffle groups were bands of brothers, self-realised and answerable only to one another, a trait that would give these young teens the confidence to write their own songs and take on the world in the decade that followed.

2 1

COUNTRY, BLUEGRASS AND BLUES

Despite the presence of role models such as Nancy Whiskey and Shirley Douglas in the Chas McDevitt group, and Hylda Sims and Shirley Bland of the City Ramblers, the amateur skiffle scene was almost exclusively the preserve of young men. Undeterred by this, publications aimed at young women sought to cash in on the craze, carrying features promoting the fashion styles that were seen in the skiffle clubs. In May 1957, a four-page special in *Reveille* magazine gave tips on how to dress for a skiffle gig, alongside reports from the skiffle scenes in Edinburgh, Glasgow, Leeds and Bradford, Sheffield, Manchester, Nottingham, Leicester, Birmingham, Bristol and London. The report stated that the recently opened Cavern jazz club in Liverpool was now holding a weekly skiffle night every Friday.

Mirabelle, a comic for teenage girls launched in 1956, carried an eight-page feature that promised to reveal 'how to be pretty at a skiffle party'. Celebrity hairdresser Mr Teazie Weazie was on hand to show how to get a 'fresh 'n' cool' skiffle bob and there were fashion tips on 'how to be a skiffle girl from head to toe'. However, actually playing an instrument wasn't encouraged. Bob Cort's guide to forming a skiffle group was strictly for the guys, instructing *Mirabelle*'s readers that the solo singer should step forward for *his* solo spots.

The skiffle craze may have been driven by teenagers but its effects reached down to pre-teens, a fact evidenced by the number of toy guitars that appeared on the market in the wake of the boom. Most popular was a twenty-three-inch hollow-body four-string manufactured in plastic by Selcol. Sporting f-holes and the words 'Skiffle Junior' on the body, its most striking feature is an illustration of a young man playing the guitar while two girls smile down upon him from either side. But look closely and you will notice that the outline of this instrument is identical to that of one of the twentieth century's most iconic figures.

Before it produced the Skiffle Junior, Selcol had been selling a Mickey Mouse guitar that was similar in size and spec. This explains the odd body shape – rather than the normal curves you'd find on a Spanish guitar, the Skiffle Junior had two rounded protuberances where the body met the neck, which had been included to accommodate Mickey's ears.*

For all this youthful interest in making music, the management at the BBC were sceptical about the need for a radio programme specifically aimed at a teenage audience, believing that as it was parents who paid the licence fee, they should be catering to adult tastes. However, with *Six-Five Special* regularly attracting 12 million viewers, the BBC were persuaded and the first weekly radio show for teenagers was broadcast at 10 a.m. on Saturday 1 July 1957. *Saturday Skiffle Club* kicked off at the height of the craze, providing thirty minutes of live guitar-led music in a slot previously occupied by Howard Thomas at the Wurlitzer organ. It was the brainchild of producer Jimmy Grant, who had witnessed the popularity of skiffle as a judge at contests held at the Streatham Locarno. Brian Matthew, who presented the show, wrote that it was 'quite unlike anything that had been heard on radio before'.

Chas McDevitt, the City Ramblers, the Vipers and even Ken Colyer

---

* In 1964, Selcol would make a fortune selling a Beatles toy guitar of similar proportions. Close inspection reveals that the Spanish-shaped front of this guitar doesn't quite match the body, which still retains room for the ears of the world's most famous mouse.

himself all appeared during the first month, and soon it was the most popular music show on the Light Programme, easily outperforming Victor Silvester's *Music for Dancing* and *The Ted Heath Show*. However, it wasn't strictly skiffle. The third show featured a twenty-one-year-old Glaswegian whose February 1957 single 'California Zephyr' was credited to Jimmy Jackson's Rock 'n' Skiffle. The number, written by Hank Williams, was a train song alright, but the way Jimmy played it was neither skiffle nor rock 'n' roll – it was more akin to western swing, the country pop sound that Bill Haley had peddled before he got hip to what kids really wanted to listen to. Confusingly, Jackson was billed as 'skiffle with a jazz beat' and backed on record by Mick Mulligan's trad jazz band. Never able to settle on one genre, he later made an appearance on the *Six-Five Special* album, singing 'Six-Five Jive' backed by the honking horns of Don Lang and his Frantic Five, sounding like a teenage lounge singer.

Johnny Duncan, another *Saturday Skiffle Club* regular, was more successful at mixing his genres, reaching number two in the UK charts in July 1957 with a country pop version of a calypso song. Many of those who heard 'Last Train to San Fernando' must have assumed that Duncan was referring to somewhere in Texas, where he was raised. In fact, the San Fernando of the title is the second largest city on the Caribbean island of Trinidad. The song was written by the Mighty Dictator, one of a number of calypsonians who came to prominence in the 1940s, and successfully recorded by the Duke of Iron.

Denis Preston, who had recorded Duncan as part of the Chris Barber Skiffle Group in September 1956, encouraged him to go solo, producing his first single, a cover of Hank Williams's 'Kaw-Liga', which made a feature of Johnny's country falsetto. Never claiming to be a skiffler, Duncan named his group the Blue Grass Boys and the line-up featured a fiddle player. When the debut single tanked, Preston drew on his years of experience producing calypso records

for Parlophone and Melodisc. It made commercial sense: 'Last Train to San Fernando' was ostensibly a railroad song and skifflers loved those. It also had a calypso flavour, touching on a rhythm which was popular in the skiffle clubs.

Duncan smoothed out the Caribbean rhythm and changed the emphasis on the way he sang 'San Fernando', but kept some of the Duke of Iron's scat singing, much to the delight of schoolboys across the nation. 'We just thought it was so funny,' recalled Ian McLagan, future keyboard player with the Small Faces, thinking back to when he was twelve years old. 'Hearing someone sing "biddy-biddy bum-bum" on the radio. He said bum! Hilarious.' The song spent seventeen weeks in the charts and turned Duncan into an overnight star. His follow-up single, 'Blue Blue Heartache', might have qualified as a rockabilly song, had it not been for the fiddle. Duncan's next release, 'Footprints in the Snow', revealed that his singing style, which had originally referenced Lonnie Donegan, was now closer to that of blue-grass singer Bill Monroe, who had a hit with the song in 1945. He further developed his country-and-western persona on a BBC radio programme entitled *Johnny Duncan's Tennessee Song Bag*.

Dickie Bishop, Duncan's erstwhile colleague in the Barber Skiffle Group, made his debut on *Saturday Skiffle Club* in September 1957. After six months touring as part of Donegan's band, Bishop had formed his own skiffle group, the Sidekicks, which included Bob Watson, one of the founders of the Round House Skiffle and Blues Club, on guitar. The two of them wrote 'No Other Baby', which sounded more like a Buddy Holly B side than any skiffle number. Bobby Helms, who had scored a hit in the US charts with 'Jingle Bell Rock', released a cover version which scraped into the lower reaches of the Top Thirty, stealing Bishop's thunder. The song made a deep impression on some listeners – Paul McCartney recorded it for his 1999 LP *Run, Devil, Run*, releasing it as the album's only single.

Since Bob Watson had stepped back from his role at the Round House, his place was taken by Alexis Korner, who struck up a part-nership with Cyril Davies. Both passionately wanted to play the blues, but found themselves drawn inexorably into the vortex of the skiffle craze. In November 1956, Alexis and Cyril had recorded four tracks with Beryl Bryden's Back-Room Skiffle Group, playing guitar and harmonica respectively. When Watson left the Round House to join Dickie Bishop's Sidekicks in early 1957, Cyril Davies saw his chance to dispense with the 's' word once and for all – even though it was drawing big crowds to the club.

'Cyril said to me one day, "Look man, I'm tired of all this skiffle stuff,"' recalled Alexis Korner. '"If I close this place down, will you come in with me and open it up as a blues club?" So I said, "Sure, why not. Let's open a blues club." So he closed down the Skiffle and Blues Club, which was packed every Thursday night. We closed it for a month and opened it up again as the Blues and Barrelhouse Club, and three people came on the opening night. Three people. And there was four of us on the stage.'

On 13 February 1957, while the club was closed, the friends got together to record their first album, taking most of their material from Lead Belly's repertoire. The line-up – two guitars, bass and washboard – was classic skiffle and the tracks they recorded have that flavour, but there was no way that Cyril would have owned up to being in a skiffle group. The resulting album was credited to Alexis Korner's Breakdown Group featuring Cyril Davies. *Blues from the Roundhouse* was a classic DIY indie record. Released on the 77 Records label, it was only available through Doug Dobell's record shop in Charing Cross. Given that Cyril Davies's name was misspelled on the cover, it was perhaps convenient that, to avoid paying purchase tax, only ninety-nine copies were pressed.

Despite the paucity of promotion (and copies), the release caught the attention of Decca Records, who offered the band a contract on condition they change their name to the Alexis Korner Skiffle Group. It must have been anathema to Davies, but the chance to record for a 'real' label was too much to resist. Still utilising a washboard player for percussion, they cut four songs for Decca's Tempo imprint in July 1957. The subsequent EP was rather confusingly called *Blues from the Roundhouse Volume 1*, but at least they spelled Cyril's surname right this time. And whatever the group was called, skiffle never sounded bluesier.

Meanwhile, Russell Quay was trying to take the music in another direction, using his column in *Weekly Sporting Review & Show Business* to proclaim the arrival of a new style distinct from skiffle and rock 'n' roll: spasm music. Claiming roots in the jump jazz of

1920s Chicago, Quay described what clothes the fashion-conscious spasm fan was wearing, as well as explaining how to dance the Jerk.

Despite Quay's best efforts, the difference between skiffle and spasm was difficult to discern. The real distinction was the source from which groups took their inspiration. For the younger generation of skifflers, early Lonnie Donegan, along with the Vipers, was the origin of much of their material. Quay's City Ramblers had a much broader repertoire, taking in trad jazz, folk, blues and gospel.

Following the success of their variety tour, Quay opened the Skiffle Cellar at 49 Greek Street on 13 April 1957, offering skiffle seven nights a week. Within a couple of months, membership had topped a thousand. Because the club had no alcohol licence, it became a magnet for teenage skiffle groups wanting a taste of the Soho scene. Such

The Skiffle Cellar, 49 Greek Street, Soho

was their number – over two hundred turned up in the first two weeks – that Quay gave one whole night over to new bands, whose fifteen minutes of fame more often than not included a rendition of 'Don't You Rock Me Daddy-O'.

In August 1957, the City Ramblers were invited to take part in the Sixth World Festival of Youth and Students in Moscow, travelling on a train across Europe with a British delegation including Bruce Turner's Jump Band, Al Jenner's jazz band and folk singers Ewan MacColl, Peggy Seeger and Guy Carawan. The Soviet Union was going through a temporary thaw in relations with the West, following Khrushchev's denouncement of Stalin's brutality in January 1956. The new regime relaxed controls on tourism and the arts, promoting the youth festival as the new outward-looking face of the Soviet people. Thirty thousand young people came to Moscow from all over the world, while an estimated 3 million Muscovites attended events across the city, eager to experience foreign culture after years of living in a closed society.

The Moscow cinema production studio, Mosfilm, was busy throughout the festival, filming many of the visiting acts in a studio environment. Once the event was over, these performances were liberally used in Soviet cinema's equivalent of *Rock Around the Clock*. Starring twenty-one-year-old Lyudmila 'Lyusya' Gurchenko, *Girl with a Guitar* is a typical tale of boy meets girl in music shop. Together they plan to take part in a big music festival and, after overcoming resistance from parents and the dead hand of bureaucracy, they make it to the festival and become stars.

Gurchenko's previous film, *Carnival Night*, had a similar plot, taking advantage of the Khrushchev thaw to entertain the audience while gently satirising the Soviet system. It was wildly popular and *Girl with a Guitar* attempted to follow its success with another teen musical. Unfortunately, by the time it was released in late 1958, the

Soviet Union's heavy-handed reaction to the Hungarian Uprising had dropped the temperature of East–West relations. The Politburo decided that Gurchenko was too flamboyant for their tastes. She was denounced in *Komsomolskaya Pravda*, the official organ of the Communist Union of Youth, for her lack of patriotism and the film, deemed too Western, was not recommended for wide distribution.

The last third of *Girl with a Guitar* takes place against the backdrop of the festival, with artists from around the world performing on screen. The whole thing is filmed in vivid colour and contains numerous cutaways to audience members, each dressed in their national costume, avidly applauding the acts. Towards the end, the City Ramblers suddenly appear, dressed in matching check shirts, playing three guitars, tea-chest bass and washboard, singing Jelly Roll Morton's 'Doctor Jazz'.

Returning to the Skiffle Cellar, where membership had now reached 1,500, Quay hosted the cream of the skiffle scene – Chas McDevitt, the Vipers, Dickie Bishop and Johnny Duncan all feature on a handbill from the period. A cohort of younger outfits that they had inspired were following close behind.

Les Hobeaux were a bunch of students from the London Polytechnic who busked around the West End, winning the International Skiffle Competition at the 1957 Soho Fair. Spotted by Paul Lincoln, they were booked to support the Vipers at the 2 I's and, after a successful run, they took over as resident group when the Vipers left to go on tour. Built around seventeen-year-old Les Bennetts, a talented guitarist, they represented the second wave of skiffle groups who emerged through the skiffle contests. With a line-up of three guitars, bass and drums, Les Hobeaux also featured a black lead singer, Keith Lardner, the only person of colour to become prominent in the scene.

According to Chas McDevitt, the group were responsible for the first four-letter word in British pop, two decades before the Sex Pistols

Soho Skiffle

LES HOBEAUX   "HIS MASTER'S VOICE"
                     EXTENDED PLAY 45 r.p.m. RECORD

encountered Bill Grundy on live TV. At their first recording session, for HMV in 1957, Bennetts was dismayed to find himself demoted to rhythm guitar on 'Mama Don't Allow' in favour of session player Roy Plummer. When the group performed the song live, they would cue the guitar solo by shouting 'Play it, Fags' – the nickname of Bennetts, a heavy smoker. Whether out of malice or mischief, the vocalists called out for Fags on the recording and, sixty years later, you can still hear Bennetts mumble, 'Fuck off,' like a grumpy bulldog.

Another second-generation skiffle group gave Joe Meek his first chance to produce a record. Desperate to convince Denis Preston to allow him total control in the studio, he cooked up a song called 'Sizzling Hot' with Charles Blackwell and set about looking for a bunch of likely lads to perform it. He found what he was looking for in the shape of the Station Skiffle Group, runners-up in the Bury St Edmunds skiffle contest. Meek had already had a hand in some skiffle hits – 'Last Train to San Fernando' had benefited from his recording techniques, as had several of Lonnie Donegan's chart-toppers, including 'Cumberland Gap' – so Preston trusted his judgement.

As the Station Skiffle Group had already released a number of songs on the Esquire label, Meek convinced them to change their name to Jimmy Miller and the Barbecues. It was a fitting sobriquet as, when the single came out in September 1957, it sounded like someone was frying a pan of sausages in the background. Joe Meek had made history, being the first British engineer to produce his own records, but he hadn't yet perfected the sound that would bring him international success in the early 60s.

The do-it-yourself nature of skiffle led groups to explore the possibilities of independently releasing their own records. Although the trend was never as widespread as during the punk rock years – there simply wasn't an alternative distribution network in 1957 – the introduction of the 7" 45 rpm vinyl format offered an independent route to record making.

Brian Jackman had done two years' national service in the Royal Navy before he caught the skiffle bug after hearing 'Rock Island Line' on the radio. 'It wasn't like anything I'd ever heard,' he recalled. 'It made my hair stand on end.' He and a bunch of friends from work went to see the Vipers at the 2 I's coffee bar in Soho. 'One Friday night, we all queued for a ticket and went down into this tiny cellar and there they all were, crammed up against the back wall. They were amazing – song after song and the whole place was buzzing. We came out thinking that was fantastic! And my mate Ron said, "Listen, why don't we do that? Get some cheap old guitars, learn the three-chord trick and form our own group?" It was as simple as that.'

Soon, he and his workmates had commandeered the loft at Leonard Hills Technical Publishing, in Eden Street NW1, as a rehearsal space. 'We used to pile up there after work, get a few beers in and eventually we built up a repertoire – train songs, Hank Williams numbers,

The Eden Street Skiffle Group jam with their mentor, Wally Whyton (*centre*).
Brian Jackman plays guitar (*standing, right*)

country and western, calypso – we even ended up playing "La
Bamba", for godsakes.' Calling themselves the Eden Street Skiffle
Group, they became eager apprentices to the Vipers. 'I used to go to
Wally Whyton's house off Tottenham Court Road where he lived with
his mum. They had a basement flat and while he taught me stuff, his
mum would feed me stew. Wally was my skiffle hero.' The group was
fronted by three guitar-playing vocalists – Jackman, Ron Lawrence
and Hamish Maxwell – backed by Micky Hopkins on mandolin, John
Willard on bass and Bob Jones on washboard. Their ability to sing
in harmony made them stand out from the run-of-the-mill groups,
winning them a residency at the Skiffle Cellar, regular appearances on
Saturday Skiffle Club and a spot on the Skiffle Jamboree Tour alongside Chas McDevitt, Les Hobeaux and the City Ramblers.

In 1957, they were approached by Headquarter and General
Supplies, based in Coldharbour Lane, Brixton – a firm with roots in

the military that traded in army surplus in the years after the Second World War. By the late 50s, they were selling watches, radios, binoculars, cine cameras and records via their mail-order catalogue. Hoping to cash in on the skiffle craze, the company offered to release an album by the Eden Street Skiffle Group in the form of ten 7" flexi-discs. Generally used for promotional purposes, flexi-discs were a cheap way of distributing a recording, allowing songs or messages to be attached to magazines and other products, such as breakfast cereal boxes.

Melody Cards of London had utilised this technology to produce a skiffle-inspired birthday card embossed with a 78 rpm recording of a song called 'The Washboard Birthday Special'. A skiffle flexi was also available to anyone who collected the wrappers from Nestlé's sixpenny milk chocolate bar. Send off the wrappers and a postal order for one shilling and sixpence and you would receive a disc of the Pan Skiffle Group singing 'Poor Howard'. Both of these flexi-discs were mounted on plastic.

The flexi-discs employed for the Eden Street album were paper-thin, with the track moulded into one side of a clear, square plastic sheet. Each had the name of the track engraved in the run-out groove. The discs came in a 7" sleeve with slots cut into each corner. In order to give the disc the rigidity necessary to make it move under the weight of the needle arm, the four corners of the flexi had to be slid into the slots in the sleeve and the whole thing placed on the turntable.

Entitled *Skiffle Album No. 1* and available by mail order only for ten shillings, it leaned heavily on songs made famous by Lead Belly, as well as featuring several gospel songs sung in a campfire style. They even took on Harry Belafonte's calypso ballad 'Judy Drownded'. However, as Headquarter and General Supplies Ltd wasn't a regular record company and didn't have a promotions department to push the release, this bold experiment in independent record making was doomed to fail.

Just one level up from H&GS was 77 Records, who had put out *Blues from the Roundhouse* by Alexis Korner's Breakdown Group featuring Cyril Davies. In 1957, 77 released an album by Guy Carawan, a thirty-year-old Californian who had graduated with a degree in sociology from UCLA, fallen in with Pete Seeger and discovered folk music. A banjo player, he was among the left-leaning musicians from around the world who travelled to Moscow for the World Festival of Youth and Students in 1957, where he met Peggy Seeger. Denis Preston put them into the studio with Scottish ballad singer Isla Cameron to record an EP entitled *Peggy Seeger Presents Origins of Skiffle* for his Nixa Jazz Today series. Joe Meek engineered the session and, other than adding a snare drum played with brushes, was uncharacteristically restrained, allowing Seeger's teen-folk voice to ring clear as she showed those three-chord boys how to play the songs that formed the bedrock of every amateur skiffle group's repertoire.

First up was 'Freight Train', which Seeger herself had introduced to the UK by playing it in coffee bars when she first arrived in 1956.

Unlike Chas McDevitt's chirpy version which had hit the Top Ten, Seeger utilised the alternating bass finger-picking style of Elizabeth Cotten. Next up was a song that Lonnie Donegan had taken to number one. Sung in a minor key, with Guy Carawan taking the lead, their version of 'Cumberland Gap' rang with the high lonesome sound of Appalachia.

Side two opened with 'Sail Away Lady', the song that had provided the framework for the most popular skiffle hit of all, 'Don't You Rock Me Daddy-O'. While most groups played 'Daddy-O' in the rough-and-ready style of the Vipers, Seeger took the song back to its sea shanty roots, fast-strumming her banjo at the top of each line of the chorus, like the swirl of a dancing girl's skirt. The final track highlighted another song that had been a Top Ten hit for Lonnie Donegan: 'Bring a Little Water, Sylvie'. For their version of this Lead Belly song, Peggy, Isla and Guy took their cue from a 1953 release by big brother Pete Seeger's band, the Weavers.

While Peggy Seeger was highlighting the American roots of skiffle, the man responsible for initiating the craze was delving into a fine old

English tradition. Lonnie Donegan had scored five Top Ten hits in 1957, two of them number ones, but the King of Skiffle had his eyes set on an even greater prize. As Christmas approached, he was to be found starring in pantomime at the Chiswick Empire, playing Wishee Washee to Maureen Kershaw's Aladdin.

22

EXPRESSO BONGO

In 1956, a book entitled *My Old Man's a Dustman* was published by André Deutsch. It told the story of two friends who protected their corner of post-war London like a cockney Don Quixote and his Sancho Panza. The Old Cock is a veteran of the First World War, an anarchist prone to outrageous oratory, employed as watchman on the council rubbish tip. His sidekick is a product of the Blitz who has never spoken since being caught out in the open during an air raid. He takes his name from the initials on the shoulder of the jacket he always wears: Arp. They spend their days sorting the rubbish, quietly putting their broken, discarded world into some semblance of order, while modernity and bureaucracy chip away at their little fiefdom.

At one point in the story, the Old Cock sings a song from the trenches, a bowdlerised version of which would provide Lonnie Donegan with his biggest hit single some four years later:

> *My old man's a dustman*
> *He fought in the Battle of Mons,*
> *Killed five thousand Germans*
> *With only fifty bombs.*
> *One lay here,*
> *One lay there,*
> *One lay round the corner,*
> *One poor fellow with a bullet up his arse*
> *Was crying out for water . . .*

The novel was the work of Wolf Mankowitz, a writer of Russian Jewish descent, born in the heart of London's East End in 1924. An Oxford graduate, he used an interest in Wedgwood porcelain as the basis for his debut novel, *Make Me an Offer*, published in 1952. His second, *A Kid for Two Farthings*, was made into a film in 1956, directed by Carol Reed. Mankowitz provided the screenplay and, recognising that things had changed in the three years since he wrote the novel, introduced rock 'n' roll into a story that had originally been a nostalgic look back at the Yiddish East End of his childhood. The kid of the title is a young goat with a single horn, mistaken by a local boy for a baby unicorn. His belief that this mythical animal will bring good fortune to everyone in the neighbourhood is the hook on which Mankowitz hangs his fable of working-class hopes and dreams. It's a bittersweet tale of lost innocence against a backdrop of cultural change, represented by the dull thump of jive music that permeates the young boy's bedroom at night, an irresistible force that betokens adolescence and modernity.

Mankowitz often featured characters trying to make a living on the fringes of the post-war economy – street traders, hustlers and others surviving on little more than their wits. Following the publication of *My Old Man's a Dustman* he turned his attention to the other end of town, writing a musical satire set in the coffee bars, strip joints and exclusive clubs of Soho. *Expresso Bongo*, which opened at the Saville Theatre in the West End on 23 April 1958, is a snapshot of the moment when the focus of the British music industry switched from adults to teenagers.

At the time, Mankowitz was hosting his own weekly programme on the independent television network. Entitled *Conflict*, it allowed him to address the issues that underpinned his work – class, culture and the new – through in-depth interviews with figures from politics, media and the arts. It was a position that left him well placed to observe the gap between generations that was being created by the burgeoning power of the teenage consumer. In the late 50s, many British movies, shows and variety tours aimed at the youth market were little more than naked cash-in attempts by older people. *Expresso Bongo* was different, taking a step back and casting a wry eye over the shabby characters who set out to make money by exploiting youth culture.

The songs were mostly show tunes, written by Julian More, David Heneker and Monty Norman, none of whom was under thirty. As a result, little of the soundtrack for the musical reflects teenage tastes at the time. However, Mankowitz must have been alert to what was happening as the story uses the skiffle scene as its backdrop.

The musical opens in a Soho jazz cellar, where a tired Dixieland jazz band are playing their final concert. Looking for something new, their small-time agent, a 'Soho Square shark' named Johnnie, begins to frequent coffee bars, discovering a youth he christens 'Bongo Herbert'. Johnnie visits Bongo's parents in Hoxton and promises to get him on the television – 'the hot cod's eye, which watches every home in Britain'. Later, we find Johnnie visiting his girlfriend Maisie, a stripper at the Intime Non-Stop Nude Revue on Brewer Street.*

In a move copied from the Tommy Steele playbook, Johnnie books Bongo into an upper-class nightspot, invites the press and employs a bunch of debutantes to go crazy and mob Bongo when he sings. Suddenly, Johnnie's boy is a national celebrity and everybody wants a piece. However, Johnnie's contract with Bongo turns out to be worthless – Herbert was underage when he signed – and soon he loses control of his charge to bigger sharks. In the process Herbert Rudge travels from his working-class roots to the very top of society, prefiguring the

---

* The same week that the curtain went up on the musical, Paul Raymond opened his first strip club in Walker's Court, an alleyway that connects Brewer and Berwick Streets, just a stone's throw from the Round House. *Melody Maker* ruefully observed that there would soon be as many strip shows as skiffle bars in Soho.

huge upheavals of the 1960s, when pop celebrity would replace breeding as Britain's greatest social lubricant.

Though some of the songs may sound quaint now, *Expresso Bongo* was hailed at the time as the first low-life British musical since *The Beggar's Opera*. Milton Shulman, theatre critic of the *Evening Standard*, called it 'a raucous, rhythmic paean of disgust aimed at the shoddy side of the entertainment business. In its misanthropic tour of the gutters of the West End, it washes up an unsavoury flotsam of sharp agents, talentless artists, love-starved women, greedy managers, shady café proprietors and dim debutantes. If they had a redeeming feature among them it would be stolen off their backs.'

Expresso Bongo ran for 316 performances at the Saville, with critics comparing it favourably with musicals such as *Guys and Dolls* and *Pal Joey*. It was voted British Musical of the Year by *Variety*, pushing the hugely popular *My Fair Lady* into second place, and within a year it was in the cinemas, starring the teenager who had risen from the coffee bars to challenge Tommy Steele as Britain's most loved home-grown pop idol – Cliff Richard.* In an irony that would not have been lost on Mankowitz, the plot and songs were altered to create a vehicle for the latest pop sensation.

Directed by Val Guest, who collaborated with Mankowitz on the screenplay, the film went into production in September 1959. Although Peter Sellers was first choice to play Johnny, the role eventually went to Laurence Harvey, who had recently been nominated for an Oscar as the heartless social climber Joe Lampton in *Room at the Top*. Born Zvi Mosheh Skikne in Lithuania in 1928 to Jewish parents who migrated to South Africa when he was five, Harvey had an ear for the Yiddish slang that often peppered the work of Wolf

---

* Cliff Richard had already appeared in a British movie, *Serious Charge*, in a cameo as a hoodlum who does little but sing three songs at a youth club, among them his first number one, 'Living Doll'.

Mankowitz. Both men were outsiders who sought, in different ways, to pass themselves off as English gentlemen.

Harvey based his accent on that of Mankowitz himself, sometimes needing to speak to the writer by phone before a particular scene in order to attain an authentic timbre. Always seen in a pork-pie hat, bow tie and cheap suit, Harvey's Johnny Jackson is a chippy protagonist and knowing narrator, a similar role to that played by Malcolm McLaren in *The Great Rock 'n' Roll Swindle* some twenty years later.

Only four numbers were retained from the stage version, three of which – 'Nausea', 'I Never Had It So Good' and 'Nothing Is for Nothing' – appear fleetingly. Bongo's syrupy paean to motherhood, 'Shrine on the Second Floor', does get the full treatment and is the only one of the original songs sung by Cliff Richard. Guest used a number of songwriters to provide material for the film, but chose to wait until almost halfway through before letting Richard loose on his first number, Norrie Paramor's somnambulant ballad 'A Voice in the Wilderness'. This was a satire with songs, he seemed to be saying, not some mere pop-star vehicle for the kids. Mankowitz makes a brief appearance in the film as a sandwich-board man wandering the streets of Soho.

Expresso Bongo premiered on 20 November 1959 to acclaim from critics who recognised that, despite the introduction of Cliff Richard, the film had retained an edge. The generational conflict – played out between Tin Pan Alley and skiffle in the movie – could also be found in contemporary plays such as *Look Back in Anger* and novels like *Absolute Beginners*. While Val Guest and Wolf Mankowitz would go on to make more films together, most notably the classic British sci-fi flick *The Day the Earth Caught Fire*, *Expresso Bongo* remains the best movie about the roots of British pop.

Cliff is backed in the movie by the Shadows, a bunch of former skifflers who had been drawn to London by the light of the 2 I's jukebox. Hank Marvin (born Brian Rankin in 1941) played banjo in the Crescent City Skiffle Group, winners of a skiffle contest at South Shields Pier Pavilion in May 1957. When the group broke up, he was invited by school friend Bruce Welch to join the Railroaders, who played their skiffle in the working men's clubs around Newcastle. On Hank's sixteenth birthday his parents gave him an archtop guitar and within a couple of weeks he and Bruce had dropped out of school to concentrate on playing music. The Railroaders reached their zenith at the Edmonton Granada in north London on 6 April 1958, when they were knocked out of the never-ending national skiffle contest. Deflated, the group broke up that night, but Hank and Bruce decided to stay on in London, becoming regular fixtures at the 2 I's, performing as an Everly Brothers-style duo.

Enhancing his considerable playing skills by sticking an electric pick-up onto his guitar soon brought Hank offers of work. On 28 June, a front-page story in the *Melody Maker* announced that 'bassist Jet Harris and 16-year-old guitarist Hank Marvin had joined the Vipers'. The interminable amateur contests that had kept Britain's premier skiffle ensemble on the road for sixteen months had petered out, the long-promised grand final never materialised and the Vipers were left drained and depleted. When two members quit, Wally Whyton, Johnny Booker and John Pilgrim decided to jump on the rock 'n' roll bandwagon by going electric. Marvin and Harris – who had been playing with Tony Crombie and his Rockets – were brought in to beef up the sound and Vipers washboard player Pilgrim purchased a set of drums. After a spot on *Saturday Skiffle Club*, the group headed to Birmingham for a week's residency at the Hippodrome.

The booking was a complete disaster. The little amplifiers that they had bought were too small for the venue and blew up when pushed to their limits. Pilgrim's drumming wasn't up to the standard of his washboard playing and when the group played 'Johnny B. Goode', the skiffle diehards in the audience saw it as a betrayal. On returning to London, Marvin made his excuses and left the group, while Pilgrim was sacked. The Vipers would muddle on for another few months, by which time Hank Marvin and Bruce Welch had been hired to back a former member of the Dick Teague Skiffle Group who had seen the rock 'n' roll light: Cliff Richard. Originally called the Drifters, when later joined by Jet Harris and Tony Meehan (who had briefly replaced John Pilgrim as drummer for the Vipers), they became the Shadows.

With his black-rimmed spectacles and Fender Stratocaster – one of the first in the UK – Hank Marvin had clearly modelled himself on Buddy Holly. The Texan's first single caught the ear of many skifflers when it entered the UK charts in December 1957. 'Peggy Sue' had the frantically strummed energy of skiffle and its three chords were within the grasp of most skiffle players. Best of all, Holly didn't have the well-honed, tanned James Dean image that seemed to be the template for so many American rockers. Instead, he had the look of someone who might have been raised during a time of food rationing – a slight, bespectacled youth empowered by an electric guitar.

When he and his band, the Crickets, appeared on ATV's *Sunday Night at the London Palladium* on 2 March 1958, the nation's youth saw a new kind of rock 'n' roller – no Presley-style histrionics and no Haley-style corn, just three guys furiously playing guitar, double bass and drums with no frills. Holly's solos were quick switches between chords, none of that fancy single note stuff. For anyone who played in a three-chord guitar group, Buddy Holly's sound was accessible. Surely this was what electric skiffle sounded like? For many of the teenage strummers who had been inspired to pick up a guitar by Lonnie Donegan, seeing Buddy Holly and the Crickets was a Damascene moment.

The two men hit it off when the Crickets toured the UK in March 1958, with Donegan taking his group to see the show. On 14 March,

Holly reciprocated. After his show at the Woolwich Granada in south-east London, he headed to the Dominion Theatre in Tottenham Court Road, where the National Jazz Federation had organised a midnight benefit concert for Big Bill Broonzy. The sixty-four-year-old bluesman, whose tours of the UK had made him hugely popular with British jazz fans, was suffering from throat cancer and needed help to pay his mounting medical costs. Any residual hostility between Ken Colyer, Chris Barber and Lonnie Donegan was forgotten as each brought his own band to play in support of Big Bill. The show was a sell-out and Holly was only able to gain entrance by claiming to be a good friend of Lonnie's. Another member of the audience that night was a nineteen-year-old Liverpudlian who would remain a lifelong Lonnie Donegan fan – future Radio 1 DJ John Peel, on his first trip to London.

The King of Skiffle had ended 1957 with the release of 'Jack o'Diamonds', a Texas gambling song popularised by Blind Lemon Jefferson, and kicked off 1958 with 'The Grand Coulee Dam', both songs taken from the *Six-Five Special* movie, a spin-off from the TV show. The latter was written by Woody Guthrie as part of a project sponsored by the Bonneville Power Administration, a government agency tasked with producing and marketing hydroelectric power in America's Pacific north-west.* Donegan would have been famil-iar with the tune, as Guthrie had borrowed the melody from the American railroad song 'Wabash Cannonball', which Lonnie used to

---

* The Grand Coulee Dam was built on the Columbia River in Washington state during the 1930s, and in 1941 Woody Guthrie was hired to write a batch of songs for a proposed documentary about its construction. The fact that he was only employed for a month was no drawback to Guthrie, a man who seemed to write a song almost every day of his life. In just three weeks he wrote twenty-six numbers and, although the documentary never saw the light of day, the songs that Guthrie wrote in the month that he spent on the Columbia River include some of his most evocative work, 'Pastures of Plenty', 'Hard Travellin'' and 'Roll On, Columbia, Roll On' among them.

sing with the Chris Barber Skiffle Group. However, where Guthrie sings his version of 'The Grand Coulee Dam' in a level, folksy manner, Donegan employs the trick that first brought him to the attention of the record-buying public. Starting at a gentle lilt, he ratchets up his vocal style with each verse, giving the song a dynamic climb not heard on the original. The single reached number six in the UK charts in April 1958.

Donegan returned to Woody's songbag for his next single, 'Sally Don't You Grieve'. The Dustbowl Balladeer had recorded the song with Cisco Houston in 1944, when the two of them were serving in the Merchant Marine, shipping out of New York on convoys ferrying troops and materiel to Britain to bolster the fight against fascism. As a result, Guthrie's version is peppered with references to Hitler and the Japanese Emperor Hirohito. Donegan wrote new verses, dropping all mention of the Second World War, and played the song with a swing that took it closer to the gospel roots Guthrie may have been drawing on when he composed it. It got to number eleven in the UK singles chart in July 1958.

Between these two hits, Nixa released a four-track live EP, recorded at the Conway Hall in London over a year previously, on 25 January 1957. Donegan's sudden rise to fame had created such a demand for live performances that it had become increasingly difficult to get the group into the studio to record a follow-up to *Lonnie Donegan Showcase*. Denis Preston proposed to get around this by recording a live album. Donegan was perhaps the most charismatic British performer of the period, driving audiences wild up and down the country. If this could be captured on record, the resulting album would be a smash.

Preston called on his most experienced live engineer, Joe Meek, who had cut his teeth placing microphones and mixing sound for weekly live music broadcasts on Radio Luxembourg. Donegan's backing band of Nick Nicholls on drums, Mickey Ashman on double bass and Denny Wright on guitar had recently been augmented by the addition of Dickie Bishop, who had played Cisco to Lonnie's Woody in the Chris Barber Skiffle Group, and his vocals added an extra dimension to the group that had so impressed George Harrison and Paul McCartney at the Liverpool Empire just a few months previously.

Nine tracks were recorded that night, but only four were released some fifteen months later, on the *Live at Conway Hall* EP. The lead song, 'Mule-Skinner Blues', first recorded in 1930 by Jimmie Rodgers, features some beautiful harmonies between Donegan and Bishop, as does their take on the gospel song 'Glory'. Two songs from Lead Belly's repertoire, 'On a Monday' and 'Old Hannah', complete the disc. But what happened to the rest of the tracks? Alan Freeman's sleeve notes claim that the audience's enthusiasm was such that their applause drowned out the music. But was that really the reason? Given that Joe Meek was one of the best sound recordists working in Europe at the time, it seems highly unlikely that he would have placed the mics in a position where they could get overloaded.

When the full set was released on CD in 2006, the sound on the missing tracks showed no evidence of being drowned out by the crowd. In their sleeve notes Paul Pelletier and Roger Dopson postulate that the decision not to release all the tracks was more to do with the fact that, within a month of the recording, Dickie Bishop had left to set up his own skiffle group, releasing 'Cumberland Gap' in direct competition to Donegan's version. Bishop featured on almost all of *Live at Conway Hall*, even singing one solo himself. Why would Nixa want to help promote a rival? Whatever the reason, by the time the EP saw the light of day in the spring of 1958, Bishop was no longer a threat as none of his singles had charted. Lonnie was still the king.

23

FOR PEACE AND HARMONY

Lonnie Donegan's success may have made him a household name, but he went to considerable lengths to remain connected to his fans, encouraging them to set up skiffle clubs wherever he went on tour. By late 1957, his fan club had over two thousand members, each paying five shillings for a membership card, a blue guitar-shaped enamel badge with his initials on, and a twelve-page magazine, printed three times a year. The October 1957 issue contained an easy-to-follow guide on how to play 'Rock Island Line' and 'I'm Alabamy Bound', as well as photos from a party for members that Lonnie hosted at the Cavern Club, described as 'Liverpool's underground jazz club'. Donegan also outlined his plans to personally attend club meetings when playing in towns where there were more than fifty members.

By spring 1958, the clubs were becoming more organised. Encouraging youngsters to 'meet socially, discuss and listen to folk and skiffle music, form their own groups and dance etc', the Club Office in London undertook to pay for the hiring of a hall and to send a free copy of every Lonnie Donegan release to each club. Members were instructed to elect their own officers, to charge each member one shilling to attend – guests were allowed, although they had to pay two shillings and sixpence – and to spend any money raised on the purchase of books and records.

In the summer 1958 issue of the club magazine, Lonnie outlined how he thought the meetings should be conducted. Records were to be played as people arrived, followed by a general discussion, and then two or three skiffle groups should perform. The winter edition carried the contact details of clubs in Birmingham, Bristol, Cardiff, Glasgow, Leeds, Liverpool, Manchester, Sheffield, Shrewsbury and Worcester.

These autonomous gatherings gave teenagers an opportunity to meet outside of the confines of church-run youth clubs, where activities were organised and approved by adults. They would also prove a good training ground for those who would play a part in organising the folk clubs that grew out of the skiffle boom in the early 60s.

But it wasn't only Lonnie Donegan's fan club that was inspiring young people to come together. Between 15 May and 19 June 1957, the British government, in the face of mounting international efforts to ban the testing of atomic weapons, detonated three hydrogen bombs above Malden Island, an uninhabited British possession in the central Pacific Ocean. The deployment of the H-bomb stirred up public opposition at home. The National Council for the Abolition of Nuclear Weapon Tests, who had led the campaign against testing, decided that it made more sense to oppose the existence of nuclear weapons rather than merely protesting against the tests and, in February 1958, transformed itself into the Campaign for Nuclear Disarmament.

From the very beginning, CND attracted huge numbers of young people. Having survived the Second World War as children, they were outraged that their parents' generation were contemplating another conflict – one which had the potential to wipe out all life on Earth. It was the first mass political movement in Britain to engage the nation's youth and its focus was the Aldermaston Marches.

In 1950, the British government established the Atomic Weapons Research Establishment at the former RAF base at Aldermaston in Berkshire, some fifty miles due west of London. CND chose the AWRE as the focus for a march from Trafalgar Square over the Easter Bank Holiday weekend of 1958. The organisers believed that music should be a central component of the event. Flyers sent out by CND

contained a line for people to fill out which read: 'I can play . . . .
and am willing to be in a band'.

A few weeks before the march, Gerald Holtom, a quietly spoken
commercial artist from Twickenham, came to the first meeting of
the London Region CND with a strip of black cloth about six yards
long and eighteen inches wide, designed to be carried on poles by two
people. On the black cloth were the words 'Nuclear Disarmament'
and each end featured a strange symbol that Holtom had conceived,
based on the semaphore signals for N (an inverted V) and D (a vertical line), surrounded by a circle.

When thousands gathered in Trafalgar Square on Good Friday,
similar banners were handed out bearing slogans such as 'From Fear
to Sanity', 'Against H-bombs for Britain, USA, Russia', 'First Step to
Peace' and, presaging a widely used slogan of the 60s, 'Make Friends
Not Enemies'. CND also produced several hundred placards bearing
Holtom's 'broken cross' peace symbol, first seen that weekend and
destined to become an icon of the alternative society.

Over four days, a crowd sometimes numbering six thousand
marched down the A4 arterial road towards Reading, the nearest
major town to Aldermaston. Local supporters organised food and
shelter for the marchers, while pubs along the way made their toilets
available. Fred Dallas and his Original Riverside Skiffle Group were
part of an advance guard, sent into towns ahead of the march to welcome them in.

John Hasted mounted an amplifier in a pushchair and led his
London Youth Choir on the march, singing a number specially written for them by John Brunner called 'The H-Bomb's Thunder'. Set to
the tune of the old American union song 'The Miner's Lifeguard', it
became the rallying song of CND. Out of respect to the religious paci-
fists attending the march, it was decided that, it being Good Friday, the
marchers should observe a contemplative silence until they reached

Shepherd's Bush, some five miles to the west. The City Ramblers clearly didn't get the memo, for as soon as Canon Collins of St Paul's Cathedral had bidden the marchers on their way, the Ramblers struck up with the spiritual 'Study War No More' as the crowds filed out of the square. The *Daily Telegraph* reported that the marchers 'skiffled their way along' through the streets of west London.

The next day, headlines declared the Easter weather to have been the worst for a century. Snow had fallen in Kew Gardens in west London on Saturday as the marchers passed on their way towards Aldermaston. Despite the terrible Bank Holiday weather, spirits were kept high by musicians, both on the march itself and in the crowds that gathered in support along the way. The *Daily Telegraph* observed that, on arrival at Reading, marchers were greeted by 'five guitars, a washboard and three dozen people singing a Negro spiritual'.

The presence of musicians is well documented in *March to Aldermaston*, a thirty-three-minute black-and-white documentary film of the event. Credited to the Film and TV Committee for Nuclear Disarmament, the footage was shot by a large team of film-makers led by documentary producer Derrick Knight, while Tony Richardson took over at the editing stage. His old collaborator from the Free Cinema days, Karel Reisz, was also involved in the production. The first musician to be seen in the film is Ken Colyer, leading his Omega Brass Band, in their uniform of white shirt, black tie and white 'milkman's hat', through the streets of west London, bringing a touch of the New Orleans marching band tradition to the cause of nuclear disarmament. Various trad jazz bands appear along the route, while guitars and washboards are clearly visible among the younger marchers, as are a huge number of duffel coats. At one point, a guy holding a trumpet and surrounded by the rest of his band explains to some bystanders why he and his pals are marching: 'We're lovers of good music and if this hell of a lot goes up, we're not likely to hear good music any more.'

The atmosphere wasn't always positive. On one occasion some fascists lay in wait and threw a few eggs at marchers before being chased away, and in Reading a local vicar rang his church bells vigorously to drown out speakers calling for world peace. But by the time they arrived at Aldermaston, their numbers had swelled to over ten thousand and a new movement had been born. The marchers felt empowered and, all over Britain, teenagers had found a cause with which to identify.

While skifflers and trad jazzers were well represented on the march, there was no sign of the new generation of rock 'n' roll stars on the route to Aldermaston. Did they have no appetite for politics? While they might not have opposed the H-bomb, that question was answered in September 1958 when *Melody Maker* carried a front-page story in which Tommy Steele, Marty Wilde, Lonnie Donegan and a host of other prominent British artists signed a statement condemning racial prejudice. They were voicing their opposition to a series of racially motivated attacks by gangs of white youths on the West Indian community in west London.

As the British Empire began its transition to the Commonwealth following the loss of India in 1947, British citizenship was granted to all colonial subjects under the Nationality Act of 1948. As soon as this became law, adverts were placed by the UK Ministries of Health and Labour in Caribbean newspapers seeking to recruit nurses, hospital auxiliary staff and domestic workers. In 1956, London Transport began bringing men and women from Barbados to work as bus conductors, station staff and canteen assistants.

Many who came to Britain from the Caribbean were well educated and highly qualified but willing to accept low-status jobs in the hope of gaining promotion or finding more suitable employment. Instead, they found discrimination. Paid lower wages than their white colleagues, passed over for promotion despite being better qualified, they were often denied accommodation on grounds of race, rooms suddenly becoming unavailable when the landlord saw a black face. Inevitably, many Caribbean immigrants found themselves living in some of the worst housing in London.

Now an upmarket area, Notting Hill in the late 1950s was a slum. Chronically overcrowded in the interwar years and badly damaged by the Blitz, it was a place of cheap lodgings and squalor. When, in July 1957, the Conservative government lifted controls on rent that had been in place since the war, unscrupulous landlords were quick to see how they could exploit immigrants desperate for accommodation. The legislation only applied to new tenants, so Peter Rachman, who owned over a hundred large houses in the Notting Hill area, began forcing out white residents whose tenancies protected them from rent increases. He then subdivided these properties into smaller flats and let them to West Indians for a higher premium.

A long-term resident of the area, Arnold Leese was the founder, in 1929, of the Imperial Fascist League, whose symbol was a swastika imposed over the Union Jack. Once a rival to Oswald Mosley as the leading figure of British fascism, Leese was jailed in 1947 for helping members of the Waffen SS escape from prisoner-of-war camps in Britain. Following his death in 1956, his house in Notting Hill became the base of operations for the White Defence League, led by Colin Jordan, a virulent racist and anti-Semite. Under their slogan 'Keep Britain White', the WDL campaigned for an end to immigration and the repatriation of all 'coloured' immigrants already living in the UK.

Mosley himself was active in the area, seeking to unite the remnants of his pre-war British Union of Fascists under the new banner of the Union Movement. During the 1930s, Mosley had relied on his blackshirts to rough up the opposition. In 1958, it was the Teddy Boys who did his dirty work, roaming the streets in gangs looking for people to intimidate.

Tensions were rising through the summer of 1958, with both the White Defence League and the Union Movement holding meetings and distributing leaflets in the Notting Hill area. At the end of July, a group of Teddy Boys attacked a cafe in nearby Shepherd's Bush. On 23 August, after closing time, a gang of nine white youths aged between seventeen and twenty toured the streets in a car, armed with iron bars, starting handles, chair legs and a knife. They later told the police that they were 'nigger-hunting' – whenever they saw a West Indian man walking alone they attacked. Five of their victims needed hospital treatment, three of whom were seriously injured.

The violence came to a head on the night of 30 August, when a young white Swedish woman was attacked by a group of local white youths unhappy at her marriage to a Jamaican, who they claimed was her pimp. When the police arrived and, aiming to defuse the situation, arrested the woman, the crowd moved on to nearby Bramley Road, where a mob of around four hundred armed with iron bars and knives began attacking houses occupied by West Indian tenants.

Mosley's Union Movement were quick to capitalise on the unrest. The next day, their newspaper, *Action*, was being hawked on every street corner by young men shouting slogans such as 'Down with the niggers' and 'Keep Britain white'. As night fell, crowds of white youths again gathered and another night of racist violence ensued, which the *Manchester Guardian* reported 'left five black men lying unconscious in the streets of Notting Hill'. The disturbances attracted more racists to the area, eager to join in the attacks. But the West Indian community also drew support from places such as Brixton, from where members of the Afro-Caribbean community came to help organise resistance.

On 3 September, heavy rain seemed to dampen passions, but the next day was among the most ferocious, with petrol bombs thrown into the homes of West Indian families. After five days of mob rule on the streets of west London, the authorities were finally able to restore order on 5 September. Miraculously, no one had been killed, but the scenes of violent hatred had sent shockwaves across British society. Among the first to respond were the jazz and pop communities. Denis Preston pulled together a statement condemning the racial attacks, which appeared on the front page of *Melody Maker* on 6 September. Under the headline 'Race Riots', Britain's pre-eminent music paper declared itself to be disturbed both by the interracial rioting and 'the absence of any civic, spiritual, industrial or political move' to condemn the racism. It printed the artists' statement in full:

'At a time when reason has given way to violence in parts of Britain, we the people of all races in the world of entertainment, appeal to the public to reject racial discrimination in any shape or form. Violence will settle nothing: it will only cause suffering to innocent people and create fresh grievances. We appeal to our audiences everywhere to join with us in opposing any and every aspect of colour prejudice wherever it may appear.'

Among the twenty-seven prominent artists who signed the statement were Chris Barber, Lonnie Donegan, Humphrey Lyttelton, Matt Monro, Harry Secombe and Peter Sellers of the Goons, Tommy Steele, Dickie Valentine and Marty Wilde.

The statement was followed by the formation of the Stars Campaign for Interracial Friendship (SCIF), organised by Preston and Fred Dallas, along with mixed-race jazz couple John Dankworth and Cleo Laine, hugely popular Trinidadian pianist Winifred Atwell, jazz singer George Melly, Ken Colyer, and Russell Quay and Hylda Sims of the City Ramblers Skiffle Group. Initial meetings were held in Dankworth's office in Tin Pan Alley and, as well as musicians, the group attracted actors such as Laurence Olivier, who became chair of the organisation, and writers Colin MacInnes and Eric Hobsbawm, the latter then reviewing jazz records under the pen name Francis Newton.

SCIF's first initiative was to organise a fundraising gig at the Skiffle Cellar. They also produced an eight-page illustrated broadsheet that was distributed around the streets where the violence had occurred, as well as in the skiffle and jazz clubs of Soho. It contained the group's mission statement: '[Our] aims are to promote understanding between races and banish ignorance about racial characteristics; to combat instances of social prejudice by verbal and written protests; to set an example to the general public through members' personal race relations; and to use all available means to publicise their abhorrence of racial discrimination.'

Organising gigs in Soho was a start, but to have any real effect SCIF needed to take their message to the streets of Notting Hill, where the White Defence League and the Union Movement were still active. Colin MacInnes, whose *Absolute Beginners* would feature the riots as the climax of the narrative, was renowned among SCIF activists for loading his car with leaflets and personally delivering them to households in the streets where violence had erupted.

The key to SCIF's engagement with Notting Hill was Claudia Jones, a forty-three-year-old activist from Trinidad, whose parents had taken her to live in New York when she was nine years old. In 1936, looking for organisations that actively opposed racism, she joined the Young Communist League, rising to become a member of the National Committee of the Communist Party of the USA in 1948. During the McCarthyite repression, she was jailed four times because of her convictions, before being deported. When the authorities in Trinidad refused to allow her admission, she was offered residency in the UK on humanitarian grounds, arriving in London in late 1955.

A journalist by trade, Jones founded the first wholly black newspaper in Britain, the *West Indian Gazette and Afro-Asian Caribbean News*, which was based over a barber's shop in Brixton. Gravitating towards the Communist Party of Great Britain, she met Eric

Hobsbawm and became an early member of SCIF. Jones provided the organisation with contacts in the Afro-Caribbean community in west London, helping to organise the first SCIF event in the area, a Christmas party for 250 children of all races held at Holland Park School on 23 December 1958.

This was quickly followed by the opening of the Harmony Club, a social space where teenagers from different backgrounds and races could get together to enjoy music provided by the stars of the day. The club was hosted by Jo Douglas, one of the original presenters of *Six-Five Special,* and opened on Mondays and Fridays at St Mark's Church Hall, Notting Hill. Club chairman Harvey Hall declared that 'this will not be a select club . . . Teddy Boys will be welcomed.' This was a direct challenge to the fascists operating in the area who relied on the thuggish element among local Teddy Boys to do their dirty work.

In the weeks that followed, black and white activists involved with SCIF received letters from fascist groups threatening violence, and threats were made to burn down the church hall that housed the club. Tensions in the area were heightened further in April 1959, when Union Movement leader Oswald Mosley declared that in the forthcoming general election he would stand for the parliamentary constituency of North Kensington, which included Notting Hill.

A week later, the BBC television programme *Panorama* brought SCIF members together with Colin Jordan of the White Defence League to discuss the issue of race relations. Johnny Dankworth made it clear that SCIF was an anti-fascist initiative. 'The objectives of the campaign are largely to counteract any cranky organisations which try to preach the gospel of a master race anywhere. Such organisations as [the WDL] seem laughable on the face of it but they aren't really laughable because Adolf Hitler started a similar organisation about twenty or twenty-five years ago which caused the deaths of millions and millions of people and the sufferings of millions more.'

In the end, the Harmony Club only lasted six weeks. Its problem, argued Alexis Korner, was that it was just too successful: 'We were limited to just fifty [members] and we got hundreds.' SCIF continued its activities at the Skiffle Cellar in Soho, hosting regular events aimed at openly challenging the colour bar.

In the districts most affected by the riots, local black activists took the lead, most notably Claudia Jones, who went on to found the Notting Hill Carnival. Mosley was decisively beaten by the Labour Party at the general election of October 1959, coming last with just 7.5 per cent of the vote. SCIF had run its course, the first high-profile, artist-led, anti-racist, anti-fascist campaign seen in the UK. Two decades later their cause would be taken up again with the formation of Rock Against Racism and the Anti-Nazi League, once again bringing artists and fans together in the fight against discrimination.

The first generation of British teenagers had found their collective voice in opposition to nuclear weapons, and the skifflers had been in the front rank. Popular music was emerging as an international language through which young people spoke to one another across borders, questioning everything that the older generation threw at them, seeking to create a better world than that which they'd inherited.

SKIFFLE ON THE SKIDS

'Skiffle on the Skids', proclaimed the front page of *Melody Maker* on 17 May 1958, atop a report on the declining fortunes of artists who, just a few months before, had been filling theatres across the land. Skiffle had swept all before it during 1957, with the Vipers, Johnny Duncan and Chas McDevitt all scoring several hits. Head and shoulders above the competition stood Lonnie Donegan, with five Top Ten singles, two of which had reached number one. But as 1958 progressed, only Donegan continued to have hits, and when, in October, *Saturday Skiffle Club* was relaunched on the BBC Light Programme as the more pop-oriented *Saturday Club*, it became clear that the skiffle boom had passed its peak. Yet just as the British were beginning to tire of hearing American folk songs in their charts, a folk song reached number one in the US.

Originally performing as the Calypsonians, the Kingston Trio took their name from Kingston, Jamaica, and hoped to hitch a ride to fame on the calypso craze that was gathering momentum in 1957. Gaining an audience on the Californian folk circuit, they released an album of mostly traditional songs in June 1958. Their clean-cut image and college-boy harmonies made them easy on the ear and, unlike other American folk singers of the late 50s, they avoided any overtly political references in their material. Popular with DJs, their wholesome version of 'Tom Dooley' reached the top of the *Billboard* charts in November.

The song tells of the murder of Laura Foster in Wilkes County, North Carolina, in 1866 by former Confederate soldier Tom Dula, for

which crime he was tried and hanged. The version recorded by the Kingston Trio was first collected from an old-time Appalachian banjo player named Frank Proffitt, of Pick Britches Valley, North Carolina. Born in 1913, he learned the song from his immediate family, some of whom had known both killer and victim. Donegan, perhaps sensing his chance to get revenge on those American artists who had recorded copycat versions of 'Rock Island Line', swiftly released his own take on 'Tom Dooley', which reached number three in the UK charts in December 1958, topping the efforts of the Kingston Trio, who only managed to get to number five.

The contrast between their arrangements of the song underscores

359

the differing manner in which the musicians of the American folk revival and British skiffle boom handled roots material. Where the Kingston Trio are sombre, as if playing at Laura Foster's funeral, Donegan employs a relentless rhythm, yelping and growling the lyrics, constantly pushing the pace of the song. Both versions have their merits, but Donegan's is closer in style and delivery to that of fiddle and guitar duo Grayson and Whitter, who made the first recording of the song for Victor in 1929.

Despite the transatlantic success of 'Rock Island Line' and 'Freight Train', skiffle never took hold in the US. There were those around the fringes of the music industry who used the term, but their efforts bore little resemblance to what was happening in the UK. In April 1957, crooner Steve Lawrence released a single called 'Don't Wait for Summer', backed by Dick Jacobs and His Skiffle Band. Jacobs was a thirty-nine-year-old New York A & R man who had introduced string arrangements to Buddy Holly's recordings. The sleeve of his 1957 EP *Dig That Skiffle* features washboard, banjo, bongos and guitar, but a cursory listen reveals that Jacobs had never heard the Vipers in full flight. The title track comprises a male chorus simply repeating the words 'Dig that skiffle' over a hokey electric guitar phrase, while the rest of the tracks are schmaltzy easy listening. You don't rock me, daddy-o.

Milt Okun was another music industry back-room operator, a successful arranger and producer of folk artists in the 50s and 60s. He was the moving force behind the Skifflers, who sounded more like the Weavers than anything a British teenager might recognise as skiffle. American jazz archive label Riverside sought to cash in on the craze by reissuing some Roy Palmer recordings from 1931 that featured the word 'skiffle' prominently on the sleeve. However, this was Chicago skiffle, barrelhouse piano instrumentals of the kind played by Dan Burley and His Skiffle Boys.

The water was further muddied when, in 1957, Folkways issued an album entitled *American Skiffle Bands*, which featured archive recordings by the Memphis Jug Band, Cannon's Jug Stompers and the Mobile Strugglers. It was a good enough collection of music that had been popular in the 1930s, but the fact remained that, before Lonnie Donegan hit the *Billboard* charts, no one in America would have referred to this music collectively as skiffle.

Which is not to say that some American artists weren't influenced by what was going on in the UK. In his autobiography, *The Mayor of MacDougal Street*, folk singer Dave Van Ronk reveals that the first record he made was inspired by Donegan's success with 'Rock Island Line'. Released on a small-time New York label named Lyrichord, *Skiffle in Stereo* featured a group of young jazz fans, including Van Ronk and Samuel Charters, who would go on to become one of the great authorities on African American roots music. Despite the title, this was more of a jug band record, a fact recognised by the name the group chose to appear under – the Orange Blossom Jug Five.

American youth may not have been bitten by the skiffle bug in quite the same way as their British contemporaries, but some US teens were becoming interested in the kind of material that skifflers were drawing on. Greenwich Village was the epicentre of this scene on the east coast and Washington Square was its Ground Zero, a place where young amateur folk singers and players could gather freely at weekends to perfect their skills among supportive souls.

The opening of the Folklore Center on MacDougal Street in February 1957 provided a focal point for teenagers hungry to learn more about old-time music. Proprietor Izzy Young offered advice and information, as well as organising concerts. By the late 50s, the old guard of American folk, artists who had promoted music with a left-wing consciousness during the 30s and 40s, were beginning to fade away. In their place rose a new generation of musicians who, like the skifflers in the UK, were drawn to the old-time music. The New Lost City Ramblers – Tom Paley, John Cohen and Mike Seeger, brother of Peggy and Pete – were multi-instrumentalists who specialised in banjo, fiddle and guitar. The same age as Ken Colyer, Chris Barber and Lonnie Donegan, they shared the anti-commercial instincts of their British counterparts.

In the sleeve notes to their eponymous debut album, released on Folkways in 1958, Tom Paley outlined the group's philosophy. 'Our principal reasons for playing together are a liking for the sound of old-timey string bands, perhaps best exemplified by the North Carolina Ramblers and Gid Tanner's Skillet Lickers, and a feeling that this

Skiffle is pushed down the bill by British teen stars

sound has just about disappeared from the current folk scene. There are many fine individual performers about and quite a number of good groups too, but the groups have virtually all followed either the Bluegrass trend of Scruggs & Flatt and Bill Monroe or the slick, modernized, carefully arranged approach of the Weavers and the Tarriers. We have no objections to either of these schools, but the older style seems deserving of resurrection.'

Like Ken Colyer, the members of the New Lost City Ramblers individually sought out the ageing artists who still played the music that they loved, although unlike Colyer they didn't have to cross an ocean to do so. Old-time players like Doc Watson, Roscoe Holcomb and Clarence Ashley were still active in their Appalachian communities, and in the years that followed, Paley, Cohen and Seeger would be instrumental in bringing these artists to national prominence. But whereas skiffle's back-to-basics ethic had inspired hundreds of thousands of British kids to pick up a guitar, the example of the New Lost City Ramblers went largely unheeded. In the first year that their album was on sale, it sold fewer than 350 copies. The American folk revival would instead be inspired by the slick, modernised and carefully arranged Kingston Trio. By the end of 1959, they had four albums in the *Billboard* Top Ten, a feat never equalled before or since. Four years after Lonnie Donegan had charted with an old Lead Belly song, American musicians had begun to find similar success in mining their own past for hits.

As more folk-style songs entered the American charts in the wake of the Kingston Trio's success, Donegan sensed a new source of material. After releasing his take on Skeets McDonald's regional hillbilly hit 'Fort Worth Jail', Lonnie scored his biggest hit for two years, reaching number two with 'The Battle of New Orleans', which Johnny Horton had recently taken to the top of the American charts.

Peter Sellers would mercilessly satirise this switch from singing

Lead Belly material to recording US hits in a sketch on his best-selling album *Songs for Swinging Sellers*. Purporting to be an interview between a clipped BBC type and the skiffle star 'Lenny Goonigan', Sellers – doing both voices – brilliantly captures Donegan's whiny voice and notoriously defensive nature. When the BBC type asks where he discovered his current hit single, Goonigan replies, 'It was an obscure folk song hidden at the top of the American hit parade.' Donegan was not amused, especially when it turned out that Wally Whyton of the Vipers had a hand in the script.

When Johnny Horton scored another hit single with an old country number called 'Sal's Got a Sugar Lip', Donegan swiftly followed suit. The song was originally performed by the Carlisle Brothers, Cliff and Bill, two Kentucky singers whose material often relied on sexual innuendo. Their version of the song, recorded in the 1930s, was entitled 'Sal's Got a Meatskin', which, the lyric informs us, she keeps 'hid away' – her hymen, in other words. The audience at the Royal Aquarium, Great Yarmouth, were doubtless unaware of this fact when Donegan performed the song for them during his 1959 summer season there, but the live recording of 'Sal's Got a Sugar Lip' made during the run got to number thirteen in the UK charts that September.

Donegan's final single of the year was another of the Kingston Trio's run of hits, this time from the pen of their most favoured songwriter, Jane Bowers. 'San Miguel' found Lonnie crooning in a cod-Spanish accent, rolling his 'r"s for all he was worth while mispronouncing the 'Meeg-el' of the title as 'Mig-well', making it sound like a village in Bedfordshire rather than some distant Mexican pueblo.

'San Miguel' was the last of Donegan's singles to be credited to his skiffle group. Chris Barber's old banjo player was now a bona fide star with his own weekly TV show. *Putting On the Donegan* made its debut in 1959 as a half-hour variety show screened in a weekly prime-time 8 p.m. spot. The man who had been horrified to discover his blues hero, Lonnie Johnson, performing in a white tuxedo when he shared a stage with him at the Festival Hall in 1952 was now seen in tux and bow tie every Friday night on commercial television.

———

In truth, skiffle had been mutating for some time. One thread of this process can be discerned in the pages of a fanzine produced by a fifteen-year-old working-class Londoner. Michael Moorcock would go on to become one of Britain's greatest science-fiction writers, but his first publications were fanzines that he typed, illustrated, duplicated and distributed himself. One was entitled *Jazz Fan*, 'an irregular publication circulated mainly in fandom but chucked at anyone who is interested. Articles or art work connected with jazz, skiffle and r&r welcomed.'

Born in 1939, Moorcock was a regular face on the Soho teen scene. Legend has it that it was he and fledgling jazz drummer Charlie Watts who first suggested to Tommy Steele that he should try his luck at the 2 I's. Available by post from the Moorcock family home in Norbury, SW16, and distributed free at gigs, *Jazz Fan* number 7, produced at the height of the skiffle boom in May 1957, contained a couple of pages reviewing the newest skiffle releases. The following issue found Moorcock declaring the Cotton Pickers – regulars on the West End circuit and featuring Tommy Steele's old mucker Mike Pratt – to be performing 'the most authentic interpretation of American folk-songs ever to appear under the name SKIFFLE'.

But by February 1958, the magazine had changed its name to *The Rambler* and, although the cover illustration depicted a jazz quartet, the focus of its content had moved towards traditional folk music. An article written by Sandy Paton, a twenty-eight-year-old folk singer

The Rambler fanzine, February 1958

visiting from the US, bemoans the fact that America has no equivalent to the Soho coffee bar where teenagers could nurse a cappuccino
all night long while listening to live guitar music, maybe even get up
and play themselves. Paton also complains that skifflers don't know
any traditional British folk songs. By March 1958, *The Rambler* had
become a fanzine about the burgeoning London folk scene, with an
enthusiastic young Moorcock encouraging his readers to hear folk
music at former skiffle strongholds such as the Breadbasket, the
Round House and the Princess Louise.

Ewan MacColl had been intermittently hosting events at the Theatre Royal in Stratford in east London under the banner of 'Ballads and Blues' since 1954, latterly billing the event as 'folk music, jazz, work songs and skiffle'. In late 1957, he moved to the Princess Louise, where, on 24 November, he opened one of the first folk clubs in Britain. Four months later, Eric Winter described the pub as 'overflowing with refugees from the skiffle craze . . . indistinguishable in dress or appearance from a Tommy Steele fan club, drinking in and applauding large instalments of the Child Ballad Collection'.

The club retained some of skiffle's infectious enthusiasm. 'There are generally about thirty bods with guitars and when they remember, performers shout out the chord sequences and everyone joins in,' wrote MacColl in a letter to Peggy Seeger in 1957.

While MacColl was willing to accommodate the inclusive spirit of skiffle, which insisted that anyone could pick up a guitar and play, he was less tolerant of the skifflers' tendency to sing in an Americanised accent. MacColl saw the commercial onslaught of American culture as a threat to the indigenous folk music of the UK. He was not alone in this concern – it was even shared by some folklorists in the US – but few went as far as he did to counter it. As early as March 1958, he was arguing that singers who performed at the Ballads and Blues Club should sing material from their own culture. English singers should sing English songs, Irish singers Irish songs, and so on. Only American singers were allowed to sing the blues. Peggy Seeger explains how the policy came about:

'I think it was Long John Baldry singing "Rock Island Line" that brought matters to a head. His accent just cracked me up. I was laughing so hard they had to take me out of the room. The next week I was hauled before the club's Audience Committee, who took me to task saying no matter how funny you think it is, you don't start laughing in the middle of a performance. I said what was so funny was that Lead

Belly used to visit our house, I'd listened to Lead Belly from the time I was little, so I know what that song should sound like. We had a French guy on the committee and he said, "Well, in that case I would be very grateful if you did not sing any French songs, Peggy." Then another member of the committee said, "Well, that guy who came a while ago" – referring to Theo Bikel – "who sings Russian songs? I speak Russian and his Russian accent is dreadful."

'Bert Lloyd sang Australian songs but he'd been down there and he could mimic an Australian accent very well. Ewan could do a Scots accent beautifully, but when someone said to me that I shouldn't sing French songs, I kind of got a bit irritated by that and I turned to Ewan and said, "Well, I wish you'd stop singing 'Sam Bass was born in Indiana, it was his native home' with a fake American accent," and we should've tumbled around laughing because it was so funny.

'Instead, we decided that on stage, only on stage, you sang in a language you understood and a language the vowels of which you used in your speech. This immediately hauled Bert back to Australian and English, Ewan to Scots and English. He had to stop singing Irish songs and I was to stop singing all those songs that Pete [Seeger] sings, which I had been singing for a long time, and concentrate on American songs mostly from the east coast. I could never sing Woody Guthrie because I didn't have that Oklahoma accent.'

This prescriptive approach was full of glaring contradictions. How could MacColl, an internationalist by conviction, impose a nationalist policy on those who came to sing at his club? And if there were to be restrictions based on regional and national identity, then why not also recognise gender, class and religion? 'The Policy' did have the effect of sending young singers off to explore their own cultural heritage, but was it really necessary for MacColl and Seeger – two great artists who spent their lives challenging authority – to set themselves up as the Folk Police?

Across the UK, young people who had been inspired to play American folk music by Lonnie Donegan were starting to explore their own tradition. Norma Waterson, born in 1939, had been taught to play guitar by her first husband and formed a skiffle group with brother Mike, sister Lal and banjo player Pete Ogley. Called the Mariners, they played anywhere they could in their native Hull: coffee bars, street corners, pubs and at the Albion Jazz Club. On a trip to London, Norma and her husband, a guitarist in a Dixieland jazz band, visited the Studio 51 club in Soho, where Ken Colyer held court with his Jazzmen. Norma was surprised to find traditional folk musicians in a jazz club: 'In the interval, we thought it would be skiffle, but this man and woman got up – the woman looked like my granny with jet-black hair. The guy played the fiddle and she played the banjo. She began singing and I was lost. She sang "She Moves Through the Fair". It was Margaret Barry and Michael Gorman.'

At the instigation of their banjo player, the Mariners had been playing mostly American folk music. 'Pete Ogley used to play a long-neck banjo and all the songs in our set were Pete Seeger songs, so when Pete O's wife told him he couldn't play with us any more, the whole set was gone and we were left with an English-only repertoire. We were lucky in that the local library had a good music section and we went and had a look, and there was one of Frank Kidson's books [of English folk songs collected in the 1890s] and we took it out and thought, "This is really what we want."'

Renaming themselves the Folksons and making a point of singing in their own accents, they opened Hull's first folk club, the Folk Union One, in the city's Baker Street Dance Hall. They soon made contact with a group of young men in Liverpool who were also making the transition from skiffle to folk.

On a visit to Paris, Alan Sytner had been highly impressed with the jazz clubs on the Left Bank of the Seine, especially one built into an underground cave, Le Caveau de la Huchette. Returning home to Liverpool, he began searching for a venue with a similar ambience, opening the Cavern Club in August 1956. The first night featured music from the Merseysippi Jazz Band and the Coney Island Skiffle Group, among others. The Cavern was a jazz club, but the popularity of skiffle meant that Sytner was soon running a whole night dedicated to this teenage music.

Among the popular skiffle acts at the Cavern was the Gin Mill Skiffle Group, comprising friends who had met at teacher training college. Tony Davis and Mick Groves began their career playing during the intervals in the Merseysippi Jazz Band's set, but soon drew their own devoted audience. They were introduced to English folk music by Redd Sullivan, at that time a regular singer with John Hasted's skiffle group at the Forty-four Club in Soho.

'Redd was a stoker on the Elder Dempster Line and came into Liverpool occasionally with the boat, and that's how he came across us,' recalls Mick Groves. 'It was Redd that actually said to Tony

Redd Sullivan (*centre*) sings with the John Hasted Skiffle Group, 1956. Hasted on banjo (*right*)

and I, "What are you two English schoolteachers doing singing these American things? Nothing wrong with them but why are you doing that? Why don't you sing your own songs from here, from Liverpool?" We said, "What do you mean?" And he said, "Sea shanties, songs about the sea," and we just went on from there to start looking at sea shanties, which became part of our early repertoire.

'The local members of the English Folk Dance and Song Society used to meet every week in the Friends' Meeting House, right across the street from the Empire. Tony and I went along, and they used to sit around a baize table, the old men in their suits and the women in their best coats and hats, and sing traditional folk songs from a book. Sullivan arrived for a few days and we said, "It's this folk thing tonight, do you want to come along and talk to them about the songs that you do?" So he came, and they started by doing their usual singing rounds and then welcomed him, and he said his piece and sang a couple of music-hall songs and shanties. When he finished they all applauded and this woman said, "I don't know what we are doing here trying to sing folk songs when surely we have to listen to people who have lived it."'

Inspired by the new material they discovered at Sullivan's suggestion, Tony and Mick opened a folk club in a basement below Sampson and Barlow's restaurant on London Road in Liverpool city centre in September 1958.

Leon Rosselson was a member of one of several skiffle groups that had splintered off from the left-wing London Youth Choir. The Southerners eschewed the skiffle songs that they heard on the radio, preferring material that reflected their political beliefs, such as 'Union Miners Stand Together', Joe Glazer's 'Put My Name Down' and anything by Woody Guthrie. Otherwise, they followed the classic skiffle group path, entering a national competition – albeit in their case one organised by the *Daily Worker* – and auditioning unsuccessfully for

Saturday Skiffle Club. They were ideally placed to participate in the Aldermaston Marches, having already performed at numerous peace rallies with the London Youth Choir.

Rosselson has long maintained that skiffle plus CND led to an outpouring of new topical songs at the end of the 1950s, long before the American protest song boom began. 'For a short time, skiffle, musically primitive as it was, broke the power of the commercial music industry, which didn't happen with Elvis Presley, Bill Haley and all that,' he recalls. 'It was, as they say, empowering, turning consumers into participants, and indirectly, I think, leading to the new song boom. If you could make your own music, you could write your own songs.'

The skiffle boom may have been over, but for a generation of youngsters empowered by learning to play guitar, their adventure was just beginning.

25

MAXIMUM R & B

If the folk clubs gave skifflers a means by which to explore their past, there were others who used skiffle as a bridge to the future, embracing rock 'n' roll as an escape from childhoods blighted by rationing and war. Tony Sheridan, one of a number of teenagers swept into Soho by the skiffle craze, had managed to find a niche for himself at the 2 I's. Born in Norwich in 1940, Anthony Esmond Sheridan McGinnity went to art school in 1956, where he formed a skiffle group called the Saints. Heading down to London to seek fame and fortune in November 1957, they failed their audition at the Skiffle Cellar. Disheartened, three of the group headed back to Norwich, but Sheridan elected to stay. He found lodgings in a room above a pub with fellow group member Kenny Packwood and the two friends became regulars at the 2 I's.

Tony Sheridan served his apprenticeship there, becoming much in demand as a backing musician – the only English guitarist who was any good during the late 50s, according to Jimmy Page. His fretwork can be heard on 'Right Behind You Baby' by Vince Taylor and the Playboys, a fabulous slice of British rockabilly released in December 1958. Taylor set Soho alight when he blew in from Hollywood, dressed head to toe in black leather, looking like Elvis and moving like lightning. He wasn't much of a singer, but his live shows were manic and menacing, attracting as many boys as girls to see this rock 'n' roll refugee. When it later transpired that Vince Taylor was actually born Brian Holden in Isleworth, Middlesex, he fled to Paris, where his form of existential angst was taken more seriously, especially as it came dressed in leather trousers and sporting a massive quiff.

When Gene Vincent arrived in Britain in late 1959, he'd burned his bridges with his backing band the Blue Caps, and was all but washed up back home. In many ways, he was the dangerous American rocker that Vince Taylor had claimed to be, an impression underlined when Jack Good dressed Gene in head-to-toe black leather for an appearance on ITV's *Boy Meets Girl* on 15 December. Britain's premier pop impresario Larry Parnes was duly impressed and, when Vincent's manager offered to bring another of his artistes, Eddie Cochran, over for a tour, Parnes filled the undercard with young British singers from his stable. Billy Fury, Joe Brown, Vince Eager and Georgie Fame each took part when they were available. The Tony Sheridan Trio played most of the dates. When the tour ended in Bristol, Sheridan consumed half a bottle of whiskey and got so drunk he never said goodbye to his American friends.

Six weeks later, the best English rock 'n' roll guitarist of his generation was wondering what to do next when he got a call from one of the 2 I's fraternity, pianist Iain Hines. Apparently, a German club owner had turned up at the coffee bar looking for English bands to come and play in Hamburg. Bruno Koschmider was the manager of the Kaiserkeller, a strip joint on the Grosse Freiheit in the city's red-light district. Rock 'n' roll was becoming popular in Germany, but local musicians simply couldn't play it convincingly. Importing American stars was impossible, so Koschmider had come to England looking for groups who both looked the part and sounded American. He was offering good money, so Hines wasted no time in pulling together a scratch band of likely lads from the 2 I's' pool of musicians. Rick Richards, lead singer of the Worried Men, was first on his list, along with guitarist Colin Milander, bass player Pete Wharton, drummer Del Ward and the mercurial Tony Sheridan on lead guitar and vocals.

The band made their Kaiserkeller debut on Sunday 5 June 1960 as the Jets, the first British rock 'n' roll band to play in Hamburg.

Meanwhile, on 16 March 1960, Lonnie Donegan released a rewritten version of an old First World War soldiers' song, which entered the charts at number one, the first record by a British artist ever to do so. 'My Old Man's a Dustman' was a novelty number of the sort that had been sung for the past sixty years in variety halls up and down the land and, as such, represented the very music that the skifflers had fought so hard to escape from. Yet here was the King of Skiffle rubbing their noses in it, laughing all the way to the bank. Never mind that Lead Belly also sang such novelty songs; this felt like a betrayal of everything that skiffle stood for.

To make matters worse, the record was credited to Lonnie Donegan alone. When even the King of Skiffle had removed the 's' word from his record label, no one could be in any doubt that the boom was over.

'Dustman' reached the number one spot on 2 April 1960 and was still there two weeks later when the car carrying Eddie Cochran and Gene Vincent spun out and crashed into a lamp post on the outskirts of Chippenham in Wiltshire. Vincent broke his ribs and collar bone; Cochran suffered massive head injuries and died in St Martin's Hospital, Bath, the next day. The two American rock 'n' roll stars had just completed their week's residency at the Bristol Hippodrome, supported by Georgie Fame and Johnny Gentle.

Eddie Cochran was the last man standing from a dynamic group of young Americans who had defined rock 'n' roll. When he died on that Easter Sunday in England, Elvis Presley was in the army, Buddy Holly was in his grave, Jerry Lee Lewis was in disgrace and Chuck Berry was in prison. Even Little Richard, the outrageous singer and pianist who scored several British hits in the late 50s, had eschewed the Devil's music to become a preacher. All of the artists who had so excited British youth were either dead or in purgatory. After Cochran's death, people would still play rock 'n' roll in Britain, but it would be a milquetoast version aimed at children, not the dangerous music that had fired up the Teddy Boys and terrified parents. Tin Pan Alley was back in control and rebellious rock 'n' roll, like anti-commercial skiffle, was cast out of the temple.

Chris Barber had continued to promote roots music, inviting American blues and gospel singers to tour the UK backed by his trad jazz band. Following successes with Sister Rosetta Tharpe, Big Bill Broonzy, and Sonny Terry and Brownie McGhee, in 1958 Barber brought Muddy Waters to Britain for the first time. His UK reputation was based on the acoustic Stovall Plantation recordings, collected by Alan Lomax in 1941, but Muddy didn't live on no plantation any more. A resident of Chicago for fifteen years, he drove a Cadillac and, like most of the bluesmen working in the city, played an electric guitar. While some of his British fans were dismayed by this discovery, others were inspired to hear the urban blues played live for the first time. Soon Alexis Korner and Cyril Davies were using amplifiers at the Blues and Barrelhouse club, a move that would eventually lead to them being thrown out of the Round House for making too much noise.

Barber, who had recently launched a new trad jazz club, the Marquee in Oxford Street, had no such qualms. Hoping to do for the blues what he had done for skiffle, he introduced a breakdown group to his trad jazz band, featuring Korner on electric guitar, initially backing vocalist Ottilie Patterson on Muddy Waters' material. As these spots became more popular, it was decided that Korner should have the whole interval to himself. Alexis, who didn't fancy becoming the front man of his own group, came up with the idea of Blues Incorporated, an amorphous collective that could include whoever was around and willing to play. Cyril Davies was an obvious choice for the nucleus of the group, especially as he had recently switched from playing twelve-string guitar to blues harmonica. He was joined by Dick Heckstall-Smith on sax, Jack Bruce on bass and Charlie Watts on drums. The band's main singer was Long John Baldry, a former member of the Bob Cort Skiffle Group.

They made their debut opening for Acker Bilk, a trad jazz clarinettist who had recently become the first British artist to score a number one in the US with his single 'Strangers on the Shore'. Barber offered Blues Incorporated a residency at the Marquee, and it was there that they began to build a reputation. However, their growth was hampered by the fact that the club scene in the UK was dominated by trad; promoters were reluctant to book bands that used electric guitars.

Realising that there was an audience of young fans hungry for something more exciting, Korner began looking for a venue of his own. On 17 March 1962, he opened the Ealing Club in a basement beneath the ABC Bakery tearoom opposite Ealing Broadway Tube station, in the western suburbs of London. It mostly functioned as a jazz club, but Korner secured the Saturday-night spot, launching Britain's first club dedicated to R & B. The Ealing Club would become a mecca for those teenagers who had learned to play three chords on guitar during the skiffle boom.

Paul Jones was fifteen years old when he saw Lonnie Donegan at the Kings Theatre, Southsea, in June 1957. He formed a skiffle group named the Louisiana Four with school friends and began collecting Lead Belly records. At Oxford University, he and some friends got together to play the blues under the heavyweight name of Thunder Odin and the Big Secret. At a jazz and poetry event in Oxford, Paul met a twenty-year-old blues fan named Brian Jones, who hailed from Cheltenham. A former member of local skiffle band the Ramrods, he was now playing guitar in the style of Elmore James. Although he never actually joined the Big Secret on the few gigs they played, Brian became a fast friend of Paul's, sitting in on the band's more frequent rehearsal sessions. 'Cheltenham is on the same road as Oxford, so on Fridays he would hitch-hike to my flat, and if we had a party to go to we would play a few songs together,' recalls Paul.

Brian had met Alexis Korner when Blues Incorporated played at Cheltenham Town Hall with the Chris Barber Jazz Band, and Korner had offered him a floor to sleep on if he was ever in London. When Brian learned that Alexis had opened the Ealing Club, he and Paul became Saturday-night regulars. 'We used to go there every week without fail,' says Paul. 'Alexis was amazingly encouraging, he was like the godfather of the movement. He'd say to us, "Have you got a band? If you haven't, then start one." He was extremely generous and warm-hearted.'

Korner's policy of having a fluid membership for Blues Incorporated gave aspiring teenagers a chance to sing a song or two backed by the band. Paul and Brian were among their number. 'We used to hang around at the front of the stage, hoping to catch Alexis's eye, and if you were lucky he would just point at somebody and beckon, and then you'd get up and do your song.'

On 7 April 1962, the two friends got their first chance to perform, Brian on slide guitar and Paul on vocals and harmonica. As they began to play, three R & B fans from Dartford, coming down the steps into the basement, were amazed to hear a white kid playing slide guitar on Elmore James's 'Dust My Broom'. Still teenagers, Mick Jagger and Dick Taylor had been playing music together since their schooldays, while the third, Keith Richards, had learned the rudiments of guitar from his grandfather, Gus.

'The band I had with my friends, Little Boy Blue and the Blue Boys, was more like a skiffle group,' Jagger would recall years later. 'People tend to forget how enormous that was. I was in loads of skiffle groups.' Richards had recently joined the band, taking it in the direction of R & B.

The three friends made a beeline for Brian once he had finished playing. The young blues guitarist was thrilled to discover that he was not the only person in the country interested in playing this kind of music. Soon Mick, Keith and Dick were getting up to play with Blues Incorporated, while Brian formed a band with pianist Ian Stewart and guitarist Geoff Bradford. In June 1962, the six young R & B fans joined forces and, after Bradford dropped out, they made their live debut as the Rolling Stones, replacing Blues Incorporated at the Marquee Club.

———

Across the UK, other skiffle-inspired teens were plugging in their guitars and playing R & B. Van Morrison was born in Belfast in 1945 and grew up in a household surrounded by American roots music. His father was a regular customer at the Atlantic Records store on the High Street, whose owner, Solly Lipsitz, specialised in imported jazz and blues records from the US. Morrison senior was a leading figure in a coterie of roots music fans who would gather together in smoke-filled rooms to listen to hard-to-find recordings from the golden age of jazz, as well as blues and country records that were never heard on the BBC.

'When he got home from work he'd be playing records – on Saturday morning – he was playing this music all the time and I was just absorbing it,' remembers Van, who from a young age was a fan of artists such as Lead Belly, Sonny Terry and early Muddy Waters.

Already familiar with 'Rock Island Line' from his father's recordings, Van was shocked when he first heard Lonnie Donegan on the radio. 'When "Rock Island Line" came out, I couldn't believe it. Before then, I'd wanted to be a folk musician. There was no kind of scene anywhere in Belfast where you played Lead Belly songs.

Suddenly, Donegan had made it all viable. It was American music, but it wasn't. Donegan had put his stamp on it and made it British.'

It was an experience repeated in sitting rooms across the nation. 'Other people had this experience too – they heard "Rock Island Line" and something happened but they couldn't explain what it was. Like something just clicked into place. Donegan brought Lead Belly home to me.' Skiffle had introduced a whole new dynamic to the music that Van had been listening to. 'There was beat and an energy in Donegan's performance. Other records started and ended in the same place, but he travelled from A to B and you were carried along with it. At the end, you felt you'd arrived at somewhere different.'

Van wasn't too impressed when Elvis hit the charts shortly after Donegan. 'Rock 'n' roll I saw as kind of commercial because I was hearing all this blues music. People trying to copy Elvis had no chance, but skiffle seemed to me like a homegrown kind of thing that could open the door. Donegan made it possible to go through that door.'

Van formed a skiffle group in 1957 with his friends at Orangefield Secondary School. 'They hadn't a clue about Lead Belly. I had to educate them on that, but they were starting to hear stuff on the radio, like Donegan, the Vipers, Chas McDevitt and Nancy Whiskey.' Named the Sputniks after the Russian satellite launched that year, the line-up comprised two guitars, washboard, tea-chest bass and something that Van christened the zobo. 'We fished this metal tube out from the bottom of the Beechie River and played it by blowing into the end. I don't know how we didn't catch typhoid.'

The group performed mostly at parties, but did have a regular spot playing at the nearby Willowfield Cinema on Woodstock Road. 'For a while we played every Saturday matinee, setting up as soon as the B film ended, before the main picture. Our last show was in July 1960, when we played the school leaving dance.'

Van Morrison would never forget the debt he owed to the skiffle movement. In 1998, he recorded an album of songs from the skiffle period with Lonnie Donegan, who by then had been more or less written out of the story of British rock. 'Without Donegan I don't know how I would have started,' he told the *Guardian* in 2015. 'It would have been extremely difficult to even think about approaching the thing unless Donegan was there, in the beginning.'

THE BRITISH ARE COMING

On 2 March 1960, two weeks before the release of 'My Old Man's a Dustman', Associated-Rediffusion broadcast a TV documentary that shocked the nation. *Living for Kicks*, an hour-long investigation into the social and sexual lives of Britain's teenagers, was unlike anything that had ever been seen before. The programme was fronted by Daniel Farson, a thirty-three-year-old writer and broadcaster who had made a reputation for himself in the late 50s by employing a style of interviewing that lacked the deference usually shown to those from the Establishment who deigned to appear on television.

Farson took his camera crew into youth clubs in Brighton, Northampton and London, and asked teenagers what they thought about matters that were important to them: sex, culture and the attitudes of their parents. 'All we hope to do', he states in his introduction, 'is to observe a new type of teenager, a teenager who is making more money than was ever dreamt of in the old days, who has a new spending power and with that power is enjoying himself – or fails to enjoy himself – in a completely different way.'

Before his middle-aged viewers became outraged at the idea of young people having more sex, money and fun than they ever did, Farson made clear that the subjects of his documentary seemed to be slightly lost in their new-found freedom, living in their own world, apart from the rest of society. Educated at public school and with a cut-glass accent – in his introduction he pronounces 'lost' as 'lorst' – Daniel Farson was the epitome of the 1950s broadcaster, yet his sensibilities already seemed tuned into the issues that would come to dominate the culture wars of the 1960s.

He certainly understood how to create a media storm. His first interviewee was a bearded nineteen-year-old who was a regular at the Whisky-a-Go-Go coffee bar in Brighton. Royston Ellis, introduced as 'a sort of beatnik, who is also a poet', had published a book of beat poetry in 1959 entitled *Jiving to Gyp*, which he dedicated to Cliff Richard, whose band, the Shadows, sometimes backed Ellis when he read his work, creating a new hybrid of rock 'n' roll and poetry that he dubbed 'rocketry'. Gay, highly articulate and deploying the sexual frankness of his hero, Allen Ginsberg, Ellis was soon in demand as a spokesman for the new generation of teenagers.

Like Farson, he loved to provoke a reaction and, during their conversation at the beginning of *Living for Kicks*, it's difficult to work out who is exploiting whom: Farson needs Ellis to make some outrageous statements on which he can hang his narrative; Ellis needs Farson to give him the platform on which to create his beat persona. Neither is disappointed. When Ellis blithely claims that 'no teenager will marry a virgin for the simple reason that, before he marries her, he'll have sex with her', you can almost hear Farson squeal with delight. He has his headline-making quote.

As the documentary unfolds, however, it becomes clear that Ellis is no expert on teen culture. Not only do most of the teenagers interviewed refute his statement, but his assertion that Teddy Boys have completely disappeared is undermined when Farson visits a coffee-bar club in Northampton. The venue is full of bequiffed young men in drape coats and girls who say they only want to go out with a Ted. Here, just seventy miles north of London, the neo-Edwardians are still flourishing – and if you look closely at the footage, you'll see the tea-chest bass being played, which reveals that they're dancing to a skiffle band, although the skiffle boom had supposedly ended two years previously.

None of this mattered, of course. When the programme was broadcast, Royston Ellis became the face of the 'lorst' generation, suddenly everywhere on TV and radio, the toast of the teenage coffee bar, King of the Beatniks, the nearest thing to a beat poet that Britain had thus far produced.

Three months after *Living for Kicks* had sparked controversy in living rooms across the country, Ellis was booked to read his poetry at an arts festival organised by the Guild of Undergraduates at Liverpool University. Used to performing in front of a band, he arrived in the city on the lookout for a bunch of young musicians willing to back his 'rocketry'. Heading for the Jacaranda cafe in Slater Street, he chanced upon a youth in a matelot-style shirt and leather jacket, to whom he was immediately attracted. When he explained what he was looking for, the young man led him through the back streets to a dilapidated flat on Gambier Terrace, where a bunch of art students were doing their best to live an approximation of the beatnik lifestyle.

Four of the boys based at the flat were budding musicians and immediately recognised that, in Ellis, they had found someone of their own age who was able to make a living through his own creativity. Determined to find out how he'd managed such an astounding feat, they offered him a bed for the night. Ellis failed to charm the audience at Liverpool University, but the group liked him so much that they invited him to get up and recite some of his beat poetry while they played along during their gig at the Jacaranda the following night.

Ellis returned the favour by giving the lads their first drug experience, showing them how to break open a Vicks nasal inhaler and get high on the Benzedrine-impregnated strip curled up inside. Years later, Ellis would also claim that it was he, the nation's most notorious beat poet, who, recognising some kindred spirits, had suggested that the group slightly alter their name by dropping an 'e' and adding an 'a' to become the Beatles.

The genesis of the group had occurred at the height of the skiffle boom, on 6 July 1957, when the Quarrymen Skiffle Group, fronted by a sixteen-year-old Teddy Boy named John Lennon, performed at St Peter's Parish Church Summer Fete in the Liverpool suburb of Woolton. Taking the stage around 4 p.m., Lennon led the Quarrymen through a series of songs made famous by Lonnie Donegan: 'Cumberland Gap', 'Lost John', 'Rock Island Line', 'Railroad Bill', 'Putting On the Style' – which was number one at the time – and 'Bring a Little Water, Sylvie'. They punctuated these with a couple of Vipers songs, as well as attempting a few rock 'n' roll numbers.

After their set, the group were introduced to a kid named Paul McCartney, who'd come along with a friend of a friend. Lennon wasn't particularly impressed with the just-turned-fifteen McCartney, until the latter picked up his guitar, retuned it and played a convincing version of Eddie Cochran's 'Twenty Flight Rock'. Within a few weeks, Paul was a member of the Quarrymen and a photograph taken in November 1957 shows how quickly he formed a partnership with John. Lennon is no longer the only vocalist: both boys have microphones and matching attire. The rest of the group – guitar, tea-chest bass and snare drum – already look like sidemen.

Shortly after this photo was taken, in early 1958, Paul would introduce John to a guitar-playing friend of his named George Harrison. Despite being just fourteen years old, George knew more chord shapes than Lennon and McCartney combined and, despite some initial reluctance from John, he too joined the group. The fourth teenager whom Royston Ellis met at Gambier Terrace was Stuart Sutcliffe, who joined the Quarrymen on bass in January 1960, after the group had been reduced to a nucleus of three guitarists – John, Paul and George.

The Jacaranda, where Ellis had initially encountered George Harrison in his matelot shirt, was owned by Allan Williams, a thirty-year-old would-be impresario whose trips to the 2 I's in London had inspired him to open a similar basement club in Liverpool. 'The Jac' became a magnet for the city's art students, who gathered there to talk pop and politics, and for the nighthawks who wanted to avoid the more violent aspects of late-night social life – with no alcohol available at the Jac, the hard nuts tended to gather elsewhere.

In January 1960, Williams had visited Hamburg to explore the possibility of finding work in the German port city for some of the bands that he employed at the Jacaranda. It was Williams that Bruno Koschmider was looking for when he turned up at the 2 I's in May asking for musicians to come and play at the Kaiserkeller. Two months later, Koschmider was back at the Soho coffee bar: Tony Sheridan and the Jets had walked out on him and he needed to find a replacement band, *schnell*. By pure coincidence, Williams was there when Koschmider arrived, supervising an audition for his band Derry and the Seniors. As soon as they began playing in the tiny cellar, Koschmider knew he'd found his next attraction. A week later, the Seniors played their first gig on the Grosse Freiheit.

Since May 1960, Williams had been looking after John, Paul, George and Stuart's group, booking gigs for them under the name of Long John and the Silver Beetles, then the Silver Beetles and – following their encounter with Royston Ellis – the Silver Beatles. In August, Koschmider called from Hamburg asking for more bands. Business was so good since he had introduced Derry and the Seniors that he was now converting the Indra, his transvestite cabaret on the Grosse Freiheit, into a rock 'n' roll club.

The Silver Beatles jumped at the chance. Swiftly recruiting Pete Best to play drums, they piled into Williams's Morris minibus and headed for Hamburg, dropping the first part of their name into the North Sea somewhere between Harwich and the Hook of Holland. The irony of five young British lads heading to Germany for a life-changing experience cannot have been lost on the Beatles. For much of their youth they had been preparing to visit the country – in uniform.

National service in the armed forces hung like a cloud over the new generation of British boys. They knew that, before they could begin whatever careers they had planned, they would first have to endure eighteen months of being ordered about – just as they were beginning to enjoy their independence – or, much worse, become involved in one of the numerous conflicts Britain faced as she withdrew from empire. Conscription had thwarted the ambitions of the Silver Beetles once already. Their previous drummer, Norman Chapman, had been forced to leave the group when his call-up papers came through in July 1960 and he was sent to Kenya to fight the Mau Mau.

However, in May 1957, the British government had announced that no one born after 1 October 1939 would be required to do national service. John Lennon and Stuart Sutcliffe – both born in 1940 – would be among the first eighteen-year-olds not to be conscripted since the outbreak of the Second World War. The cut-off date came just in time. Had it continued for just a few more years, national service would have had a devastating effect on the development of British pop.

A love of guitar playing and American music had bridged the significant age differences between the Beatles; conscription would have ripped them apart. John Lennon would have been first to get his papers in November 1958, not returning home until April 1960, just three months before Paul McCartney was called up. By the time Paul was demobbed in December 1961, George Harrison would have been a national serviceman for nine months, only getting back to Liverpool in August 1962. Thankfully, their rite of passage would not be provided by induction into the armed forces, but by the denizens of the Hamburg Reeperbahn.

When they made their debut at the Indra on 17 August 1960, the

Beatles were not a fully developed rock 'n' roll band. They consisted of the three core guitarists from the Quarrymen Skiffle Group, plus a bass player who couldn't really play the bass and a drummer they'd never played with before. Horst Fascher, an ex-boxer who protected the boys from the rowdier elements of the Grosse Freiheit, told Beatles biographer Larry Kane that when they played those first concerts at the Indra, they still sounded like a skiffle group. 'They thought Lonnie Donegan was Elvis. All that washboard stuff. Every English boy that bought a guitar followed Lonnie Donegan. I had already heard some rock 'n' roll bands like Derry and the Seniors and Tony Sheridan and things like that. I was saying, after listening to five, six, seven songs . . . this is too much washboard music.'

Over the following years, more and more British musicians would follow the route taken by the Beatles, a metamorphosis that would see them transcend their skiffle roots to become acts capable of taking on the world. On 1 February 1964, the Beatles topped the *Billboard* charts for the first time with 'I Want to Hold Your Hand', kicking off a two-year streak which would see British acts at number one in the US for 52 weeks out of 104.

The Beatles dominated this period. In 1962, they finally found a regular drummer in the shape of Ringo Starr, who had learned his trade in the rhythm section of the Eddie Clayton Skiffle Group. And almost all the other British acts who scored US number ones in these years had their roots in skiffle too. Peter Asher of Peter and Gordon had been in a skiffle group with future folk artist Andy Irvine. Both Alan Price and Hilton Valentine of the Animals had formed skiffle groups in their native north-east. Manfred Mann were fronted by Ealing Club graduate Paul Jones, who formed his first skiffle group at school in 1957. Freddie and the Dreamers had evolved out of the Kingfishers Skiffle Group, while Wayne Fontana, of Mindbenders fame, started his career in a schoolboy skiffle ensemble called the Velfins. Karl Green of

Herman's Hermits had been inspired to pick up the guitar by Lonnie Donegan, and the Dave Clark Five began life as a skiffle group formed to raise some money for a trip to Holland. The Rolling Stones found a stable line-up in late 1962 with the addition of Bill Wyman on bass. Born in 1936, Wyman had been doing his national service in Germany when he first heard Lonnie Donegan. He built himself a tea-chest bass and formed a skiffle group in his barracks.

Of the ten British artists who topped the US charts during that incredible two-year period, only one had no connection to skiffle. Petula Clark didn't need Lonnie Donegan to open her eyes to the possibilities of being a pop star. By the time that 'Rock Island Line' hit the charts in December 1955, she had already released thirty singles in the UK.

A cursory look into the backgrounds of other UK bands that got into the US charts during the mid-60s gives even more substance to the notion that skiffle was boot camp for the British Invasion. The Searchers began life as a skiffle group; the Gerry Marsden Skiffle Group, who won a certificate of excellence at the 1957 Youth Music Festival in Liverpool, evolved into Gerry and the Pacemakers; the Swinging Blue Jeans used to play at the Cavern on skiffle night as the Bluegenes. Chad Stuart of Chad and Jeremy was an ex-skiffler, as was Billy J. Kramer. Kramer's backing band, the Dakotas, featured Mick Green, one of the great British guitarists of the period, who had begun his career as a member of a skiffle trio called the Wayfaring Strangers. The Honeycombs, whose hit single 'Have I the Right?' was produced by Joe Meek, contained a couple of ex-skifflers, and three members of the Zombies had played in the same skiffle group while at school. Ian McLagan, the keyboard player with the Small Faces, began his musical journey playing tea-chest bass. Dave Davies, lead guitarist of the Kinks, played in a skiffle outfit at school with his future bass player Pete Quaife. Graham Nash and Allan Clarke of the Hollies formed a skiffle duo in Manchester called the Two Teens. Roger Daltrey made his first guitar from a block of wood and founded his own skiffle band called the Detours, which later evolved into the Who.

It wasn't just the pop bands of the 60s who owed a debt to skiffle. When the focus of the music scene shifted from singles to albums as the decade wore on, ex-skifflers were in the front rank. Syd Barrett was inspired to pick up a guitar by his brother's skiffle band, and other members of Pink Floyd also cut their teeth on Lonnie Donegan's repertoire. Jack Bruce of Cream played his cello as a bass in his school skiffle band, while Roy Harper, Bert Jansch and Joe Cocker were all swept along by the craze.

Jimmy Page had already enjoyed an illustrious career before he joined Led Zeppelin, but his first TV appearance, in 1957 aged thirteen, was with his schoolboy skiffle group. *All Your Own* was a BBC production for children that offered youngsters the opportunity to show off their skills in such pastimes as making models, rearing pets and playing musical instruments. It was presented by the avuncular Huw Wheldon, who would quiz his young guests on how they had achieved such prodigious feats and what they intended to be when they grew up. Jimmy and his JG Skiffle Group played a couple of songs, 'Momma Don't Allow No Skiffle Playing Round Here' and Lead Belly's 'Cottonfields', after which Page informed Wheldon that, rather than be a musician, he was going to do biological research. Happily for us, he was able to combine both.

As the 70s dawned, British kids who had been inspired by skiffle continued to light up the charts on both sides of the Atlantic. The cover of David Bowie's 1972 album *The Rise and Fall of Ziggy Stardust and the Spiders from Mars* was designed by his old friend George Underwood, with whom Bowie had made his debut performance in August 1958 singing several Lonnie Donegan songs at the Bromley Boy Scouts' annual summer camp on the Isle of Wight.

Underwood also designed sleeves for ex-skiffler Marc Bolan and for Mott the Hoople, whose lead singer, Ian Hunter, was a veteran of the national skiffle contests with his group Apex. Rod Stewart described his time in the Kool Kats Skiffle Group as 'seven guitars and one bloke on tea-chest bass'. His guitar player in the Faces, Ronnie Wood, had made his musical debut aged nine, playing washboard in his brother Ted's Candy Bison Skiffle Group, which performed between films at the local cinema. Even Elton John confessed he owed a huge debt to Lonnie Donegan.

Skiffle's influence extended into the mid-70s, twenty years after the original boom. One of the biggest bands of the period, the Bee Gees, had begun life as a Manchester skiffle group called the Rattlesnakes, formed by the brothers Gibb when they returned from Australia in 1955. The influence of skiffle was also felt across Europe. Björn Ulvaeus of Abba was inspired to form his first group after his cousin returned home from a holiday in England with an armful of skiffle records. The two key protagonists in Dr Feelgood had first encountered one another when playing in rival skiffle outfits on Canvey Island, where tea-chest basses were still in use in the mid-60s. With their menacing demeanour and sparse, spiky sound, the Feelgoods were precursors of a back-to-basics movement that sought to sweep away the rock stars of the 1960s. Yet for all its Year Zero antagonism towards what came before, punk rock had much in common with the original do-it-yourself music.

In September 1976, the 100 Club in London's Oxford Street played host to the fledgling UK punk scene. The bill, consisting of the Sex Pistols, the Clash, Buzzcocks, the Damned, the Vibrators and Subway Sect, represented almost every punk band in the land. The promoters were so short of acts that they gave stage time to an unknown group of individuals, only one of whom could play an instrument. Siouxsie and the Banshees had never performed together before, but Sid Vicious on drums, Steve Severin on bass and Marco Pirroni on guitar improvised a twenty-minute set while front woman Siouxsie Sioux intoned the Lord's Prayer.

A time-travelling teenage skiffler, beamed into the 100 Club that night from the 1950s, would have seen much that was familiar. Punk wasn't manufactured by the music business, it was raucous, ragged and out of control and you only needed to know three chords on the guitar to play it. Like skiffle, it set out to democratise popular culture, taking the onus away from trained musicians up on the bandstand and putting instruments into the hands of thousands of British teenagers who had no formal musical training – empowering them to perform. And like skiffle had done in the 50s, punk confused the grown-ups; they said it wasn't real music, that the musicians couldn't really play, that it was just a noisy racket.

The sense that British pop culture had come full circle was underlined the following evening, when the 100 Club played host to Ken Colyer's Jazzmen. Did the forty-eight-year-old trumpet player shake his head and tut disapprovingly when told about the antics of the night before? Or did the man once shunned for playing purposefully primitive music recognise some kindred spirits? Ken Colyer prized authenticity over popularity and had a chip on his shoulder as big as any punk rock front man's. The spark that he kindled turned into a wildfire that quickly spread beyond his control, sweeping through the Soho clubs and out into the provinces. Colyer had originally reached for skiffle to make a connection with the past, but the kids who picked up guitars after hearing 'Rock Island Line' used it to escape the drab world of post-war austerity, a process that led them to create some of the greatest British pop, rock and folk music of the following decades.

ACKNOWLEDGEMENTS

As someone who experienced the rise of punk rock in late-1970s Britain, as both a fan and a musician, I have always viewed skiffle as a similar phenomenon. Both were movements that came from outside the music industry, breaking down the barrier between performer and audience, eschewing commerciality in favour of a do-it-yourself approach based more on enthusiasm than musical skill. My experiences during the punk rock years gave me an insight into how an egalitarian youth movement could spread from the West End of London out to the suburbs and provinces, empowering those it touched to climb up on stage and make their own music.

However, perspectives on the cultural significance of skiffle were hard to come by in the late twentieth century, when the whole phenomenon was reduced to passing references in the biographies of 1960s rock stars. This was remedied in 1997, when Chas McDevitt published *Skiffle: The Definitive Inside Story*. McDevitt's account lived up to its subtitle, his background in jazz giving him insights into the roots of the scene, while his transatlantic success with 'Freight Train' allowed him to tell the story of how skiffle tried to come to terms with the pop music of the day.

McDevitt's book was followed a year later by *The Skiffle Craze*, written by Mike Dewe. Born in 1940, Dewe was one of the thousands of boys who had been inspired to pick up a guitar by artists like McDevitt, spending their short careers playing intermittently on the local amateur circuit before fading into obscurity. As a result, Dewe's

393

book is focused on the grass roots, his narrative peppered with 'skiffle reminiscences' – panels containing first-hand accounts of skiffle contests and self-made instruments.

I avidly read both books and was pleased to see Van Morrison record the *Skiffle Sessions* album with Lonnie Donegan and Chris Barber in 1998. The English Folk Dance and Song Society invited me to write an article for their house magazine early in the new millennium, and I chose skiffle as my subject. It was in the course of researching that piece that I first grasped the significance of Ken Colyer's pilgrimage to New Orleans. Speaking to the Ken Colyer Trust, I discovered that one of his original Crane River Jazz Band colleagues, bass player Julian Davies, lived a few miles from me in west Dorset. Julian kindly assented to be interviewed and, over cups of tea in his house in North Allington, he began my education in trad jazz.

Like many brought up on 60s pop music, I regarded trad with contempt. Just as punk was a rejection of the pretentious prog-rock scene, I understood that British beat music – and especially our R & B bands – was a reaction to the trad boom, whose popularity had preceded the appearance of the Beatles and the Stones. It was a prejudice reinforced by seeing the likes of Acker Bilk and Kenny Ball on TV variety shows in the early 70s. Trad seemed backward-looking, middle-aged, square.

Julian changed my perspective. Through his enthusiasm, I came to see trad jazz as a classic 'back to basics' movement, akin to what the Ramones and Dr Feelgood were doing in the mid-70s when they stripped the edifice away from rock music, making it exciting again by taking it back to its roots. When, in 2008, I was invited to make a documentary for BBC Radio 4, I chose as my subject the life and legacy of Ken Colyer.

Three years ago, when performing at the Tønder Folk Festival in Denmark, I heard the distinctive sound of what sounded like a skiffle group emanating from the main stage. On investigating, I discovered that it was a performance by the Carolina Chocolate Drops that had caught my ear. The band, consisting of young black musicians, had formed in 2005 to play jazz, blues, folk and country in the African American string band tradition. Not only did they sound like a skiffle group, but their intent seemed to come from a similar place.

A month later, I was in Nashville, Tennessee, as the guest of the Americana Music Association, presenting an award at their annual jamboree. The AMA have done great work over the past few years, nurturing a new scene for younger, edgier bands that don't fit into country music's more commercial image. Their notion of what constitutes Americana is broad, encompassing folk, jazz, blues, soul, country and western, rock 'n' roll, rhythm and blues, zydeco and more.

When I asked them to define this new genre, what I heard immediately made me think of skiffle. According to the AMA, Americana is any contemporary music based on the roots music of the US that lives in a world apart from the pure forms of the genres upon which it draws. Wasn't that what Lonnie Donegan was creating back in 1954, when he recorded 'Rock Island Line'? I was so taken with this idea that I returned to my hotel room to dash off a column for the *Guardian* website claiming that the Brits had invented Americana. Tongue-in-cheek though that argument may have been, my encounters with the Carolina Chocolate Drops and the AMA ignited a desire to both explore and relate the back story of skiffle, investigating the forces that had come together to create the cultural space for it to emerge in 1950s Britain.

There is, to my mind, no greater authority on the pop music of this period than Pete Frame, genealogist of British rock music, whose hand-drawn family trees have graced the pages of numerous music magazines since the mid-70s. His magnum opus, *The Restless Generation*, published in 2007, tells the story of youth culture in the

50s with the forensic detail of one who was there at the time and experienced the great sense of relief as jazz, skiffle, rock 'n' roll and pop helped a generation of war babies slough off the restricting skin of post-war British society. This was my guiding star in the writing of this book, a constant source of reference, along with the McDevitt and Dewe tomes. *Goin' Home: The Uncompromising Life and Music of Ken Colyer*, the definitive biography of the man, written by Mike Pointon and Ray Smith, was a huge help for the early chapters, as was Samuel Charters's brilliant history of New Orleans jazz, *A Trumpet Around the Corner*.

I was privileged to speak with a number of skiffle veterans and their family members, who did their best to recall events that happened sixty years ago: Chris Barber, Dickie Bishop, Joe Boyd, Billy Burnette, Shirley Collins, Maureen Donegan, Ron and Claudia Gould, Mick Groves, Ray and Eva Harvey, Fred Hellerman, Brian Jackman, Paul Jones, Chas McDevitt, Pete Maynard, Van Morrison, Dave and Christine Mutton, Richard Preston, Leon Rosselson, Peggy Seeger, June Shelley, Hylda Sims, Ann Sunshine, Norma Waterson, Bob Watson and Martyn Wyndham-Read.

Jeff Place, archivist and curator of the Smithsonian Center for Folklife and Cultural Heritage in Washington, DC, helped me make sense of Lead Belly's many recordings of 'Rock Island Line'. David Nathan and Mike Rose at the National Jazz Archive corresponded with me on Lonnie Donegan's early involvement with the NFJO. Keith Ames and Karl Magee at the Musicians' Union and John Williamson at Glasgow University provided valuable background to the AFM/MU ban.

I'm indebted to Ian Anderson, editor of *fRoots* magazine, for giving me access to the Eric Winter archive that he curates and for allowing me to use a number of images I found there. Laura Smyth at the Vaughn Williams Memorial Library was most helpful on the history of the English Folk Dance and Song Society. Rick Blackman was good enough to give me sight of the manuscript for his forthcoming book *Forty Miles of Bad Road: SCIF and the Notting Hill Riots* and to allow me to cite it as a source for the activities of the Stars Campaign for Interracial Friendship. Martyn Colyer, son of Bill, very kindly gave me access to his photo archive and permission to use images.

Paul Adams at Fellside Recordings, who currently release Ken Colyer's recordings, was a mine of information and contacts, as was skiffle veteran Derek Mason. Cyril Davies's biographer Todd Allen gave me some background on his subject. Roger Trobridge from the Cyril Davies website put me in touch with Bob Watson and Dickie Bishop. Nora Guthrie hooked me up with Fred Hellerman. Bob Dylan's bass player Tony Garnier overheard me talking about Lonnie Donegan and told me how Paul Burlison used to wax lyrical about the time the Rock 'n' Roll Trio backed Lonnie in 1956. Paul kindly put me in touch with Billy Burnette. Peter Donegan arranged for Lonnie's first wife, Maureen, to speak to me. Ivan Beavis put me in touch with Tom Greenwood, who agreed to let me use photographs taken by his father, Ernie.

Jim Irvin provided some helpful background about the Pye record label. John Harris and Tom Holland were instrumental in pointing me towards some illuminating books. Barb Ingalls kindly did some research for me in Detroit, and Samantha Pearce did a great job in transcribing interviews. I spent a considerable amount of time in the British Library wading through music papers and journals from the 1950s, and the staff there were always helpful.

Among the team at Faber, my editor, Dave Watkins, has been a constant source of support and guidance. Eleanor Rees brought her copy-editing skills to the project, knocking the narrative into shape, and Ian Bahrami was a meticulous proofreader and fact checker. Thanks are also due to Luke Bird, who designed the jacket, Kate

Ward, text designer, Dan Papps, who handled the publicity, and Lee Brackstone, publisher of the Faber Social list.

But my biggest debt of gratitude is to my partner, Juliet, without whose love, support and understanding this book would never have been written.

NOTES

CHAPTER 1

5 *the Rock Island Bridge case drew national attention*: David A. Pfeiffer, 'Bridging the Mississippi: The Railroads and Steamboats Clash at the Rock Island Bridge', *Prologue Magazine*, Vol. 36, No. 2 (Summer 2004)

7 *the Rock Island operated 3,568 miles of track*: Bill Marvel, *The Rock Island Line*, Indiana University Press, 2013, pp. 53, 56

8 *The verses spoke of the different characters*: Stephen Wade, *The Beautiful Music All Around Us: Field Recordings and the American Experience*, University of Illinois Press, 2012, p. 49

CHAPTER 2

19 *to spend whatever money he'd saved from his job*: Pete Frame, *The Restless Generation*, Rogan House, 2007, p. 3

20 *had put his two elder brothers into children's homes*: Mike Pointon and Ray Smith, *Goin' Home: The Uncompromising Life and Music of Ken Colyer*, Ken Colyer Trust, 2010, p. 45

21 *But instead of the RAF, he attempted to join the Merchant Navy*: Frame, *The Restless Generation*, p. 6

21 *Now don't be angry*: Frame, *The Restless Generation*, p. 6

22 *Talking to Ken, he was intrigued to discover*: Pointon and Smith, *Goin' Home*, p. 49

24 *Within a couple of numbers, the band were playing with a power*: Pointon and Smith, *Goin' Home*, p. 56

25 *After what he later referred to as 'a lot of argy-bargy'*: Frame, *The Restless Generation*, p. 9

26 *Ken and Bill teamed up with another shipmate*: Pointon and Smith, *Goin' Home*, p. 258

27 *Ken said very little to us*: Pointon and Smith, *Goin' Home*, p. 64

27 *We chatted and got along quite well*: Pointon and Smith, *Goin' Home*, p. 64

30 *We're talking about kids – fifteen, sixteen, seventeen*: Pointon and Smith, *Goin' Home*, p. 74

31 *Big Bill Broonzy was another favourite*: Frame, *The Restless Generation*, p. 19

31 *The Cranes were grudgingly allowed to play*: Pointon and Smith, *Goin' Home*, p. 75

33 *And Bill Colyer came along too*: Pointon and Smith, *Goin' Home*, p. 82

34 *A good New Orleans band has no stars*: Frame, *The Restless Generation*, p. 16

34 *Even Humph, although he always denied it*: George Melly, *Owning Up: The Trilogy*, Penguin Books, 2000, p. 416

35 *Having lost his front teeth*: Samuel Charters, *A Trumpet Around the Corner*, University Press of Mississippi, 2008, p. 332

35 *we didn't call him 'Bunk' for nothing*: cited in Charters, *A Trumpet Around the Corner*, p. 94

37 *You see those fellows standing behind him*: Pointon and Smith, *Goin' Home*, p. 54

38 *If the employer desires to bring in a complete band*: Hansard, 11 February 1929

39 *The crowd of over 1,700 were ecstatic*: Martin Cloonan and Matt Brennan, 'Alien Invasions: The British Musicians' Union and Foreign Musicians', *Popular Music*, Vol. 32, Issue 2

40 *In England, owing to the unfortunate restrictions*: *Melody Maker*, 28 March 1953

CHAPTER 3

42 *the orchestra was composed of three pieces*: Lynn Abbott and Doug Seroff, *Out of Sight: The Rise of African American Popular Music 1889–1895*, University Press of Mississippi, 2002, p. 444

42 *Jones was enjoying success with his new song*: Abbott and Seroff, *Out of Sight*, p. 162

42 *the most common term used to describe these informal events was a 'break-down'*: Abbott and Seroff, *Out of Sight*, p. 443

43 *'Jazz' as a musical term was rarely heard before 1920*: Burton W. Peretti, *The Creation of Jazz*, University of Illinois Press, 1994, p. 22

43 *a placard that read 'Don't Patronise This Jass Music'*: Charters, *A Trumpet Around the Corner*, p. 116

45 *When the Spanish ruling class sought to marginalise French settlers*: http://www.neworleansonline.com/neworleans/history/people.html

46 *reclassified as 'negro' by Louisiana state law*: Charters, *A Trumpet Around the Corner*, p. 38

46 *won't lower the tone of your event by vulgar improvisation*: Charters, *A Trumpet Around the Corner*, p. 56

47 *a very high-class musician*: Lee Collins, *Oh Didn't He Ramble*, University of Illinois Press, 1989, p. 33

47 *by 1900 this red-light zone was generating more revenue than any other district of the city*: 'Storyville, New Orleans', Wikipedia

47 *a celebration of 'open and notorious depravity'*: Abbott and Seroff, *Out of Sight*, p. 295

47 *a habit he'd acquired from performing in rowdy red-light district dance halls*: George 'Pops' Foster, quoted in Tom Stoddard, *The Autobiography of Pops Foster: New Orleans Jazzman*, University of California Press, 1971, p. 16

48 *He wasn't really a [trained] musician*: Peretti, *The Creation of Jazz*, p. 101

49 *Known as 'spasm bands', the more proficient were hired*: Peretti, *The Creation of Jazz*, p. 28

49 *When bands from New Orleans made whistle stops in La Place*: Peretti, *The Creation of Jazz*, p. 18

49 *But Lena was having none of it*: John McCusker, *Creole Trombone – Kid Ory and the Early Years of Jazz*, University of Mississippi Press, 2012, p. 56

50 *It was Bolden's loud playing that caught their ear*: McCusker, *Creole Trombone*, p. 58

50 *four of whom were African Americans*: McCusker, *Creole Trombone*, p. 66

50 *He referred to this mixture of influences as 'soft' ragtime*: McCusker, *Creole Trombone*, p. 103

52 *Looking for a name that described their sound*: Charters, *A Trumpet Around the Corner*, p. 132

52 *It was only when the manager appeared*: Charters, *A Trumpet Around the Corner*, p. 136

54 *Prohibition, introduced in 1920, further undermined their opportunities*: Charters, *A Trumpet Around the Corner*, p. 302

56 *Rather like a primitive religion*: Dave Gelly, *An Unholy Row*, Equinox Publishing, 2014, p. 23

CHAPTER 4

58 *You'll get what men I send you and you'll accept them*: Ken Colyer, *When Dreams Are in the Dust*, Ken Colyer Trust, 1989, p. 151

63 *British cornettist Ken Colyer sends this first-hand account*: *Melody Maker*, 13 December 1952

65 *[Ken and I visited] places like*: Pointon and Smith, *Goin' Home*, p. 100

65 *I was given a quiet word of warning*: Pointon and Smith, *Goin' Home*, p. 103

68 *The people in the group are*: Pointon and Smith, *Goin' Home*, p. 141

CHAPTER 5

70 *he and his friends sometimes saw*: Chris Barber, *Jazz Me Blues*, Equinox Publishing, 2014, p. 4

71 *The difference between the scratchy old 78 rpm records*: Barber, *Jazz Me Blues*, p. 8

72 *It was, by his own admission, a terrible trombone*: Barber, *Jazz Me Blues*, p. 10

NOTES

72 *strange, wild, smoking black cigarettes*: Harry Shapiro, *Alexis Korner: The Biography*, Bloomsbury, 1996, p. 43

73 *Alexis had attended the King Alfred Grammar School*: Shapiro, *Alexis Korner*, p. 39

75 *Although the young Donegan loved Crumit's novelty songs*: Frame, *The Restless Generation*, p. 50

75 *Alex invited him over for a jam session*: Frame, *The Restless Generation*, p. 36

77 *Donegan heard Hank Williams, the Carter Family and Tennessee Ernie Ford*: Patrick Humphries, *Lonnie Donegan and the Birth of British Rock & Roll*, The Robson Press, 2012, p. 48

78 *At Wood Green, I would sing the songs*: Frame, *The Restless Generation*, p. 54

78 *No, I just want you*: Humphries, *Lonnie Donegan*, p. 53

79 *OK, I was terrible*: Frame, *The Restless Generation*, p. 58

79 *All the things that Lonnie had been reaching for*: Melody Maker, 7 June 1952

81 *Lonnie wasn't too disappointed*: Barber, *Jazz Me Blues*, p. 22

82 *Barber's band thought he was mad*: Frame, *The Restless Generation*, p. 65

83 *Straight away we sounded marvellous*: Frame, *The Restless Generation*, p. 66

CHAPTER 6

85 *We are going to try to popularise New Orleans music*: Melody Maker, 21 March 1953

86 *with the glamour of his New Orleans adventure behind him*: Melody Maker, 4 April 1953

87 *Playing every night in Denmark*: Barber, *Jazz Me Blues*, p. 26

87 *Whenever there was a gap*: Pointon and Smith, *Goin' Home*, p. 160

90 *This instrument was going to change the world*: Ken Colyer: He Knew, All Out Productions, 2008

91 *If you don't believe this kind of music could be a draw in London*: Jazz Journal, July 1953

92 *the 'parlor social', the 'gouge' and the 'percolator'*: Paul Oliver, *The Story of the Blues*, Northeastern University Press, 1969, p. 83

97 *Burley's South Side Shake album, which appeared on Circle Records*: Karl Hultberg, *Rudi (& Me): The Rudi Blesh Story*, Ragtime Society Press, 2013, p. 40

CHAPTER 7

99 *An LP of New Orleans jazz*: Melody Maker, 1 August 1953

99 *Let us not carp, gentlemen*: Pointon and Smith, *Goin' Home*, p. 159

100 *His wife Delphine said as much*: Pointon and Smith, *Goin' Home*, p. 18

101 *Barber easily identified the cause of the friction*: Pointon and Smith, *Goin' Home*, p. 160

102 *Well, that's not difficult*: Frame, *The Restless Generation*, p. 72

NOTES

102 *While the band has made great progress*: Melody Maker, 23 May 1954

102 *For that kind of music*: Frame, *The Restless Generation*, p. 73

102 *[Ken] always had to have a lot*: Pointon and Smith, *Goin' Home*, p. 166

104 *From the start of this session*: Uncredited sleeve note, *Back to the Delta*, Decca Records LF 1196

105 *it might help if the band sat down to play*: Pointon and Smith, *Goin' Home*, p. 175

CHAPTER 8

112 *A cinema used barbed wire*: 'Barbed Wire Foils Teddy-suit Gang at Cinema', *Daily Sketch*, 15 March 1954

115 *Clearly, all of the classic elements of Teddy Boy style*: 'Why All This Talk of Change?', *Sunday Pictorial*, 11 January 1953

117 *Youths wearing Edwardian dress will not be admitted*: www.edwardianteddyboy.com

119 *We did not need to take up the conventional class attitudes of British film-making*: Free Cinema, BFIVD717

121 *These figures will have raised eyebrows*: Picture Post, 29 May 1954

123 *before I get called up, blown up or married*: quoted in Bill Osgerby, *Youth in Britain Since 1945*, Blackwell, 1998, p. 20

123 *teenagers, viewed from the shelter of this middle-class enclave*: Peter Lewis, 'Mummy, Matron and the Maids: Feminine Presence and Absence in Male Institutions', quoted in Osgerby, *Youth in Britain*, p. 27

CHAPTER 9

126 *he affected a bohemian style*: Christina L. Baade, *Victory through Harmony: The BBC and Popular Music in World War II*, Oxford University Press, 2012, p. 123

126 *Preston, a committed anti-racist*: Baade, *Victory through Harmony*, p. 124

127 *What we were doing at Melodisc*: Lloyd Bradley, *Sounds Like London*, Serpent's Tail, 2013, p. 47

128 *Trinidadian vocalist Young Tiger*: John Cowley, 'London Is the Place for Me: Caribbean Music in the Context of Empire 1900–60', in Paul Oliver (ed.), *Black Music in Britain*, Open University Press, 1990, p. 70

132 *Humph complained in vain*: New Musical Express, 14 January 1955

CHAPTER 10

150 *During the first ten months of 1955 over 46 million records had been sold in the UK*: Record Mirror, 5 November 1955

152 *there's a demon in this man Colyer*: Record Mirror, 6 August 1955

153 *the utterly stupid antics of fans and fannies*: Record Mirror, 12 November 1955

155 *it has even been suggested that 'Rock Island Line'*: 'Trad Man in the Top Twenty', *New Musical Express*, 27 January 1956

156 *The general 'pop' public*: *Record Mirror*, 31 December 1955

CHAPTER 11

158 *Marx lives in one of the worst*: quoted in Edmund Wilson, *To the Finland Station*, Harcourt Brace, 1940, p. 243

158 *the free port that every city must have*: Ian Nairn, *Nairn's London*, Penguin, 1966, p. 74

162 *singing easily, loudly, all together*: Martha Gellhorn, 'So Awful to Be Young', *Encounter*, May 1956, p. 42

CHAPTER 12

176 *I don't think it's a particularly good recording*: 'Trad Man in the Top Twenty', *NME*, 27 January 1956

181 *No more fear for me now*: John Szwed, *The Man Who Recorded the World*, Arrow Books, 2011, p. 252

181 *The fact that he'd deprived blues fans*: Frame, *The Restless Generation*, p. 54

185 Woody Guthrie's Blues *was Elliott's first record*: Hank Reineke, *Ramblin' Jack Elliott: The Never Ending Highway*, The Scarecrow Press, 2010, p. 66

185 *We met a most intriguing character*: *Jazz Journal*, November 1955, p. 25

186 *the review was written by one Alan Lomax*: *The Times*, 28 December 1955

187 *a person supporting Communist movements*: Peter Cox, *Set into Song: Ewan MacColl, Charles Parker, Peggy Seeger and the Radio Ballads*, Labatie Books, 2008, p. 33

CHAPTER 13

190 *The fact that records by English 'skiffle' groups*: *Jazz Journal*, April 1956, p. 2

191 *a phenomenon almost exclusively of the British jazz world*: Paul Oliver, 'Hometown Skiffle', *Music Mirror*, February 1956, p. 8

193 *You're the first man to have made any money out of the guitar*: Spencer Leigh, *Puttin' On the Style: The Lonnie Donegan Story*, Finbarr International, 2003, p. 37

194 *A former employee confided*: Jim Irvin, unpublished sleeve note, quoted in *The Story of Pye Records*, Sequel Records, 1998

196 *On Monday last the Races began at the Curragh*: quoted in Seán Ó Cadhla, 'In Search of the Original "Skewball"', in *Ethnomusicology Ireland* 2, 3 July 2013

197 *it is the most widely known of the chain-gang songs*: J. and A. Lomax, *American Ballads and Folk Songs*, Macmillan, 1934, p. 68

197 *'It was terrific being on those records*: Leigh, *Puttin' On the Style*, p. 38

198 *as a jazz record, it can only be described as phoney*: *Record Mirror*, 28 April 1956

199 *the single had received a tremendous reception*: 'Don and Donegan are Fighting Out a Record Battle over "Rock Island Line"', *NME*, 16 March 1956

201 *So I signed a contract for American representation*: Frame, *The Restless Generation*, p. 91

202 *Donegan had parted company with the Chris Barber Jazz Band*: *NME*, 11 May 1956

203 *Jazz is your bread and butter*: Leigh, *Puttin' On the Style*, p. 40

CHAPTER 14

206 *obvious commercial intent*: Craig Morrison, *Go Cat Go! Rockabilly Music and Its Makers*, University of Illinois Press, 1998, p. 1

208 *We thought it was a rock 'n' roll record*: Humphries, *Lonnie Donegan*, p. 139

209 *They were sensational musicians*: Frame, *The Restless Generation*, p. 92

209 *What is a Lonnie Donegan?*: Humphries, *Lonnie Donegan*, p. 138

211 *a wiry guy with that intense Murder, Inc. face*: Bill Graham and Robert Greenfield, *Bill Graham Presents: My Life Inside Rock and Out*, Da Capo Press, 1992, p. 88

212 *The story was deemed serious enough*: *Billboard*, 9 June 1956

212 *All the coloured acts were backed by an orchestra*: Leigh, *Puttin' On the Style*, p. 39

214 *We love what you're doing, man*: Leigh, *Puttin' On the Style*, p. 39

CHAPTER 15

216 *A family with the wrong members in control*: George Orwell, *The Lion and the Unicorn: Socialism and the English Genius*, Searchlight Books, 1941, p. 35

217 *There would be no going back to the past*: Spike Milligan, foreword to Christopher Pearce, *Fifties Source Book*, Grange, 1998

219 *Oh no! Not the ironing board*: 'Pamela Lane: Obituary', *Guardian*, 21 November 2010

220 *all scum and a mile wide*: Kenneth Tynan, *Observer*, 13 May 1956

220 *It's just a travesty of England*: Arthur Miller, *Timebends: A Life*, Harper & Row, 1987, p. 417

224 *Pop Art is:* Richard Hamilton, letter to Peter and Alison Smithson, 16 January 1957, in *Collected Works 1953–1982*, Thames and Hudson, 1982, p. 28

228 *Bill Haley shouted out*: Frame, *The Restless Generation*, p. 218

229 *I'm surprised and a little shocked*: '"Rock" and Wreck in Film Frenzy', *Manchester Guardian*, 4 September 1956

229 *[Rock 'n' roll] is deplorable*: *Daily Mail*, 5 September 1956

230 *Opposite the cinema in the early evening*: *Manchester Guardian*, 11 September 1956

230 *it would have been much better if the police had been allowed to deal with you*: *Manchester Guardian*, 12 September 1956

231 *when they got to 'See You Later, Alligator'*: 'This Crazy Summer's Weirdest Craze', *Daily Express*, 12 September 1956

232 *Even without Sunday*: 'Rock Film Off for the Day' *Manchester Guardian*, 17 September 1956

232 *The press have offered a challenge to the teddy boys*: 'Rock'n'roll Scenes: Press Blamed', *Manchester Guardian*, 19 September 1956

233 *Much of the hooliganism has drawn strength*: *The Times*, 15 September 1956

234 *We sang 'Tea for Two' and 'Avalon'*: 'Elvis the Pelvis and the Big Beat', *Manchester Guardian*, 8 November 1956

CHAPTER 16

236 *What we nowadays call English folksong*: A. L. Lloyd, *The Singing Englishman*, Workers Music Association, 1944, p. 4

240 *Londoners can go and hear folk singers*: *Sing*, November/December 1954, p. 71

243 *John Hasted was one of those co-ordinating people*: Frame, *The Restless Generation*, p. 110

CHAPTER 17

259 *'Don't worry,' he assured Booker*: Frame, *The Restless Generation*, p. 132

269 *after getting an autograph for himself*: http://www.triumphpc.com/mersey-beat/beatles/lonniedonegan-beatles2.shtml

269 *from approximately the last weeks of 1956*: Mark Lewisohn, *The Beatles – All These Years*, Vol. 1: *Tune In*, Little, Brown, 2013, p. 100

271 *British skiffle is, most certainly, a commercial success*: 'Skiffle or Piffle?', *Melody Maker*, 23 July 1956

CHAPTER 18

274 *Had I not gone on holiday*: Dave Thompson, *Joe Meek – The Ultimate Listening Guide*, Kindle, 2013, p. 12

274 *had a drum sound*: John Repsch, *The Legendary Joe Meek: The Telstar Man*, Cherry Red Books, 2001, p. 48

284 *one of the most astonishing performances in all recorded music*: Humphries, *Lonnie Donegan*, p. 148

284 *a joint live review of Donegan and Steele*: 'Rock'n'Roll (Or Was It Skiffle?) Comes to Town', *Melody Maker*, 8 December 1956

CHAPTER 19

286 *a place of our own*: 'Skiffle: It's the New Note at Night', *Daily Herald*, 6 November 1956

293 *I've got a very good ear for a melody*: Frame, *The Restless Generation*, p. 226

298 *played a passable version of the National Anthem*: Chas McDevitt, *Skiffle: The Definitive Inside Story*, Robson Books, 1997, p. 42

CHAPTER 20

303 *At Christmas people were walking around*: 'This'll Make You Skiffle', *News of the World*, 14 May 1957

304 *Unlike the older skiffle groups*: John Hasted, 'A Singer's Notebook', *Sing*, April/May 1957

306 *I did it from the beginning because I believed in it*: 'Skiffle on Trial', *Melody Maker*, 9 March 1957

306 *It's all very well, some say*: '"Conceited? They Always Say That When You're Successful" Says Lonnie Donegan', *Melody Maker*, 4 May 1957

306 *Harry Belafonte, whose album* Calypso *had vied with Presley's*: 'Will Calypso Knock the Rock?', *Melody Maker*, 16 March 1957

307 *The failure of calypso to ride to the rescue*: 'Has Trad Jazz Had It?', *Melody Maker*, 15 June 1957

307 *Hardly a week goes by*: 'Skiffle Intelligentsia', *Observer*, 16 June 1957

308 *amateur performers singing in modest public houses*: 'Skiffle Success with Young England', *The Times*, 17 July 1957

308 *For nearly a decade, my wife and I played*: 'Skiffle Won't Die', *Melody Maker*, 6 July 1957

308 *Are we to let youth become the sole judge*: Jack Payne in *Melody Maker*, 23 June 1956, p. 5

315 *If one must categorise skiffle*: Graham Boatfield, 'An Eye upon Skiffle', *Jazz Journal*, August 1957, p. 5

317 *the cheapest Sunday concert*: *Weekly Sporting Review & Show Business*, 28 December 1957

318 *these busy boys were also making frequent appearances at the Skiffle Cellar*: *Barking Advertiser*, 20 December 1957

320 *we felt that was an injustice*: McDevitt, *Skiffle*, p. 196

CHAPTER 21

321 *the recently opened Cavern jazz club in Liverpool was now holding a weekly skiffle night*: *Reveille*, 23 May 1957

321 *Bob Cort's guide to forming a skiffle group*: *Mirabelle*, 22 July 1957

322 *quite unlike anything that had been heard on radio before*: Brian Matthew, *This Is Where I Came In*, Constable, 1991, p. 121

325 *Cyril said to me one day*: Roger Dopson, *Blues from the Roundhouse* CD, GVC 1006

326 *Claiming roots in the jump jazz of 1920s Chicago*: *Weekly Sporting Review & Show Business*, 31 January 1958

330 *the vocalists called out for Fags on the recording*: McDevitt, *Skiffle*, p. 85

NOTES

CHAPTER 22

339 *there would soon be as many strip shows as skiffle bars in Soho*: 'On the Beat', *Melody Maker*, 26 April 1958

340 *a raucous, rhythmic paean of disgust*: *Expresso Bongo*, sleeve notes of original cast recording

CHAPTER 23

347 *guests were allowed, although they had to pay two shillings and six pence*: *Lonnie Donegan Club*, Vol. 2, No. 1

348 *The winter edition carried the contact details of clubs*: *Lonnie Donegan Club*, Vol. 2, Nos 2 and 3

348 *The organisers believed that music should be a central component*: George McKay, *Circular Breathing: The Cultural Politics of Jazz in Britain*, Duke University Press, 2005, p. 57

349 *On the black cloth were the words 'Nuclear Disarmament'*: Peggy Duff, *Left, Left, Left*, Alternative Editions, 1971, p. 115

350 *The City Ramblers clearly didn't get the memo*: John Hasted, *Alternative Memoirs*, Greengates Press, 1992, p. 157

350 *the marchers 'skiffled their way along'*: 'Motley 4000 Begin H Bomb Procession', *Daily Telegraph*, 5 April 1958

350 *five guitars, a washboard and three dozen people singing a Negro spiritual*: 'Marchers' Numbers Rise to 1000', *Daily Telegraph*, 6 April 1958

350 *We're lovers of good music*: *March to Aldermaston*, Film and T.V. Committee for Nuclear Disarmament, 1959

353 *They later told the police that they were 'nigger-hunting'*: Ruth Glass, *Newcomers: The West Indians in London*, Centre for Urban Studies, University of London Press, 1960, p. 135

353 *left five black men lying unconscious*: *Guardian*, 24 August 2002

354 *Among the twenty-seven prominent artists who signed the statement*: 'Race Riots', *Melody Maker*, 6 September 1958

355 *[Our] aims are to promote understanding between races*: Glass, *Newcomers*, p. 198

356 *this will not be a select club*: 'Harmony Club on Monday', *Kensington Post*, 16 January 1959

356 *received letters from fascist groups threatening violence*: Marika Sherwood, *Claudia Jones: A Life In Exile*, Lawrence & Wishart, 1999, p. 116

356 *The objectives of the campaign*: *Panorama*, BBC TV, 13 April 1959

CHAPTER 24

361 *The Orange Blossom Jug Five*: Dave Van Ronk with Elijah Wald, *The Mayor of MacDougal Street*, Da Capo Press, 2006, p. 91

NOTES

365 *an irregular publication circulated mainly in fandom*: Michael Moorcock, *Jazz Fan*, Issue 7, May 1957

367 *overflowing with refugees from the skiffle craze*: Eric Winter, 'The Flowers of Manchester', *Manchester Guardian*, 3 March 1958

367 *There are generally about thirty bods with guitars*: Ben Harker, *Class Act: The Cultural and Political Life of Ewan MacColl*, Pluto Press, 2007, p. 128

CHAPTER 25

378 *The band I had with my friends, Little Boy Blue and the Blue Boys*: Dora Loewenstein and Philip Dodd, *According to the Rolling Stones*, Phoenix, 2004, p. 13

378 *I was in loads of skiffle groups*: Chris Salewicz, *Mick & Keith*, Orion, 2002, p. 21

381 *Without Donegan I don't know how I would have started*: *Guardian*, 5 June 2015

CHAPTER 26

385 *Taking the stage*: Lewisohn, *The Beatles – All These Years*, Vol. 1: *Tune In*, p. 128

388 *They thought Lonnie Donegan was Elvis*: Larry Kane, *When They Were Boys: The True Story of the Beatles' Rise to the Top*, Running Press, 2013, p. 173

BIBLIOGRAPHY

Abbott, Lynn, and Seroff, Doug, *Out of Sight: The Rise of African American Popular Music 1889–1895*, University Press of Mississippi, 2002

Abrams, Mark, *The Teenage Consumer*, LPE Papers, 1959

All Out Productions, *Ken Colyer: He Knew*, Radio programme, 2008

Baade, Christina L., *Victory through Harmony: The BBC and Popular Music in World War II*, Oxford University Press, 2012

Barber, Chris, *Jazz Me Blues*, Equinox Publishing, 2014

BBC TV, *Panorama*, 13 April 1959

Bird, Brian, *Skiffle – the Story of Folk Song with a Jazz Beat*, Robert Hale, 1958

Blackman, Rick, *Forty Miles of Bad Road: SCIF and the Notting Hill Riots*, Redwords Publications, 2017

Bradley, Lloyd, *Sounds Like London*, Serpent's Tail, 2013

Charters, Samuel, *A Trumpet Around the Corner*, University Press of Mississippi, 2008

Cloonan, Martin, and Brennan, Matt, 'Alien Invasions: the British Musicians' Union and Foreign Musicians', *Popular Music*, Vol. 32, Issue 2, May 2003

Cohen, Norm, *The Long Steel Rail*, University of Illinois Press, 1981

Collins, Lee, *Oh, Didn't He Ramble*, University of Illinois Press, 1989

Colyer, Ken, *When Dreams Are in the Dust*, Ken Colyer Trust, 1989

Cowley, John, 'London Is the Place for Me: Caribbean Music in the Context of Empire 1900–60', in Paul Oliver (ed.), *Black Music in Britain*, Open University Press, 1990

Cox, Peter, *Set into Song: Ewan MacColl, Charles Parker, Peggy Seeger and the Radio Ballads*, Labatie Books, 2008

Davies, Hunter, *The Quarrymen*, Omnibus Press, 2001

Dewe, Mike, *The Skiffle Craze*, Planet, 1998

Dopson, Roger, notes to *Blues from the Roundhouse* by Alexis Korner's Breakdown Group, CD GVC 1006, 2009

Dopson, Roger, notes to *Midnight Special: The Skiffle Years* by Lonnie Donegan, CD ACTRCD9013, Acrobat Music, 2008

Duff, Peggy, *Left, Left, Left*, Alternative Editions, 1971

Dunn, Anthony J., *The Worlds of Wolf Mankowitz*, Valentine Mitchell, 2013

BIBLIOGRAPHY

Dupin, Christophe, notes to *Free Cinema*, DVD, BFI BFIVD717, 2006

Ellis, Royston, *The Big Beat Scene*, Music Mentor, 2010

Ferris, Ray, and Lord, Julian, *Teddy Boys – A Concise History*, Milo Books, 2012

Film and TV Committee for Nuclear Disarmament, *March to Aldermaston*, 1959

Frame, Pete, *The Restless Generation*, Rogan House, 2007

Gellhorn, Martha, 'So Awful to Be Young', *Encounter*, May 1956

Gelly, Dave, *An Unholy Row*, Equinox Publishing, 2014

Glass, Ruth, *Newcomers: The West Indians in London*, Centre for Urban Studies, University of London Press, 1960

Glicco, Jack, *Madness After Midnight*, Bestseller Library, 1952

Goddard, Simon, *Ziggyology: A Brief History of Ziggy Stardust*, Ebury Press, 2013

Graham, Bill, and Greenfield, Robert, *Bill Graham Presents: My Life Inside Rock and Out*, Da Capo Press, 1992

Hamilton, Richard, *Collected Works 1953–1982*, Thames and Hudson, 1982

Harker, Ben, *Class Act: The Cultural and Political Life of Ewan MacColl*, Pluto Press, 2007

Hasted, John, *Alternative Memoirs*, Greengates Press, 1992

Hultberg, Karl, *Rudi (& Me): The Rudi Blesh Story*, Ragtime Society Press, 2013

Humphries, Patrick, *Lonnie Donegan and the Birth of British Rock & Roll*, The Robson Press, 2012

Irvin, Jim, *The Story of Pye Records*, Sequel Records, 1998

Kane, Larry, *When They Were Boys: The True Story of the Beatles' Rise to the Top*, Running Press, 2013

Keepnews, Orin, and Grauer, Bill, *A Pictorial History of Jazz*, Spring Books, 1958

Kitchener, Bill (ed.), *The Oxford Companion to Jazz*, Oxford University Press, 2000

Larkin, Colin, *The Virgin Encyclopedia of Fifties Music*, Virgin Books, 1998

Leigh, Spencer, *Puttin' On the Style: The Lonnie Donegan Story*, Finbarr International, 2003

Lewisohn, Mark, *The Beatles – All These Years*, Vol. 1: *Tune In*, Little, Brown, 2013

Lloyd, A. L., *The Singing Englishman*, Workers Music Association, 1944

Loewenstein, Dora, and Dodd, Philip, *According to the Rolling Stones*, Phoenix, 2004

McAleer, Dave, *Hit Singles: Top Twenty Charts from 1954 to the Present Day*, Carlton Books, 2003

McCusker, John, *Creole Trombone: Kid Ory and the Early Years of Jazz*, University of Mississippi Press, 2012

McDevitt, Chas, *Skiffle: The Definitive Inside Story*, Robson Books, 1997

MacInnes, Colin, *Absolute Beginners*, Allison & Busby, 1959

MacInnes, Colin, *England, Half English*, Chatto & Windus, 1986

412

McKay, George, *Circular Breathing: The Cultural Politics of Jazz in Britain*, Duke University Press, 2005

Mankowitz, Wolf, *My Old Man's a Dustman*, André Deutsch, 1956

Marvel, Bill, *The Rock Island Line*, Indiana University Press, 2013

Matthew, Brian, *This Is Where I Came In*, Constable, 1991

Melly, George, *Owning Up: The Trilogy*, Penguin Books, 2000

Miller, Arthur, *Timebends: A Life*, Harper & Row, 1987

Moorcock, Michael, *Jazz Fan*, May 1957

Moorcock, Michael, *The Rambler*, January 1958

Morrison, Craig, *Go Cat Go! Rockabilly Music and Its Makers*, University of Illinois Press, 1998

Ó Cadhla, Seán, 'In Search of the Original "Skewball"', *Ethnomusicology Ireland* 2, 3 July 2013

O'Donnell, Jim, *The Day John Met Paul*, Penguin, 1996

Oliver, Paul, *The Story of the Blues*, Northeastern University Press, 1969

Orwell, George, *The Lion and the Unicorn: Socialism and the English Genius*, Searchlight Books, 1941

Osgerby, Bill, *Youth in Britain Since 1945*, Blackwell, 1998

Pearce, Christopher, *Fifties Source Book*, foreword by Spike Milligan, Grange, 1998

Peretti, Burton W., *The Creation of Jazz*, University of Illinois Press, 1994

Pfeiffer, David A., 'Bridging the Mississippi: The Railroads and Steamboats Clash at the Rock Island Bridge', *Prologue Magazine*, Vol. 36, No. 2, Summer 2004

Pointon, Mike, and Smith, Ray, *Goin' Home: The Uncompromising Life and Music of Ken Colyer*, Ken Colyer Trust, 2010

Reineke, Hank, *Ramblin' Jack Elliott: The Never Ending Highway*, The Scarecrow Press, 2010

Repsch, John, *The Legendary Joe Meek: The Telstar Man*, Cherry Red Books, 2001

Romney, Jonathan, and Wooton, Adrian (eds), *Celluloid Jukebox: Popular Music and the Movies Since the 50s*, BFI, 1999

Salewicz, Chris, *Mick & Keith*, Orion, 2002

Shapiro, Harry, *Alexis Korner: The Biography*, Bloomsbury, 1996

Sherwood, Marika, *Claudia Jones: A Life in Exile*, Lawrence & Wishart, 1999

Szwed, John, *The Man Who Recorded the World*, Arrow Books, 2011

Thompson, Dave, *Joe Meek – The Ultimate Listening Guide*, Kindle, 2013

Thorp, Raymond, *Viper: Confessions of a Drug Addict*, Robert Hale, 1956

Uncredited sleeve note to *Back to the Delta* by Ken Colyer's Jazzmen, Decca Records, LF 1196, 1954

Van Ronk, Dave, with Wald, Elijah, *The Mayor of MacDougal Street*, Da Capo Press, 2006

Vinen, Richard, *National Service: Conscription in Britain 1945–1963*, Allen Lane, 2014

413

BIBLIOGRAPHY

Wade, Stephen, *The Beautiful Music All Around Us: Field Recordings and the American Experience*, University of Illinois Press, 2012

Warwick, Neil, Kutner, Jon, and Brown, Tony, *The Complete Book of the British Charts: Singles and Albums*, Omnibus Press, 2004

Wilson, Edmund, *To the Finland Station*, Harcourt Brace, 1940

Wolfe, Charles, and Lornell, Kip, *The Life and Legend of Leadbelly*, Harper Collins, 1992

INDEX